MW00678480

THE OFFICIAL
WORLD WAR II GUIDE
TO THE ARMY AIR FORCES

AAF

FRANKLIN DELANO ROOSEVELT
Commander-in-Chief of the Army and Navy

THE OFFICIAL
WORLD WAR II GUIDE
TO THE ARMY AIR FORCES

AAF

A DIRECTORY, ALMANAC AND
CHRONICLE OF ACHIEVEMENT

BONANZA BOOKS
New York

A Lou Reda Book.

Originally published as *The Official Guide to the Army Air Forces*

Copyright © MCMXLIV by Army Air Forces Aid Society
All rights reserved.

This 1988 edition is published by Bonanza Books, distributed by Crown
Publishers, Inc., 225 Park Avenue South, New York, New York 10003,
by arrangement with Lou Reda Productions, Inc.

Printed and Bound in the United States of America

Library of Congress Cataloging-in-Publication Data

Official guide to the Army Air Forces.
　AAF : the official World War II guide to the Army Air Forces.
　　p.　　cm.
　"A directory, almanac, and chronicle of achievement."
　Reprint. Originally published: Official guide to the Army Air Forces. New York,
N.Y. : Simon and Schuster, 1944.
　Includes index.
　ISBN 0-517-66803-3
　1. United States. Army Air Forces—History—World War, 1939–1945.
I. United States. Army Air Forces.　II. Title.　III. Title: Army Air Forces.
IV. Title: Official World War II guide to the Army Air Forces.
UG633.0315　1988
358.4′00973—dc19　　　　　　　　　　　　　　　　　　　　　88-3802
　　　　　　　　　　　　　　　　　　　　　　　　　　　　　　CIP

ISBN 0-517-66803-3

h g f e d c b a

PREFACE

On June 30, 1910, the entire strength of the United States Army (Signal Corps) consisted of one officer, nine enlisted men, one Wright airplane, one Baldwin airship, and three captive balloons. In December 1938 Army Air Forces personnel (officers and enlisted men) numbered 21,125; by December 1943 they reached 2,373,882, with an annual appropriation of $23,655,998,000 in funds for Army aviation in 1944.

If you were among the men and women of the Army Air Forces in World War II, you know much of the story of the AAF—how its incredible growth and remarkable technological and organizational achievements led to a victory on behalf of the world. But as a part of the AAF, you probably tended to know only what you needed to know. Considering the general attitude toward secrecy, and the prevailing fear of spreading information, you were unlikely to learn much about the history or the function of the organization as a whole, unless you read a book released by and on behalf of the Army Air Forces Aid Society.

The Official Guide to the Army Air Forces was published in 1944 to serve as an authoritative reference to a vast fighting organization—the mightiest air force in the world. Now, forty-four years after its original publication, *The AAF Guide* still stands firmly as a historical document: the record of a remarkable achievement and a testimonial to the American ability to organize and produce under fire. And the organization and technology that developed under the impetus of war today serve our country as the modern Air Force—dedicated to the safety and well-being of millions of Americans.

On December 7, 1941, the AAF faced the challenge of the century. The sudden transition from peace to war posed enormous problems. As with an animal freed from a cage after a long captivity, neither the teeth nor the claws of the AAF were strong enough for immediate and effective use. Although production facilities had been increased by 400 percent between 1939 and 1941, the majority of the materials produced had been sent to England under the lend-lease program and other defense agreements. But the new planes had already been battle-tested, and although they were not formally a part of the AAF's strength, the expansion of production facilities brought about by lend-lease had prepared the nation for the far greater expansion necessary. It is the unique privilege of *The AAF Guide* to give you the story and the statistics of this remarkable growth with all the immediacy and voice of a nation at war.

But the true credit for the AAF's achievement is readily acknowledged here, and gracefully given—to the individuals who fought on behalf of the whole:

> "The massed power of our air forces and the fighting strength of their units are built upon the accomplishments of individual crewmen. Although virtually every move in combat is related to the operation of a machine, our machines are useless without men to run them—men who are willing to put their lives on the line when the situation demands."

The Official Guide to the Army Air Forces—or, as it has been retitled for current publication, *The Official World War II Guide to the Army Air Forces*—is a fascinating and comprehensive guide to how the separate components of the AAF meshed to become a vast fighting machine. Whether you fought in the war, or whether you've just read about it, this book tells you what you want to know about the AAF.

BUD MASTERSON

New York
1988

FOREWORD

AAF is more than the abbreviated term for the Army Air Forces. It is a symbol of massed American striking power. Fundamentally, the AAF is a people's air force, and its bombs dropping on the enemy represent the work of millions of Americans in and out of uniform.

In a democracy it is fitting that the people should have the opportunity to obtain a thorough understanding of their military air organization. This book furnishes that opportunity. It coordinates the many aspects of our activity and provides an integrated picture of the AAF as it is today.

This book is a useful, accurate guide to our operations and should be of wide personal interest to those who know the AAF through relatives and friends in the service. It will be especially valuable to those who hope to become directly associated with us. To the officers, men and women of the AAF it should serve as a helpful work of reference.

H. H. ARNOLD
General, U. S. Army
Commanding General, Army Air Forces
1944

CONTENTS

THE OFFICIAL
WORLD WAR II GUIDE
TO THE ARMY AIR FORCES

AAF

ON TARGET

AN INTRODUCTION TO THE AAF

If you would know the Army Air Forces today, consider first a global network of men and airplanes, supply lines, communica tions routes and airbases; think of this network as a striking force that since the start of the war has made more than 700,000 combat flights, dropped more than 600,000 tons of bombs, fired more than 75,000,000 rounds of ammunition against the enemy.

Now think of a part of this striking force: of 1000 heavy bombers stretched across 100 miles of sky, with as many fighter planes forming a protective cover; 30,000 tons of metal, 11,000 fighting men and 2500 tons of high explosives roaring along in battle formation to a common objective.

Consider the objective: a production center that is a source of enemy power; a German equivalent of Detroit or Pittsburgh fashioning weapons of war for use against American troops and the troops of our Allies; a vital, strategic target protected by land and sea, accessible only through the air.

Think of the attack: 1000 bombers forcing their way to within 5 vertical miles of this enemy stronghold; men who take aim and hurl their bombs down those 5 miles onto the target; metal and men who will be back over the target tomorrow or the next day, who are capable of repeating the performance again and again, of shifting their attack to other targets at will; think in terms of repeated bombings; think of each mass attack as a major military campaign taking place within the space of hours.

THE CHALLENGE OF WAR

In that sober hour on Dec. 7, 1941, the challenge to the AAF was clearly outlined:

Could we, the air organization of the U. S. Army, mass and perfect the men and materials to graduate from a minor airpower to the mightiest air force the world had ever known?

Could we, with our limited strength, fight holding actions over 5 continents while we amassed the necessary resources?

Could we, in minimum time, launch an air offensive that would fatally weaken the enemy's ability to resist?

Actually, considerable planning had gone before. The nations already at war had proved that airpower would be a decisive factor in the struggle, that airpower could only be defeated by superior airpower. Ever since World War I farsighted military men and civilian students of military affairs in this country had been convinced that the airplane would have a profound effect on future warfare. During the 1920's this thinking and study began to crystallize into certain definite conclusions within the AAF. We believed:

That the most efficient method of waging war was to destroy the enemy's weapons while they were still in production, thus depriving his armies of those weapons and eventually rendering him powerless.

That airpower, capitalizing upon its inherent long-range strategic capabilities and operating in sufficient strength, could accomplish this objective.

That precision bombing was the heart of such airpower and the key to our operations.

That airpower, operating in cooperation with ground and sea units, could be a decisive factor by isolating the battle area and participating on the battlefield.

That land-based aircraft, with emphasis on the long-range, high altitude heavy bomber, would be the backbone of our air force, and that super-bombers would be required.

That the maximum strength of our weapon could be realized and its limitations offset by our ability to make sustained mass attacks.

THE AIR WAR PLAN

More than 3 months before Pearl Harbor, the AAF, in response to an instruction of the President, submitted to the War Department an air war plan based on the following assumptions:

That we might be at war with Germany and Japan simultaneously.

That Germany, as the center of the Axis system and its principal military power, would have to be dealt with first.

That a land invasion of Germany would take considerable time to prepare.

That a sustained and powerful bombing assault against specific targets might make an invasion unnecessary, or if necessary, would play a vital role in any such effort.

That a specific number of bombardment planes could be set up as the power element of an air offensive.

That in addition to bases in Britain, efforts should be made to develop bases in the Near East; and to obtain Atlantic and Western Mediterranean bases—if necessary by land, sea and air action.

That a long-range, heavily armed escort fighter would be needed to offset German defenses.

That a "strategic defensive" would be necessary in Asia until Germany was defeated.

The plan, as submitted, called for the creation of an air force numbering more than 2,000,000 men and upwards of 88,000 planes.

The value of an air offensive was predicated on the conviction that the German industrial effort, and consequently the continued existence of the German army, was dependent on the following elements: the electric power system, the transportation system, the oil and petroleum system, civilian morale.

We believed that destruction of specified targets in the first 3 categories would paralyze the functioning of each, and that the same result could be accomplished by a collapse of enemy civilian morale.

We realized that it might be desirable to accomplish certain "intermediate" objectives, as: neutralization of the German air force, attack on airbases, attack on aircraft factories (engine and airframe), and attack on aluminum and magnesium plants producing the essential metals from which airplanes are built.

In order to secure our bases and maintain supplies, we recommended "diversionary" objectives such as submarine bases, surface sea craft, "invasion" bases.

PLAN OF IMMEDIATE ACTION

A week after the U. S. was attacked, the AAF submitted the following recommendations:

> Since the Axis powers command a substantial advantage in forces available for immediate use, protection of the military and industrial strength of the U. S. is the FIRST consideration; protection of the British Isles, as a base for future offensive operations, is the SECOND consideration.
> Offensive action against the sources of Axis military strength is mandatory, if we are to win.

As steps in the creation of an air force for the preservation of national security and the defeat of the Axis powers, we recommended the acquisition of 88,000 planes and—stepping up the pre-Pearl Harbor estimate—2,900,000 men and officers. We further recommended the providing of air defense for the U. S., Panama and Hawaii; the providing of hemisphere defense; the providing of supplies necessary to secure bases in Britain and the Near East; the maintenance of lines of communication; the reinforcing of the Philippines; the providing of shipping needed for the offensive; and the construction of bases in Alaska and the Aleutians for an ultimate offensive against Japan.

Since all military plans are subject to alteration in the face of action before the enemy, new ways must be devised for attaining the objective, new plans drawn to conform with changing circumstances. Objectives originally tagged "diversionary" or "intermediate" may for immediate reasons become "primary," thus influencing other elements of a plan. However, the overall strategy remains unchanged.

THE FIRST RUSH OF WAR

Pearl Harbor converted our long-deliberated PLAN of action into ACTION itself. In the sudden transformation from a nation at peace to a nation at war, our air program was like an animal unleashed from its cage after long confinement, but with neither his teeth or claws sharp enough or strong enough to be immediately effective.

The very nature of the war made it necessary that we, as the flying force of the nation, should bear the brunt of the enemy's first rush of conquest. Our efforts during the first 6 months of war were valiant but meager when measured by today's standards. Yet we did delay the enemy, and in some measure held him and interfered with his plan of domination. We built up the hard way the combat experience required to put our own plan into full-fledged action.

In the early days of expansion everything we wanted was needed "yesterday"; and mostly we wanted strength. The quotas we set up were of necessity as changeable as our initial organization charts. And while we were still CREATING the essential industrial means, the enemy was in a position to USE his means to push us further and further back from the points from which we could launch a future offensive.

Between 1939 and 1941 the production facilities at our disposal had increased 400%, but the lion's share of that expansion had gone to Great Britain under "defense aid" and lend-lease agreements. Yet, foreign purchases of the nation's aircraft had given us the valuable asset of battle-tested planes. And although lend-lease had cost us immediate strength, it had also prompted expansion of our original production facilities and prepared us for the far greater expansion needed.

Our training facilities were wholly inadequate for the job ahead, but we could utilize those of private and commercial flying that fortunately had been built up in the peacetime years; we could make use of the nation's educational system, could transform hotels into training centers. The "combat aircrew," as we know it today, was unknown in early 1942. Balance was lacking among the necessary components of the AAF—the airmen, technicians, ground crews—and we didn't have enough planes with which to instruct our men. But a training program initiated in 1939 had given us a nucleus of skilled personnel; and every rural and city area of the nation could contribute to a vast pool of trainable men, many of whom not only had a keen interest in the airplane, but a similarly valuable aptitude for things mechanical.

We lacked both transport facilities and bases. Naval strength had to be devoted largely to securing lines of communication; this not only placed a heavier burden on air operations but also gave the enemy a chance to wage submarine warfare, which in turn absorbed some of our aerial operations and by necessity diverted them from industrial targets. However, after the first threat of direct attack had passed, the location of the U. S. guaranteed security for the production program that lay ahead. We could grow without the destructive time-loss factors of bomb-harried production which both Great Britain and Germany had suffered. The British Isles could become one huge airbase for strategic bombing operations. In the South Pacific we could benefit from the aid offered by Australia. Throughout the world we had other Allied nations to assist us in our prosecution of the war.

THE NETWORK IN ACTION

After we had pushed through the first year of combat, gradually the cycle of war began to turn to our advantage. Our accumulation of strength began to mesh with the concepts of our war plan; combat experience meshed with training, supply and communications with the establishment of bases—until the global network took shape.

Early in 1944 we massed our first 100-mile procession of bombers. Simultaneously, we were preparing to strike in even greater numbers, were flying even larger bombers, and were planning to carry massed aerial attack across the world to Japan. But early 1944 was the start of the real air offensive.

Today, while 1000 of our bombers stretch across the sky over Germany, all over the globe our men are making themselves understood in Hindustani, Italian, Arabic, Bengali, Eskimo, pidgin English; and our planes are making themselves understood in the tropics, arctic and desert; over sea, mountain and glacier.

In China, at this moment, some of us may just be landing medium bombers after raiding Japanese warehouses in Indo-China. Every ounce of gasoline our planes used—like the gas for the jeeps and trucks on the airfields in China, like the gas for the heavy bombers just now taking off for a dawn mission to bomb Formosa—was carried over the Himalayas by air. In India our transports are coming in after a day of shuttling these supplies. Several thousand miles to the southeast, on a Pacific island once headquarters for the Japanese, others of us are being briefed to sweep over an enemy harbor and, from zero altitude, attack his shipping. On a tiny island in the Arabian Sea we sit out a sandstorm and wait for the evening transport. On the hot Tunisian desert we are still busy looking for salvageable items from the year-old wrecks of enemy planes. Over the Central Pacific our night search planes, with their equipment that sees better in the dark than any man has ever seen in daylight, are on patrol. On the west coast òf the U. S., while another shift is coming off work in the great airplane factories, thousands of us are taking off in training flights in small aircraft that out-perform the combat planes our pilots flew in the last war. In a New York City procurement office a colonel dictates a request for 4 million rivets. In the Aleutians the "I Bombed Japan" club is initiating some new members. We are over Kansas on our first solo; high over central Germany with enemy fighters attacking; low over a Japanese airfield strafing planes on the runway; far out over the Pacific with an enemy warship clearly fixed in the cross-hairs of our bombsight. We are the AAF.

In this book we tell about our men and our planes—who they are and what they do—and about our whole global network.

WHAT WE ARE

We have a saying in the AAF that 10 men in a bomber will never replace a combat aircrew. Similarly, more than 2⅓ million men and 100,000 airplanes will never replace an air force.

The AAF is, first of all, a huge team. Teamwork is the cornerstone of all our activities—in the air and on the ground. No one man in a bomber crew can carry out a mission by himself. Unless the work of each member is planned, disciplined and coordinated with the others, all will fail. One man cannot win a battle, but one man can lose it.

Between plane and plane, teamwork is as necessary as it is between man and man. A cohesive formation of bombers is essential for mass bombing and for self-protection. If one aircraft fails to maintain its appointed position it jeopardizes not only itself but the entire formation, and perhaps the success of the mission. Fighters must work closely with the bombers they are escorting. They fly in teams, cover one another, attack in unison.

AAF aircrews have no monopoly on teamwork. It must exist between them and their ground men, among the ground crews themselves; and among the forces back home—both military and civilian—which develop and build the planes, ship the supplies and train the men. Nor is teamwork confined to any one branch of the armed forces. Essential to success in the war is AAF teamwork with the ground armies, with the Navy, and with Allied forces in combined air-sea-ground operations.

OUR ORGANIZATION

Evolution of the AAF—The AAF stems from modest beginnings. Created in 1907 as a tiny branch of the Signal Corps, the Army air arm mushroomed during World War I to what then seemed giant proportions. During the latter months of the war the Air Service was set up as a separate branch of the Army, distinct from the Signal Corps. In 1926 it was renamed the Air Corps. In 1935 a combat air organization was established to complement the Air Corps—the General Headquarters (GHQ) Air Force. Later renamed the Air Force Combat Command, this was a unified combat force composed of the various fighting air units. It was an early testing ground for the strategical and tactical doctrines on which our present aerial offensives were conceived.

With the creation of the Air Force Combat Command, the Air Corps concentrated on supply and training functions. From its Materiel Division and its training centers grew the continental commands of the AAF which have been chiefly responsible for building the AAF into the fighting machine it is today.

Shortly after Pearl Harbor, the U. S. Army was reorganized. The Air Corps and Air Force Combat Command were merged into the Army Air Forces. The Infantry, Cavalry, Field Artillery and other surface combat elements were merged into the Army Ground Forces. The supply and service agencies—Quartermaster, Ordnance, Chemical Warfare, etc.—were merged into the Services of Supply, subsequently renamed the Army Service Forces. Responsibility for coordinating the 3 forces was lodged in the General Staff, a body composed of equal numbers of air and ground officers.

The military air arm currently consists of the following elements: the Commanding General, AAF; the Deputy Commander; the Air Staff; 4 continental air forces; 6 AAF commands and certain other AAF agencies which are engaged in various specialized activities; and 11 combat air forces in the theaters of operations.

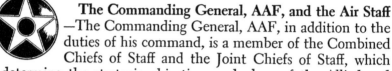 The Commanding General, AAF, and the Air Staff —The Commanding General, AAF, in addition to the duties of his command, is a member of the Combined Chiefs of Staff and the Joint Chiefs of Staff, which determine the strategic objectives and plans of the Allied and American armed forces (see page 33). The Air Staff is the arm of the Commanding General which enables him to direct and control all the far-flung parts of the AAF. It translates the war plans laid down by the President and the higher planning agencies into concrete courses of AAF action. It keeps in close touch with the theaters of operations in order to see that production and training programs are geared to the changing requirements of the war. Months in advance it plans where, when and what kinds and quantities of planes and men will be needed. It develops and maintains a synchronized schedule taking into account the multiple factors affecting fully trained and equipped air units. This schedule serves as the basis for specific directives from the Commanding General to AAF agencies in the field.

The Headquarters of the AAF, in Washington, D. C., includes the Commanding General, AAF, the Deputy Commander and the Air Staff. The Air Staff consists of a Chief of Air Staff (who is also the Deputy Commander, AAF), assisted by 4 Deputy Chiefs; 6 Assistant Chiefs of Air Staff, each responsible for a main phase of AAF operations; and several special officers, each a specialist in a particular field.

COMMANDING GENERAL, AAF
General H. H. Arnold

OFFICERS OF THE AIR STAFF

DEPUTY COMMANDER, AAF, AND CHIEF OF AIR STAFF: Lt. Gen. B. M. Giles—Assists and advises the Commanding General; directs, supervises, coordinates activities of the Air Staff, the commands and the continental air forces.

DEPUTY CHIEFS OF AIR STAFF: Brig. Gen. W. E. Hall, Brig. Gen. H. S. Hansell, Jr., Brig. Gen. P. Timberlake, Brig. Gen. D. Wilson—Assist the Chief of Air Staff in the performance of his duties.

ASSISTANT CHIEF OF AIR STAFF, PLANS: MAJ. GEN. L. S. KUTER—
Recommends strategy and deployment of air combat units; interprets approved war plans in terms of air combat requirements.

ASSISTANT CHIEF OF AIR STAFF, OPERATIONS, COMMITMENTS AND REQUIREMENTS: MAJ. GEN. H. A. CRAIG—Translates approved air war plans into an integrated AAF program covering personnel, equipment, trained units and replacement crews; establishes tactics and techniques of aerial warfare, standards and characteristics required of aircraft and combat units; plans; orders the creation of units, and the movement of units and aircraft to overseas theaters.

ASSISTANT CHIEF OF AIR STAFF, PERSONNEL: MAJ. GEN. J. M. BEVANS —Plans, establishes policies for and supervises the AAF personnel program, both military and civilian; supervises recreational and morale activities; administers personnel operations for the personnel of the Air Staff.

ASSISTANT CHIEF OF AIR STAFF, INTELLIGENCE: BRIG. GEN. T. D. WHITE—Establishes policies and plans for air intelligence activities, including counter-intelligence, photo-interpretation and intelligence training; collects, evaluates and disseminates information bearing on the air war.

ASSISTANT CHIEF OF AIR STAFF, TRAINING: MAJ. GEN. R. W. HARPER —Establishes training schedules and policies and supervises AAF training activities; stimulates and coordinates the development and use of training aids, such as texts, training films, synthetic training devices and posters.

ASSISTANT CHIEF OF AIR STAFF, MATERIEL, MAINTENANCE AND DISTRIBUTION: MAJ. GEN. O. P. ECHOLS—Establishes plans and policies for all supply activities of the AAF, including the development, procurement and production of aircraft and related equipment, the supply and maintenance of all such supplies within the continental U. S., and air transportation to overseas theaters; also works in close coordination with the Army Service Forces in the furnishing of supplies and services by other branches of the War Department to the Army Air Forces.

CHIEF, MANAGEMENT CONTROL: BRIG. GEN. B. E. GATES—Advises on organizational, administrative and procedural matters; prepares recommendations to obtain the most efficient utilization of AAF manpower; obtains and maintains current statistical information relative to all AAF activities.

AIR INSPECTOR: BRIG. GEN. J. W. JONES—Develops plans and policies for all AAF inspections; conducts periodic and special inspections of AAF activities for the Commanding General.

AIR SURGEON: MAJ. GEN. D. N. W. GRANT—Plans and directs all medical facilities and personnel of the AAF, including aeromedical research.

CHIEF, BUDGET AND FISCAL OFFICE: BRIG. GEN. L. W. MILLER—Supervises and administers all AAF budget and fiscal matters.

AIR JUDGE ADVOCATE: BRIG. GEN. L. H. HEDRICK—Acts as legal counsel of the AAF.

AIR COMMUNICATIONS OFFICER: BRIG. GEN. R. M. McCLELLAND—Determines policies and programs for air communications activities, including radio, radar, teletype, pigeons, etc.

CHIEF, OFFICE OF LEGISLATIVE SERVICES: COL. W. S. EGE—Handles matters involving relationships with Congress, including proposed legislation.

SPECIAL ASSISTANT FOR ANTIAIRCRAFT: MAJ. GEN. H. R. OLDFIELD—Advises on all antiaircraft activities affecting the AAF.

CHIEF, SPECIAL PROJECTS: COL. F. T. DAVISON—Performs such special projects as the Commanding General may from time to time assign.

CHIEF, OFFICE OF FLYING SAFETY: COL. G. C. PRICE—Develops and carries out a flying safety program for the prevention of aircraft accidents; develops and enforces procedures for the control of military air traffic.

CHIEF, OFFICE OF TECHNICAL INFORMATION: LT. COL. R. D. SMITH—Under direction of AAF Public Relations Board plans and supervises AAF public relations and related activities.

The AAF Commands and the Continental Air Forces—During the prewar period and the early months of the war, the AAF concentrated on growing. In 1943, as it approached its scheduled size, it gradually shifted its emphasis from training to operations. But even after it has reached its peak, it must continue to train men and produce planes and equipment in order to maintain its combat forces at full strength. New and better planes must replace old ones as well as those damaged and destroyed; new crews must be trained to replace those lost in action and those relieved from combat duty.

THE PLACE OF THE AAF IN THE WAR DEPARTMENT

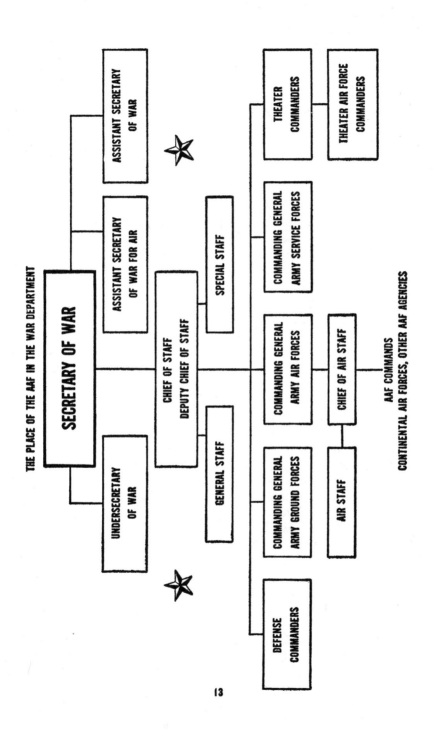

In charge of building and maintaining combat air forces are the several AAF commands, the 4 air forces in the continental U. S., and certain other AAF field agencies. Subject to the overall directives and programs of the Commanding General, AAF, the commander of each of these organizations has full authority and responsibility for organizing his command and developing methods and procedures for accomplishing his objectives.

The 4 continental air forces originated as Air Districts under the old GHQ Air Force in the winter of 1940–41. Set up as air combat organizations, each was assigned a certain area of the U. S. in which to operate. Thus the 1st Air Force operates along the eastern seaboard; the 2nd in the northwestern and mountain areas; the 3rd in the southeastern area; and the 4th along the west coast and in the southwest. During the early part of the war, a major responsibility, particularly of the 1st and 4th Air Forces, was to guard against possible attack on the continental U. S. Today, although they still maintain a defensive force, their main job is the organizing and training of air units for overseas combat.

Each command and air force has its own headquarters and its own subordinate field organization. These organizations are characterized by the nature of their varying activities. The Materiel Command, for example, which deals primarily with private industries, functions through procurement districts located at or near principal industrial centers. These districts maintain offices in the various aircraft factories. The Air Service Command has 11 air depots as well as a number of special depots and stations. Each major AAF installation has a supply and maintenance organization which draws on an appropriate air depot for supplies and heavy maintenance work.

The 4 continental air forces operate through sub-commands or wings, each of which supervises airbases of a particular type or in a particular area. The Training Command is organized into several sub-commands, including 2 technical training commands, each operating technical schools in a specified area of the continent, and 3 flying training commands, each operating flying schools in a specified area.

The Air Transport Command is composed of a ferrying division which ferries new airplanes from factory to destination, either in the U. S. or abroad; a domestic transportation division for the transport of supplies and passengers in the continental U. S.; and several foreign wings, each operating transport routes over a specified region of the world.

THE AAF COMMANDS AND CONTINENTAL AIR FORCES

TRAINING COMMAND—Fort Worth, Tex.; Lt. Gen. B. K. Yount. Organized—Tech. Tr. Comd. 26 Mar. '41; Flying Tr. Comd. 23 Jan. '42; combined into Training Comd. 7 July '43. Function—Training of pilots, bombardiers, navigators, gunners, mechanics and other ground technicians; basic training of all incoming personnel; officer candidate training.

I TROOP CARRIER COMMAND—Indianapolis, Ind.; Brig. Gen. F. W. Evans. Organized—As Air Transport Comd. 30 Apr. '42; redesignated I Troop Carrier Comd. 20 June '42. Function —Organization and training of troop carrier, glider and medical air evacuation units and crews; joint training with Army Ground Forces of airborne units.

AIR TRANSPORT COMMAND—Washington, D. C.; Maj. Gen. H. L. George. Organized—As Ferrying Comd. 29 May '41; redesignated Air Transport Comd. 20 June '42. Function—Ferrying of new aircraft from factory to using locations all over the world; world-wide air transport service for personnel, supplies and mail.

MATERIEL COMMAND — Wright Field, Dayton, Ohio; Maj. Gen. C. E. Branshaw. Organized— As Air Corps Materiel Division 15 Oct. '26; redesignated Materiel Comd. 9 Mar. '42. Function — Research, development and procurement of aircraft and related equipment.

AIR SERVICE COMMAND—Patterson Field, Fairfield, Ohio; Maj. Gen. W. H. Frank. Organized —As Air Corps Provisional Maintenance Comd. 15 Mar. '41; as Air Corps Maintenance Comd. 29 Apr. '41; redesignated Air Service Comd. 17 Oct. '41. Function—Distribution and supply to AAF units of AAF equipment and supplies; maintenance and repair of aircraft; training of service, supply and maintenance units for assignment overseas.

PROVING GROUND COMMAND—Eglin Field, Fla.; Brig. Gen. G. Gardner. Organized—As Air Corps Proving Ground 15 May '41; redesignated Proving Ground Comd. 1 Apr. '42. Function—Operational tests and studies of aircraft and aircraft equipment.

1ST AIR FORCE—Mitchel Field, Hempstead, L. I., N. Y.; Maj. Gen. F. O'D. Hunter. Organized—As NE Air District 16 Jan. '41; redesignated 1st Air Force 9 Apr. '41. Function—Organization and training of bomber, fighter and other units and crews for assignment overseas; participation with Army Ground Forces in combat training maneuvers; provision of units and planes for defense of the continental U. S.

2ND AIR FORCE—Colorado Springs, Colo.; Brig. Gen. U. G. Ent. Organized—As NW Air District 16 Jan. '41; redesignated 2nd Air Force 9 Apr. '41. Function—Same as 1st Air Force.

3RD AIR FORCE—Tampa, Fla.; Maj. Gen. W. T. Larson. Organized—As SE Air District 16 Jan. '41; redesignated 3rd Air Force 24 May '41. Function—Same as 1st Air Force.

4TH AIR FORCE—San Francisco, Calif.; Maj. Gen. W. E. Lynd. Organized—As SW Air District 16 Jan. '41; redesignated 4th Air Force 31 Mar. '41. Function—Same as 1st Air Force.

OTHER AAF AGENCIES

AAF BOARD, Orlando, Fla.—Development and determination of AAF military requirements.

TACTICAL CENTER, Orlando, Fla.—Testing and demonstrating tactical unit organization, equipment and techniques; training of selected AAF, Army and Navy personnel in air tactics and doctrine; training of air intelligence officers and air inspectors.

REDISTRIBUTION CENTER, Atlantic City, N. J.—Processing and assignment of AAF personnel returned from overseas; operation of rest camps for such personnel.

ARMY AIRWAYS COMMUNICATIONS SYSTEM WING, Asheville, N. C. —Provision of world-wide system of communications along military airways, including ra-

dio stations, airbase control towers, beacons, teletype systems, radio ranges and other communications facilities.

WEATHER WING, Asheville, N. C. —Provision of scientific weather information service for the AAF and the rest of the Army.

SCHOOL OF AVIATION MEDICINE, Randolph Field, Tex.—Training of AAF medical personnel; research and development in science of aviation medicine.

FIRST MOTION PICTURE UNIT, Culver City, Calif.—Production of motion pictures for the training and orientation of AAF personnel.

AERONAUTICAL CHART PLANT, St. Louis, Mo.—Procurement, reproduction and distribution of aeronautical charts for AAF operations around the world.

THE PARTS OF AN AIR FORCE

To understand precisely what an air force is and what makes it tick, it is necessary to know the units which comprise it and how they are organized to work together.

The Airplane and Crew—Basic unit of all aerial combat organizations is the individual airplane and its combat crew. In the fighter airplane, the crew is a one-man organization—the pilot, who also acts as his own navigator, gunner, radio-operator and even bombardier. In contrast, a heavy bomber has a crew of 10 or more highly specialized men. The medium bomber normally has a crew of 6.

The Flight—Two or more airplanes may be organized, for tactical purposes, into a flight. This means that they train, fly and fight together. One of the planes is the flight leader; its pilot, the flight commander, directs the operations of the entire flight. The flight, as a sub-division of the next larger unit, the squadron, simplifies the problem of control by the squadron commander, who would otherwise have to deal directly with a large number of individual airplanes. A heavy bomber flight usually consists of 4 or more airplanes which in combat may fly in pairs, trios, or fours known as elements of the flight.

The Squadron—The smallest air force unit having both tactical and administrative duties is the squadron. Unlike the flight, it includes ground personnel whose duties are to administer the squadron and to furnish necessary ground service. When necessary, it can be stationed at an advanced base and operate on its own resources for a short period. The make-up of a squadron is determined by the type of airplane used and the nature of its mission. Basic types of flying squadrons include very heavy, heavy, medium and light bomber, 2-engine fighter, single-engine fighter, night fighter, troop carrier, tactical reconnaissance, photo-reconnaissance, transport and ferrying squadrons.

While the composition of these different types varies widely both in equipment and personnel, squadrons of a given type are

MAKE-UP OF TYPICAL HEAVY BOMBER CREW—B-17

TITLE	RANK AND DUTY	GUN POSITION
Pilot	1ST. LT.—Commands airplane and crew; pilots airplane.	
Copilot	2ND LT.—Assists pilot in flying plane; operates fire control.	
Bombardier	2ND LT.—Locates, identifies and bombs target; directs plane while over target.	Chin turret
Navigator	2ND LT.—Navigates plane to target and home.	Alternate on chin turret
Aerial engineer-gunner	T/SGT.—Handles and corrects mechanical troubles in flight; checks airplane before flight; gunnery.	Top turret
Ass't aerial engineer-gunner	S/SGT.—Assists aerial engineer-gunner; gunnery.	Waist gun
Radio operator-mechanic gunner	T/SGT.—Operates all radio communications; makes necessary radio repairs; gunnery.	Radio hatch gun
Ass't radio operator-mechanic gunner	S/SGT.—Assists radio operator-mechanic gunner; gunnery.	Ball turret
Armorer-gunner	T/SGT.—Maintains and repairs armament, including guns, gunsights, turrets, bomb racks, etc.; gunnery.	Waist gun
Ass't armorer-gunner	S/SGT.—Assists armorer-gunner; gunnery.	Tail gun

(Note: Ranks and duty assignments vary somewhat in different organizations. Officer ranks are all one grade higher if the airplane is a flight leader.)

similar. Tests and experience determine the number of planes which should be grouped in one squadron for maximum efficiency in combat, and what personnel, equipment and supplies are required to keep the planes flying. Such determinations become standard. They are published in Tables of Organization (T/Os) which state the number of personnel in each specialty and in

each rank, and in Tables of Equipment (T/Es) which authorize
equipment by type and quantity for each kind of squadron.

The squadron has a commanding officer and a group of subordinate officers to assist him to plan and to carry out the squadron's mission. Its activities normally fall into 4 basic divisions:

1. THE TACTICAL DIVISION includes an operations and an intelligence
section and all the aircrews. The operations officer usually acts as
the squadron commander's chief assistant. He directs the training of all the crews and prepares the detailed plans for all missions. The intelligence officer collects and provides necessary information relative to the enemy, the war situation, targets, etc.
The operations officer is also assisted by a communications officer, an armament officer, an oxygen officer and perhaps other
specialists.

2. THE ADMINISTRATIVE DIVISION handles all the office work required
for squadron administration, and such housekeeping activities as
squadron supply, transportation and mess. It is headed by the
squadron executive and includes the squadron adjutant.

3. THE SERVICE DIVISION consists of chemical, medical and ordnance
services, and includes the squadron flight surgeon and the squadron ordnance officer.

4. THE TECHNICAL DIVISION is responsible for all ground maintenance and servicing of airplanes and equipment. It normally
handles the supply of technical aircraft equipment and parts.
This division is headed by the squadron engineering officer. It
may also include armament, communications and photographic
sections.

Service and Repair—The service and repair personnel of a
squadron are organized into ground crews, each of which is normally responsible for the service and maintenance of a particular
plane. Ground crews consist of aircraft mechanics and specialists
in propellers, instruments, armor, etc. Each ground crew is supervised by a crew chief and the crew chiefs are supervised by a line
chief—a master sergeant.

The personnel of each squadron are divided into an air echelon
and a ground echelon. The air echelon may fly when the squadron
moves from one station to another. It includes the squadron commander, the aircrews, the engineering officer, the flight surgeon,

key ground mechanics and specialists. The ground echelon, which includes the rest of the squadron, travels by boat, rail or truck.

The Group—Next organizational level above the squadron is the group. This usually consists of from 2 to 4 combat squadrons and a group headquarters. It is both tactical, in that it provides a grouping of aircraft to perform combat missions together, and administrative, in that it forms a nucleus for administrative services for all its squadrons. All squadrons in a particular group fly the same type of planes; groups, like squadrons, are referred to by type of plane—heavy bomber group, light bomber group, fighter group, etc.

When an entire group is stationed at one large airbase, the ground personnel of the various squadrons may be pooled to provide consolidated maintenance, mess, transportation, personnel and other services. However, squadrons are sometimes stationed at separate bases and must furnish these services wholly or in part. All squadrons of a group train together and the group usually moves and fights as a unit. It is a vital organization in combat operations and is the basic yardstick in AAF planning.

Higher Levels of Command—Above the group level, the organizational layers in different air forces reflect a variety conditioned by the requirements of a particular theater and its air strength. Normally, 2 or more groups constitute a wing, a non-administrative body concerned chiefly with tactical plans and operations. Similarly, 2 or more wings are usually grouped with auxiliary units to form a command, which is a large striking organization of one major category of air strength. In some cases where a particular type of aviation is too unwieldy, in point of size, for a single command to control, air divisions may be formed between the wing and command levels. The air force itself is the next level, usually composed of 3 or more commands.

It is difficult to avoid oversimplification in describing these organizations. In practice, they follow no standard formula. If direct air force control is desirable, a group or wing may be attached directly to an air force. Dominance of one type of activity may cause an air force to be formed within a theater air force. Because of this, tactical and strategic air forces were formed in Africa and in England. (For explanation of strategic and tactical operations see page 255.)

STRENGTH OF TYPICAL AAF UNITS IN MEN AND PLANES

Note: Does not include reserve aircraft and extra combat crews assigned to some theaters.

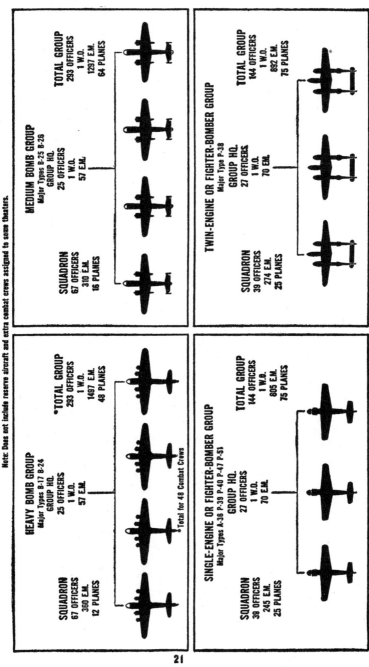

HEAVY BOMB GROUP
Major Types B-17 B-24

SQUADRON
67 OFFICERS
360 E.M.
12 PLANES

GROUP HQ.
25 OFFICERS
1 W.O.
57 E.M.

*TOTAL GROUP
293 OFFICERS
1 W.O.
1497 E.M.
48 PLANES

*Total for 48 Combat Crews

MEDIUM BOMB GROUP
Major Types B-25 B-26

SQUADRON
67 OFFICERS
310 E.M.
16 PLANES

GROUP HQ.
25 OFFICERS
1 W.O.
57 E.M.

TOTAL GROUP
293 OFFICERS
1 W.O.
1297 E.M.
64 PLANES

SINGLE-ENGINE OR FIGHTER-BOMBER GROUP
Major Types A-36 P-39 P-40 P-47 P-51

SQUADRON
39 OFFICERS
245 E.M.
25 PLANES

GROUP HQ.
27 OFFICERS
1 W.O.
70 E.M.

TOTAL GROUP
144 OFFICERS
1 W.O.
805 E.M.
75 PLANES

TWIN-ENGINE OR FIGHTER-BOMBER GROUP
Major Type P-38

SQUADRON
39 OFFICERS
274 E.M.
25 PLANES

GROUP HQ.
27 OFFICERS
1 W.O.
70 E.M.

TOTAL GROUP
144 OFFICERS
1 W.O.
892 E.M.
75 PLANES

Supporting Units—The bomber or the fighter squadron is only relatively and temporarily self-sufficient. It cannot supply itself with the bombs, bullets and gasoline necessary to fly missions day after day. It cannot carry the heavy equipment necessary to overhaul a fouled engine or scrape a smooth runway out of a jungle. For these needs and others, combat units depend upon ground organizations, or supporting service units.

Specially trained units supply and, if necessary, repair bombs, guns and other ordnances; chemicals, medical supplies, radios and telephones. Truck units move up men and supplies from the rear and transport back salvaged equipment. Military police furnish ground protection to bases and aircraft. Weather detachments provide vital forecasts for the planning of missions. Communications units perform any number of duties. Other units provide the ordinary needs of living: food, clothing, shelter. Supporting units range all the way from work battalions to highly skilled groups of topographic engineers, meteorologists, photographers and radar specialists.

Certain specialized units in an overseas air force are attached directly to combat units or to higher headquarters. Most of them, however, become part of the air force air service command (see page 178). This command is on the same level as the bomber and fighter commands and performs duties equally essential; it draws heavily upon the supplies and services of the Army Service Forces in the theater. In a theater where the only American forces are the air force, however, it may have to provide all the supplies and services itself.

ORGANIZATION FOR AIR WAR

The Air Forces in Combat Theaters—Each theater of operations normally has one or more air forces. The air force commander normally is responsible to the theater commander for air operations. In addition to commanding the air force, he advises the theater commander on air matters.

No two air forces are identical. Each is conditioned by its strategic situation, geographic and climatological conditions, enemy operations and tactics, and other factors. As the war progresses and the strategic situation changes, rapid shifts occur in the location, nature and use of the different air forces. The commanding general of an air force determines its organization.

All units of an air force are combined under a single commander for the accomplishment of a common objective. The essential offensive element of air organization is a bombing force for strategic attacks well behind the enemy's front lines on industrial and transportation centers and other key targets. This force may be organized as a strategic air force (such as the 8th and 15th Air Forces) consisting of heavy and sometimes medium bomber units, fighter units for escort, and photographic aviation. In other cases, these attacks are carried out by a bomber command of an air force with fighter escorts drawn from the fighter command.

In a theater where an air force is operating with ground forces, a tactical air force becomes a basic component of the theater air force. It usually contains light and medium bomber units, fighter-bomber units, reconnaissance units, fighter units and troop carrier units. When, as in the New Guinea campaign, transportation of men and equipment by air is an important element of operations, a troop carrier command or a troop carrier wing may be established directly under the air force.

An air force normally possesses an air defense command, which includes fighter groups as well as various ground defense organizations. This command's mission is to protect air and ground installations and communications from enemy attack. The air force air service command controls the service units assigned to an air force and is responsible for providing services and supplies to the entire air force.

Another important air force activity is reconnaissance, including photographic reconnaissance. Vital both to air and ground operations, a reconnaissance group or wing may be attached directly to the air force headquarters. Construction of airbases is ordinarily planned and controlled by air force headquarters. Training is a continuous air force activity.

GENERAL PLAN OF ORGANIZATION NORTHWEST AFRICAN AIR FORCES, SPRING, 1943

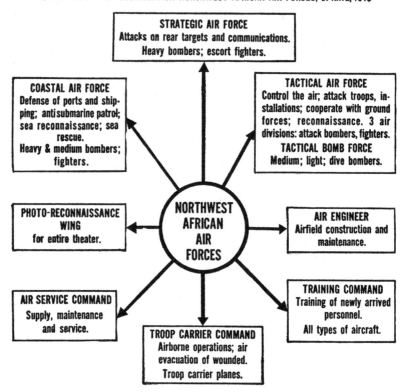

The North African Experience—Basic requirements of air force organization are flexibility and adaptability. A specific example of the adaptation of air force organization to a particular military situation is the experience of the Northwest African Air Forces in 1942–43.

The forces originally available to the Allied Air Commander in North Africa included the bomber, fighter, air support, service commands and troop carrier wing of the U. S. 12th Air Force; and, among British air units, the Army Cooperation Command as well as coastal defense, photo-reconnaissance and service units.

As the campaign progressed it became apparent that these forces would have to be integrated. In attacks against rear targets, fighter aircraft had to be used in conjunction with heavy bombers. In missions against enemy ground and air forces in the battle area, fighters had to team up with medium and light bombers. In defense against enemy air attack, fighters had to be used alone.

The bomber command was confronted by similar demands for flexibility. For attacks on enemy shipping and enemy ports, a striking force of bombers was required. For coordinated mass attacks on enemy forces in the battle area, medium and light bombers had to be removed from the control of scattered army commanders in the field and concentrated under a single air control. Another air force mission, the defense of Allied shipping and Allied ports in North Africa, required various types of aircraft.

In February 1943, the month which marked the turning point of the African campaign, all the air elements in the theater were reorganized on the basis of types of tasks to be performed rather than types of aircraft employed.

A strategic air force of heavy bombers and escort fighters was established for attacks on enemy shipping, ports and bomber bases in Sardinia and Sicily. Air units previously assigned to ground commanders were fused in a tactical air force under air command. Its tasks included operations against enemy air forces, bombing and strafing attacks on enemy armies and transportation lines, and reconnaissance and mapping. Moreover, a tactical bombardment force to bomb enemy ground forces was set up under the direct control of the tactical air force, while a coastal air force was set up to defend Allied ports and shipping.

This reorganization safeguarded and enhanced the peculiar advantages of the air weapon in regard to mobility and flexibility by retaining central planning and control in the strategic air force and the tactical bomber force. Units and airplanes were not frozen under any command; they were used where they could function most effectively. In attacking key targets, the tactical air force and the strategic air force furnished each other with bombers and escort fighters. This kind of collaboration was also reflected in the relationship between the tactical air force and surface forces. It has become a model for combined action. It is no exaggeration to say that the Northwest African Air Forces furnished the pattern for subsequent operations in Sicily and Italy, and that the plan of air organization for the assault on western Europe follows similar principles of flexibility and collaboration.

HOW AN AIR FORCE OPERATES

The Principle of Command—The North African air campaign was won by an air force composed of several hundred thousand men, operating equipment worth several hundred million dollars over an area of thousands of square miles. For all its immense size, it was won by an air force operating as one unit, controlled and directed by one man.

Obviously, no single commander can personally direct all the men in such a force. Nevertheless his plan and his will must control every man. The device which makes this possible is the organization of units and levels of units under a plan known as the principle of command. According to the principle of command, every unit has a single commander who is completely responsible for his command and who directs the actions of his subordinates. By this method no man receives instructions from more than one immediate commander.

The number of individuals one commander can personally direct and control is limited. When it exceeds that limit, it is subdivided into groups, each one under a subordinate commander. This subdividing continues all the way down the line. Since a squadron commander cannot personally direct all 300 or more of his men, he organizes his squadron into sections. When his planes are in flight, it is difficult to control directly the movement of more than a few of them; therefore the planes are grouped into flights, each under a flight commander. Since the flight commander cannot personally direct the aiming of all the guns or the opening of all the bomb bays of all the planes in his flight, he deals with the airplane commander of each plane—the pilot. The pilot in turn commands the aircrew of his plane. In the largest planes, crews are subdivided into sections so that the airplane commander will not have more than 3 or 4 subordinates with whom to deal.

The Use of Staff—Although a commander must see to it that his orders are carried out and must take full responsibility for the way they are carried out, he alone cannot possibly solve all the problems of his command. For this he requires expert advice and assistance from his staff.

The purpose of a staff is to assist the commander in the performance of his command duties.

In the AAF, an airplane commander does not require a formalized staff, nor does a flight commander. The various assistants to a squadron commander advise him but are not, in the strict sense, a staff to him because their chief responsibilities are operational—the carrying out of orders. In a group and in all higher levels, however, every air commander has a sizeable staff.

The staff does not, of itself, possess any authority. It may issue orders to subordinate commanders, but in so doing it merely carries out the wishes of its commander and employs the authority of his position. Its duties may be broadly defined as assisting the commander of the unit by (1) advising him on policy matters and on strategic and tactical plans, (2) maintaining current information and keeping him informed at all times, (3) elaborating upon his general plans and preparing appropriate orders to carry them out, and (4) following up to see that his orders are properly executed.

Staff Organization—The duties of staff officers are logically divided into 4 main categories, or staff sections. For convenience of reference, these sections are commonly referred to in the wing and higher levels by number as A-1 (personnel); A-2 (intelligence); A-3 (operations and training); and A-4 (supply). Similar staff sections in the groups are designated as S (for staff) —S-1, S-2, S-3 and S-4.

A-1, OR S-1, is concerned with all policies and plans relating to personnel. These include such matters as personnel authorizations, procedures, classifications, procurement, assignment, promotions, leaves, rewards, citations, honors, punishment, religious and recreational services, morale, Army postal service, custody of prisoners of war, quartering of soldiers, relations with civil government and civilians, maintenance of order and discipline, burials and similar matters.

A-2, OR S-2, keeps the commander informed as to the situation and capabilities of the enemy. This office is concerned with photographic intelligence and reconnaissance, interrogation of prisoners of war, issuance of intelligence reports, maintenance of pertinent maps and charts, interrogation of pilots after return from missions and intelligence training of all personnel. It also makes studies of enemy targets, handles policies and regulations relating to security and counter-intelligence and advises the commander on public relations matters. A most important function of a squadron intelligence officer is to brief combat crews prior to missions, providing them with relevant information on the enemy.

A-3, OR S-3, is concerned with all plans and policies pertaining to the organization and movement of the unit or subordinate units, to their training, and to combat operations. This office prepares the tactical plans for all combat missions. It must keep informed as to the strength and state of training of units, the availability and condition of aircraft and other equipment, and combat readiness generally. It is concerned in all matters pertaining to flying, such as oxygen equipment, communications, weather, flight control, flying safety and others.

A-4, OR S-4, performs all staff functions pertaining to supply and maintenance. This office must keep thoroughly familiar with the status of all supplies, determine supply requirements and prepare logistical plans to support tactical operations. It is responsible for policies, organizations, facilities and personnel for servicing and maintenance of aircraft; for procurement, distribution, transportation, storage, reclamation and salvage of supplies; for construction and maintenance of airbases, supply depots and other facilities.

It should be noted that while the squadron does not have a formalized staff, its principal officers are grouped along the same general lines as the staff sections.

PATTERN OF COMMAND AND STAFF RELATIONSHIPS IN AN AIR FORCE

LINE OF COMMAND

STAFF

			PERSONNEL ★	INTELLIGENCE ★	OPERATIONS ★	SUPPLY ★
THEATER COMMANDER						
COMMANDING GENERAL AIR FORCE	CHIEF OF STAFF		A-1	A-2	A-3	A-4
COMMANDING GENERAL COMMAND	CHIEF OF STAFF		A-1	A-2	A-3	A-4
COMMANDING GENERAL WING	CHIEF OF STAFF		A-1	A-2	A-3	A-4
COMMANDING OFFICER GROUP	EXECUTIVE*		S-1	S-2	S-3	S-4
COMMANDING OFFICER SQUADRON	EXECUTIVE*		ADJUTANT	INTELLIGENCE OFFICER	OPERATIONS OFFICER	ENGINEERING OFFICER SUPPLY OFFICER TECH. SUPPLY OFFICER
FLIGHT COMMANDER						
AIRPLANE COMMANDER						

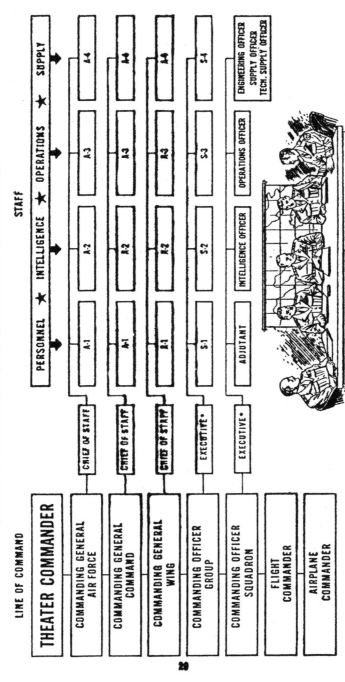

* THIS POSITION MAY BE HELD BY AN EXECUTIVE OR OPERATIONS OFFICER OR MAY BE DIVIDED BETWEEN THEM, ONE SERVING AS GROUND EXECUTIVE, THE OTHER AS AIR EXECUTIVE.

29

The Special Staff—In addition to the general staff sections described, each commander is provided with a group of specialized officers, commonly referred to as the special staff. These officers advise the commander and his staff on matters in which they are particularly qualified. Some of them are also responsible for carrying out operations in their particular fields. The special staff usually includes some or all of the following:

ADJUTANTS GENERAL OR ADJUTANTS • Handling of official correspondence; authentication and distribution of orders; maintenance and custody of records, rosters, reports; office procedure and administration.

INSPECTORS GENERAL OR INSPECTORS • Inspections and investigations for the commander of the internal situation of his command.

FINANCE OFFICERS • Pay of troops and maintenance of a finance service.

JUDGE ADVOCATES • Legal counsel to the commander and his staff; administration of military justice; the handling of all other legal matters.

STATISTICAL CONTROL OFFICERS • Provision of factual data necessary for effective management.

WEATHER OFFICERS • Provision of information, forecasts and advice on weather.

COMMUNICATIONS OFFICERS • Advice and staff supervision of air communications.

SURGEONS • Advice and information on the health and physical fitness of all personnel, sanitation, aviation medical problems, evacuation of sick and wounded, and medical training; technical supervision of medical troops, facilities and supplies.

SPECIAL SERVICE OFFICERS • Development and maintenance of the mental and physical well-being of the troops by utilization of welfare, recreation, orientation, information and morale activities.

PROVOST MARSHALS • Assistance in supervision and operation of all police matters.

PHOTOGRAPHIC OFFICERS • Advice and technical supervision of photographic activities.

CHAPLAINS • Provision of religious and morale guidance to all personnel of the command.

CHEMICAL OFFICERS • Advice on all matters pertaining to chemical warfare.

AIR FORCE ENGINEERS • Technical advice on engineering matters and command of engineer troops in the construction of air-bases, landing fields and related facilities.

ORDNANCE OFFICERS • Advice on all ordnance matters and technical supervision of ordnance activities.

QUARTERMASTERS • Advice on all quartermaster matters and technical supervision of quartermaster troops.

The Inspection System—A primary means of control, which has long been established in all military organizations, is that of inspection. Inspection in the AAF starts at the very bottom—the mechanic inspecting a plane, the sergeant inspecting the military bearing of his men. At higher levels the commander of every unit must make frequent inspections of the units immediately below him and occasional inspections of all subordinate units.

However, the commanding officer of a large organization lacks the necessary time to make frequent inspections. For this reason the commander of each unit is assisted by an inspector, or a staff of inspectors whose full-time responsibilities are to keep him currently informed of the condition of his command and to initiate corrective action wherever necessary.

There are 3 main types of inspection in the AAF: administrative inspection, designed to determine the degree of efficiency of administration and to assure compliance with orders and regulations; technical inspection, concerned with the condition of aircraft, aircraft parts and techniques employed in their maintenance; and tactical inspection, which is the inspection of an entire unit to ascertain the efficiency with which it can perform its primary mission and its readiness for active combat service.

A specialized type of inspection made by the Air Inspector of the Commanding General, AAF, is known as the Preparation for Overseas Movement (POM) Inspection. This is a thorough and detailed inspection which is made of every AAF unit before it is sent overseas. In this inspection every factor bearing on the ability of the unit to perform its assigned job is checked—from the condition of the teeth of every man, the completeness of every record, the spark plugs in every plane, to the combat effectiveness of every aircrew. An inspection of this type culminates in a detailed report which is submitted to the Commanding General, AAF. Upon the basis of this information, it is determined whether the unit should or should not be sent overseas, and appropriate action is recommended to the War Department General Staff.

Statistical Control System—Basis for all decisions and for all plans of a unit commander is accurate and complete information. He must know exactly what his subordinate units are able to do—how many planes they are able to put in the air, how many trained crews are ready to go on a mission, what shortages or deficiencies of supplies, equipment or personnel might impede operations. To furnish such factual data, a statistical control system has been established throughout all echelons of the AAF. It is a system for the collection, compilation, analysis and presentation of statistical data concerning: personnel, housing, training, operations, aircraft, equipment, supply and maintenance.

Summary reports on all AAF operations are regularly furnished to the Commanding General, AAF, in Washington, D. C. These provide him and his staff information upon which are based the strategic, tactical, production, training and personnel plans of the AAF.

Budget and Finance—Financial control is exercised in the AAF through its budget and fiscal system. Budget and fiscal officers are assigned to each of the higher levels of command; through their allocation of funds and accounting of expenditures, they are able to maintain for their commanders complete control over the fiscal aspects of their organizations.

Army Air Forces Board—The Army Air Forces Board is the AAF laboratory group for tactical research and experimentation. The board utilizes the personnel and facilities of the AAF Tactical Center and the Proving Ground Command to conduct tests which precede its decisions and recommendations. Directives issued by the board form a basis for determining operational suitability of individual aircraft and items of equipment, and for developing improved operational technique. The key assignments on the board—tactics, organization, equipment, aircraft, armament and ordnance, and communications—are held by officers with combat experience who are specialists in their fields.

PLANNING A TOTAL WAR

A bomber formation bombs a small railroad bridge south of Mandalay. A cloud of B-17s and B-24s batters an airplane factory deep in Germany. Several groups of medium bombers attack a storage dump in northern France. All of these operations seem unrelated except for the common denominator that they are air attacks on enemy targets. But why these particular targets? How does the AAF happen to have these particular planes, personnel and bases in these particular war areas? How was it decided what types of planes, and in what numbers, should be provided for such operations?

The first of these questions is a matter of target selection. The second is one of deployment of available forces. The third is one of program. The answers to all of them must be determined in the light of an overall war plan for the defeat of the enemy. This war plan must take into account all the forces available for use against the enemy: Army, Navy and Allied forces. It must be correlated with productive resources, manpower, shipping facilities and other broad factors in an all-out war.

Combined and Joint Chiefs of Staff—Ultimate responsibility for our war plan rests in the Commander-in-Chief—the President—together with the governmental leaders of our Allies. Their broad strategic decisions are implemented by the Combined Chiefs of Staff, the highest military planning body of the United Nations. The Combined Chiefs of Staff includes the top commanders of the American and British military services. Its American members include the President's Chief of Staff, the Chief of Staff of the U. S. Army, the Commanding General, AAF, and the Commander-in-Chief of the U. S. Fleet. In itself, this American group comprises the Joint Chiefs of Staff, which is the planning body for all U. S. forces.

The Combined Chiefs of Staff normally does not name specific targets for air attack, but does indicate the priorities of different types of strategic targets in the various theaters. This body also makes overall plans which in turn determine the conduct of tactical air operations. On the basis of such priorities the air force commanders select individual targets and execute plans for aerial missions against them.

The General Staff and the Air Staff—The War Department General Staff is the planning agency for the U. S. Army. It coordinates planning problems relating to air, ground and service activities. It maintains direct contact with all the theaters of operations, determines what units will be sent to what theater, correlates supply and transport requirements with tactical plans, steers the entire Army training program to meet anticipated war needs. The Air Staff of the Commanding General, AAF, works in close coordination with both the Combined and Joint Chiefs of Staff and the War Department General Staff. The Air Staff prepares and submits to these agencies recommendations relative to the AAF program, the employment of airpower and the deployment of AAF units. It interprets the decisions of these planning bodies into specific courses of AAF action and follows through to see that they are successfully accomplished.

WORKING WITH OTHERS

Nothing better illustrates the fact that this is a war of a whole people than the teamwork between the military forces and civilian agencies. The continuous, hour-to-hour interdependence of the AAF with countless other organizations touches almost every aspect of our national life. Within the Army itself, the AAF, the Army Service Forces and the Army Ground Forces work as one team.

The Army Service Forces provides our food, our clothing and other everyday essentials for the AAF. The Corps of Engineers has built many of our airbases and has provided us with trained personnel to build new ones in combat zones. The Ordnance Department designs and procures our bombs, and Chemical Warfare Service provides incendiaries and other chemicals, and is responsible for protective measures against gas attack. The Signal Corps and our own communications system work hand in hand in developing and installing the latest communications equipment. The training of service personnel for AAF units has been to a large extent a joint undertaking. The AAF and the Army Ground Forces work closely together in joint training activities. AAF tactical units regularly participate in ground force maneuvers. AAF units and equipment are also used in the training of airborne troops, including glider troops and paratroopers. A worldwide weather service for the entire Army is furnished by the AAF. Similarly, the Air Transport Command provides for speedy air transportation of key personnel and critical supplies for the entire Army as well as for other agencies.

Army and Navy combine in the planning of aircraft production, raw materials and facilities. The AAF supervises the production of several types of planes for the Navy and the Navy reciprocates on other types. During the first year and a half of war, the AAF Antisubmarine Command provided an air patrol along vital sea lanes. The cooperative interchange of information, techniques and tactics between Navy and AAF is illustrated in the joint staff training of Army and Navy officers at the AAF Tactical Center, the development of training devices, exchange of maps and charts, communications and radar developments.

Through the mechanism of lend-lease, the AAF has participated in the strengthening of all our Allies. Working in collaboration with representatives of other United Nations, AAF has programmed, procured and supervised the production of thousands of airplanes for other countries, and has provided for their shipment. It has also trained thousands of fliers for Canada, England, China, France and other Allies.

The civil agencies, both public and private, with which the AAF works are legion. Government agencies include the War Production Board, the Joint Aircraft Committee, the War Manpower Commission and many other Federal agencies. The National Advisory Committee on Aeronautics, established in 1915, has provided invaluable aid in aeronautical developments, many of which are now standard in the AAF. The Civil Aeronautics Administration and the AAF work together in the development and utilization of civil air facilities, the training of pilots, the control of air traffic and related activities.

An outstanding example of civil participation in the AAF program is the Civil Air Patrol (CAP). This organization consists of volunteer civilians, many of them fliers using their own planes. The Civil Air Patrol has operated in close collaboration with the AAF on various types of projects since the war began and it was made an AAF auxiliary by Executive Order on April 29, 1943. During the bitterest part of the antisubmarine campaign, from March 1942 to August 1943, it provided an antisubmarine air patrol which totalled more than 24 million miles of over-water flying and spotted 173 submarines. The Civil Air Patrol provides an extensive air courier service for the transport of critical supplies, parts and mail between AAF bases as well as for other agencies. Other important Civil Air Patrol contributions include training of pre-induction personnel (see page 121), search missions for lost aircraft, a southern air patrol over the Mexican border.

Combined Operations—The ultimate flowering of teamwork is reflected in combined military operations of ground, sea and air forces. The necessity for timing, for integrated planning and for joint action in such operations involves more than mere cooperation between one service and another. Combined operations, such as those carried on in the island offensives in the Pacific and in the conquest of North Africa, require the application of military power in mass and speed as one force. In North Africa, combined ground-air operations were developed to a point where the ground commander and the air commander worked in the same headquarters; the ground plan and the air plan were one plan. Except for strategic air attacks behind enemy lines, virtually all the major offensive operations of the United Nations have been combined operations—air-ground, air-sea, or air-sea-ground.

WHO WE ARE

We total more than two and a third million individuals. We hail from every part of the country and we have been sent to almost every part of the globe. Soon one-half of our number will be on duty outside our borders.

Nine out of every ten of us were gathered into the AAF in the last four years—since June of 1940 when our expansion program began. Yesterday we were the clerks, salesmen, students and farm hands of the nation. Today we are the pilots, gunners, radio operators and maintenance men of the AAF.

Working alongside us and contributing notably to the accomplishment of our program are some 500,000 civilian employees at AAF stations, ranging from unskilled laborers to highly specialized technicians. Additional thousands serve in auxiliary capacities—including natives of the arctic, desert and tropics.

Ours has been a twofold problem of expansion; first, that of building an immense organization from scratch; second, that of investing that untrained body with hundreds of separate skills. The possessors of these skills are not only the fighting men of the

AAF, but also the far larger number required to maintain, supply and support the fighting men.

Today our problem of expansion is licked. Our strength is at its intended peak. Our acquisition of personnel is now based on replacement.

The men who paved the way for our expansion grew up with the AAF and with the predecessor air arms from which the AAF sprang. Despite dwindling appropriations and consequent lack of personnel and equipment, these pioneers carried on the essential planning and experimenting.

Today the pioneers and the newcomers merge to form the largest air force in the world.

PROCUREMENT OF PERSONNEL

Requirements—Personnel procurement is a continuous process, subject to constant modification in its details. For example, a decision, motivated by combat experience, to add one gunner to the crew of each heavy bomber might cause a revision in the number of men to be taken into the AAF, the number of gunners to be selected from that intake, the number and size of gunnery schools to be established and the intensity of the training period for gunners already in schools.

This hypothetical case concerns the addition of just one man to a crew. Procurement changes arising from a more complicated problem such as the adoption of an entirely new airplane are naturally greater. Such changes are constantly occurring.

Once allowance has been made for such changes, and once the desired strength has been reached, the problem becomes one of keeping strength at the desired level. Here several factors enter:

AUTHORIZED STRENGTH—This quota is the minimum plus the reserves of manpower required for superiority over the enemy.

ROTATION—The rigors of aerial combat make it necessary to relieve personnel for rest after a period of service; this requires available reserve personnel.

REPLACEMENT—Replacements must be made for those unable to continue: the casualties. Such replacement varies constantly with the fortunes of war.

All these factors are affected by the course of battle. Modern aerial warfare knows no static plan.

Growth—In 1938 there were approximately 1300 officers and 18,000 men, with an additional 2800 officers and 400 men in the Reserve Corps, to begin the job of expanding the AAF to its present strength.

Various methods were used to attain this strength. Officers and enlisted men in the Reserve Corps were called into service; officers and men in other components of the Regular Army were permitted to apply for transfer into the AAF; 4000 men in the National Guard were taken in; recruiting campaigns utilizing such facilities as radio, pamphlets, posters and motor trailers were used from time to time to obtain more mechanics, radio operators or aviation cadets, depending on the urgent needs of the moment.

New officers were obtained by 2 methods: civilians with experience valuable to the technical needs of the AAF were commissioned by a special procurement organization; potential officer material among enlisted men was selected and sent to the Officer Candidate School at Miami Beach, Fla., and graduates were granted commissions.

Although the Selective Service program supplied quantities of personnel, our growing and specialized needs continuously outdistanced the supply. In the fall of 1942, a special recruiting

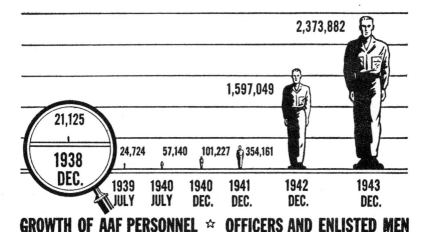

GROWTH OF AAF PERSONNEL ☆ OFFICERS AND ENLISTED MEN

campaign was undertaken to obtain sorely needed mechanics, armorers, radio technicians and other specialists. This campaign alone resulted in 128,000 enlistments. During this period, from September to December 1942, over 500,000 men were absorbed by the AAF.

Present Procurement—Selective Service is the basic procurement source for male military personnel. Those entering military service pass through its induction centers, and are assigned to one of the 3 major forces of the Army in prorated volume dependent on needs and available supply.

Those not yet of Army age may prepare themselves for future aviation training through the Civil Air Patrol training program. The original CAP enrollment comprised 40,000 cadets. Present plans call for enrollment of 250,000 by the end of 1944. High school students from the ages of 15 to 18 will be enrolled with the cooperation of civic organizations throughout the country. This training is planned on a 3-year period; future aviation cadets will have the most thorough preparation for flying studies ever furnished to citizens of this country. CAP, Chambers of Commerce, Rotary, Kiwanis, Elks, Lions and other civic organizations can furnish information on this program.

AVIATION CADETS

The AAF's principal source of flying officers and ground officer specialists has been the Aviation Cadet Recruiting Program.

This activity, temporarily suspended in March 1944, was open to civilians and enlisted men able to satisfy certain entrance requirements. Successful completion of Aviation Cadet Training qualified men to be commissioned 2nd lieutenants or appointed flight officers (see page 52). The program comprised aircrew trainees—pilots, bombardiers and navigators—and men trained in armament, communications, engineering, meteorology and photography.

At present, entrance to the Aviation Cadet Program is confined to certain AAF officers and enlisted men. However, the requirements of war may at any time prompt the re-establishment of aviation cadet recruiting.

For the most up-to-date information, civilians may consult their nearest U. S. Recruiting and Induction Center; an Aviation Cadet Examining Board; a Civil Air Patrol unit headquarters, or the adjutant of any Army post.

AAF Enlisted Personnel—The only enlisted personnel who may apply for aircrew training are enlisted men of the AAF who are combat crew members returned from overseas theaters after completion of a prescribed number of combat missions or in accordance with War Department regulations.

Application for those eligible may be made through the organization commander or at a Redistribution Station upon return to the U. S. An enlisted man found qualified and assigned to aircrew training (bombardier, pilot or navigator) may elect to train as an aviation student instead of accepting appointment as an aviation cadet. He then retains all the pay and allowances of his enlisted grade during his training period.

Officers—A very limited number of AAF officers in the grade of 2nd and 1st lieutenants are being qualified for aircrew training. These men are called student officers.

Basic Physical Requirements

VISION—*Minimum 20/20 each eye without glasses; must have perfect color vision.*

TEETH—*No minimum, if free from gross dental infections and correctible by full or partial dentures.*

HEARING—*Minimum 20/20 each ear (whispered voice).*

HEIGHT—*Minimum 60" maximum 76" (pilots minimum 64").*

WEIGHT—*Minimum 105 lbs. maximum 200 lbs. (pilots minimum 114 lbs.)—based on relation to height and age.*

Educational Requirements—Formal schooling is not required; applicants are given a qualifying examination of short-answer, multiple-choice type.

The following subjects are among those which have been

found extremely helpful for young men of school age in preparation for flying service with the AAF:

> PILOT—Science (gases, heat, gravity, stress, strain, energy, forces); mathematics (fundamental processes, formulas and equations); machine shop, bench metal work, mechanical drawing and blueprint reading, physical training.
>
> BOMBARDIER—Mathematics through trigonometry; science (properties of materials, heat, gases, forces, frictions, air currents); mechanical drawing, map and blueprint reading, physical training.
>
> NAVIGATOR—Mathematics as above; science (astronomy, weather elements, temperature, variation, air masses and currents) electricity, maps, charts and radio; geography, blueprint reading and mechanical drawing, physical training.

Tests—Applicants are given a series of psychometer and placement tests at the Basic Training Center in order to check mental and muscular coordination. Scores made on these tests determine the particular phase of flying—pilot, bombardier or navigator—in which an applicant can be best and most quickly trained. Failing to meet the minimum standards for any of these, applicants are eligible to apply for aerial gunnery training.

MILITARY PERSONNEL

Classification—From Jan. 1, 1942, to June 30, 1943, the period of greatest growth, the AAF expanded from 354,161 to 2,197,114 —or 520%. Each individual had to be interviewed, classified and assigned—1,842,953 in 18 months. The procurement program poured into uniforms a varied mass of skills, backgrounds and mental abilities, and varying degrees of education and training.

The AAF required a high level of technical aptitudes or abilities (see Military Occupational Specialties on page 45). Accepted classification procedures were not adequate to obtain suitable personnel. New methods had to be devised.

Reception centers are the first step in Army and AAF classification for the enlisted man. Here the newcomer is issued his first equipment and the Army obtains the first indication of his ability. After an introductory orientation lecture, he takes the most important of the various tests—the Army General Classification Test, known as GCT. Other tests given at the reception centers include: Oral Trades Test; General Mechanical Aptitude Test; Radio Operator Aptitude Test.

These tests are not intended to furnish proof of exact or detailed knowledge but to serve as an indication of aptitude for training in the technical categories involved.

From the reception centers the AAF receives its quota of enlisted personnel. Then additional tests are given to select men for the various technical training schools. Tests given at AAF Basic Training Centers are: Weather Aptitude Trade Test; Radio Operator Trade Test; Cryptography Test; Nut and Bolt Manual Dexterity Test; U-Bolt Assembly Test; Technical Trade Test.

AAF classification does not stop here. With each new job at each new station, individual classification is rechecked in the light of the soldier's current activities as compared to his potentialities. Officers follow the same general procedure.

Typical AAF Jobs—Listed below are more than 20 fields of skill required by the AAF. Pilot, bombardier and navigator are officer members of the aircrew. Unless indicated, all other classifications in this section are held by enlisted men. All duties are described in broad terms, with only major functions listed.

GENERAL NATURE OF DUTIES—AIR

PILOT—*Handles controls of plane and commands aircraft; in addition, fighter pilot fires guns, navigates, communicates with radio, sometimes directs and releases bombs.*

BOMBARDIER—*Directs flight of bomber when approaching and over target; operates bombsight; releases bombs; gunner during attack.*

NAVIGATOR—*Plots course of plane to and from the objective; furnishes pilot with flight directions; keeps flight log book; gunner during attack.*

AERIAL ENGINEER—*Flies with multi-engine bomber and transport; makes repairs and adjustments in flight; substitutes for or helps copilot operate flaps, landing gear, etc.; gunner during attack.*

RADIO OPERATOR—*Operates plane radio, direction finder, radio compass, etc.; relays data by radio to personnel on ground; receives weather and other information; gunner during attack.*

AERIAL GUNNER—*Mans guns; informs pilot of approaching enemy planes; services guns and turrets in flight.*

GENERAL NATURE OF DUTIES—GROUND

ARMAMENT OFFICER—*Supervises maintenance, loading and repair of armament equipment; is responsible for knowledge of latest armament devices and techniques.*

COMMUNICATIONS OFFICER—*Supervises maintenance, operation and repair of radar, radio, telegraph, teletype and directional equipment including radio compasses.*

AIRCRAFT MAINTENANCE OFFICER—*Supervises engineering ground duties of crew chiefs, aerial engineers, inspectors and mechanics.*

METEOROLOGY OFFICER—*Analyzes weather conditions; forecasts conditions along flight routes; keeps navigator informed; supervises weather technicians.*

PHOTOGRAPHY OFFICER—*Directs operations of mobile and fixed photographic laboratories and equipment; supervises aerial photographers and camera repairmen; is responsible for accurate photographic mapping of strategic areas.*

ARMORER—*Inspects, adjusts and repairs aerial machine guns, cannons, synchronizers, gun cameras, bomb racks and other armament mechanisms.*

METAL WORKER—*Repairs airbase equipment including tools; remakes certain broken and worn parts.*

WELDER—*Fuses metal parts by means of electric welding apparatus or oxyacetylene torch.*

AIRPLANE MECHANIC AND REPAIRMAN—*Checks the condition of airplanes and engines; makes repairs, replacements and adjustments; inspects electrical and control systems, undercarriage, brakes, engines and propellers.*

WIRE TECHNICIAN—*Installs, inspects, services and repairs telephone and telegraph communications systems; sets up switchboards; maintains lines over large areas.*

SYNTHETIC TRAINING DEVICE INSTRUCTOR—*Teaches instrument flying (blind flying) to pilot students through the use of the Link Trainer; instructs on other synthetic training devices.*

PARACHUTE RIGGER—*Sews and patches by hand and machine damaged parachute canopies; replaces defective shrouds; repairs harnesses; repacks parachutes.*

PHOTOGRAPHIC TECHNICIAN—*Develops films and prints pictures; assembles mosaic maps; takes motion and still photographs in flight or on ground.*

RADIO OPERATOR, MECHANIC AND REPAIRMAN—*Operates and adjusts all transmitter and receiver equipment; repairs defective radios and parts; tests circuits and tubes.*

WEATHER OBSERVER AND FORECASTER—*Analyzes weather conditions; observes instruments recording wind velocities, changes in temperature, humidity, barometric pressure, amount of rainfall and other conditions; prepares weather maps and reports.*

SUPPLY CLERK—*Receives, stores and issues equipment, material, merchandise and tools; checks incoming orders; counts, grades and weighs articles; takes periodic inventories; prepares reports.*

ADMINISTRATIVE CLERK—*Prepares reports; tabulates and posts data in record books and on bulletin boards; operates office machines; may supervise headquarters clerks.*

Distinctive Patches for Specialists—Enlisted technical specialists of the AAF in job categories of armament, communications, engineering, photography and weather are authorized to wear the patches shown below. Patches are orange on blue background and worn with lowest point 4 inches above edge of right sleeve (left breast pocket on fatigue uniform).

ARMAMENT   COMMUNICATIONS   ENGINEERING   PHOTOGRAPHY   WEATHER

MILITARY OCCUPATIONAL SPECIALTIES—After a qualifying period of time in his assigned duties, every soldier is classified according to his Military Occupational Specialty (MOS). Each specialty has a number which becomes a part of the soldier's record. Progressively, as more specialized tasks are performed, his record is supplemented by additional MOS numbers to show a complete picture of the soldier's experience. The AAF utilizes approximately 500 military occupational specialties, about evenly divided between officers and enlisted men. The following summary indicates the diversity of technicians required to accomplish the AAF mission.

OFFICER SPECIALTIES

RATED PERSONNEL—19 types of pilots from glider to 4-engine; 7 types of bombardiers and navigators; airbase commanders.

AIRCRAFT ENGINEERING—airplane maintenance engineers, inspectors and aeronautical engineers.

AVIATION ENGINEERS—inspection, mechanical, surveying, construction, camouflage and mapping engineers.

ARMAMENT AND ORDNANCE—includes torpedo, bombsight and mine specialists; bomb disposal and other ordnance officers.

COMMUNICATIONS—includes signal, message center, cryptanalytic and pigeon officers; radio, telephone, telephoto, radar and telegraph engineers.

OPERATIONS—personal equipment, flight control, priorities and traffic, and weight and balance officers.

RADAR—airborne and ground officers.

AIRCRAFT WARNING OFFICERS

PHOTOGRAPHIC—includes ground and aerial photographers, motion picture producers, technicians, laboratory supervisors.

INTELLIGENCE—historical, public relations and prisoner of war interrogation officers; photo-interpreters.

WEATHER—forecasters, climatologists, oceanographers.

FINANCE, BUDGET AND FISCAL OFFICERS

STATISTICAL OFFICERS

ADMINISTRATIVE—adjutant; publications and inspection officers, non-tactical unit commanders.

PERSONNEL—military personnel and civilian personnel officers, classification and assignment officers; psychologists.

CHAPLAINS

SPECIAL SERVICES—includes physical fitness and orientation officers.

MEDICAL—53 types including surgeons, nurses, veterinarians, sanitation engineers, dieticians, physical therapy aids and varied medical specialists.

SUPPLY—quartermaster, army exchange, salvage, laundry, technical, freight, petroleum, procurement and renegotiation officers.

TRANSPORTATION—marine officers classified as master, mate and engineer; motor and rail transportation officers.

MESS OFFICERS

LEGAL—judge advocates; legal assistance and claims officers.

CHEMICAL—aviation chemical warfare specialists.

PROVOST MARSHAL—includes military police and prison officers.

ANTIAIRCRAFT ARTILLERY OFFICERS

ENLISTED SPECIALTIES

PILOTS—*liaison and service pilots.*

AIRCREW — *gunners, photographers, radio operators, aerial engineers.*

ADMINISTRATIVE—*financial, typing and mail clerks; interpreters, translators and investigators; business machine operators; supply technicians in communications, ordnance, engineer and quartermaster equipment.*

AIRCRAFT WARNING — *controllers, aircraft observers, information center operators.*

ANTIAIRCRAFT—*includes gunners, repairmen, heightfinders, listeners, searchlight men.*

ARMAMENT AND ORDNANCE—*power turret, bombsight, munitions and armament technicians.*

BANDSMAN—*12 types classified by instrument.*

CHEMICAL—*toxic gas handlers, decontaminating equipment technicians.*

COMMUNICATIONS—*includes code, cryptographic, pigeon, signal and facsimile technicians; radar mechanics and repairmen; radar operators, radio operators; telephone and telegraph technicians.*

DRAFTSMEN—*draftsmen and photogrammetrists.*

DUTY AND INSTRUCTION—*includes military police, guards, athletic instructors, technical instructors, airplane handlers.*

ENGINEER, UTILITY AND REPAIR— *includes geodetic computers, surveyors, laundry technicians; construction men including bricklayers, camoufleurs, riggers, carpenters.*

MAINTENANCE — *includes supercharger, power plant, and fabric and dope specialists; electrical instrument, automatic pilot and fire control specialists; gyro, optical, hydraulic and mechanical instrument technicians; machinists; parachute and propeller specialists; sheet metal workers, welders, woodworkers.*

MEDICAL—*laboratory, supply, optical and dental technicians; pharmacy and veterinary specialists.*

MARINE—*includes able seamen, mates, oilers, engineers, etc.*

PHOTOGRAPHIC—*includes camera and motion picture technicians, photographers and projectionists, laboratory assistants.*

REPRODUCTION AND PRINTING—*lithographic and printing specialists.*

SERVICE AND REPAIR—*includes shoe repair, leather and canvas workers; painters; refrigeration mechanics; demolition specialists; water supply technicians.*

TRANSPORTATION — *automotive equipment operators and repairmen, diesel mechanics, motor and tractor specialists.*

WEATHER—*forecasters, observers, equipment men; radio-sonde men.*

TRAINER EQUIPMENT — *navigation trainers; instrument flying trainers; altitude chamber and flexible gunnery specialists.*

MISCELLANEOUS — *includes dog trainers, tire rebuilders, entertainment directors, physics laboratory assistants.*

AERONAUTICAL RATINGS—In order to be rated as any of the various types of flying personnel, officers, warrant officers, flight officers and enlisted men on duty with the AAF must meet certain qualifications.

PILOT—A rating of pilot in the AAF may be obtained:

☆ By successful completion of a prescribed course of instruction for heavier-than-air pilots at an AAF advanced pilot school (this method is the one from which the bulk of our pilot personnel is obtained).

☆ Upon the recommendation of a board of officers on the basis of meeting one of the following requirements:

(1) Previous aeronautical ratings held or previous aeronautical instruction passed within a specified past period; certain requirements of flying time; completion of a flight test.

(2) A rating as service pilot currently held; certain requirements of flying time; determination by the board of qualifications and readiness for assignment to the combat duties appropriate for a pilot who has graduated from an AAF advanced flying school.

(3) Graduation from a course of instruction for heavier-than-air pilots in armed forces of friendly foreign nations or the accumulation of certain required flying time with the armed forces of friendly foreign nations.

SENIOR PILOT—Requires not less than 5 years' service as rated pilot with aviation components of the military or naval services and not less than 1500 hours' logged time according to War Department records.

COMMAND PILOT—Obtainable by any rated pilot having certain combinations of the following: 10, 15 or 20 years' active duty or service with air components of the military or naval services, and 2000 or 3000 hours or more logged time according to War Department records. Credited at 100% is time flown in heavier-than-air military aircraft as pilot, copilot, or when not at the controls but acting in capacity of command pilot in unit operations of 2 or more aircraft. All other flying time in military heavier-than-air aircraft is credited at 50%. Lighter-than-air pilot time is credited at 25%. Flying time in non-military aircraft of 400 or more horsepower is credited at 100%.

SERVICE PILOT—Obtainable by individuals between 18 and 45 who have passed physical qualifications and who possess outstanding qualifications for the performance of service pilot duties as defined in AAF Reg. 35-23. Completion of a flight test and professional examination, certain flying time, and a recommendation by a board of officers is required.

SENIOR SERVICE PILOT—Obtainable by a rated service pilot who has 1500 hours' logged time according to War Department records, and has had 5 years' experience as a licensed pilot with the CAA.

LIAISON PILOT—Granted only to officers, warrant officers and enlisted men assigned to organic air observation of the Field Artillery. Liaison pilot ratings formerly granted to enlisted men in the AAF have been discontinued.

GLIDER PILOT—Requires successful completion of a prescribed advanced course of glider pilot training at an AAF special service school. Individuals may be rated glider pilot who hold ratings

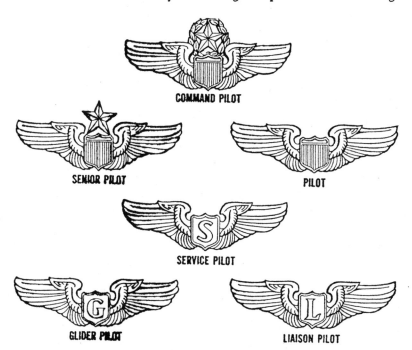

COMMAND PILOT

SENIOR PILOT

PILOT

SERVICE PILOT

GLIDER PILOT

LIAISON PILOT

as command pilot, senior pilot, pilot, service pilot or senior
service pilot and who have flown as pilot of tactical type gliders
3 hours or more and have made at least 10 landings, passed a
flight test, and are recommended by an examining board.

AIRCRAFT OBSERVER—Obtainable by individuals who hold ratings as
command pilot, senior pilot, pilot, senior balloon pilot or balloon
pilot—provided they have qualified as expert aerial gunner or
aerial sharpshooter, have been certified by their commanding
officers as competent to carry out the functions of an aircraft
observer, and satisfy one of the following additional requirements:

(1) Have served as a regularly assigned member of a combat crew
in observation and reconnaissance aviation units of the AAF;
completion of a course in aerial navigation, including celestial;
establishment of qualification as bombardier 1st class, 2nd class,
or 3rd class.

(2) Have served as a regularly assigned member of a combat crew
in a balloon squadron, and are certified by their commanding officers as competent to carry out the functions of an aircraft
observer.

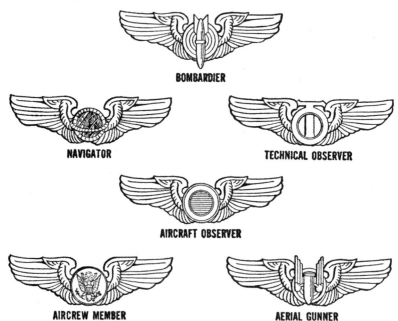

BOMBARDIER

NAVIGATOR

TECHNICAL OBSERVER

AIRCRAFT OBSERVER

AIRCREW MEMBER

AERIAL GUNNER

(3) Have graduated from the AAF tactical school and have 6 years' service as a rated pilot in the AAF.

AIRCRAFT OBSERVER (bombardier, navigator, radio observer night fighter, radio observer RCM, flight engineer)—Granted upon successful completion of the prescribed course of instruction for such ratings at an authorized AAF special service school. Rating as aircraft observer (bombardier, navigator and radio observer night fighter) is also granted to individuals who have demonstrated in a theater of operations their ability to satisfactorily perform the duties of bombardier, navigator or radio observer night fighter, are certified by their commanding officers as competent to carry out the functions proper to such ratings, and have flown 50 hours performing combat missions as bombardier, navigator or radio observer night fighter.

SENIOR AIRCRAFT OBSERVER—Obtainable by rated aircraft observers who have not less than 5 years' service as rated aircraft observer with air components of the military service and have flown as rated aircraft observer 500 hours or more.

TECHNICAL OBSERVER—Obtainable by commissioned officers who hold ratings as command pilot, senior pilot, pilot, senior balloon

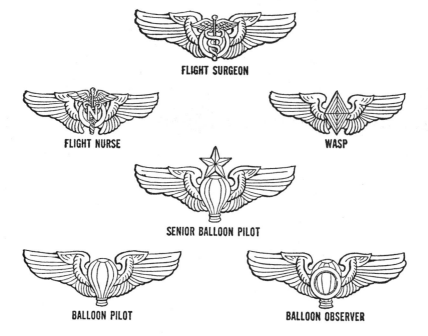

FLIGHT SURGEON

FLIGHT NURSE

WASP

SENIOR BALLOON PILOT

BALLOON PILOT

BALLOON OBSERVER

pilot or balloon pilot, whose principal duty should be that of a technical observer and whose experience with the AAF makes them especially qualified to perform technical duty incident to the operation of aircraft in flight. Requirements include certification by the commanding officer of the individual concerned that the principal duty of the individual should be that of technical observer, that he is qualified by both experience and ability to perform such duty, what specific duties are to be performed as technical observer, and a summary of the applicant's experience pertinent thereto.

SENIOR BALLOON PILOT—Obtainable by holders of balloon pilot rating who have 10 years' service with air components of the military service and who have piloted military airships or military motorized balloons for 100 hours.

BALLOON PILOT—Granted only to individuals who complete a prescribed balloon pilot course. No such course is being conducted at the present time.

(AAF Regulation 50-7 describes in detail aeronautical ratings.)

FLIGHT OFFICER—On July 8, 1942, the grade of flight officer was established. Upon graduation, aviation (flying training) cadets who have not qualified as 2nd lieutenants may be appointed flight officers with a status equivalent to that of warrant officer, junior grade. Promotion from flight officer to 2nd lieutenant is permitted.

Wearing of Aerial Gunner and Aircrew Member Badges

AERIAL GUNNER—Upon authorization by his commanding officer, a regularly assigned aerial gunner member of an aircrew, who has demonstrated his proficiency as such, may wear the badge during such time as he is assigned to such duties. Graduates of an AAF flexible gunnery school, or of an AAF instructors' school (flexible gunnery) may wear the badge during such time as they are assigned as a regular gunner member of an aircrew, are awaiting assignment to such duties, or are performing duties of an instructor in flexible gunnery.

AIRCREW MEMBER—Upon authorization by his commanding officer, a regularly assigned member of an aircrew who has demonstrated his proficiency as such may wear the badge during such time as he is assigned to such duties. Individuals authorized to wear specific badges may continue to wear such badges when no longer so assigned if they meet one of the following requirements:

(1) 150 hours' flying duty as regularly assigned aerial gunner or air-crew member.

(2) Participation as regularly assigned aerial gunner or aircrew member in 10 combat missions during which exposure to enemy fire was probable and expected.

(3) Physically incapacitated through enemy action or while discharging duties as member of an aircrew.

Army Air Forces Technician Badge—AAF enlisted technicians and mechanics have been authorized to wear a distinctive silver badge indicating the skills in which they are qualified. Qualifications: at least 6 months' service with the AAF and either graduation from an authorized course in technical training or evidence of capability in one or more of the following 24 specialties for which the badge has been designated:

 airplane armorers; airplane electrical, hydraulic and instrument specialist; airplane mechanic, machinist, metal worker and welder; airplane power plant specialist; airplane propeller specialist; ACS radio specialist; bombsight mechanic, Link Trainer instructor, parachute rigger, photographer, photographic laboratory technician, power turret and gunsight specialist, radio V-I mechanic, radio V-I observer, radio mechanic, radio operator, teletypewriter mechanic, weather forecaster, observer.

PAY AND INSIGNIA OF RANK OR GRADE

OFFICERS—Commissioned, warrant and flight. The following chart showing rank identifying insignia (worn on garrison caps and outer clothing), and rates of pay and allowances, does not include pay increases based on length of service, etc. Information in the chart on the next page is base pay only.

ENLISTED MEN—Grades are known by both name and number, i.e. enlisted man, 7th grade, is a private; 6th grade, a private 1st class. The chart on page 55 shows grades, identifying chevrons (worn on sleeves of outer clothing) and pay scale of enlisted men.

AVIATION CADETS—Base pay $75 per month and a subsistence allowance of $1 per day. (As with officers, aviation cadets, after graduation, are granted $250 clothing allowance.)

Rank	Insignia	Yearly Pay	Rent Allowance (Mo.) with dependents	single
General	✯✯✯✯	$8,000	$120	$105
Lt. General	✯✯✯	8,000	120	105
Maj. General	✯✯	8,000	120	105
Brig. General	✯	6,000	120	105
Colonel	🦅	4,000	120	105
Lt. Colonel	(Silver)	3,500	120	105
Major	(Gold)	3,000	105	90
Captain		2,400	90	75
1st Lieutenant	(Silver)	2,000	75	60
2nd Lieutenant	(Gold)	1,800	60	45
Warrant Officer (chief)	(Brown)	2,100	75	60
Warrant Officer (j.g.)	(Brown)	1,800	60	45
Flight Officer	(Blue)	1,800	60	45

In the above, all officers with dependents receive $42 per month (30 day period) subsistence allowance; single officers, $21. (Exception: Lt. Col. and Maj., married, receive $63.)

FLYING PAY—Flying officers and enlisted men receive an increase of 50% of their base pay when by orders of competent authority they are required to participate regularly and frequently in aerial flights and when as a result of orders they do participate in such flights. Non-flying officers receive flying pay at the rate of $60 per month when they participate in regular and frequent aerial flights ordered by competent authority.

Rank	Sleeve Insignia	Monthly Base Pay
Private (7th grade)	no chevrons	$50
Private first class (6th grade)		54
Corporal (5th grade)		66
Sergeant (4th grade)		78
Staff Sergeant (3rd grade)		96
Technical Sergeant (2nd grade)		114
Master Sergeant, First Sergeant (1st grade)		138

Pay scale noted above shows base pay amounts. This is the lowest amount paid to each grade. To this may be added other amounts for flying pay, longevity, etc., descriptions of which follow.

LONGEVITY—Every enlisted man receives an increase of 5% of his base pay for each 3 years of service up to 30 years.

FOREIGN SERVICE—The base pay of officers is increased by 10% (enlisted men 20%) for any service while on sea duty or duty in any place beyond the continental limits of the U. S. or in Alaska.

ALLOWANCE FOR DEPENDENTS (Class F Allotment)—Under the Oct. 26, 1943 amendment to the Servicemen's Dependent Allowance Act of 1942, dependents of enlisted men receive increased benefits. Several classes of benefits are allowed—for wife and children, for parents, brothers and sisters whose chief support is the serviceman, and for combinations of these family relationships. Men with dependents allow the government to deduct $22 per month from pay, the remainder of the amount received by the family is contributed by the government. A wife will receive $50 per month; with one child, $80, and $20 for each additional child. A mother as a dependent will receive $37, in cases of total dependency, $50.

CHAPTER CONTINUED ON PAGE 89

OUR LEADERS

Brief Biographies of Some AAF Men with Key Assignments*

ARNOLD, General Henry H.

COMMANDING GENERAL, AAF

First airman to achieve the rank of General and one of the nation's first military pilots, Gen. Arnold serves on the Combined Chiefs of Staff and the Joint Chiefs of Staff.

Gen. Arnold was born in Gladwyne, Pa., June 25, 1886. He graduated from the U. S. Military Academy and was commissioned 2nd Lt. Inf. June 14, 1907; served in the Philippines; was detailed to the Signal Corps in April, 1911. After completing flying instruction at Dayton, Ohio, in June, 1911, Gen. Arnold became an instructor at the Signal Corps Aviation School; he was promoted to 1st Lt. in April, 1913. In February, 1917, after serving in the Philippines and California, he went to the Panama Canal Zone to organize and command the aviation service there. He was promoted to Capt. in May, 1916; to Maj. (temp.) in June, and to Col. (temp.) in August, 1917.

With U. S. entry into the World War, Gen. Arnold was placed in charge of the Information Service, Aviation Division, Signal Corps; later appointed Executive Officer; then, Assistant Director, Office of Military Aeronautics. In 1925 he became Chief, Information Division, Office Chief of Air Corps. He commanded Air Corps troops at Ft. Riley, 1926 to 1928, graduated from the Command and General Staff School in June, 1929, and until 1936 held command posts at Fairfield, Ohio, and at March Field, Calif. Gen. Arnold received the 1934 Mackay Trophy award in recognition of his leadership of the U. S. Army Alaskan flight of that year. He was promoted to Brig. Gen. (temp.) in February, 1935.

Service as Assistant Chief of the Air Corps was followed by appointment as Chief of the Air Corps, Sept. 29, 1938. He was designated Acting Deputy Chief of Staff for Air in October, 1940, and appointed Chief of the AAF in June, 1941. He became a permanent Brig. Gen. in December, 1940; permanent Maj. Gen., February, 1941; Lt. Gen. (temp.), December, 1941. When the War Department was reorganized March 9, 1942, Gen. Arnold became Commanding General of the AAF; in March, 1943, he was promoted to General (temp.). *Ratings:* Command Pilot, Aircraft Observer, Technical Observer. *Decorations:* DFC, DSM, Air Medal.

*Ranks and assignments as of May 1, 1944. Space limitations do not permit a complete listing of Army Air Forces' leaders.

LOVETT, Hon. Robert A.

ASS'T SECRETARY OF WAR FOR AIR

Born Huntsville, Tex., Sept. 14, 1895. Graduated Yale Univ., 1918. Post-graduate courses Harvard Law School (1919-1920) and Harvard Graduate Sch. of Business Administration, 1920-1921. Naval pilot, ensign in 1917; served in France and awarded French wings. Established U. S. Naval Air Service Transition Flying School same year. Promoted to Lt. Commander and received Navy Cross in 1918. Between 1921 and 1940 engaged in philanthropic interests and served as director and trustee of numerous corporations. He resigned from business activities and obtained leave of absence from other interests in 1940 to accept appointment as Special Assistant to the Secretary of War; was appointed Assistant Secretary of War for Air in April 1941.

McNARNEY, Lt. Gen. Joseph T.

DEP. CHIEF OF STAFF, U. S. ARMY

Born Emporium, Pa., Aug. 28, 1893. Graduated USMA and commissioned 2nd Lt. Inf. June 12, 1915. Completed flying training and received rating of Jr. Military Aviator in April 1917. Served in France during World War I. Graduated Army War College 1930. Served in War Plans Division, General Staff, 1939, and appointed member of Joint Army and Navy Planning Committee. Member of Special Observers Group, London, 1941. Member of Roberts Commission 1941-42. Designated Dep. Chief of Staff, U. S. Army, March 1942. *Ratings:* Command Pilot, Technical Observer, Aircraft Observer.

GILES, Lt. Gen. Barney McK.

DEPUTY COMMANDER AAF, CHIEF OF AIR STAFF

Born Mineola, Tex., Sept. 13, 1892. Attended East Texas College and Univ. of Texas. Appointed flying cadet and commissioned 2nd Lt. Aviation Section of Signal Corps Reserve April 9, 1918. Received Reg. Army commission July 1, 1920. Served in France and in Coblenz, Germany. During 1918-19. Organized and commanded 4th Air Service Area Command and designated Commanding General of 4th Bomber Command 1942. Made Commanding General 4th Air Force, San Francisco, Calif., Sept. 1942. In March 1943 became Ass't. to Chief of Air Staff and in July 1943 named Chief of Air Staff. *Ratings:* Command Pilot, Technical Observer, Aircraft Observer. *Decorations:* DFC, Air Medal.

EMMONS, Lt. Gen. Delos C.

COMMANDING GENERAL, WESTERN DEFENSE COMMAND

Born Huntington, W. Va., Jan. 17, 1888. Graduated USMA and commissioned 2nd Lt. Inf. June 11, 1909. Executive officer for Ass't. Secretary of War for Air 1928-31. Commanding General, GHQ Air Force March 1939. Assigned Chief of Air Force Combat Command June 1941 and designated Commanding General, Hawaiian Dept. Dec. 1941. Named Commanding General Western Defense Command Sept. 1943. *Ratings:* Command Pilot, Aircraft Observer. *Decorations:* DFC, DSM, Air Medal.

YOUNT, Lt. Gen. Barton K.

COMMANDING GENERAL, AAF TRAINING COMMAND

Born Troy, Ohio, Jan. 18, 1884. Attended Ohio State Univ. Graduated USMA, commissioned 2nd Lt. Inf. June 14, 1907. Member Board of Officers for reorganization of Air Service 1918-19. Ass't. Military Attache for Aviation, Paris 1925-29; served as Technical Expert at Geneva Disarmament Conference. Graduated Army War College 1936. Commander Air Corps Training Center, Randolph Field, Tex., 1938. Appointed Ass't. to Chief of Air Corps July 1938. Placed in charge of all training activities of the Air Corps 1939. Commanded Panama Canal Dept. Air Force Oct. 1940; Southeast Air District Dec. 1940. Commanding General of AAF Flying Training Command March 1942. In July 1943 became Commanding General, AAF Training Command. *Ratings:* Command Pilot, Technical Observer, Aircraft Observer.

HUNTER, Maj. Gen. Frank O'D.

COMMANDING GENERAL, 1st AIR FORCE

Born Savannah, Ga., Dec. 8, 1894. Enlisted as flying cadet, and commissioned 1st Lt. Aviation Section, Signal Corps Reserve, Sept. 12, 1917. Reg. Army commission as 1st Lt. Air Service July 1, 1920. Shot down 9 planes in World War I. Military Observer in London 1940. In May 1942 became Commanding General of the 8th Air Force Fighter Command. Returned to U. S. in Sept. 1943 and designated Commanding General 1st Air Force. *Ratings:* Command Pilot, Aircraft Observer, Technical Observer. *Decorations:* DSC with 4 Oak Leaf Clusters, Silver Star, Legion of Merit, Purple Heart, French Croix de Guerre with Palm.

60

ENT, Brig. Gen. Uzal G.

COMMANDING GENERAL, 2ND AIR FORCE

Born Northumberland, Pa., March 3, 1900. Attended Susquehanna Univ. Served as enlisted man in Inf., Aviation and Balloon companies 1918-19. Graduated USMA and commissioned 2nd Lt. Air Service June 1924. Military attache at Lima, Peru, 1940. Assigned to 9th Air Force, Middle East Command, Oct. 1942. Returned to U. S. and designated Commanding General 2nd Air Force Jan. 1944. *Ratings:* Command Pilot, Aircraft Observer, Balloon Pilot, Balloon Observer. *Decorations:* DSM with Oak Leaf Cluster, DSC, DFC with Oak Leaf Cluster, Air Medal with Oak Leaf Cluster.

LARSON, Maj. Gen. Westside T.

COMMANDING GENERAL, 3RD AIR FORCE

Born Vernalis, Calif., April 18, 1892. Attended Polytechnic College of Engineering at Oakland, Calif. Enlisted Aviation Section Signal Corps Reserve Oct. 19, 1917, and completed flying training at Park Field, Tenn. Commissioned 2nd Lt. May 18, 1918. Served at Park, Ellington and Kelly fields, and in Panama Canal Zone 1920-28. Commanded 13th Bombardment Group, Langley Field 1941. Designated Commanding General: 1st Bomber Command 1942; Antisubmarine Command, 1942-43; 3rd Air Force, Tampa, Fla., Sept. 1943. *Ratings:* Command Pilot, Aircraft Observer.

LYND, Maj. Gen. William E.

COMMANDING GENERAL, 4TH AIR FORCE

Born Santa Fe, Kan., Sept. 10, 1893. Attended Univ. of Seattle. Commissioned 2nd Lt. Inf. Idaho Nat'l guard April 4, 1917. Served in France during World War I. Graduated Naval War College June 1938. Air Base Commander, Wheeler Field, Hawaii 1939. Commanding General 7th Bomber Command in Hawaii, and in Nov. 1942 named Army Air Officer on staff of Commander-in-Chief of Pacific Fleet. Commanding General 4th Air Force July 1943. *Ratings:* Command Pilot, Aircraft Observer. *Decorations:* Silver Star (awarded in 1918), DFC, Air Medal with Oak Leaf Cluster, Purple Heart.

GEORGE, Maj. Gen. Harold L.
COMMANDING GENERAL,
AIR TRANSPORT COMMAND

Born Somerville, Mass., July 19, 1893. Commissioned 2nd Lt. Aviation Section, Signal Corps, March 29, 1918. Served in War Plans Division, Air Service, 1925-29. Chief of Bombardment and Air Force Instruction and Director of Air Tactics and Strategy, Maxwell Field, Ala. 1932-36. Commanding General Ferrying Command March 1942; Air Transport Command Aug. 1942. *Ratings:* Command Pilot, Aircraft Observer. *Decoration:* Silver Star.

EUROPEAN—MEDITERRANEAN

SPAATZ, Lt. Gen. Carl
COMMANDING GENERAL,
U. S. STRATEGIC AIR FORCES IN EUROPE

Born Boyertown, Pa., June 28, 1891. Graduated USMA and commissioned 2nd Lt. Inf. June 12, 1914. Stationed Schofield Barracks, Hawaii 1914-15, then detailed as student at Aviation Sch. San Diego, Calif. Served in France during World War I and credited with 2 German planes. Commanded Kelly Field, Tex., 1920-21. Special Military Observer in England 1940. Chief Materiel Division of Air Corps Oct. 1940. Chief of Air Force Combat Command Jan. 1942. Commanding General 8th Air Force May 1942; Northwest African Air Forces, Nov. 1942. In Jan. 1944 became Commanding General of U. S. Strategic Air Forces in Europe. *Ratings:* Command Pilot, Aircraft Observer. *Decorations:* DSC, DSM, DFC, Legion of Merit.

EAKER, Lt. Gen. Ira C.
COMMANDING GENERAL,
MEDITERRANEAN ALLIED AIR FORCES

Born Llano, Tex., April 13, 1896. Commissioned 2nd Lt. Inf. Reg. Army Nov. 15, 1917. Commanded Mitchel Field, N. Y., 1921-23. Named Commander of Bombardment European Theater, July 1942 and later Commanding General of 8th Air Force. Designated Commander Mediterranean Allied Air Forces in Jan. 1944. *Ratings:* Command Pilot, Technical Observer, Aircraft Observer. *Decorations:* Silver Star, DFC with Oak Leaf Cluster, Legion of Merit.

62

DOOLITTLE, Lt. Gen. James H.
COMMANDING GENERAL, 8TH AIR FORCE
Born Alameda, Calif., Dec. 14, 1896. Attended Univ. of Calif. Enlisted as flying cadet, Signal Corps Reserve, Oct. 6, 1917. Commissioned 2nd Lt. March 11, 1918. Entered MIT 1923 and received Master's and Doctor's degrees 1924 and 1925. Resigned Reg. Army commission on Feb. 15, 1930 and commissioned a Maj., Spec. Res. Ordered to active duty as Maj. July 1, 1940. On April 18, 1942 led first aerial raid on Japanese mainland. Commanded 12th Air Force Sept. 1942. Commanding General: NW African Strategic Air Force March 1943; 15th Air Force Nov. 1943; 8th Air Force Jan. 1944. *Rating:* Command Pilot. *Decorations:* Medal of Honor, DSM, Silver Star, DFC with Oak Leaf Cluster, Air Medal with 3 Clusters.

TWINING, Maj. Gen. Nathan F.
COMMANDING GENERAL, 15TH AIR FORCE
Born Monroe, Wis., Oct. 11, 1897. Graduated from USMA and commissioned 2nd Lt. Inf. Nov. 1, 1918. Served at March Field, Calif., and in Hawaii 1927-32. Designated Director of War Organization and Movement AAF 1942. Appointed Commanding General 13th Air Force Jan. 1943. July 1943 assigned Commander of Aircraft in Solomon Islands, in which capacity he directed all air strength in that area. Became Commanding General 15th Air Force Jan. 1944. *Ratings:* Command Pilot, Aircraft Observer. *Decorations:* DFC, Legion of Merit with Oak Leaf Cluster, Air Medal.

BRERETON, Lt. Gen. Lewis H.
COMMANDING GENERAL, 9TH AIR FORCE
Born Allegheny, Pa., June 21, 1890. Graduated U. S. Naval Academy 1911. Resigned as ensign, commissioned 2nd Lt. Coast Arty. Corps Aug. 17, 1911. During World War I saw action in France. Air Attache, American Embassy, Paris, 1919-22. Commanding Officer France Field and Panama Air Depot, and Acting Air Officer Panama Canal Department 1931-35. In July 1941 assigned to command 3rd Air Force. Commanding General: 10th Air Force March 1942; 9th Air Force, Oct. 1942. *Ratings:* Command Pilot, Technical Observer, Aircraft Observer. *Decorations:* DSC, Silver Star with Oak Leaf Cluster, DSM, DFC, Air Medal, Purple Heart, French Croix de Guerre with 2 Palms.

CANNON, Maj. Gen. John K.

COMMANDING GENERAL, 12TH AIR FORCE

Born Salt Lake City, Utah, March 9, 1892. Graduated Utah Agricultural College 1914. Commissioned 2nd Lt. Inf. Reserve Nov. 27, 1917. Director of Flying, later of Training, Randolph Field, Tex., 1931-35. Chief of U. S. Military Mission to Buenos Aires 1938. Commanding General 1st Interceptor Command, Mitchel Field, N. Y., Feb. 1942. Became Commanding General 12th Air Force Dec. 1943. *Ratings:* Command Pilot, Aircraft Observer. *Decorations:* DSM, Air Medal, Legion of Merit.

ANDERSON, Maj. Gen. Frederick L. Jr.

DEPUTY COMMANDER FOR OPERATIONS,
U. S. STRATEGIC AIR FORCES IN EUROPE

Born Kingston, N. Y., Oct. 4, 1905. Graduated USMA and commissioned 2nd Lt. Cav. June 9, 1928. Graduated Advanced Flying Sch., Kelly Field, Tex. Sept. 1929. Served in the Philippines until 1934. Director of Bombardier Instruction Air Corps Tactical Sch. July 1940. Deputy Director of Bombardment, Hq. AAF, in Jan. 1942. Assigned as Commanding General of 8th Bomber Command. Became Deputy Commander for Operations USAFE in July 1943. *Ratings:* Command Pilot, Technical Observer, Aircraft Observer. *Decorations:* Silver Star, DFC, Legion of Merit, Air Medal.

VANDENBERG, Maj. Gen. Hoyt S.

DEPUTY COMMANDER-IN-CHIEF,
ALLIED EXPEDITIONARY AIR FORCES

Born Milwaukee, Wis., Jan. 24, 1899. Graduated USMA and commissioned 2nd Lt. Air Service June 12, 1923. Served in Hawaii 1929-31. Graduated Army War College 1939. Operations and Training Officer (A-3) Air Staff, Washington, D. C., March 1942. Assigned to United Kingdom and assisted, in plans for African invasion June 1942. Chief of Staff 12th Air Force Oct. 1942. Returned to U. S. and designated Deputy Chief of Air Staff Aug. 1943. Became Deputy Commander-in-Chief Allied Expeditionary Air Forces March 1944. *Ratings:* Command Pilot, Technical Observer, Aircraft Observer. *Decorations:* DSM, Silver Star, DFC, Legion of Merit, Air Medal.

64

ASIATIC

STRATEMEYER, Maj. Gen. George E.

COMMANDING GENERAL,
EASTERN AIR COMMAND

Born Cincinnati, Ohio, Nov. 24, 1890. Graduated USMA and commissioned 2nd Lt. Inf. June 12, 1915. Commanding Officer, Air Service Mechanical Sch. Kelly Field, Tex. 1917 and Commanding Officer, Chanute Field, Ill., 1921. Instructor at USMA until 1929. Graduated Army War College 1939. Chief Training and Operations Division, Office of Chief of Air Corps April 1941. Commanding General, Southeast Air Corps Training Center Jan. 1942. Chief of Air Staff June 1942. Air Advisor to Commanding General, China-Burma-India Theater July 1943; Commanding General, Eastern Air Command, Aug. 1943. *Ratings:* Command Pilot, Aircraft Observer. *Decorations:* DSM, Air Medal.

DAVIDSON, Maj. Gen. Howard C.

COMMANDING GENERAL, 10TH AIR FORCE

Born Wharton, Tex., Sept. 15, 1890. Graduated USMA, commissioned 2nd Lt. Inf. June 12, 1913. Served at Tours and Paris 1917-19. Ass't Military Attache, London 1922-26. Commanding Officer Bolling Field, D. C., 1928-32. Commanded 19th Bombardment Group 1935-36. Graduated Army War College June 1940 and ordered to Hickam Field, Hawaii as Commanding Officer. Commanding General: Hawaiian Interceptor Command Dec. 1941; 7th Air Force June 1942; AAFTTC Mississippi Delta Area Nov. 1942; 10th Air Force July 1943. *Ratings:* Command Pilot, Aircraft Observer.

CHENNAULT, Maj. Gen. Claire L.

COMMANDING GENERAL, 14TH AIR FORCE

Born Commerce, Tex., Sept. 6, 1890. Attended Louisiana State Univ. and Normal College. Commissioned 1st Lt. Inf. Reserve Nov. 27, 1917. Instructor and Director of Flying at Brooks Field, Tex., until 1930. Author: Role of Defensive Pursuit 1935. Retired April 30, 1937 and went to China; made a Brig. Gen. in the Chinese Air Force and placed in charge of AVG (Flying Tigers). Recalled to active duty April 1942. Commanding General: AAF in China July 1942; 14th Air Force, March 1943. *Ratings:* Airplane Pilot, Aircraft Observer. *Decorations:* DSM, DFC.

KENNEY, Lt. Gen. George C.

COMMANDING GENERAL, 5TH AIR FORCE

Born Yarmouth, Nova Scotia, Aug. 6, 1889. Attended MIT. At outbreak of World War I enlisted as flying cadet; commissioned 1st Lt. in Aviation Section, Signal Corps Reserve, Nov. 5, 1917. Served in France and Germany 1917-19; credited with destruction of 2 enemy aircraft. Graduated Army War College June 1933. Ass't Attache for Air in Paris in 1940. Commanding General 4th Air Force April 1942. Commanding General Allied Air Forces in Australian theater; 5th Air Force Sept. 1942. *Ratings:* Command Pilot, Aircraft Observer. *Decorations:* DSC with cluster, DSM, Silver Star, DFC, Purple Heart.

HARMON, Lt. Gen. Millard F.

COMMANDING GENERAL, U. S. ARMY FORCES IN SOUTH PACIFIC

Born San Francisco, Calif., Jan. 19, 1888. Graduated USMA, commissioned 2nd Lt. Inf. June 12, 1912. Saw action at Somme during World War I. Ass't Prof. Military Science & Tactics, Univ. of Washington 1923-24. Graduate Army War College June 1925. Commanded Luke Field, Hawaii and 5th Bombardment Group 1936-38. Air Observer and member Harriman Commission 1941. Commanding General 4th Interceptor Command of 4th Air Force April 1941; 2nd Air Force July 1941. Chief of Air Staff, Washington, D. C., Jan. 1942. Commanding General U. S. Army Forces in South Pacific Area July 1942. *Ratings:* Command Pilot, Technical Observer, Aircraft Observer. *Decorations:* Navy DSM, French Croix de Guerre with bronze star.

HARMON, Maj. Gen. Hubert R.

COMMANDING GENERAL, 13TH AIR FORCE

Born Chester, Pa., April 3, 1892. Graduated USMA, commissioned 2nd Lt. Coast Arty. Corps June 12, 1915. Became Chief of Air Staff Air Service Command, Third Army 1919. Aviation Officer, U. S. Liquidation Committee London 1919-20. Instructor USMA 1929-32. Commander 19th Bombardment Group 1936-37. Graduate Army War College July 1938. Chief of Operations, Personnel, Washington, D. C. 1937-40. Commanding General: Gulf Coast Training Center 1941; 6th Air Force 1942; 13th Air Force Jan. 1944. *Ratings:* Command Pilot, Aircraft Observer. *Decorations:* Legion of Merit, Air Medal.

66

HALE, Maj. Gen. Willis H.
COMMANDING GENERAL, 7TH AIR FORCE
Born Pittsburg, Kan., Jan. 7, 1893. Lt. in Philippine constabulary 1913 to March 20, 1917 when commissioned 2nd Lt. Inf. Reg. Army and promoted to 1st Lt. same date. Served in China and France 1917-18. Prof. Military Science and Tactics Yale Univ. 1920-22. Graduated Army War College June 1937. Inspector General of GHQ Air Force, Langley Field, Va., 1939-40. Chief of Staff 3rd Air Force, Tampa, Fla., 1940-41. Commanding General 7th Air Force Hawaii July 1942. *Ratings:* Command Pilot, Aircraft Observer. *Decorations:* DSM, Legion of Merit, Purple Heart, Navy Cross.

JOHNSON, Maj. Gen. Davenport
COMMANDING GENERAL, 11TH AIR FORCE
Born Tyler, Tex., March 28, 1890. Graduated USMA, commissioned 2nd Lt. Inf. June 12, 1912. Military Observer with French Army during World War I. Graduated Army War College June 1929. Commanded 3rd Attack Group to July 1932. Commanding Officer Hamilton Field, Calif., 1937. Ass't to Chief of Air Corps in Washington, D. C., 1940. Commanded 6th Air Force, Panama, C. Z., 1942. Became Director Military Requirements Hq. AAF Nov. 1942. Commanding General 2nd Air Force Feb. 1943; 11th Air Force Sept. 1943. *Ratings:* Command Pilot, Aircraft Observer. *Decorations:* Silver Star, Air Medal, French Croix de Guerre.

MIDDLE EAST

GILES, Brig. Gen. Benjamin F.
COMMANDING GENERAL, U. S. ARMY FORCES, MIDDLE EAST
Born Mineola, Tex., Sept. 13, 1892. Attended Univ. of Tex. and commissioned 2nd Lt. Inf. Res. April 28, 1917. Served in France during World War I. Commissioned 2nd Lt. Air Service, Reg. Army July 1, 1920. Chief of Aviation Division, Nat'l. Guard Bureau 1939. Commanding General: Hq. North Atlantic Wing, Air Transport Command Aug. 1942; 9th Air Force Troop Carrier Command Oct. 1943; U. S. Army Forces, Middle East Feb. 1944. *Ratings:* Command Pilot, Aircraft Observer. *Decorations:* DSM, Air Medal.

SOUTH ATLANTIC

WALSH, Maj. Gen. Robert LeG.

COMMANDING GENERAL,
U. S. ARMY FORCES, SOUTH ATLANTIC

Born Walla Walla, Wash., July 25, 1894. Graduated USMA and commissioned 2nd Lt. Cav. June 13, 1916. After service in France during World War I he was assigned to Division of Military Aeronautics in Washington, D. C., 1919-20. Ass't Attache for Air at Paris and Madrid 1929-31. Commanded Albrook Field, C. Z., 1933-35. Graduated Army War College 1940. Commanding General: South Atlantic Wing, Air Transport Command June 1942; U. S. Army Forces South Atlantic Nov. 1942. *Ratings:* Command Pilot, Aircraft Observer. *Decoration:* Legion of Merit.

CARIBBEAN

BRETT, Lt. Gen. George H.

COMMANDING GENERAL,
CARIBBEAN DEFENSE COMMAND

Born Cleveland, Ohio, Feb. 7, 1886. Graduated VMI 1909. Appointed 2nd Lt. Philippine Scouts March 22, 1910; 2nd Lt. of Cav. Reg. Army 1911. Commanded Crissy Field 1921-24. Graduated Army War College June 1936. Ass't to Chief of Air Corps Jan. 1939. Chief of Air Corps May 1941. Became Deputy Supreme Commander of Allied Forces in South Pacific and in April 1942 named Chief of Allied Air Forces in Australia. Named Commanding General Caribbean Defense Command and Panama Canal Dept., Nov. 1942. *Ratings:* Command Pilot, Technical Observer, Aircraft Observer. *Decorations:* DSM, Silver Star, DFC.

WOOTEN, Brig. Gen. Ralph H.

COMMANDING GENERAL, 6TH AIR FORCE

Born Tate Co., Miss., Aug. 30, 1893. Graduated A & M College of Texas, 1916. Commissioned 2nd Lt. Inf. Reg. Army Aug. 8 1917; Chief of Military Procurement and Transportation, Washington, D. C., 1924-28. Military Attache, Santiago, Chile, 1929-33; 1938-41. Graduated Army War College June 1937. Air Officer General Hq., 1941. Assigned AAF Technical Training Command, Miami Beach, Fla., March 1942. Jan. 1943 Commanding General 6th Air Force Service Command and Chief of Staff 6th Air Force. Named Commanding General 6th Air Force Nov. 1943. *Ratings:* Command Pilot, Aircraft Observer.

BOMBER CREW, basic unit of the AAF offensive, is a tight-knit team. Each man is expert in his specific duty: all work in close coordination.

Gen. Arnold has said, "Nowhere in the world are the lives of men as interdependent as in a bomber on a mission." Above, a mission is over.

BOMBER PILOT, commander of the airplane, has the responsibility of flying the plane to the target and bringing it home again. The lives of the crewmen depend upon the pilot's skill and judgment.

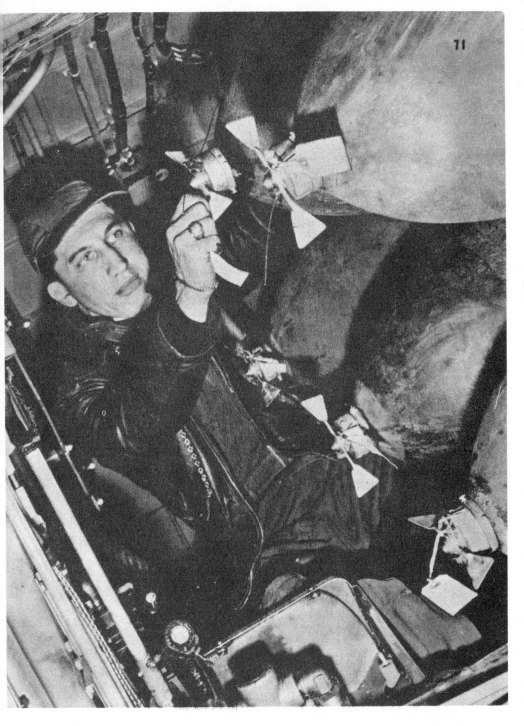

THE BOMBARDIER, here pulling safety-pins on bombs during flight, takes over plane on bombing run, aims and drops bombs. Accuracy of his calculations determines success of the mission.

GETTING THERE and getting back depends on the navigator. From the takeoff on, he determines and logs plane's position, direction.

LINK WITH the ground is the radio operator. In constant contact with ground controls, he sends and receives all radio messages.

AERIAL GUNNER *must drive off enemy planes attacking bomber. His oxygen mask makes thin upper air breathable; metal-lined flak vest guards against flak fragments; warm clothing protects him from intense cold. Plane's floor is strewn with discarded shell cases.*

WITHOUT ground crews there could be no flying, no bombing. Combat wear necessitates constant checking and repairing of aircraft. In all war theaters, from desert (above) to Arctic (below) ground crews toil at their unending maintenance. At right, an engine change.

WOMEN in the AAF fly and keep 'em flying. Air Wacs fill over 200 important job categories like weather observation (above) and make it possible to release men for combat duty. Wasps (below) do 10 non-combat flying jobs like ferrying, tow-target and courier.

RADIO navigational aids and weather data are transmitted to AAF and Allied aircraft by Army Airways Communications System. Stations are located in 48 states and 52 foreign countries, many in lonely wilds. Pacific station above is reinforced against bomb fragments.

IN TRAINING, students get enough theory to understand their jobs, perfect their knowledge with practical experience. Training aids like dummy battleship for bombardier trainees (above) are widely used. Civilian factory schools (below) help train AAF technicians.

AFTER a crammed day of flying, ground school, calisthenics and drill, night often finds pilot trainees waiting to take off on a cross country flight (above). Overland hops in darkness teach students to maintain formation and to navigate without landmarks.

GUNNERY STUDENT trains with targets moving on the ground. Later he will fire from plane at target towed by another airplane.

UNDER BATTLE ZONE conditions Operational Training Units give men final training before combat. Life is primitive, tools crude.

SUPPLY BY AIR has proved a deciding factor in many battles of this war. Today the AAF flies 110,000 miles of air transport routes.

AIR EVACUATION speeds battle wounded from fronts to hospitals. Flight nurses and medical personnel attend evacuees during flight.

CARGO PARACHUTES, capable of dropping loads to 3000 pounds, answer the problem of supplying troops in inaccessible regions.

TO SUPPLY the AAF, dumps and depots are needed in all parts of the globe. Below, bombs lie under palm camouflage on Pacific isle.

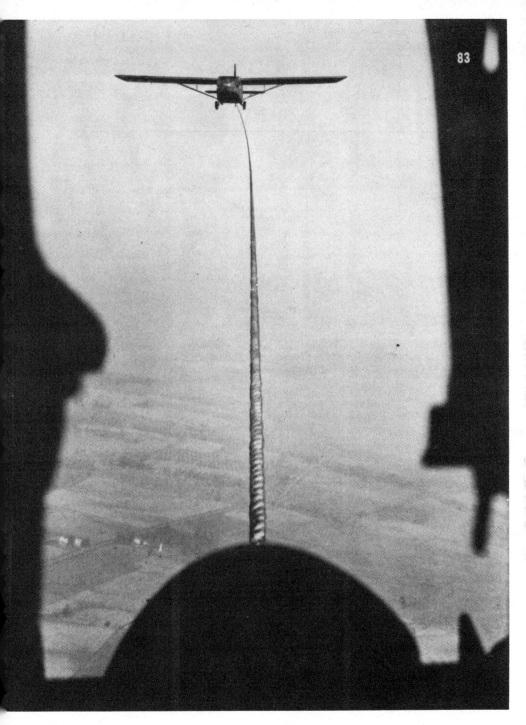

GLIDERS, used to carry troops and supplies, can land in short spaces, on nearly any terrain. When tow rope is released, pilot maintains forward movement by controlling rate of descent. The glider above (YCG-13) can carry 4 tons of equipment or 30 equipped troops.

TO SPEED the work of building forward airbases, aviation engineers and heavy equipment like this bulldozer often travel by air.

EMPLOYMENT of native labor for airfield construction has helped keep our aircraft in position for continuous attack on the enemy.

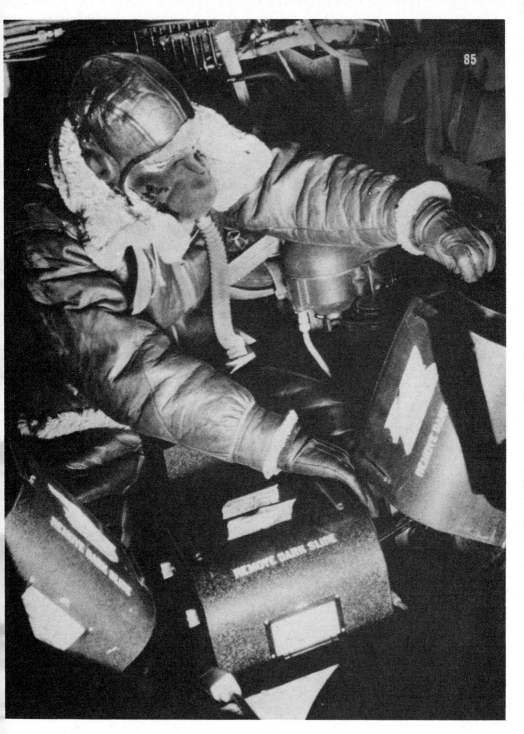

PHOTO-RECONNAISSANCE planes photograph target before a mission, return afterwards to take pictures of damage. The tri-metrogon camera (above), combining 3 synchronized mechanisms, enables one airplane to photograph 8000 square miles of terrain in one hour.

CHOW CALL comes as a welcome break in the day's work at AAF stations everywhere. Here North African desert serves as messhall.

SPORTS follow AAF around the world, help relieve nervous fatigue brought on by combat. Volleyball game below is in Aleutians.

NAMES on planes are serious (Eagle's Wrath), frivolous (Wham Bam), historical (Tom Paine), often meaningful only to the crew.

BEFORE mission crews are briefed about routes, target, enemy. Below, navigators are synchronizing their watches after briefing.

STOCK-IN-TRADE of the fighter pilot is the combined skill of pilot, navigator, radio operator, gunner. Attack is his business.

LIKE SHEPHERD DOGS protecting a flock, fighters hover above, below and on the flanks of bomber formations to ward off attackers.

HUMAN RELATIONS

In the last analysis, AAF effectiveness rests upon the individual soldier and the efforts he expends in his assignment. A discontented soldier, or a sick soldier, is seldom a good soldier. The AAF therefore takes a special interest in the use of leisure time, personal and family problems, recreation and worship.

Special Service—The duties of special service officers with the AAF are many-sided. The 2 main sections of the special service division, however, are physical fitness and orientation.

An extensive physical fitness program for all AAF personnel is supplemented by intra- and inter-unit athletic competition. A physical fitness test is given each quarter to check the progress or improvement which may have resulted from this sustained conditioning program.

Early in the war the need for current films and periodicals, for touring stage entertainment and for recreational supplies of all kinds was recognized by the AAF. Indoctrination, educational programs of orientation, and Army Institute courses are available to the men; from ping-pong to text-books, the problems of leisure time are given constant attention. In the forward stations for example, one of the first buildings constructed is often an enlisted men's squadron dayroom.

Chaplains—The provision of spiritual guidance for the men is essential at all Army stations, whether at a permanent base in the U. S. or an isolated outpost on New Britain or Iceland. The AAF chaplain at island stations of the South Pacific is likely to make his visits via bomber. More than 1600 chaplains serve with the AAF.

Personal Affairs—To provide assistance and advice on personal and financial matters for the soldier and his dependents, a Personal Affairs Division has been created, with Personal Affairs Officers in the field. When an individual joins the AAF, Personal Affairs is interested in seeing that:

He is adequately protected by U. S. Government insurance.
Legal beneficiaries are designated to receive gratuity pay in event of his death.

He has made a will, and if necessary, granted a power of attorney.
He has filed Class E allotment for dependents' support.
Dependency benefits are applied for if he is eligible for them.
He has arranged for a joint bank account.

During the individual's active service, a check is made to see that allotments and dependency benefits are paid promptly.

If he becomes a non-fatal casualty and is discharged from the Army, Personal Affairs seeks to re-establish him as a self-supporting member of society and assist him, when eligible, in securing Veteran's Administration benefits of pension, domiciliary care and vocational rehabilitation, and other benefits from the individual's home state and other agencies.

Redistribution—Redistribution is a program original with the AAF. It is a process involving interview, classification, rehabilitation or medical care, and reassignment to duty of men returning from overseas. The objectives of the plan:

☆ Proper conditioning before assuming new duties.

☆ New and correct assignments—right man for right place.

☆ Finest possible treatment for battle casualties.

☆ Guidance toward correct civilian employment in the event of discharge because of physical disability.

Main Steps in the AAF Redistribution Program (see chart):

(1) Overseas AAF Stations—Complete physical examination; returnees draw clothing and equipment for journey.

(2) Embarkation ports (aerial or water)—Physical check-up for communicable diseases; assignment to groups according to home locations.

(3) Debarkation ports (aerial or water)—Physical check-up; disposition according to physical condition.

(4) Home on furlough, or

(5) General Hospitals—Treatment for the sick and disabled.

(6) AAF Convalescent Centers—Physical rehabilitation; treatment, rest and observation; vocational guidance.

(7) AAF Redistribution Stations—Orientation; personal interviews; physical examination; assignment; rest and recreation.

AAF OVERSEAS UNITS

AAF REPLACEMENT CONTROL DEPOTS

OVERSEAS PORTS OF EMBARKATION

by water   by air

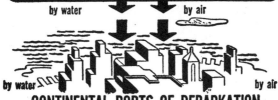

by water   by air

CONTINENTAL PORTS OF DEBARKATION

GENERAL HOSPITAL

HOME (FURLOUGH)

AAF CONVALESCENT CENTER

AAF REDISTRIBUTION STATIONS

FURLOUGH

REST CAMP

DISCHARGE

ASSIGNMENT

AAF HOSPITALS

Today the AAF has 238 hospitals, 375 infirmaries, 150 dispensaries and 8 convalescent centers within the U. S.—well over twice the bed capacity available at the time of Pearl Harbor.

Seventy-four AAF hospitals, of which 61 have been approved as teaching institutions, serve as regional hospitals. These are equipped for specialized surgery and treatment and staffed with highly-trained specialists. There is a regional hospital within easy distance of every AAF station hospital in the U. S. When a station hospital patient requires special treatment he can be moved to a regional hospital. If it is inadvisable to move the patient, the specialist from the regional hospital goes to the station hospital. Inter-hospital travel is done by air whenever necessary.

WOMEN IN UNIFORM

Nearly 30,000 women in uniform are entitled to wear the regulation AAF shoulder patch: the Air Wacs, the Women's Airforce Service Pilots (Wasps), and the members of the Army Nurse Corps assigned to the AAF.

WOMEN'S ARMY CORPS—Members of the Women's Army Corps serving with the Army Air Forces—the Air Wacs—comprise almost one-half of the Army's entire WAC personnel. Wacs have served with the AAF longer than with any other branch of service.

Where and How to Apply—Application blanks may be obtained from any Army recruiting and induction station. It is now possible to apply not only for the AAF but also for the job for which the recruit is best qualified and which she wants, and for the station she desires if it is within the service command in which she enlists.

Requirements for Air Wacs—To enlist as an Air Wac, a woman must meet all the requirements for enlistment in the Women's Army Corps and also qualify for one of the jobs listed.

AGE—*20 to 49 years inclusive.*

CITIZENSHIP—*Must be a citizen of the U. S. and furnish satisfactory proof of citizenship and age.*

MARRIAGE—*May be married or single.*

DEPENDENTS—*Must be without children under 14 years of age.*

EDUCATION—*Two years of high school and a satisfactory aptitude rating are sufficient. High school requirement may be waived in the case of those whose general classification and other aptitude tests show ability of equivalent nature.*

HEALTH—*Satisfactory health and average height and weight required.*

General Fields in Which Air Wacs Are Recruited

Medical and hospital technicians; personnel; photography; drafting; radio operators; radio and electrical repair; telephone operators; gasoline motor and light machinery operators; instrument repair; general clerical; typing-clerical; statistical and financial; stenography; tabulating machine operators; teletypewriter operators; drivers; supply and stock clerks.

Specific Jobs for Air Wacs—Air Wacs are classified in the same manner as male personnel of the AAF (see page 45), and are engaged in more than 200 separate job categories. Some of the technical jobs are listed below:

Aerial photographer; airplane fabric & dope worker; airplane electrical specialist; airplane engine mechanic; airplane propeller specialist; bombsight mechanic; camera technician; cartographer; control tower operator; cryptographer; cryptoanalyst; draftsman; Link Trainer instructor; parachute rigger and repairman; photographic laboratory technician; radio mechanic; radio operator; sheet metal worker; weather observer.

Uniform, Pay and Allowance—Rank, identifying insignia and pay for Air Wacs are the same as those applying to male personnel. (See page 54.) Uniforms are feminine adaptation of the male officers' and enlisted men's clothing.

Training for Air Wacs—Every Wac is given a basic training period of 6 weeks or more, including military drill, Army organization and other primary subjects. Air Wacs are also given on-the-job training in many technical subjects and may be sent to specialized training courses which will aid them in their work.

AAF NURSES—At the present time, more than 6500 nurses are on duty with the AAF. Of this number, 500 are flight nurses serving throughout the world wherever we are evacuating wounded by plane. The remainder, all members of the Army Nurse Corps, are on duty at AAF station hospitals.

Training, Duties, Pay—When assigned to the AAF, Army nurses are sent to one of 11 different AAF nurses' training centers for 4 weeks of military indoctrination, training and physical conditioning before being sent to various AAF station hospitals throughout the U. S.

Members of the Army Nurse Corps are granted the privileges of the service as prescribed by their rank. They do not hold commissions as do WAC and male officers, but hold appointments in the Medical Corps. Nurses are accorded full membership privileges in officers' clubs.

Pay is the same as that of Army officers (see pay tables on page 54) except in the instance of flight nurses, who draw $60 per month extra when they are placed on flying status.

Flight Nurses—After 6 months' duty in an AAF hospital, members of the ANC are eligible to make application for flight nurse training. The physical examinations required prior to assignment are the same as all other flying personnel must pass. In addition, the nurses must be recommended by the senior flight surgeon of their command as being particularly adapted to duty in the air evacuation service.

If they meet these requirements, the nurses are sent to the School of Air Evacuation, Bowman Field, Ky. Here they undergo 8 weeks of academic, professional, military and physical training to prepare them for the strenuous duties ahead. Subjects in which they are required to be proficient include emergency medical treatment, intravenous therapy, tropical medicine, field sanitation, and compass, map and aerial photography orientation. Upon graduation, they are rated flight nurses and are permitted to wear gold combat observers' wings with the ANC insignia superimposed. (See page 51.)

By the end of 1943, there were flight nurse units in every theater of operations where units of the AAF were assigned. Flight nurses arrived in the Sicilian and Italian campaigns as soon as it was possible to send transport planes to the front.

Within 3 days after the initial landing in the Tarawa-Makin campaign, the wounded were evacuated to Hawaii aboard 4-engined transport planes with flight nurses in attendance.

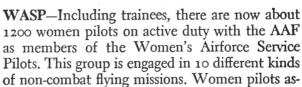

WASP—Including trainees, there are now about 1200 women pilots on active duty with the AAF as members of the Women's Airforce Service Pilots. This group is engaged in 10 different kinds of non-combat flying missions. Women pilots assigned to the Air Transport Command ferry 43 different types of aircraft, everything from small PTs to our fastest fighters and our heavy cargo and bombardment planes, from factories to points throughout the country and to bases in Canada. Wasps take meteorologists up for weather observations and fly administrative missions in 8 domestic AAF weather regions; they transport equipment, break in engines with slow-time flying at 20 different Training Command bases and perform various courier duties.

Training—Primary, intermediate and advanced training for the Wasps is conducted at Avenger Field, Sweetwater, Texas, by the AAF Training Command. The 27-week course is required regardless of previous flying experience. It includes flying training, ground school, instrument instruction, and is generally the same as that given to aviation cadets. When necessary, Wasps receive additional transitional flying instruction at the particular station to which they are assigned. Special missions, such as tow target work, may require training at B-17, B-24, B-26, or C-60 schools.

Pay and Status—Although Wasps are on Civil Service status (as of spring 1944), they are entitled to the privileges of officers when on an Army base and must conform to military regulations when on duty. They are paid $150 a month while in training; $250 a month when placed on operational duty. WASP wings are the standard AAF silver wings with a lozenge in the center (see page 51).

Entrance Requirements—Entrance requirements (as of Spring, 1944):

35 hours' flying time (CAA certificate)—Height: 62½ inches, minimum—Age: 18 years 6 mos. to 35—Education: high school or equivalent—Personal interview with official WASP representative—Must pass a physical examination for flying and aviation cadet qualifying examination.

CIVILIAN PERSONNEL

Civilian employees play an important role in the AAF. In 1940 when the AAF had 51,000 military members, the civilian employees numbered 8000; today, with more than 2⅓ million in uniform, AAF civilians total 350,000 within the U. S. Add to this figure those employed by the arms and services at AAF installations and the estimate is 500,000. An important 18% of the AAF wear mufti; half or more are women.

Some 183,000 civilians are working in Air Service Command depots throughout the country in maintenance, repair and supply of aircraft, engines and radios. Over 34,000 are connected with the procurement activities of the Materiel Command. The Training Command employs approximately 64,000, not only in offices but as instructors and mechanics.

Civilian experts in the National Advisory Committee for Aeronautics (NACA) are designing and testing the equipment of tomorrow. Our weather school programs were planned and executed largely by civilian meteorologists. The high priority enemy industrial targets we bomb are selected partly by civilian economists and industrialists who advise military strategists. In all phases of AAF work civilian experts act as consultants to the military.

Just as the military personnel receive awards for outstanding service, so too do civilian employees of the AAF. This custom was initiated on Dec. 8, 1943. Civilian decorations are shown below.

6 MONTHS SATISFACTORY   **MERITORIOUS**   **EXCEPTIONALLY MERITORIOUS**

VOLUNTEERS WITH THE AAF

Ground Observer Corps—The Ground Observer Corps consists of civilian men and women of all ages who, without pay, kept thousands of observation posts up and down our coasts in continuous 24-hour operation from the day we entered the war until the fall of 1943. When threat of enemy aerial attack on our shores diminished with our offensive actions abroad, it was decided to reduce the burden on existing commercial telephone facilities and to release this large pool of military and civilian manpower for other essential war work by placing the GOC on an alert status. Since Oct. 4, 1943, members of the corps have manned their observation posts at intervals for test and training in place of the previous 24-hour-a-day basis.

AAF AWARDS FOR CIVILIAN VOLUNTEERS SERVING WITH THE AIRCRAFT WARNING SERVICE.

IV FIGHTER COM.   I FIGHTER COM.

Aircraft Warning Corps—The Aircraft Warning Corps includes all those volunteers in filter and information centers of our continental fighter commands who are on the receiving end of the ground observers' reports. At its peak this corps numbered more than 25,000. Like the GOC, the Aircraft Warning Corps is now also on an alert status; those assigned to filter centers serve on the same days that ground observers are on duty. Information centers differ in this respect: radar information comes in 24 hours a day; continuous operation of that portion of the AWC is required to plot radar information.

AAF Women Volunteers—Some 25,000 women members of AAF families are engaged in a wide variety of volunteer activities throughout the country. At almost every AAF base and in many communities a local AAF women's club is the hub around which revolve welfare projects for AAF personnel. To coordinate the work of these hundreds of local AAF women's groups, the National Association of Air Forces Women was organized on Feb. 8, 1944. The major responsibilities of the groups serving with it are outlined in the chart that follows.

ORGANIZATION	NATIONAL ASSOCIATION OF AIR FORCES WOMEN	AAF WOMEN'S CLUBS
MEMBERSHIP	Women members of immediate families of personnel who are or have been on active duty with the AAF.	Women members of AAF families, in conformance with local club policy.
MAJOR ACTIVITIES	Coordinates the work of all AAF women's volunteer activities throughout the country by serving as a medium to: ☆ Direct the standardization of activities undertaken by AAF women's clubs. ☆ Train its members in a unified system of volunteer work. ☆ Assist in the welfare and rehabilitation of all AAF personnel. Included on the executive board of the NAAFW are representatives of the Women's Volunteer Branch of the Personal Affairs Division, Red Cross, Spotters, and public relations activities. Serving on its advisory board are women representatives of all AAF commands and air forces. Local AAF women's clubs are the mediums through which the National Association of Air Forces Women sponsors its activities. Corresponding address: National Association of Air Forces Women, Box 23, Ft. Myer, Va.	Operating at AAF posts and in communities, with officers elected from among their members, these groups promote educational, social and recreational activities which may include assistance to such projects as: kindergartens, lending libraries, flower committees, clothing and toy exchanges, study clubs, lectures, garden clubs, athletic clubs, decorating service clubs on post, Bond sales, U.S.O. activities, welfare work, mending service, issuance of ration books, Christmas wrapping, club canteens, information desks, Music-for-the-Services.

WOMEN'S VOLUNTEER BRANCH AAF PERSONAL AFFAIRS DIVISION	SPOTTERS (personnel)	RED CROSS ACTIVITIES
AAF Women Volunteers	AAF Women Volunteers	AAF Women Volunteers

WOMEN'S VOLUNTEER BRANCH AAF PERSONAL AFFAIRS DIVISION	SPOTTERS (personnel)	RED CROSS ACTIVITIES
Organizes and supervises activities of volunteer units of women for service with the AAF Personal Affairs Division in the field. Assists convalescent training counselors in educational activities as may be necessary or desirable for AAF men in convalescent centers; establishes contacts in homes of the convalescent and rehabilitated under supervision of Personal Affairs Officer. Assists in community chest and war bond drives. Arranges for hospitalization and medical care where needed. Follows up on maternity cases. Arranges for better housing. Calls on bereaved families. Establishes day nurseries if not otherwise provided for. Provides clerical assistance where needed. Works in conjunction with Advice and Claims and Placement and Education branches of Personal Affairs Division. Assists chaplain when requested.	This organization: Makes initial contact with each AAF wife as she arrives at a post by means of letter, personal call, informal party, etc. Keeps a local address file and records data on AAF women, listing training and qualifications for specialized work. Helps AAF women find their place in the local war effort and Army activities. Supplies other organizations, upon request, the names of trained women available for volunteer work. Maintains national headquarters for information on organization of Spotters' units. Address: Box 42, Ft. Myer, Va.	Volunteer special services: Dieticians' Aides. Home Service—counsel and assistance to families of men in armed forces. Hospital and Recreation — Gray Ladies. Canteen Corps. Canteen Aides. Motor Corps. Production Corps —surgical dressings, knitting, sewing. Staff Assistance—helping in various types of office work. Volunteer Nurses' Aides. Volunteer participation in: Blood Donor Service. Camp and Hospital Council Service. Disaster Preparedness and Relief. Red Cross drives. Courses in accident prevention, first aid, home nursing, nutrition, water safety, etc.

ARMY AIR FORCES AID SOCIETY

The Army Air Forces Aid Society, whose address is Washington 6, D. C., was incorporated in the District of Columbia March 9, 1942, for the purpose of relieving distress of AAF personnel, including those who have honorably served with the AAF, and their dependents.

The Society, composed of persons interested in the AAF, has 4 classes of membership, each having the same rights and privileges, the difference in the classes being the fee or annual dues paid by the member. Patron members pay an initial fee of $100; life members pay $50; benefactor members and members-at-large pay annual dues of $5 and $1 respectively.

The Board of Trustees of the Society is as follows:

General Henry H. Arnold
Mrs. Henry H. Arnold
Maj. Gen. James M. Bevans
Hon. John M. Costello
Mrs. Howard C. Davidson
Mrs. James H. Doolittle
Mr. Robert V. Fleming
Lt. Gen. Barney M. Giles

Mr. Robert A. Lovett
Brig. Gen. Bennett E. Meyers
Mr. Floyd B. Odlum
Capt. Eddie Rickenbacker
Brig. Gen. Cyrus R. Smith
Mr. Thomas J. Watson
Mr. Charles E. Wilson

After the war the Society plans:

☆ To assist AAF personnel and their dependents in obtaining government benefits to which they may be lawfully entitled.

☆ To assist in providing for education, vocational rehabilitation and job placement.

☆ To provide financial assistance in worthy cases.

The Army Air Forces Aid Society is at present accepting voluntary memberships and contributions for future use toward the fulfillment of its mission when other agencies currently performing similar functions cease to operate.

HOW WE TRAIN

In the AAF we must be more than individuals organized into teams. We must be trained individuals and trained teams. More than 500 separate skills contribute to the success of a routine bombing mission—skills ranging from that of a drill sergeant helping to make recruits into soldiers to that of a bombardier synchronizing the cross-hairs on his target.

Our training problem has been further complicated by the highly technical nature of many of these duties, by the need for vast expansion, and by our oldest enemy—lack of time. Based on pre-Pearl Harbor figures, we have experienced as much as a 20,000% increase in the training of some specialists. In other specialties, in which training did not even begin until after 1941, the increase cannot be measured percentage-wise.

The statistics of our training expansion would give pause to an Einstein. During the first 2 years of war one million men—nearly half our total strength—were engaged in AAF training either as trainers or trainees. During the peak year of 1943, 120,000 aircrew trainees flew more than 3 billion miles in the U. S.—as though the entire population of Savannah, Ga., seized by an uncontrollable impulse and equipped with the necessary priorities, flew 134,000 trips around the equator.

The Training Program—The AAF training program has been a continuing experiment in mass education. Originally small, scattered and loosely coordinated, the bulk of it had by early 1942 been unified under 2 new commands—the Technical Training Command and the Flying Training Command. The Technical Training Command used every available type of educational facility to train hundreds of thousands of technicians in duties ranging from repairing an airplane engine to roasting a Thanksgiving turkey. It leased 68 civilian mechanics schools, turned factory shops into classrooms, and increased the number of its own schools from 3 to 33. It bought or leased 452 hotels and converted them into combination schools and barracks. Within 2 years of its inception, it turned out some 600,000 graduates. Men unable to attend technical schools for reasons of time and space learned on the job by working alongside training-school graduates.

First problem of the Flying Training Command was the construction of sufficient fields to train pilots, bombardiers and navigators. In the South, as training stations sprang up, aviation cadets arrived at half-completed fields; training planes flew over bulldozers at work laying runways. By 1943 the Flying Training

AAF TRAINING COMMAND

Figures below, showing total number of training course graduates in 1941 and 1943, reveal tremendous expansion of AAF Training Command program. Most impressive increase was production of gunners and technicians, for whom there was not even a formal training program in 1941.

1941	1943	1941	1943	1941	1943	1941	1943	1941	1943
7244	65,797	601	15,928	310	16,057	0	91,595	0	544,374
PILOT		NAVIGATOR		BOMBARDIER		GUNNER		TECHNICIAN	

Command's yearly output had rocketed to 65,797 pilots, 16,057 bombardiers, 15,928 navigators.

Once the Flying and Technical Training Commands had trained individuals in their particular skills, there remained the final training task of teaching them to employ these skills with combat equipment under combat conditions and of welding them into operational teams. The 4 domestic air forces trained new fighter and bombardment groups and also replacements for aircrews lost in battle or returned home from overseas groups.

The Troop Carrier, Air Transport and Air Service Commands fused technical and flying school graduates into specialized units. Such units as reconnaissance, air warning and fighter control were activated and trained. Many units were composed of specialists trained by the Army Service Forces—Signal, Ordnance, Chemical Warfare, Engineers, Medical, Finance, Quartermaster and Transportation.

Training Commands Merged—In July of 1943 the Flying and Technical Training Commands were merged into the AAF Training Command. In December the training of all but a few Army Service Forces-trained specialists was taken over by the AAF. The formation of new units dropped off and gave way to a stepped-up replacement training program. (Exception: the B-29 Superfortress unit program which got underway late in 1943 and is now in full swing.)

Today, combat has replaced training as the AAF's largest function. As more and more of our men go overseas, the training program will contract further. Because of new combat lessons, new techniques and new methods, however, it always will be a vital factor.

INDIVIDUAL TRAINING

Every man assigned to the AAF learns at the outset to be a soldier. He takes a 5 weeks' basic military course which includes 73 hours of drills and marches; 15 hours of physical training; 54

hours of marksmanship; 13 hours of military procedure; 8 hours of first aid; 12 hours of sanitation; 3 hours of personal adjustment; 5 hours of care of clothing and equipment; 5 hours of defense against chemical attack; 5 hours of individual security and camouflage; 4 hours of map and photo-interpretation; and 4 hours of defense against air attack.

Basic training for men enlisted for aviation cadet training also includes exhaustive physical, psychological and mental tests to determine their fitness for the flying program and to ascertain the specialty for which they are best suited. After basic training each man is ready to begin training in his specialty. The individual training schedule is divided into 2 major categories: Flying Training, and Technical, Administrative and Service Training.

FLYING TRAINING: Pilots

PREFLIGHT SCHOOL—10 weeks' course: sea and air recognition, 30 hours; code, 48 hours; physics, 24 hours; math, 20 hours; maps and charts, 18 hours; daily physical and military training.

PRIMARY FLYING SCHOOL—10 weeks' course: 70 hours in 125 to 225 horsepower open cockpit biplanes or low-wing monoplanes; 94 hours academic work in ground school; 54 hours military training.

BASIC FLYING SCHOOL—10 weeks' course: 70 hours in a 450 horsepower basic trainer; 94 hours in ground school; 47 hours military training. By the end of basic school trainees have learned to fly a plane competently. Further training will teach them to fly a warplane the AAF way. Before the end of basic, trainees are classified—on the basis of choice and instructors' reports—for single-engine training (fighter pilot) or 2-engine training (bomber, transport or 2-engine fighter pilot).

ADVANCED FLYING TRAINING—10 weeks' course (single-engine and 2-engine): 70 hours of flying; 60 hours of ground school; 19 hours military training. Single-engine trainees fly 600 horsepower AT-6s and take a course in fixed gunnery. Two-engine trainees fly AT-24s, AT-17s, AT-9s, or AT-10s. Based on performance and choice, they are earmarked for heavy or medium bombardment, transport, troop-carrier or 2-engine fighter. At the end of advanced training the graduates, single- and 2-engine, are awarded the silver pilot's wings of the AAF and appointed flight officers or commissioned 2nd lieutenants.

Flight is simulated when student, enclosed under canopy, uses instruments to maneuver the Link on its swivel mount. Needle on instructor's desk records the Link's action.

LINK TRAINER

TRANSITION FLYING TRAINING—Before they begin to train in units, pilots learn to fly the type of warplane they will handle in combat. For example, those marked for B-26 assignment take a 10 weeks' transition course of which 105 hours are spent flying B-26s and the rest in ground school. B-17 and B-24 pilots also get 105 hours 4-engine flying time and additional ground school training in a 10 weeks' post-graduate transition course. Fighter pilots get a 5 weeks' transition course; single-engine pilots fly 10 hours in P-40s; P-38 pilots take 10 hours in P-322s (modified P-38s). Gunnery is a part of fighter transition training. At the conclusion of transition training, pilots report to unit training groups where they are welded into fighting teams.

Navigator and Bombardier Training

PREFLIGHT SCHOOL—10 weeks' course: Trainees attend the same preflight school. Both bombardiers and navigators take 48 hours of code; 28 hours of mathematics; 24 hours of maps and charts; 30 hours of aircraft recognition; 12 hours of naval recognition; 12 hours of principles of flight; 20 hours of aero-physics; 9 hours of altitude equipment.

GUNNERY SCHOOL—6 weeks' course: Because every bomber crew member must be an expert gunner, navigator and bombardier trainees are sent to a flexible gunnery school after preflight school. They learn weapons, ballistics, turret operation and maintenance; gun repairs; air, sea and land recognition; shooting from a moving base and from a turret; firing from the air at ground objects, at tow targets and at other planes with a gun camera. After gunnery school bombardier and navigator trainees separate and each takes a specialized advanced course.

BOMBARDIER SCHOOL—20 weeks' course: Following gunnery school, bombardier trainees spend 120 hours in AT-11 training planes on practice bombing runs and 718 hours in ground school. The latter consists of: navigation, 96 hours; bombing, 388 hours; navigation and bombing and related training (code, meteorology, air and sea recognition), 234 hours. At the conclusion of the course trainees are awarded bombardier's silver wings, appointed flight officers or commissioned 2nd lieutenants, and sent on to unit training.

NAVIGATOR SCHOOL—20 weeks' course: Following gunnery school navigator trainees spend 104 hours in the air on practical navigation problems, and 782 hours in ground school. The latter includes: pilotage, 8 hours; instruments, 83 hours; dead reckoning, 54 hours; radio, 8 hours; celestial navigation, 53 hours; meteorology, 47 hours; code and recognition, 9 hours each. Upon completing the course, trainees are awarded navigator's wings, appointed flight officers or commissioned 2nd lieutenants, and advanced to unit training.

BOMBARDIER-NAVIGATOR SCHOOL—12 weeks' course: Each month a specified number of graduate navigators (180 monthly on March 1, 1944) receive full bombardier's training, excluding navigation in which they are already proficient. Bombardier-navigator training provides the doubly-trained officers needed for B-29s and for lead planes in medium bomber missions.

Glider Pilots—AAF enlisted men between the ages of 18 and 26 who have had 125 hours flying time either in a glider or power aircraft are eligible for glider pilot training. (Quotas are at present filled.) The 6 months' course is divided as follows:

First 2 months are devoted to ground training. Trainees take commando-type training in personal combat and weapons. During the next month they learn glider repair and maintenance. The following month they fly powered aircraft; then they spend a month learning to fly gliders and studying meteorology, navigation and selected academic subjects. The final month is devoted to advanced glider flying, the trainees becoming proficient in the tactical uses of gliders. When advanced training is over, they are awarded silver glider pilot's wings, appointed flight officers or commissioned 2nd lieutenants, join troop carrier units for training as team members.

Radar Observer, Night Fighter—Aviation cadets with special qualifications who are eliminated from flight training for reasons which do not disqualify them from further aircrew duties are eligible to train as radar observers, night fighter. Because their work requires a thorough knowledge of flying technique, they must have had at least 50 hours' flying time. They first take a 6 weeks' gunnery course, followed by 9 weeks' radar operations. Training is designed to enable them to fly with a pilot in a 2-seated night fighter and direct the pilot to enemy aircraft by means of radar. Radar observers are appointed flight officers or commissioned 2nd lieutenants and proceed to operational training with night fighter units.

Aircrew, Enlisted Men—All enlisted members of an aircrew are aerial gunners; only the career-gunner, however, is exclusively a gunner. The others are trained in a technical specialty before they become gunners.

At the end of the basic training period, men chosen to train as career-gunners are eligible to enter the 6 weeks' gunnery school. (For outline of gunnery course, see page 105 under Navigator and Bombardier.) Airplane armorer-gunner trainees take a 20 weeks' course in the operation and maintenance of airplane armament. Airplane mechanic-gunner trainees take 27 weeks' training in airplane inspection and maintenance. Radio operator mechanic-gunner trainees get 20 weeks of combat crew radio operation and repair. At the conclusion of their technical training, specialist-gunner trainees go to gunnery school.

TECHNICAL, ADMINISTRATIVE AND SERVICE
TRAINING: Officers and Officer Trainees

AAF ADMINISTRATIVE OFFICERS CANDIDATE SCHOOL—16 weeks' course: From the ranks of enlisted men, both in this country and overseas, come qualified candidates for this school, commonly called OCS. The course is divided into two 8 week periods. For the first 8 weeks all candidates study the requisites for administration of AAF units: classification, military discipline, sanitation, squadron duties, voice and command, arms and marksmanship, first aid, protection against chemical attack, guard duty, camouflage, and maps and charts. At the end of 8 weeks candidates are assigned to specialized training in the type of administration for which they are best qualified: adjutant, personnel, intelligence, mess management, physical training, statistical, supply, or training. During the last 8 weeks 10 days are spent in field training. Upon graduation all candidates are commissioned 2nd lieutenants.

AVIATION CADETS, GROUND—These are selected enlisted men or officers with special educational qualifications. Before they begin cadet training, they generally have spent several months in the service, at the very least 8 weeks of basic training. After a 12 weeks' special basic training course, they proceed to specialized technical courses, after which they are commissioned 2nd lieutenants. Cadets attend one of the following schools: Photographic Laboratory Commanders School, 16 weeks; Communications Officers School, 18 weeks; Armament Officers School, 19 weeks; Engineering Officers School, 20 weeks; Weather Officers School, 33 weeks; Radar Officers School (3 types), 38, 42 and 48 weeks.

RESIDENT GRADUATE TRAINING PROGRAM—Medical officers who enter the service directly from their final year at medical school or from internship, work for the first 6 months under the supervision of experienced medical officers in an AAF hospital. This half year's training supplies the practical experience necessary to fulfill the duties of medical officers.

NURSES TRAINING PROGRAM—30 days' course. Upon assignment to the AAF, nurses are given a course in military organization, sanitation, food inspection and hospital procedures. After completing the course, they report for duty at AAF hospitals.

AAF ENGINEERING SCHOOL—3 months' course. At Wright Field, Ohio, the Materiel Command gives a course in aeronautical engineering for pilots with BS degrees. The curriculum is designed to make students more valuable for Materiel Command duties.

Enlisted Men—The preparation of enlisted men for ground duty is the AAF's largest single training job; 314 separate skills are taught in 80 different types of courses. A digest of the courses is listed below:

Communications (radio, telegraph, telephone, radar): 26 courses ranging from 4 to 44 weeks; airplane repair and maintenance: 15 courses, 5 to 29 weeks; armament and equipment: 5 courses, 8 to 23 weeks; weather: 2 courses of 11 and 33 weeks; photography: 5 courses, 2 to 16 weeks; aviation engineers: 8 courses, 4 to 12 weeks; motor transport: 4 courses, 5 to 10 weeks; Link Trainer: 4 courses, 8 to 12 weeks; miscellaneous: 7 courses, 3 to 9 weeks.

There are no schools, as such, for the training of AAF enlisted medical personnel. Enlisted men qualified for medical work are placed in AAF hospitals, train under supervision on the job, are awarded technicians' ratings when they achieve proficiency.

UNIT AND CREW TRAINING

The second part of AAF training—unit and crew training—is devoted to making coordinated, effective teams out of soldier-specialists—teams within airplanes, teams of airplanes, teams of airplanes and ground personnel, teams of ground personnel alone.

Immediately after Pearl Harbor there was a pressing need for complete new units: fighter, bombardment, transport, reconnaissance, troop carrier. These units were supplied by the operational unit training (OTU) program. Simultaneously, a replacement unit training (RTU) program was initiated to provide replacements for overseas aircrews which had been lost in battle or returned home for reassignment. By the end of 1943 most of the authorized new units had been formed. Stepped-up air action increased the demand for replacements, and RTU became a larger program than OTU.

Today, except for B-29 units and a few others, all air unit and crew training is RTU. Because the low casualty rate among AAF ground personnel obviates the need for an extensive replacement training program, the training of ground units, which have no flying personnel or airplanes, is almost entirely OTU.

Following is an outline of unit and crew training divided into the 2 main classifications of air units and ground units.

AIR UNIT TRAINING

Bombardment: Medium, Heavy and Very Heavy—In the days when medium and heavy bombardment OTU was functioning, units were formed by breaking off cadres or skeleton units from groups within the 4 domestic air forces and supplementing this experienced nucleus with new graduates of flying and technical schools. Ground and flying personnel were trained together, and the unit was capable of administering, feeding, clothing and housing itself. The unit went overseas after 90 days of training.

Under the present RTU system, flying personnel (pilots, navigators, bombardiers, gunners) report to groups within the 4 domestic air forces. They are trained by instructor crews, many of them with combat experience. Administration and maintenance work are done by a ground echelon which is a regular part of the group. Trainees undergo a 90-day course, divided into 3 overlapping phases: First, the trainees increase their proficiency in individual skills, learn to work as a team, and become familiar with equipment and techniques. Second, formation flying is stressed. Finally, trainees move to a training area which approximates a battle zone, fly long formation bombing missions by day and night, learn to live, work and fight under combat conditions.

When there is time between the date an aircrew completes its training and the date it is to report at an overseas base, the crew will often train with a tactical air division. Tactical air divisions operate in conjunction with Army Ground Forces in maneuver areas, act as flying partners to the ground troops in war games. Fighter units also train when they can with tactical air divisions; whenever it can be arranged, fighters and bombers fly together in joint training exercises.

The sole remaining bombardment OTU—the formation of B-29 (very heavy) Superfortress units—recruits pilots with at least 300 hours 4-engine flying time from staff and instructor positions at B-17 or B-24 transition schools or from 4-engine combat groups. Copilots are new graduates of 4-engine transition schools. Other members of the B-29 aircrew are 2 bombardier-navigators, an aerial engineering officer, a radio operator-mechanic and gunners. The aircrews are joined by technical, administrative and supply personnel who have had experience in the ground echelons of 4-engine groups. Training time for the whole B-29 unit is 4 months.

Fighter, Fighter-Bomber and Night Fighter—Fighter and fighter-bomber RTU training resembles bombardment RTU except for these 2 differences: first, because all aircraft in these categories are single-seaters, only pilots are trained; second, training is measured in hours as well as months (a pilot must get at least 60 hours' flying experience). This level, however, is constantly being raised. The present goal is 120 hours.

Although fighters have been used advantageously as fighter-bombers, their primary role is air fighting. Training, therefore, must accomplish 2 things: teach a pilot to position his aircraft properly, and to aim and fire his guns accurately.

The fighter and fighter-bomber OTU program is about complete, but night fighter OTU is still an active program. Night fighter aircrews take a 4 months' OTU course. They fly 2-engine P-70s or P-61s and specialize in night operations. The crew consists of a pilot and an observer (see page 274) who also doubles as a gunner. Crews are taught to seek out and attack enemy planes. The ground complement of a night fighter unit joins the unit halfway through the course and trains with it for the final 2 months. Night fighter RTUs—aircrew only—train 5 months.

Reconnaissance—Two types of groups are trained:

PHOTO-RECONNAISSANCE—Pilots with at least 40 hours' flying time in a P-38 take an 8 weeks' course. They fly an F-5 (converted, unarmed P-38), practice high altitude flying, learn the technique of taking air-photos and become proficient in evasive action. Complete B-24 crews also receive 8 weeks' training. In an F-7 (converted B-24) they learn photo-mapping. In photo-mapping the plane flies over the area to be photographed until pictures are made of every square foot of it. Then the pictures are mounted in a mosaic to provide a photographic map.

TACTICAL RECONNAISSANCE—Here, photography is secondary; the main job is observation. Pilots with at least 60 hours' experience in a P-51 train for 6 weeks in an F-6 (converted P-51). They fly at medium and low altitudes, become experts in recognition and orientation, learn to detect camouflage and how to adjust long-range artillery fire and naval gunfire. They use cameras chiefly for confirmation of what they have seen, but their primary task is to seek out objectives on the ground.

Combat Camera Crews—Crews of officers and enlisted men with long photographic and motion picture experience are trained in a 10 weeks' course. They learn by taking newsreel and still pictures of simulated combat action and are assigned as camera units with overseas air forces.

Troop Carrier Units—Troop carrier training is now almost entirely RTU. Pilots marked for troop carrier are graduates of advanced 2-engine flying schools. After taking 30 days' transition training in C-47s, they are sent to train in a troop carrier unit. At the end of 2 months, they are joined by their crew members—copilot, engineer, radio operator and, in some cases, navigator. When the new crew is ready to fly as a team, it begins to practice dropping small units of airborne ground forces stationed at adjoining fields. This troop-carrying operation increases in size as training progresses. A glider element joins the crews and the troop carrier teams learn to tow gliders. Working as a unit, in airplanes and gliders, they are taught the specialized techniques they will employ in combat—air discipline, low altitude flying, all-weather operations, weapons, communications, navigation, glider and paratroop landings, supply by air, air evacuation (see page 196) and identification of air and ground objects.

When crews have completed their training (5 months for pilots, 3 for other crew members), they are assigned to troop carrier units overseas.

Air Transport Units—Since the planes flown by the Air Transport Command range from bantamweight primary trainers to giant 4-engine cargo planes, the ATC training program is diverse. Pilots flying for ATC are classified into 5 categories identified by the type of planes flown, as follows:

CLASS ONE—Small, single-engine trainers; CLASS TWO—2-engine advanced trainers and small 2-engine cargo planes; CLASS THREE—heavy 2-engine cargo planes; CLASS FOUR—2-engine fighters and medium bombers; CLASS FIVE—heavy bombers and 4-engine cargo aircraft. Upon attaining the rating of Class Five pilot, the ATC pilot can fly any plane in the AAF.

From the day he starts his training with ATC as Class One pilot, he is a student, constantly learning by working at his job. He becomes steadily more proficient through progressive transition from Class One to Class Five, from the lightest to the heaviest type aircraft. Every flight he makes is a training flight. In addition to on-the-job training in the air, intensive ground school courses in aircraft engineering, instruments, navigation and meteorology are completed. All pilots must go through this entire sequence, the length of time required depending on the ability of the pilot to advance, availability of aircraft and flying conditions. Pilots are trained individually for single-engine domestic flying but crews are trained as units for bombers and multi-engine transports. These crews, including pilots, copilots, navigators, radio operators and flight engineers, train as units for several weeks in a specialized school.

In addition to flight personnel, ATC trains ground personnel in such fields as traffic, travel and insurance, loading, flight control, weather forecasting, engineering, communications, personnel, administration, supply and mess.

GROUND UNIT TRAINING

The training of ground units (units containing no flying personnel and no aircraft) is usually a 2-phase process. First, technical school graduates report to a training base operated by a domestic ground group. Under the direction of the parent group the individuals are formed into squadrons (not groups, as is the case with combat units) and train as such during the first phase. In the second phase the squadrons are sent to domestic bases where they learn to coordinate their particular functions with the work of other types of squadrons. This is called combined training. Following is a table of principal types of ground units trained and length of training in weeks:

TYPE OF UNIT	FUNCTION	Unit	Com-bined
		WEEKS OF TRAINING	
Airborne engineer aviation battalion	Rehabilitates captured airfields; constructs advance airbases	11	0
Airdrome squadron, special	Operates advance & auxiliary airbases	9	4
Aircraft warning unit	Radar detection of friendly and enemy aircraft	6	4
Airways detachment	Maintenance of transient aircraft	13	0
Aviation squadron	Housekeeping; general labor functions	9	4
Chemical company, air operations	Loads airplane spray tanks with liquid smoke, chemicals; operates chemical warehouses	15	6
Chemical depot company	Stores & issues chemical ammunition & equipment	10	4
Chemical maintenance company	Repairs & salvages chemical warfare equipment	10	4
Depot repair squadron	Major aircraft repairs	8	16
Depot supply squadron	Supply for major repairs	8	16
Engineer aviation battalion	Constructs, maintains, defends airbases	11	0
Engineer aviation camouflage battalion	Supervises camouflage activities	11	0
Engineer aviation fire fighting platoon	Fire fighting & crash crew service	6	0
Engineer depot company	Operates engineer supply depot	11	0
Engineer topographic company	Prepares charts, maps, photomosaics	11	0
Engineer utilities detachment	Provides & maintains water & electric facilities	11	0

TYPE OF UNIT	FUNCTION	WEEKS OF TRAINING Unit	Combined
Fighter control unit	Directs aircraft by radio-telephone; furnishes navigational aids	6	0
Headquarters squadron, service group	Administration; transportation of service group	8	16
Medical dispensary, aviation	Functions as dispensary	8	0
Medical sections, service or depot group	Performs medical duties for service or depot groups	8	16
Medical supply platoon	Stores, issues medical supplies	6	0
Military police company	Guards installations, conducts criminal investigations	10	0
* Ordnance ammunition company	Stores, issues & maintains ammunition	16	8
* Ordnance maintenance company	Repairs, maintains ordnance materiel	16	8
Quartermaster company, service group	Stores & issues general supplies	8	8
Quartermaster service company	Forms general labor pool	5	8
Quartermaster truck company	Transports troops, ammunition, equipment	8	8
Service squadron	Aircraft maintenance & repair	8	16
Signal company	Procures, installs, operates communications facilities	12	5
Signal company depot	Installs, does major repairs on radio & radar communications	12	14
Signal construction battalion	Constructs heavy wire installations, strings cables	8	9
Signal radio interception company	Intercepts and analyzes enemy radio traffic, operates direction finders	6	0
Station complement squadron	Provides continuous operation of airbase	16	0

* Receive unit training from Army Service Forces.

OVERSEAS TRAINING

AAF training may be compared to assembly line production. The parts of the machine are forged in the individual training program and assembled in the unit and crew training program. The last step is modification: making alterations in the finished product necessary for the particular requirements of each overseas theater. Modification is done in training centers in the theaters.

In the British theater, for example, the 8th Air Force operates a combat crew replacement center to which every new crew reports for additional training before it begins combat operations. The course has 2 purposes—first, to correct any flaws of individual crew members; second, to indoctrinate every man in the procedures and problems of the theater.

First the crews hear lectures which provide them with general information about the theater. They receive instruction in the use and care of high altitude personal equipment, bailing out, prisoner of war procedure and escape techniques, observation and reporting of intelligence data, air and naval recognition, geography of Europe, and German air fighting methods. After the lecture session the individual crew members—pilot, bombardier, navigator, radio operator, mechanic and gunners—get intensive checks in their specialties to make sure that they meet the standards for combat proficiency. Faults are corrected before the crewman is sent to combat.

AAF TACTICAL CENTER

The AAF Tactical Center, headquartered at Orlando, Fla., occupies an area of 8000 square miles—approximately the size of Sicily. Here a threefold program is conducted: the training of cadres to form the nuclei of new units, the training of individuals in highly specialized duties and the testing of new tactics and techniques under combat conditions. Since its inception in late 1942, the Tactical Center at Orlando has turned out more than 35,000 graduates, made about 500 tactical tests.

The Tactical Center's training program is divided into academic and practical phases. Lectures and classes are held in the AAF School of Applied Tactics; field problems are worked out in a simulated theater of operations.

Cadres reporting from operational units take a one-month

course—2 weeks of academic work and 2 weeks in the simulated theater of operations learning battle tactics, communications, control systems, emergency procedures, intelligence methods and defensive safeguards.

An important training function of the Tactical Center is helping to coordinate the AAF with other services. Many courses, including some under the Army-Navy Staff College, are taught to officers from all branches of the Army, Navy and Marines.

For AAF officers, the Tactical Center also conducts several special short courses: senior officers, 10 days; staff officers, 14 days; tactical inspectors, 15 days; administrative inspectors, 4 weeks; technical inspectors, 4 weeks; intelligence officers—combat intelligence, 8 weeks; photo-interpretation, 8 weeks; airbase intelligence, 4 weeks; prisoner of war interrogation, 4 weeks; senior medical officer, 6 days; staff weather officers, 2 weeks; personal equipment officers (oxygen devices, electric heating clothing, life vests and other personal equipment) 2 weeks. More than 30 other specialized courses are given in the AAF Tactical Center.

OTHER TRAINING PROGRAMS

SPECIAL TRAINING

School of Aviation Medicine—Three courses are taught at the School of Aviation Medicine, Randolph Field, Tex. A 9 weeks' aviation medical examiners' course teaches AAF medical officers (men who were physicians in civilian life) the special sciences necessary to safeguard the health of aircrews—physiology of altitude, effects of gravity and decompression. They are also taught to administer rigid physical examinations to aircrew members. Aviation medical examiners may become flight surgeons after a year's experience, including 50 hours' flying time and may wear flight surgeons' gold wings (see page 51).

A 6 weeks' aviation physiologists course trains doctors and physiologists in research methods. Their work, after graduation, is to ascertain whether new techniques and equipment can safely be used within the limits of physiological capability. Aviation physiologists also conduct the altitude training program. Another 6 weeks' course trains enlisted medical technicians to help aviation medical examiners in aircrew physical examinations.

School of Air Evacuation—To teach the methods of transporting patients by air to hospitals far behind the lines, the AAF School of Air Evacuation was set up in June 1943 at Bowman Field, Ky. In a 2 months' course, flight surgeons, nurses and enlisted men learn field medical technique, care of airborne patients, preparation of medical records, camouflage, protective measures and problems of the battle zone.

AAF Staff Course—As our overseas operations expanded, a need arose for skilled young officers to assume staff duties in higher echelons—wing and above. In July 1943 an AAF Staff Course for captains, majors and, in some cases, colonels between the ages of 25 and 35, was established. The selected officers—many of them with combat experience, all with command experience—take a 3-phase course: First, a 2 weeks' course at the AAF Tactical Center (see page 116) to learn the duties of a staff officer in a combat theater. Next, a 2 weeks' tour of stations to observe the work of the Materiel Command, the Antiaircraft School, the Airborne Command, an amphibious force and a port of embarkation. Finally, 4 weeks are spent at AAF headquarters studying personnel, intelligence, training, operations, commitments and requirements, materiel, maintenance and distribution, and plans.

Emergency Rescue Training—Any AAF man forced down on land or sea can be sure that he will be the object of a search. A whole training program is devoted solely to preparing special squadrons for searching out and rescuing stranded personnel. The program is divided into 2 parts: aircraft and marine.

Members of aircraft rescue squadrons are pilots, navigators, flight surgeons, sea search radar observers, and enlisted technicians who perform maintenance and administrative functions. Pilots first report to the Navy's air training station at Pensacola, Fla., where they take a 10 weeks' course in flying seaplanes. Mechanics take a 6 weeks' course in seaplane maintenance. Then all flying, medical and ground personnel spend 45 days learning to function as a unit.

Sea rescue squadrons are composed of AAF officers and men

who have had extensive nautical experience in civilian life. The training period is 24 weeks: the first 6 on the basic principles of seamanship and sea rescue; the next 12 on instruction of each individual crew member in his particular duty; the final 6 on unit training.

Convalescent Training—The tedium of convalescence has been profitably relieved in AAF hospitals by a program of convalescent training. The training program includes courses in code, chemical warfare, camouflage, map reading, calisthenics, first aid, booby traps and land mines, aircraft identification, geopolitics, weather, arctic and tropical medicine, foreign languages, mathematics and physics.

Patients well enough to leave their beds attend lectures and training films. When a patient must remain in bed, the training is brought to his bedside. Lectures and demonstrations are given in the wards; even complete airplane mock-ups have been set up in hospital bays.

Besides increasing the soldier's knowledge, convalescent training has definite therapeutic advantages. It has shortened the average convalescent period by 30 to 40% (scarlet fever convalescence, for example, has been cut from 33 to 23 days). Hospital readmissions have dropped a full 25%. In a large number of cases the need for a convalescent furlough has been eliminated, enabling the soldier to return more quickly to duty.

Rehabilitation—The AAF's obligation to its war-wounded, physical and psychological, does not end with hospitalization and treatment. Eight large convalescent centers have been established in the U. S. to recondition casualties so they can once more perform useful work in the AAF or, if they are unfit for further military duty, in civilian life.

Patients sent to convalescent centers from overseas hospitals are kept busy. Light calisthenics, useful work in manual crafts shops and gardening projects, and lectures and demonstrations on military subjects are part of the daily hospital routine. Patients who have undergone amputations are taught the use of artificial limbs by skilled instructors. By easy stages they master the techniques, develop confidence in themselves and acquire a high degree of proficiency. As soon as a patient's health permits, he begins a course of actual job training. If it has been decided to return him to AAF duty, he is given a refresher course in the specialty to which he will be assigned. If the patient is to be honorably discharged, he is given guidance in a skill that will help assure him employment in civil life.

INSTRUCTORS TRAINING

Instructors for pilot, navigator, bombardier and gunnery schools are trained at AAF central instructors schools. Both newly commissioned officers and aircrew members returned from combat are taught instruction methods. The pilot instructor course is 4 weeks, navigator 9 weeks and bombardier 9 weeks. Ground school instructors at pilot training fields take a 4 weeks' course in the latest academic instruction methods at the pilots' central instructors school. Gunnery central instructors school, the only one for enlisted men, conducts a 4 weeks' course.

Because all-weather operations require a sound knowledge of instrument flying, an instrument central instructors school was opened in early 1943. In spite of flying blind through all kinds of weather, students there flew over 250,000 hours during the first year without even a minor accident.

FOREIGN STUDENT TRAINING

In 1943 some 6500 foreign students were trained at approximately 50 AAF stations in the U. S.; 2800 were trained the year before. In the early months of the war before our training expansion got under way, about one-third of U. S. airfields were being used to train foreign students.

Students from all participating nations except the British and Dutch take their training, whether flying or technical, alongside American trainees in regular AAF training installations. The British and Dutch use AAF equipment and airplanes, but conduct their own programs.

Training of all foreign students, including British and Dutch, is under AAF supervision, with training costs being charged in the main against lend-lease. Upon completing their courses, foreign students return to the air forces of their own nations—except the Chinese who report to the Chinese-American wing attached to the U. S. 14th Air Force in China.

TRAINING AIDS

AAF training aids are divided into 5 classifications:

PUBLICATIONS—Hundreds of highly technical publications have
been printed in attractive illustrated forms.

POSTERS—A staff of skilled artists prepares posters which deliver
important training messages in graphic, forceful manner.

FILMS—Training films are produced in conjunction with the AAF
motion picture unit. Combat movies taken by AAF overseas
cameramen are often spliced into training films. In the past
year more than 150,000,000 feet of training film were distributed to AAF stations here and abroad.

RECOGNITION DEVICES—A flash system of aircraft recognition has
been developed. In the flash method a silhouette of an airplane
is flashed on a screen for a fraction of a second, allowing only
enough time to pick out major identifying features. After a student has learned by the flash system, he is able to recognize any
aircraft in a minimum of time. Picture cards and models of
planes, ships and ground equipment are also included under recognition devices.

MECHANICAL DEVICES—These are specialized training equipment:
Link Trainers (see page 105), navigation, bombing and gunnery
trainers, and all other mechanical training devices which are not
actual operational equipment.

Aids to training are coordinated and supplied through the AAF
Training Aids Division, located in New York City.

YOUTH TRAINING GUIDED BY THE AAF

Two civilian training programs, the High School Victory Corps
and the CAP (Civil Air Patrol) Cadets, are engaged in preparing
young men and women for future duty in the AAF. The AAF
training organization has only an advisory connection with both
programs. Members of the Victory Corps are students in about
20,000 high schools who take courses which increase their aptitude for military training. Credit is given in the school curriculum. The AAF course includes mathematics, physics, physical
training, elementary aeronautics.

CAP cadet training is an extracurricular program for boys and
girls 15 to 18. In localities where the High School Victory Corps
training is given, a boy or girl must be a member in order to be
eligible for CAP cadet training. The cadets wear CAP uniforms,
meet regularly for evening classes in armories or auditoriums, are
instructed by members of the CAP. The 4 required courses are
military, physical training, code and aircraft identification. As the

student progresses, he may begin preflight training—elementary navigation, elementary meteorology, first aid, principles of flight.

PREVENTION OF FLYING ACCIDENTS

The flying safety record for the last half of 1943 was 6 fatal accidents per 100,000 hours flown, the same as the record for the prewar decade 1931–1940, and considerably less than the overall rate for 1942 and 1943. This safety record was accomplished in spite of the tremendous expansion in the training program, the vast increase in numbers of aircraft and the increasing mechanical complexities of flying.

The Office of Flying Safety (formerly Flight Control Command) conducts a 5-phase flying safety program:

ACCIDENT REPORTING—All accidents are reported first by radio and wire, and later on a standard questionnaire known as Form 14. This information provides both an up-to-the-minute and a detailed account of the accident situation from which studies are made to assist in determining the necessity for preventive measures.

FIELD SAFETY OPERATIONS—Statistical information on the nature and causes of accidents is combined with the experience of safety officers in the field. These, veteran pilots, assist the continental air forces and the Training Command in accident prevention. This is accomplished through observation of training and operating procedures, resulting in corrective measures and recommendations for modification of aircraft or changes in training policy.

SAFETY EDUCATION—By emphasis, repetition and inspiration, pilots and instructors are encouraged and assisted in obtaining sound flying knowledge. The media for this program consist of training aids, films, posters and other educational aids.

FLIGHT CONTROL—The flight control system utilizes all available aerial navigational aids, meteorological data and experience, and technique in the dispatching and control of military flights. Flight control requirements are determined and flight control procedures, methods and practices established for the AAF.

MEDICAL SAFETY DIVISION—Operating under the medical policies of the Air Surgeon, medical investigations of aircraft accidents are made upon which to determine the need for protective devices, emergency equipment and safety procedures.

WHAT WE FIGHT WITH

In the AAF we enter into a partnership with our machines and instruments. It is a close relationship, at times conducted virtually on a man-to-man basis, and our mechanical needs are great, both in quality and numbers. It takes some 500,000 separate items to keep the AAF in operation. One 4-engine bomber requires enough aluminum for 55,000 coffee percolators; enough alloy steel to make 6800 electric irons; enough steel for 160 washing machines; enough rubber to recap 800 automobile tires; enough copper for 550 radio receivers.

To provide us with the necessary aircraft and corollary equipment, a civilian army of several million men and women work around the clock in more than 15,000 factories throughout the nation. To keep this huge production wheel turning, some 60 billions of dollars have been appropriated in the last 3 years. In 1939, a total of 568 military aircraft was produced in the U. S. In the summer of 1940 our production goal was set at 50,000 planes—a figure soon boosted to 125,000.

Our program for global air supremacy called for planes superior

MILITARY AIRCRAFT PRODUCTION

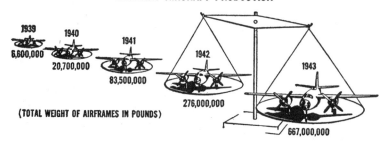

1939
6,600,000

1940
20,700,000

1941
83,500,000

1942
276,000,000

1943
667,000,000

(TOTAL WEIGHT OF AIRFRAMES IN POUNDS)

to anything the enemy could put in the air against us. It called principally for long-range bombers and fighters to strike deep into the enemy homeland; for land-based aircraft, since only from land bases can aircraft carry the great weight of explosives necessary to produce any considerable effect on strategic targets.

Along with the war of production and combat goes the war of experimental development, of design and research, to provide the planes that will be in the air tomorrow.

Procurement and production of AAF aircraft, equipment and accessories are supervised and administered by the Materiel Com-

RATIO OF AIRCRAFT TYPES ACCEPTED

1943

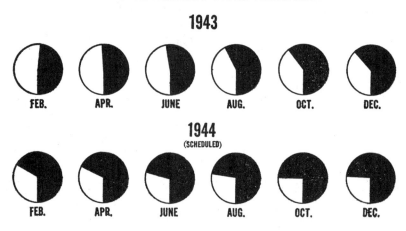

FEB.   APR.   JUNE   AUG.   OCT.   DEC.

1944
(SCHEDULED)

FEB.   APR.   JUNE   AUG.   OCT.   DEC.

KEY: Black area represents combat planes; White area represents other types.

mand, which also has the major responsibility for aircraft development, engineering and inspection.

Production directives reach the Materiel Command with technical instructions as to the quantity of each airplane by type, its performance requirements and its delivery schedules. The actual administration and supervision are done by 3 sections of the command: production engineering, production control, industrial planning.

AAF procurement is administered by procurement district offices throughout the U. S. Supervision of these districts, originally under civilian inspectors, now is conducted by AAF officers who are also stationed at manufacturing plants.

Designations of Aircraft—Letters are assigned to aircraft according to the mission each type is designed to perform; numerical designations refer to particular models. Thus, bombers bear the designation "B" for bombardment, as the B-17 or B-25. "P" stands for pursuit, although pursuit planes are now called fighter planes (P-40, P-51, P-38). This system of nomenclature was adopted in the middle 1920's, and theoretically, numerical designations indicate the order in which designs were accepted by the AAF for certain types of aircraft. However, numbers are often assigned to designs which are subsequently cancelled. Therefore the number 17 in B-17 does not necessarily identify this model as the 17th bomber design produced for the AAF.

"A" stands for attack planes (A-20, A-24) whose mission is low altitude bombing, dive-bombing, or strafing. A P-51 modified for dive-bombing is known as an A-36.

Other designations include: "C" for cargo aircraft (C-47, C-87); UC for utility cargo (UC-78); "F" for photo-reconnaissance (F-5 is the P-38 photo-type plane); "R" for rotary wing aircraft; "G" for gliders ("CG," cargo glider; "TG," training glider); "O" for observation; "L" for liaison; "AT," "BT," "PT" for advance, basic and primary trainers; "X" indicates plane is experimental; "Y" is for service test aircraft. Dropping of "X" and "Y" indicates plane is in production; "Z" indicates it has been declared obsolete.

When a number is followed by a letter, it means that a production modification such as a change in engine, armament or internal equipment has been effected on this particular type of plane.

The B-17G, for example, indicates the seventh step of modification in the production model, "G" being the series letter.

MILITARY AIRCRAFT

DESIGNER	AAF DESIGNATION	APPROVED NAME
BOMBERS		
Boeing	B-17	Fortress
Douglas	B-18	Bolo
Douglas	B-23	Dragon
Consolidated	B-24	Liberator
North American	B-25	Mitchell
Martin	B-26	Marauder
Boeing	B-29	Superfortress
Vega	B-34 (O-56)	Ventura
Douglas	A-20 (P-70)	Havoc
Douglas	A-24	Dauntless
Curtiss	A-25	Helldiver
Lockheed	A-29 (AT-18)	Hudson
Martin	A-30	Baltimore
Vultee	A-31, A-35	Vengeance
Brewster	A-34	Bermuda
North American	A-36 (P-51)	Mustang
FIGHTERS		
Lockheed	P-38	Lightning
Bell	P-39	Airacobra
Curtiss	P-40	Warhawk
Republic	P-47	Thunderbolt
North American	P-51 (A-36)	Mustang
Northrop	P-61	Black Widow
Bell	P-63	King Cobra
Douglas	P-70 (A-20)	Havoc
LIAISON		
Taylorcraft	L-2 (O-57)	Grasshopper
Aeronica	L-3 (O-58)	Grasshopper
Piper	L-4 (O-59)	Grasshopper
Vultee	L-5 (O-62)	Sentinel

DESIGNER	AAF DESIGNATION	APPROVED NAME

OBSERVATION

Vultee	O-49	Vigilant
Curtiss	O-52	Owl
Lockheed	O-56 (B-34)	Ventura
Taylorcraft	O-57 (L-2)	Grasshopper
Aeronica	O-58 (L-3)	Grasshopper
Piper	O-59 (L-4)	Grasshopper
Vultee	O-62 (L-5)	Sentinel

TRAINERS

North American	AT-6	Texan
Beech	AT-7	Navigator
Beech	AT-10	Wichita
Beech	AT-11	Kansan
Boeing	AT-15	Crewmaker
North American	AT-16	Harvard
Cessna	AT-17	Bobcat
Lockheed	AT-18 (A-29)	Hudson
Vultee	AT-19	Reliant
Fairchild	AT-21	Gunner
North American	BT-9, BT-14	Yale
Fleetwing	BT-12	Sophomore
Vultee	BT-13, BT-15	Valiant
Stearman	PT-13, PT-17 PT-18, PT-27	Caydet
Fairchild	PT-19, PT-23 PT-26	Cornell
Ryan	PT-21, PT-22	Recruit

TRANSPORTS

Beech	C-43	Traveller
Beech	C-45	Expediter
Curtiss	C-46	Commando
Douglas	C-47	Skytrain
Douglas	C-49, C-53	Skytrooper
Douglas	C-54	Skymaster
Lockheed	C-56, C-60	Lodestar
Lockheed	C-63 (AT-18) (A-29)	Hudson
Lockheed	C-69	Constellation
Curtiss	C-76	Caravan
Consolidated	C-87	Liberator
Grumman	OA-9	Goose

Removal of camouflage paint from almost all of its aircraft was ordered by the AAF in December 1943. It is estimated that removal of the familiar greenish-gray paint gives AAF planes a slight increase in top speed, a weight reduction in fighter types of approximately 15 to 20 pounds, and in heavy bombardment types of from 70 to 80 pounds. The action was taken upon recommendations of combat commanders. Only specialized planes overseas will retain their camouflage, and in the continental U. S. practically all aircraft will roll off the assembly lines a metal color.

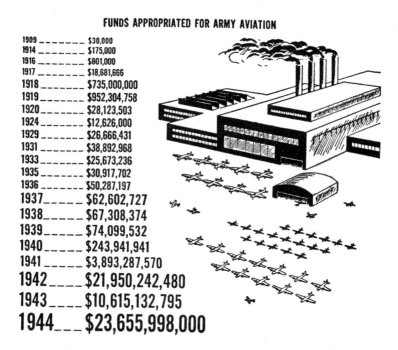

FUNDS APPROPRIATED FOR ARMY AVIATION

1909	$30,000
1914	$175,000
1916	$801,000
1917	$18,681,666
1918	$735,000,000
1919	$952,304,758
1920	$28,123,503
1924	$12,626,000
1929	$26,666,431
1931	$38,892,968
1933	$25,673,236
1935	$30,917,702
1936	$50,287,197
1937	$62,602,727
1938	$67,308,374
1939	$74,099,532
1940	$243,941,941
1941	$3,893,287,570
1942	$21,950,242,480
1943	$10,615,132,795
1944	$23,655,998,000

"Buy a Bomber" Plans—The AAF has received several thousand military airplanes through voluntary cash contributions and special War Bond purchases sponsored by communities, organizations and other groups.

Under the cash plan, citizens have made outright gifts of more than $3,000,000 for the purchase of planes for the AAF. These contributions have been made both in cash and in the form of manhours through voluntary payroll deductions. Wherever possible, the AAF makes available a specific plane, marked with an appropriate inscription up to 25 words, for a dedication ceremony.

The bond purchase "Buy a Bomber" plan reached the $550,-000,000 mark early in 1944. This represents more than 3000 individual planes, with requests for participation coming in at the rate of about 300 a month. Planes financed through War Bond purchases can be painted with the name of the sponsoring community or non-commercial organization.

Quotas set for the purchase of various types of planes for the AAF under these plans are as follows:

PLANE	CASH	BONDS
Trainer	$10,000	$15,000
Fighter	50,000	75,000
Medium bomber	150,000	175,000
Heavy bomber	250,000	300,000

Arrangements for cash purchases are made through the office of the Assistant Secretary of War for Air. AAF acceptances of War Bond financed planes are handled in cooperation with the U. S. Treasury Department.

Performance and Characteristics—Aircraft characteristics, such as armament installations, are undergoing constant modification. In our B-25s, the bombardier and his compartment were eliminated on some models for installation of a 75 mm cannon and fixed .50 caliber guns. Because many different modifications are constantly being made, the accompanying chart presents only the normal equipment found on each aircraft type.

A plane's performance primarily is affected by its gross weight, speed and altitude. A bomber carrying a maximum bomb load of 3 tons cannot fly as high as when it carries only one ton of bombs. When a fighter flies at high speed, it reduces its range by burning up gasoline faster. A plane has greater range and speed at 30,000 feet, where air is thin, than at 10,000 feet where more power is expended to overcome resistance of denser air. For these reasons, it does not necessarily hold true that a bomber can carry its maximum bomb load at its maximum speed and altitude for its maximum range. Figures in the chart must be considered as presupposing specific operational conditions.

TYPE	ENGINE	DIMENSIONS		MAX. SPEED	WEIGHT (lbs.)	OPERATIONAL CEILING
		Wing Span	Length			
B–17G	4–Wright 1200 hp radial	103'10''	74'9''	300+	60,000	30,000
B–24J	4–P&W 1200 hp radial	110'	66'4''	300+	60,000	30,000
B–25G	2–Wright 1700 hp radial	67'6''	53'5''	300+	35,000+	25,000
B–26B	2–P&W 2000 hp radial	71'	58'2''	300+	35,000	20,000
B–29	4–Wright 2200 hp radial	141'3''	99'	Restricted: Very heavy; effective speed; high altitude.		
A–20G	2–Wright 1700 hp radial	61'4''	48'	320+	25,000	20,000+
P–38J	2–Allison 1520 hp in-line	52'	37'10''	420+	18,000	40,000
P–39Q	1–Allison 1325 hp in-line	34'	30'2''	375	8500	35,000+
P–40N	1–Allison 1325 hp in-line	37'4''	33'4''	350+	9500+	30,000
P–47D	1–P&W 2000 hp radial	40'8''	36'1''	420+	13,500	40,000
P–51D	1–Rolls Royce 1500 hp in-line	37'	32'3''	425	10,000	40,000
P–61	2–P&W radial air cooled	Restricted: Long-range; effective speed and rate of climb.				
P–63	1–Allison 1500 hp in-line	Performance data restricted.				
C–46	2–P&W 2000 hp radial	108'	76'4''	265	45,000	25,000+
C–47	2–P&W 1200 hp radial	95'	64'6''	200+	29,000	22,000+
C–54A	4–P&W 1350 hp radial	117'6''	93'10''	250+	60,000	20,000+
C–69	4–Wright 2200 hp radial	123'	95'1''	300+	90,000+	30,000

TACTICAL RADIUS	BOMB LOAD (lbs)	ARMAMENT	CREW	REMARKS	TYPE
700	6000	13–.50 cal guns; turrets.	9–11	Optional: external bomb racks.	B–17G
750	6000	10 or more .50 cal guns; turrets.	9–11	Cargo type: C-87; 1000 mile radius.	B–24J
400	2000	12–.50 cal guns; turrets.	5–6	Attack type: 75 mm cannon; 14–.50 cal guns.	B–25G
350	2000	12–.50 cal guns; turrets.	6	Provision for torpedo.	B–26B
		Heavy armor and armament.		4–blade props.	B–29
250 FB 600 E	2000	5 to 9–.50 cal guns; turrets.	3	Night fighter P–70: 4–20 mm cannon.	A–20G
250 FB 400+ E	2000	1–20 mm cannon; 4–.50 cal guns.	1	Photo type F–5: belly tanks, no guns.	P–38J
100 E	500	1–37 mm cannon; 4–.50 cal guns.	1		P–39Q
150 E	1000	6–.50 cal guns.	1		P–40N
250 FB 350 E	1000	8–.50 cal guns.	1		P–47D
250 FB 600 E	1000	6–.50 cal guns.	1	Photo type: F–6 (51B). Dive bomber: A–36 (51A).	P–51D
		heavy armor.	3	Night fighter; twintail and booms.	P–61
		1–37 mm cannon; 4–.50 cal guns.	1	Improved supercharger.	P–63
800			3–4	36+ men or 15,000+ lbs. cargo.	C–46
750			4	28 men or 6000 lbs. cargo; hospital, 18 litters.	C–47
1000			6	36 men or 8000 lbs. cargo.	C–54A
			9	Pressurized cabin.	C–69

ABBREVIATIONS

E—escort
FB—fighter-bomber
FLG—fixed landing gear
Cont—Continental
Lyco—Lycoming
P&W—Pratt and Whitney

NOTE: Suffix letter after plane denotes model on which maximum information could be released as of April 15, 1944.

TYPE	ENGINE	NORMAL RANGE	CRUISING SPEED	SERVICE CEILING	GROSS WEIGHT (lbs.)	DIMENSIONS Wing Span	Length	REMARKS
LIAISON PLANES (Models L–1, 2, 3, similar to L–4)								
L–4H	1–Cont 65 hp	206	75	11,500	1220	35'2"	22'5"	FLG; 2 seat; fabric.
L–5	1–Lyco 185 hp	300+	112	15,800	2065	34'	24'1"	FLG; 2 seat; fabric.
TRAINING PLANES (selection of typical models)								
PT–17	1–Cont 220 hp	380+	100	13,200	2700	32'2"	24'10"	FLG; open ckpt; 2 seat; fabric. biplane.
PT–19A	1–Ranger 175 hp	420+	105	15,000	2500	35'11"	27'11"	FLG; open ckpt; 2 seat; plywood.
BT–13	1–P&W 450 hp	550+	140	18,000+	4100	42'	28'10"	Instrument trainer; FLG; 2 seat; metal.
AT–6	1–P&W 600 hp	750+	190	21,500	5280	42'	29'	2 seat; metal.
AT–7	2–P&W 450 hp	735	190	24,000	7700	47'8"	34'3"	Navigation trainer with celestial dome; 5-6 seats.
AT–10	2–Lyco 295 hp	750	175	15,000+	6000	37'	27'11"	Adv. 2-engine trainer; 2 seat; plywood-metal.
AT–11	2–P&W 450 hp	800+	175	20,000	8700	47'8"	34'2"	Bombardier trainer; 4-5 seats; metal.

GLIDERS

CG–4 Designer: Waco. Crew: 2. Towspeed: 150 mph. Gross weight: 7500 lbs. with useful load of 3000 lbs. or 15 equipped troops, or 6 men and jeep. Dimensions: span, 83'8" chord, 10'6".

CG–13 Designer: Waco. Crew: 2. Towspeed: 150 mph. Gross weight: 17,000 lbs. with useful load of over 9000 lbs. or 30 equipped troops. Dimensions: span, 85'8" chord, 10'6".

HELICOPTER

R–4 Designer: Sikorsky. Main rotor with 3–15 ft. blades. Engine: Warner 180 hp. Approx. speed: 90–100 mph. Weight: 2500 lbs. Length: 48 ft. Approx. range: 100 miles.

JET PROPELLED

Designer: Whittle. Mfg.: Bell. Fighter with 2 General Electric thermal-jet engines. No propellers. High speed and ceiling; heavy armor and armament.

How a Plane Is Born—New airplanes are not new in the sense of being inventions; they are the products of development.

The AAF's aeronautical technicians decide what top speed is required, what rate of climb the plane must have, how fast it may land with safety, how much space is required for taking off and landing, its range, operational ceiling, and load—including

SPEED IN MILES PER HOUR

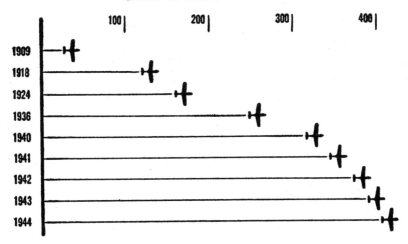

the number of crew, weight of fuel, oil, equipment, bomb load and armament.

Once 3-view drawings based on established specifications have been prepared, a wind tunnel model is constructed. The model is subjected to high-speed flow of artificial wind produced by huge fans, while accurate measuring equipment determines efficiency of the design. Next, a full-sized mock-up, or model of the craft, is constructed from wood and cheap materials to facilitate proper placement of armament and accessory equipment and to determine whether or not parts will be accessible for maintenance and repair. Final stage is production on the first model of the experimental airplane.

Modification—Modification is the tailoring job of the AAF which fills the gap between the time we decide on an alteration of a plane and the time the factory can incorporate the change into production. To modification centers, operated on contract by commercial airline companies and manufacturers, go most of our completed airplanes before shipment overseas. Here they are modernized with the best and newest equipment available.

RANGE IN MILES

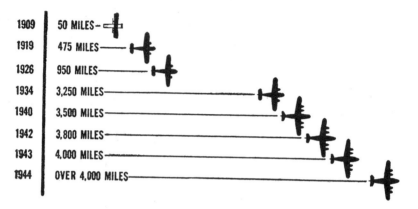

1909	50 MILES—
1919	475 MILES———
1926	950 MILES———
1934	3,250 MILES———
1940	3,500 MILES———
1942	3,800 MILES———
1943	4,000 MILES———
1944	OVER 4,000 MILES———

Planes also are dressed up or stripped down according to the military requirements and weather conditions of the theater for which they are destined. Dust filters are installed on planes scheduled for operation in dry countries while planes on their way to arctic regions are completely winterized. Modification is continued on operational aircraft by service personnel in the theaters, where many modification ideas originate.

Obsolescence—Without our modernization system, many of our planes would become obsolete as soon as newer enemy equipment was developed and before similar improvements could be made in our production aircraft. An oxygen mask that is reliable up to 25,000 feet is replaced by oxygen masks that are reliable as high as any of our airplanes can fly. Heated wing de-icing developments have made our rubber boot de-icers obsolete, so changes are being made on all types of aircraft.

Rotary Wing Aircraft—One of the newest types of aircraft in use by the AAF is the helicopter, a rotary wing design capable of vertical flight and potentially useful in liaison, reconnaissance and rescue work.

Whereas a conventional airplane relies on forward speed to produce airflow over fixed wings, the helicopter flies by rotating a series of small wings (rotors) to induce airflow over their surfaces sufficient to lift the craft into the air. Its forward motion is obtained in effect by tilting the rotor disc and its directional control by varying the pitch of the tail rotor. Like a dragonfly, it can remain stationary in a hovering position or fly forward or backward, or, unlike a dragonfly, sideways.

Similar in appearance, but different in operating principle, is the autogiro. It differs from the helicopter in that its rotor only provides lift as does the wing of an airplane, does not provide forward motion. The plane obtains its forward speed from a conventional engine-propeller power plant, must maintain forward speed to be airborne. It is incapable of zero speeds, cannot fly sideways or backward and cannot ascend vertically.

Gliders—In towed flight, gliders are dependent for forward motion upon a powered aircraft to which they are attached by a tow-rope. In free flight the glider maintains safe forward motion by means of a controlled rate of descent. A free flight glider can execute many of the maneuvers done by powered aircraft and has the added advantage of being able to land in restricted areas and on almost any type of terrain. Two types of gliders are now in use by the AAF. One can carry 15 fully-equipped infantrymen or paratroopers and another 30 troops with their heavy equipment. Equipment has been developed for picking up gliders parked on the ground by planes in flight.

ENGINEERING

The airplane fundamentally is composed of 3 major components: the airframe, the engine and the propeller. (Engine and propeller comprise the power plant.) All else on the airplane comes under the heading of accessories or equipment.

Airframes—The load-carrying structure of an airplane—the airframe—includes wings, fuselage, control surfaces and the metallic or fabric skin that covers them.

Aluminum-alloy, alclad and stainless steel are the basic materials most commonly used in airframes. Alclad, which is an aluminum-alloy sheet with pure aluminum coating, is used for skin covering. Aluminum-alloy is used for ribs, structural parts of wings and fuselages, cowlings and longerons. Stainless steel is used for parts, such as engine mounts and firewalls which must withstand high temperatures. Some wing panels are being built of stainless steel. Even within the basic components of the airframe there are many intricate parts and construction details. For example, in the metal wing tip of a P-38, there are 14 pieces of tubing, ribs and sheet skin, and 277 bolts and nuts plus hundreds of rivets.

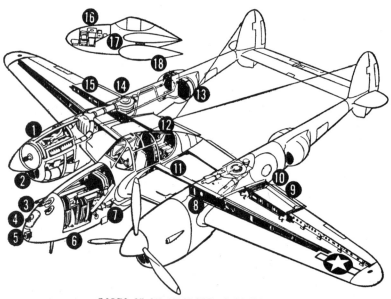

PARTS OF AN AIRCRAFT—P-38 FIGHTER

1. IN-LINE ENGINE	7. NOSE LANDING GEAR	13. COOLANT RADIATOR
2. OIL, INTERCOOLER DUCTS	8. MAIN BEAM	14. SUPERCHARGER SYSTEM
3. FOUR .50 CAL. GUNS	9. FLAPS	15. REAR SHEAR BEAM
4. ONE 20 MM. CANNON	10. MAIN LANDING GEAR	16. CAMERA NOSE F-5 MODEL
5. GUN CAMERA	11. FUEL TANKS	17. BOMB SHACKLE
6. ARMAMENT COMPARTMENT	12. TWO WAY RADIO	18. DROP TANK

Plastics and impregnated plywoods have been substituted for metals in some airframes. However, because physical properties of non-metallic materials change under radical variations of temperature and humidity, plastics and similar substitutes are not as reliable as metals for structural parts of combat aircraft.

Airfoils—Technically, an airfoil is any flat or curved surface designed to obtain reaction from the air through which it moves. The largest airfoil is the wing, which is designed to develop the major part of the lift of an aircraft.

The AAF today is using 2 types of airfoil cross sections: conventional, and low drag or laminar flow sections. The conventional airfoil has its maximum thickness about 30% of the distance from the leading edge of the wing. The laminar flow airfoil

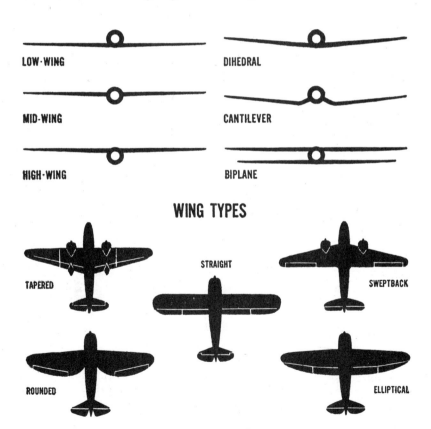

LOW-WING   DIHEDRAL

MID-WING   CANTILEVER

HIGH-WING   BIPLANE

WING TYPES

TAPERED   STRAIGHT   SWEPTBACK

ROUNDED   ELLIPTICAL

section has its maximum thickness 40 to 60% from the leading edge.

Conventional types are less sensitive to surface irregularities, and can be more easily produced. For extremely high-speed and high altitude performance, the laminar flow airfoil is being adopted because it is designed for higher speeds with a smoother flow of air over the wing.

Pressurized Cabins—Substratosphere operation has led to development of the pressurized cabin on some AAF aircraft. A pressurized cabin enables airmen to move about freely in the plane's interior, breathing normal air at high altitudes; it eliminates the need for individual oxygen supply.

There are 2 methods of pressurizing. One is an independent compressor, powered from the engine which compresses the rarefied air of high altitudes, feeding it back through ducts to the cabin itself; such air is of sufficient density and temperature to allow normal breathing. The principle is much the same as a hot air blower system. The other system utilizes the engine supercharger to divert back into the cabin part of the compressed air supplied to the engine.

Dispersed gun positions, crew locations and danger of bullet punctures that might render it inoperative, make pressurization of combat airplanes difficult.

LANDING FLAPS

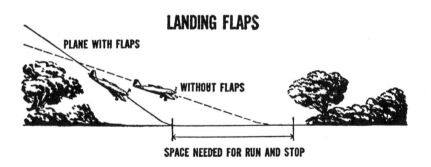

PLANE WITH FLAPS

WITHOUT FLAPS

SPACE NEEDED FOR RUN AND STOP

Flaps—Nearly every aircraft has a system of landing flaps which are lowered from the trailing edge of the wing primarily to increase the lift coefficient of the wing and thus lower stalling speed. The drag effects are beneficial to a certain extent in slowing down the aircraft. The popular Fowler flap protrudes beyond the trailing edge of the wing and hence increases total wing area. Other types fit into the underside of the wing. Dive flaps, or dive brakes, applicable on fighters and dive bombers, slow down the airplane in its dive to give the pilot more time to sight the target accurately, permit a steeper dive angle and a slower pull-out. Maneuver flaps may be used as auxiliary control surfaces which facilitate the making of sharper turns by high-speed aircraft. Flaps are operated from the cockpit.

Landing Gear—Landing gear, or undercarriage, is the airplane's means of mobility when it is on the ground. In the air, landing gear generally is retracted into the plane's engine nacelles or wings to help streamline the aircraft, although a fixed type is found on liaison and trainer type planes.

The AAF utilizes 2 general types of landing gear on its planes: conventional gear with tail-wheel or skid, and the tricycle gear with a wheel extended from the nose of the fuselage. The latter permits easier operation on small fields by eliminating the ground looping tendency common to conventional type gears; however, on rough fields the nose wheel of the tricycle gear is more susceptible to damage.

Retractable types operate electrically or hydraulically. Some gears retract outward and sideways into wing wells as on the B-24; others retract inward into wing wells as on the P-39; some pull up into engine nacelles as on the B-17.

Tires—Airplane tires wear out rapidly because of high landing and takeoff speeds and increased weights of modern aircraft. In wartime the problem is doubly serious because our combat aircraft often land on crushed rock, coral, dirt or metal runways. Many reinforcing layers of rubber, synthetic and natural, and cotton or rayon are required to withstand the impact of 30-ton bombers landing on rough strips at speeds over 100 miles per hour. Sizes of tires range from tiny ones that support the tails of training gliders and light airplanes to huge 8-foot tires on the B-19 "flying laboratory."

Engines—Before the airplane can fly it must have a source of power—the engine. Without power, the airframe is little more than a glider. Speed, altitude, performance and the amount of

RADIAL ENGINE

weight that can be sustained in flight depend upon the horse-power and number of engines installed.

Most engine development today is concentrated on 2 types: radial air-cooled and in-line liquid-cooled. While the large frontal area of radial engines tends to destroy an ideal aerodynamic design, new radial engines have a reduced frontal area and improved cowlings which compare favorably with the design of in-line engines of comparable horsepower.

Major problems that must be solved in aircraft engine designs are development of more horsepower for a given displacement,

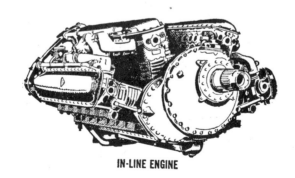

IN-LINE ENGINE

and more efficient and economical consumption of fuel; more specific problems are cooling, high altitude ignition, carburetion and supercharging. Additional fins on the cylinders have helped solve the cooling problem on radial engines; installation of special dampers and other devices has eliminated some vibrations; new fuel injection systems and new lubricating oils have eliminated other problems. Continual progress in solution of these problems has made high horsepower engines possible without increasing the pound-per-horsepower ratio.

Jet Propulsion—Perhaps the greatest development in aeronautical engineering of the last decade is the jet propelled airplane, the most interesting feature of which is elimination of the propeller. The principle of jet propulsion overcomes some of the speed limitations of the propeller-driven airplane. We can reasonably expect the jet engine to add 100 miles or more an hour to the speed of airplanes.

In its practical application, jet propulsion may be defined as any kind of reaction motor which develops forward thrust by the rearward emission of a jet of air, gas or liquid. In the AAF jet-propelled fighter, now in production, the engine is quite simple. It is a gas turbine, and the gases it creates, after driving a turbo-compressor, are discharged through a restricted tail pipe nozzle, thus giving the engine its thrust.

The engine is a modification of a British design; it presents few new problems to the pilot other than how to fly a simpler airplane.

Takeoff Rockets—Rockets may be utilized to assist takeoffs, are slung under the fuselage or wings of a fighter or bomber aircraft with conventional engine-propeller power plant. Ignited by the pilot from the cockpit, the rocket adds forward thrust to the horsepower pull of the engines, thus permitting shorter takeoff runs with maximum loads.

Superchargers—Engines, like people, must have oxygen to breathe at high altitudes; engines need oxygen to mix with gasoline to obtain a combustible mixture in their cylinders. The oxygen mask for the aircraft engine is the supercharger, of which the AAF has 2 types: the turbo-supercharger and the geared supercharger. Both compress rarefied air to a density equal to air at sea level; both function at altitudes up to 43,000 feet.

The turbo-supercharger is operated by the force of engine exhaust gases upon a turbine wheel and impeller or air compressor. The gases pass through the turbine wheel, spinning it; the wheel rotates the impeller which compresses the rarefied air. The air is then fed back into the engine in sufficient quantities to support combustion when mixed with gasoline.

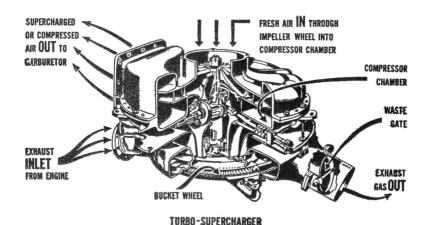

TURBO-SUPERCHARGER

The geared supercharger, as its name implies, is driven by a series of gears in train which turn its impeller, compressing the air and at the same time feeding it into the cylinders.

Aviation Fuels—Except for those airplanes which have low-horsepower engines, aircraft must be serviced with a special fuel (high octane) and not the type of motor fuel used in automobiles. The use of an inferior anti-knock value fuel in tactical aircraft would result in overheating, detonation and pre-ignition which would burn holes in pistons and cause other damage.

Octane rating is an arbitrary scale adopted to indicate the comparative performance relative to the fuel's resistance to detonation. This scale runs from zero to 100 octane. Fuels having ratings above 100 are rated on a different scale designated as the Performance Number Scale. Ninety-five per cent of the gasoline used in U. S. combat planes today exceeds the 100 octane number in anti-knock values.

The following table illustrates adaptation of fuels to type of aircraft:

AIRCRAFT	OCTANE RATING OR PER. NO.
Liaison	80-octane or all-purpose motor vehicle fuel
Primary Trainers	73-octane aircraft engine fuel
Advanced Trainers	87 to 97-octane
All Tactical Types	100/130 Performance Number

Self-sealing Gasoline Tanks—To help prevent igniting of gasoline tanks by enemy gunfire, our aircraft engineers have developed a gasoline tank which, while not bulletproof, lessens danger of explosion and prevents loss of large amounts of fuel through bullet holes. This was accomplished by inserting a series of linings of rubber and other materials in the tank. The linings are capable of sealing instantly multiple punctures made by bursts from both light and heavy machine gun fire and flak. This development has saved countless airmen and aircraft.

Droppable Fuel Tanks—The range of fighter planes, once hampered by limited fuel supply, has been increased substantially by the use of droppable auxiliary fuel tanks attached beneath wings and fuselages. Streamlined to the shape of a teardrop, these droppable tanks enable fighter planes like the P-47 and P-51 to fly long bomber escort missions. Once the fighter plane has used up its auxiliary fuel supply, the tanks are released by the pilot, enabling the plane to fight off enemy attacks and return to its base on the fuel supply in its wing tanks. Capacity varies from 150 gallons to 300 gallons. Some fighters carry 2 auxiliary tanks under the wings and one tank under the belly of the fuselage.

Propellers—The power plant of any airplane is more than just the engine. It is the combination of engine and propeller. The engine is the source of power for the propeller. The propeller transforms that energy into thrust by boring itself through the air and pulling the airplane after it.

Today the AAF has propellers which range from small wooden 2-bladed propellers less than 6 feet in diameter to giant 4-bladed all-metal propellers 20 feet in diameter. Most common in use today is the 3-bladed propeller although 4-bladed props are becoming increasingly conventional.

Pitch—Propeller blades are so constructed and operated that they may be turned at varying degrees, to take larger or smaller bites of air, thereby increasing or decreasing forward thrust. Since air density varies with altitude, it is desirable to vary the angle of the prop blade to maintain a constant degree of thrust. The angle at which the blade is set is called pitch.

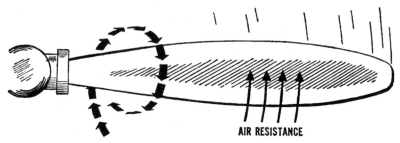

AIR RESISTANCE

VARIABLE PITCH PROPELLER

A comparatively new experiment with propellers is the use of reversible pitch control which enables the pilot to reverse completely the pitch of the blades, thereby creating negative thrust which acts as a brake to the forward movement of an airplane. The reversible pitch propeller is useful in slowing down aircraft in flight, decreasing the landing run after a plane's wheels have touched the ground and supplementing the flaps in reducing landing speed of large airplanes.

Propellers also are classified according to operating principles:

The fixed pitch propeller, as its name implies, has a fixed pitch that is stationary at all times.

The ground adjustable propeller has detachable blades, the pitch of which is changed while the plane is on the ground and the propeller is not in motion.

The two-position hydraulic propeller has a mechanism operated by a hydraulic piston which permits the pilot to control pitch during takeoff and in flight at either a predetermined low pitch or high pitch position. The low pitch position is used for takeoff and the high pitch for normal flight operations.

The hydraulic constant speed propeller is controlled in flight by a governor which automatically changes the pitch of the propeller to maintain constant engine speed. The propeller revolutions per minute may be adjusted by the pilot during flight. There are 2 types: one employing oil pressure from the engine lubricating system, the other having a self-contained hydraulic unit.

The electric constant speed propeller operates much the same as the hydraulically controlled propeller but the power for changing the pitch is provided by a small electric motor on the front of the propeller hub, which is controlled by a constant speed governor adjustable from the cockpit.

Feathering—The hydraulic and electric constant speed propellers used on multi-engine airplanes are full-feathering. A full-feathering propeller is one in which the pitch changing mechanism can turn the blades to approximately a 90-degree angle of pitch relative to the leading edge of the wing, thereby presenting a knife edge in the direction of flight. The advantages are twofold: it prevents the propeller from windmilling and causing excessive vibration in the event of engine failure and, with motion stopped, it presents the minimum amount of drag, whereas a turning propeller would create considerable resistance.

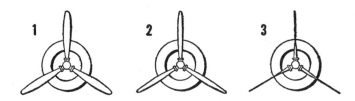

EMERGENCY "FEATHERING" OF PROPELLER

Electrical Systems—Electrical systems provide power for more than 100 pieces of equipment and accessories in an airplane. These include various types of radio equipment, all kinds of lighting equipment, practically every piece of armament; heaters, motors and other auxiliary essentials.

Motors are used for many purposes: the largest ones lift landing gear and turn gun turrets; the smallest operate gyroscopic instruments. Between these limits, motors are used for starting engines, operating bomb bay doors and cowl flaps, remote positioning of equipment, operation of ventilating fans and other functions.

A normal installation provides for one generator on each engine with a rating of 6 kilowatts (1⅓ horsepower). The units on 100 heavy bombers generate enough electricity to care for the requirements of a community of 1200 people. The electrical systems of large planes require approximately 6 miles of electrical wiring.

During the last 5 years, as aircraft demands on the electrical system have increased, generators have been reduced from a weight of 43 pounds per kilowatt to 4 pounds per kilowatt.

Hydraulic Systems—Hydraulic systems wind like intricate pipelines throughout the aircraft, supply the extra forces which easily and smoothly motivate the airplane's flaps, engine cowl flaps, dive brakes, landing gear mechanisms, bomb bay doors and turrets. It would be virtually impossible to perform these operations manually in flight due to wind resistance. For operation of the system, heavy petroleum-base oil is stored in a reservoir. When the hydraulic system is actuated by the pilot, fluid pressure is built up in a hydraulic pump, then released into the proper pipelines; the flipping of a switch or handle operates a series of diaphragms to raise or lower the flaps, landing gear, etc.

ARMAMENT

Today's warplane is virtually a flying gun platform. Our P-47s, with eight .50 caliber guns, can fire in salvo at the rate of 6000 rounds per minute, creating 96,000 pounds of impact pressure. A flight of 13 P-47s has 3 times the striking power of a machine gun unit in a German infantry regiment while a formation of 13 bombers, carrying 75 mm cannon, carries twice the firepower of the howitzers used by this same Nazi regiment.

Fixed guns are those mounted in rigid position, generally fired by remote control and set to fire in one direction in respect to the airplane. With a fixed gun the airplane itself is aimed at the target, as in single-seat fighters.

Flexible guns are those which are installed on movable mounts which enable the gun to be fired in various directions and to follow a moving target. They can be either hand-held or turret-operated.

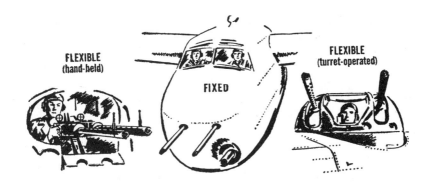

.50 CALIBER MACHINE GUN—The .50 caliber gun, capable of firing at a rate of more than 800 rounds per minute, weighs only 65 pounds. Its projectile leaves the muzzle at a speed of over 2900 feet per second and is capable of penetrating any and all parts of an airplane including the engine. The small size and light weight of the complete round (shell) permit more than 1000 rounds per gun to be carried in some planes. This gun is mounted in the fuselage or in the wings, or both, of most of our fighters. All flexible guns, both hand-held and power turret mounted, in AAF bombardment airplanes are at present .50 caliber.

GUNSIGHTS—In the last war the ordinary ring and bead sight, common to the hunter, was standard for all aircraft guns. Now the ring and bead sight is used only on hand-held guns. Reflector type and computing type gunsights in our turrets and fighter aircraft eliminate the need for lining up the gunner's eye, front and rear sights, and the target; the sight itself actually projects a sight reticle image on a transparent reflector plate which, at infinity, moves with the gunner's eye. Thus, although the gunner's head may be in continual movement in rough air, the sight line and target will remain together. New computing sights have been developed and placed in production for use in all gun positions.

AIRCRAFT ROCKETS—Investigations and experimentation with aircraft rockets are being conducted to produce new rocket projec-

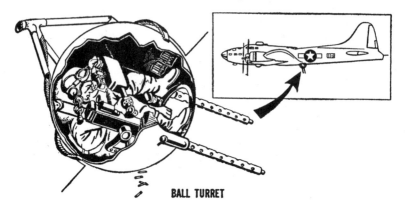

BALL TURRET

tors and projectiles not only as offensive weapons but for defensive action as well.

TURRETS—Because the high velocity of air that flows over an airplane's surfaces in flight makes it difficult to turn guns into the airstream by hand, booster motors are used to help move and aim flexible guns in aircraft. Most effective method of solving the problem has been the development of hydraulic and electrically operated gun turrets. The turret is an independent unit. It has: a seat; hand controls that turn it in azimuth and elevation and fire the guns; oxygen and interphone communication equipment; heating units for electrically heated flying suits, gunsights, ammunition belts and containers; its own armor protection; a plexiglass dome or enclosure to provide maximum visibility for the gunner. Other than remote controlled turrets which at present are limited in use, there are 6 basic types of turrets on AAF bombers: nose turrets, chin turrets, ball turrets, tail turrets, upper turrets and training types.

REMOTE CONTROLLED TURRETS—Certain new turret installations incorporate remote control mechanisms that enable the guns to be fired electrically from sighting stations apart from the turrets themselves. (By taking the gunner out of the turret, size and weight of the turrets can be reduced.) Such installations permit cleaner aerodynamic features resulting in increased speed and ranges.

AERIAL CANNON—A 75 mm cannon now is standard armament on some models of the B-25 and AAF armament experts are experimenting with the installation of still larger millimeter guns. The

75 mm gun is mounted in the forward fuselage and nose of the B-25. It is a standard M-4 cannon with a specially constructed spring that absorbs the recoil shock. The breech of the gun is located behind and below the pilot's seat. The barrel extends forward under the cockpit through the tunnel formerly used by the bombardier in reaching his nose position; the muzzle emerges from a concave port on the left side of the nose. The complete round fired by this cannon weighs 20 pounds. Each projectile is 26 inches long and weighs 15 pounds. Just above the breech of the gun is a shell rack holding about 20 shells. The rapidity of fire depends on the loading technique of the cannoneer, usually the navigator. The cannon has an effective range of about 2000 yards but can toss a projectile several miles.

The 37 mm cannon, although not a rapid-fire weapon, does fire its shells from clips of 5 in much the same manner as an automatic pistol. A new magazine employs a horse-collar clip that can feed 30 shells into the gun. The 2 types of 37 mm cannon in use today are the M-4 and M-9 guns. Both hurl the same size projectile, which weighs little more than one pound, but the M-9 has increased velocity over the M-4. Both have a penetrating force that will cut through armor plate the thickness of their diameter. It is used on the P-39. Smallest cannon in AAF fighting planes is the 20 mm rapid fire gun which uses a projectile 3 times the size and weight of the .50 caliber. This cannon has a muzzle velocity of about 2800 feet per second and the projectile can penetrate an inch of armor plate. The P-38 is equipped with a 20 mm cannon.

AMMUNITION—Three types of ammunition are used in machine guns: armor piercing, incendiary and tracer. These are used in various combinations on gun belts, the most common being 2 each of incendiary and armor piercing to one tracer.

Tracer ammunition contains a chemical composition that burns visibly from the rear forward giving the illusion of a stream of fire. They are used in observing the direction of fire, for incendiary purposes, in signalling and for the psychological effect upon the enemy.

Incendiary ammunition has the primary purpose of starting fires. The charge is designed for conflagration rather than penetration.

Armor Protection—Protection against gunfire in airplanes is provided by steel armor plate, aluminum-alloy deflector plate, bullet resistant glass and splash shields (guards bolted along the edge of armor plate). The use of each depends upon how much of the plane structure the bullet must pass through before it hits the protective material, the angle at which it hits the material, and the necessary requirements as to vision and movement.

BOMBS

Today we are using many types of specialized bombs: incendiary, fragmentation, armor piercing, semi-armor piercing, general purpose, light case blast and chemical. Approximate weights of some of these bomb types are:

TYPE BOMB	WEIGHT
Incendiary	2, 4 & 100 lbs.
Fragmentation	20 & 260 lbs.
Anti-personnel	4 lbs.
General Purpose	100, 250, 500, 1000, 2000 & 4000 lbs.
Armor Piercing	1600 lbs.

COMPARATIVE SIZES OF GENERAL PURPOSE (DEMOLITION) BOMBS

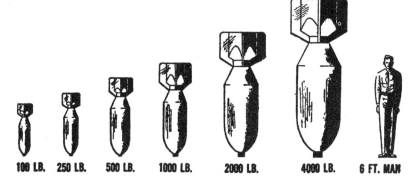

100 LB.   250 LB.   500 LB.   1000 LB.   2000 LB.   4000 LB.   6 FT. MAN

General purpose bombs are designed for the destruction or demolition of materiel targets, the destructive effect being produced chiefly by the violence of the detonation, although fragments may cause additional damage, particularly when the detonation occurs above ground. Armor piercing and semi-armor piercing bombs are designed to pierce the deck armor of battleships, heavy concrete structures, and similar highly resistant targets.

Incendiary bombs range in size from 2 to 500 lbs. Small types generally are released in an aimable cluster that disperses after leaving the aircraft. Various chemical fillings are used, the construction of the target determining which is employed. Frequently high explosive bombs are released upon a target first, followed by incendiaries; then, more explosives. The result achieved is that flaming debris and sparks are scattered throughout the devastation caused by the explosives.

Biggest of the bombs we are using today are known as block busters. These giants weigh 4000 pounds apiece and are made with a light metal casing; 77.4% of their total weight is a high explosive composition. The 2000-pound bomb has about 56% high explosive content and the 1000-pound bomb, whose metal components weigh about 435 pounds, carries a high explosive charge of approximately 530 pounds.

EXPLOSIVE TRAIN OF GENERAL PURPOSE (DEMOLITION) BOMBS

IN GENERAL, THE EXPLOSIVES IN THE SYSTEM ARE ARRANGED IN ORDER OF SENSITIVITY, FROM A
SMALL QUANTITY OF A SENSITIVE EXPLOSIVE TO A LARGE QUANTITY OF LESS SENSITIVE EXPLOSIVE

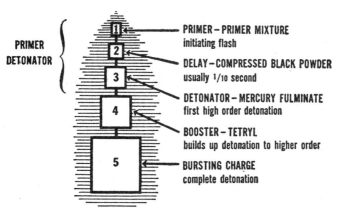

PRIMER DETONATOR {

1 — PRIMER – PRIMER MIXTURE
initiating flash

2 — DELAY – COMPRESSED BLACK POWDER
usually 1/10 second

3 — DETONATOR – MERCURY FULMINATE
first high order detonation

4 — BOOSTER – TETRYL
builds up detonation to higher order

5 — BURSTING CHARGE
complete detonation

Destructive force of bombs varies with the size and high explosive content. A 100-pound bomb with an instantaneous fuze, when dropped from a given altitude on sandy soil, will blast a crater approximately 2 feet deep and 9 feet in diameter, displacing about 40 cubic feet of dirt. A bomb weighing a full ton will blast a hole approximately 7 feet deep and 20 feet in diameter, displacing about 1300 cubic feet of dirt. On the other hand, a delayed action bomb will cause greater destruction. For instance, a 100-pound bomb with delayed action fuze, in sandy soil will make a crater 5 feet deep and 20 feet in diameter, displacing approximately 800 cubic feet of dirt. A 2000-pounder will displace more than 1600 cubic feet, resulting in a crater approximately 17 feet in depth and 50 feet in diameter at the surface.

Bomb Racks and Release Mechanism—Internal bomb racks are designed to carry all sizes of bombs in use except the 4000 pounders which are carried on special external racks. Made of steel alloys, bomb racks are part of the airplane structure, sometimes serve as reinforcements in the plane's fuselage.

The number of bombs that can be carried on a rack depends upon the diameter and length of the bomb itself. That is, more 100-pound bombs can be carried than 500-pounders because the lighter bomb is smaller in diameter; consequently more of these can be placed one above the other in bomb racks.

Shackles hold the bombs in the racks. Inside the bomber the shackle and the bomb release mechanism are like a nut and bolt. One is of little use without the other; normally bombs are hooked onto the shackle in 2 places. The small hooks, operated electrically or manually, will support several thousand pounds and, with the proper pressure, will allow the bomb to drop. On a mission the release is operated electrically. Hand mechanisms are for emergency only. Bomb bay doors are controlled by electricity on B-17s and by hydraulic systems on other planes. In both instances they are operated by a switch in the bombardier's compartment. It is mechanically impossible for a bomb to drop from its shackle when the doors are in closed position, thus safeguarding the airplane. This safety measure is made possible by a tiny switch which completes the circuit on the bomb release only when the doors are in open position.

No bomb is considered alive when it is inside the bomber. A special arming device arms the bomb fuzes only when they are free of the plane. Generally speaking, as the bomb falls, a propeller, whirled by the air, unscrews itself to arm the fuze. Upon impact of the bomb, fuzed instantaneously, the powder train of the fuze detonates the explosive charge. A time fuze in the bomb can delay its detonation for any desired length of time.

CHAPTER CONTINUED ON PAGE 170

"BECAUSE we've had the support of thousands of men and women on the production lines in our aircraft and engine factories, we have been able to build the largest air force in the world . . . have gained control of the air in every major theater . . ."—Gen. H. H. Arnold

B-24 LIBERATOR.

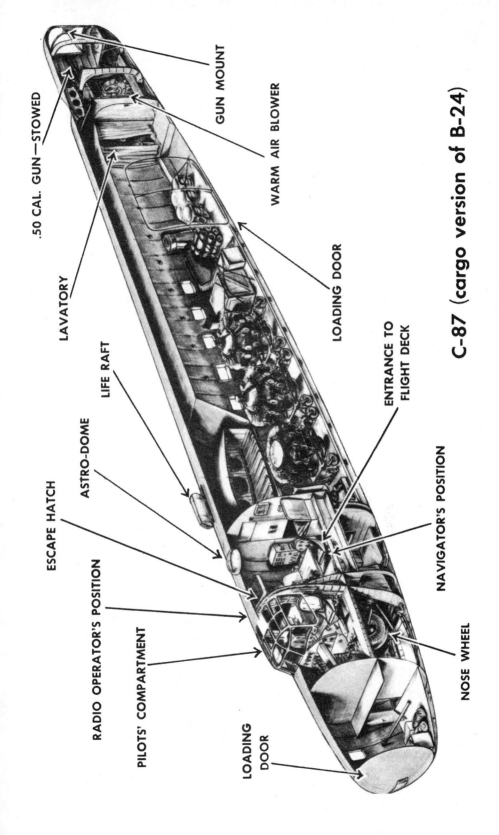

.50 CAL. GUN—STOWED

GUN MOUNT

WARM AIR BLOWER

LAVATORY

LOADING DOOR

LIFE RAFT

ENTRANCE TO
FLIGHT DECK

ASTRO-DOME

ESCAPE HATCH

NAVIGATOR'S POSITION

RADIO OPERATOR'S POSITION

PILOTS' COMPARTMENT

NOSE WHEEL

LOADING
DOOR

C-87 (cargo version of B-24)

B-17 FLYING FORTRESS

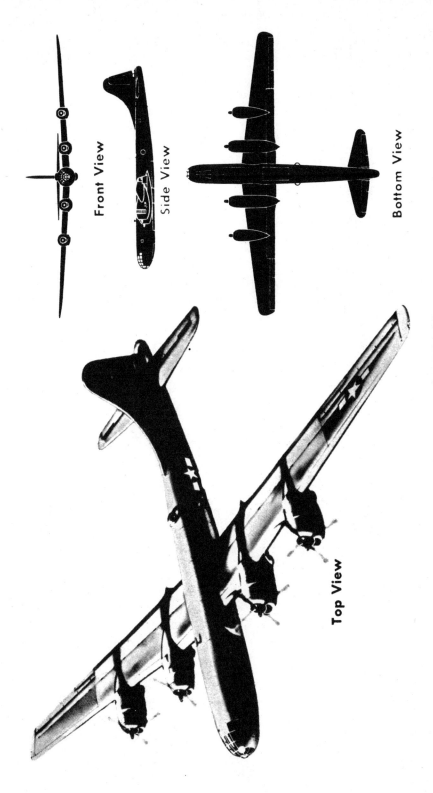

Front View

Side View

Bottom View

Top View

B-29 SUPERFORTRESS

P-51 MUSTANG

P-47 THUNDERBOLT

B-26 MARAUDER

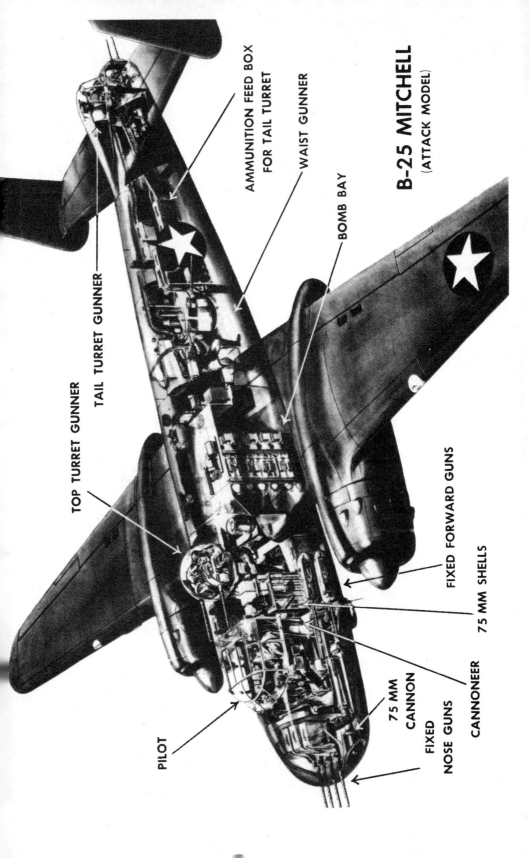

B-25 MITCHELL
(ATTACK MODEL)

AMMUNITION FEED BOX
FOR TAIL TURRET

WAIST GUNNER

BOMB BAY

TAIL TURRET GUNNER

TOP TURRET GUNNER

FIXED FORWARD GUNS

75 MM SHELLS

PILOT

75 MM CANNON

FIXED NOSE GUNS

CANNONEER

B-25 MITCHELL

P-38 LIGHTNING

P-40 WARHAWK

P-39 AIRACOBRA

P-61 BLACK WIDOW

A-20 HAVOC

C-54 SKYMASTER

C-47 SKYTRAIN

C-46 COMMANDO

CG-13 (CARGO OR TROOP GLIDER)

CG-4 (CARGO OR TROOP GLIDER)

R-4 HELICOPTER

L-5 SENTINEL

BT-13 VALIANT

AT-7 NAVIGATOR

AT-10 WICHITA

PT-17 CAYDET

AT-6 TEXAN

AT-11 KANSAN

PT-19 CORNELL

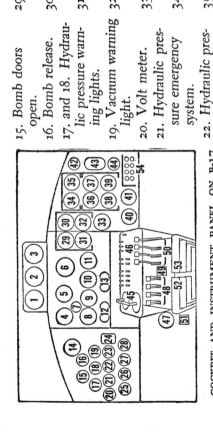

COCKPIT AND INSTRUMENT PANEL ON B-17

1. and 3. Carburetor air temperature gauges.
2. Accelerometer.
4. Radio compass indicator.
5. Turn indicator.
6. Artificial horizon or flight indicator.
7. Marker beacon.
8. Altimeter.
9. Air speed indicator.
10. Turn and bank.
11. Rate of climb.
12. Prop feather left engines.
13. Prop feather right engines.
14. PDI equipment visual indicator.
15. Bomb doors open.
16. Bomb release.
17. and 18. Hydraulic pressure warning lights.
19. Vacuum warning light.
20. Volt meter.
21. Hydraulic pressure emergency system.
22. Hydraulic pressure main system.
23. Vacuum gauge.
24. Air speed source control.
25. Pilot's oxygen flow indicator.
26. Pilot's oxygen cylinder pressure.
27. Copilot's oxygen flow indicator.
28. Copilot's oxygen cylinder pressure.
29. Manifold pressure left engines.
30. Manifold pressure right engines.
31. Tachometer left engines.
32. Tachometer right engines.
33. Flap position indicator.
34. Fuel pressure left engines.
35. Fuel pressure right engines.
36. Oil pressure left engines.
37. Oil pressure right engines.
38. Oil temperature left engines.
39. Oil temperature right engines.
40. Cylinder head temperature left engines.
41. Cylinder head temperature right engines.
42. Free air temperature.
43. Fuel tank gauge.
44. Fluorescent light control.
45. Ignition and master electric switch.
46. Switch for fuel, landing gear, etc.
47. Automatic pilot turning control.
48. Turbo-supercharger regulators.
49. Lock for mixture controls and supercharger.
50. Mixture controls.
51. Lock for throttles.
52. and 53. Throttles.
54. Carburetor air cleaner.

Instruments—Airmen depend upon instruments to get them off the ground, to keep them in the air, to keep them on the right course, to bomb their target and to return them to their base. Consequently the instruments that go into the modern fighting plane are its mechanical brains, the liaison devices between man and science. Flight instruments, navigation instruments and engine instruments are of equal importance to the success of a mission. A few fundamental flight instruments are: bank and turn indicator, air speed indicator, rate of climb indicator, flight indicator or artificial horizon, and directional gyro. They tell the

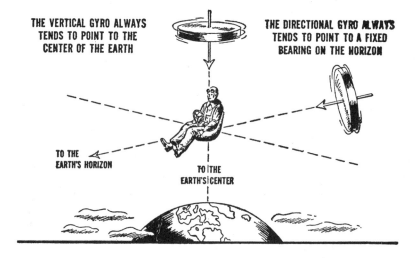

THE VERTICAL GYRO ALWAYS TENDS TO POINT TO THE CENTER OF THE EARTH

THE DIRECTIONAL GYRO ALWAYS TENDS TO POINT TO A FIXED BEARING ON THE HORIZON

TO THE EARTH'S HORIZON

TO THE EARTH'S CENTER

pilot the position of his airplane relative to its own axis, the speed at which it is being propelled through the air and its rate of climb. (For illustration of instrument panel with explanatory key see page 169.)

Engine instruments include: temperature gauges, fuel mixture indicators, oil gauges, coolant and pressure gauges; vacuum, fuel, manifold tachometers.

Navigation instruments enable our AAF fliers to make long-range flights over water and through unfavorable weather. With the aid of electronic devices, they also make possible bombing through the overcast.

The B-25 Mitchell bomber contains approximately 128 instruments—thermometers, clocks, altimeters, etc.; the B-17 has 323; the P-38 fighter 90.

Auto-Pilot—The automatic pilot which enables some of our aircraft to maintain straight and level flight, or any desired attitude independent of manual control by the pilot, is of great value in making a bombing run (see page 260) and in relieving the pilot on long flights.

Automatic pilots are of 2 types: hydraulic, usually adapted to transport planes, and the electrically controlled, usually adapted

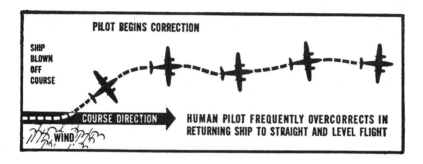

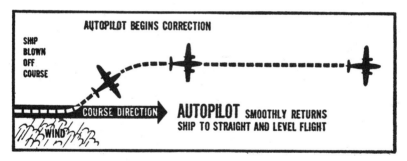

to combat aircraft. Both contain 2 vacuum-operated gyroscopes, one revolving on a vertical axis, the other on a horizontal axis. Each of these gyros has a series of pick-off control points which actuate impulses that operate the airplane's controls, ailerons, elevators and rudder. The pick-off points are operated by the changing attitude of the airplane itself.

Electronics—The unusual speed and mobility of air operations have stimulated the development of electrical devices which fall within the sphere of electronics. Such devices are used to obtain and transmit information needed to put combat aircraft in the right place at the right time; they are playing an increasingly important part in combat operations and strategic planning.

These devices are of 2 types: the first includes radio as we have always known it; the second includes new locating devices which are considered among the outstanding technical achievements of the present war.

Science is making great strides in giving eyes to aircraft operating in darkness and above the overcast. These eyes are needed for navigation, for finding and hitting the target and often for landing.

The airplane, depending on the type, may have such electronic equipment as command radio set (relatively short range); liaison radio set (short and long-range); radio compass; electronic altimeter; devices for precision and automatic navigation; devices for locating the target; identification devices to determine whether detected aircraft are friendly or hostile; devices for detecting enemy transmissions; devices for interfering with enemy transmissions; electronic gear to be dropped or parachuted for special operations.

Fire Extinguishers—Fire extinguishers are standard precautionary equipment on all aircraft because of fire hazards from inflammable gasoline and incendiary bullets. The 2 types are hand-held and built-in extinguishers. Hand-held extinguishers are located where the danger of fire is greatest in a plane. Built-in systems are used in various parts of planes but especially in engine nacelles. The engine fire extinguisher system consists of high pressure cylinders containing carbon-dioxide. These systems are controlled from the pilot's or navigator's compartment, and operated by cable controls or electricity.

Parachutes—Three types of personnel parachutes are common: seat type, back type, and chest or quick attachable type. In anticipation of war in the Pacific, the AAF substituted nylon for silk in parachutes before war with Japan had cut off our supplies from the Far East. Because it is plastic, nylon fiber does not disintegrate with age to the extent of silk fiber which is an animal matter. Silk chutes were limited to a useful life of 7 years; nylon chutes apparently last indefinitely.

Into one nylon chute goes enough material to make 100 pairs of ladies' hose; 4 times that much goes into the nylon shroud lines that hang down from the folds and support the harness, which is made of a tough cotton-nylon fabric.

The parachute used in most crew positions is the flexible back type. It conforms to the shape of the back, thereby allowing complete freedom of movement. The pack is thin, has a minimum of metal ribs to hold its shape. It enables crewmen to climb about in the small confines of bombers and gives the fighter pilot more freedom and comfort.

Some crew positions, such as the ball turret on bombers, are too small for the wearing of any parachute. Such crewmen use the quick-attachable chute which rolls up in a small pack and is snapped onto D-shaped rings that are a part of the harness worn on the chest. These harnesses are worn at all times, and the chute is stored near the escape hatchway.

The seat type parachute folds into a small pack and is harnessed around shoulders and thighs; it also serves as a seat cushion.

Aerial Delivery Parachutes—Cargo parachutes, varying in diameter from small 2½-foot chutes for dropping messages, to giant 48-foot chutes capable of dropping 3000-pound loads, are being used by the AAF to supply ground troops with equipment and materiel. A 12-foot chute is one of the latest types used for dropping sea-rescue kits.

The giant 48-foot chutes, the AAF's largest, are utilized for dropping iron matting for emergency runways, land-mines, demolition equipment, mortars and heavy war vehicles.

Parachutes used for aerial delivery are made of rayon or cotton, depending upon the weight of the equipment to be dropped. Variously colored canopies are used, each color representing a specific item of equipment or supply, to enable ground troops to identify parachutes when they land.

Oxygen Equipment—In addition to oxygen masks and regulators (see page 244), the storage of oxygen in cylinders has undergone a major change. Early types of cylinders were made of heavy steel to withstand the high pressure of 2000 pounds per square inch. When it was discovered that such cylinders would explode with the force and effect of a small shrapnel bomb upon being struck by bullets or flak, new light-weight low-pressure cylinders were developed and standardized in all of our aircraft. The change-over also facilitated refilling of the cylinders from conventional commercial storage cylinders.

Aerial Photography Equipment—Two of the most commonly used high altitude cameras are the K-3B and the K-18. Both are electrically operated. The K-3B has 24-inch lenses with 3 focal lengths; the K-18 is larger and takes a 9 by 18 inch photograph. A telephoto camera is the K-15 type; improved versions of this camera are going into use. The T-3A and T-5 cameras are special map-making cameras with multiple lenses capable of photographing hundreds of square miles in one photograph. One camera of this type is equipped to record on one film the time of day, date, serial number of the negative, altitude, speed, vertical angle of camera and other data pertaining to the mission which might be of help in working out tactical maneuvers.

High-speed continuous-strip cameras are installed in fast-flying planes for low sweeps; these cameras have wide-open lenses, the speed of shutter and plane being synchronized. They have been used at low altitudes at speeds above 400 miles per hour on moving objects such as tanks, cars and other vehicles. One picture taken from 350 feet head-on against a moving automobile on a highway was so clear that the gas ration sticker on the windshield was plainly visible.

Special stereoscopic processes enable photographs to be read in such a manner that experts can tell the height of a building or the depth of a trench.

Wright Field—Frequently referred to as the technical nerve center of the AAF, Wright Field is the home of the largest aeronautical research center in the world. Seven miles east of Dayton, Ohio, the installation was built in 1926 and named in honor of the pioneering Wright brothers who had flown their kites and gliders over this same plot of ground.

To a visitor, the 7000 acre installation, headquarters of the Materiel Command, looks like a gigantic conglomerate of surrealist Hollywood movie sets: huge caterpillar-like wind tunnels, arched hangars that dwarf the B-19, a runway that leads from the level field almost to the top of a 200 foot hill, a gaping trench excavated from the hillside as the practice firing range for experimental aircraft and a maze of weirdly shaped steel and concrete structures where propellers are whirled until they shatter and engines roar day and night.

If the equipment at the field were put into action at one time, airplanes would swoop down over the field and pick up motorless gliders, and wingless helicopters would hang in mid-air; captured German and Japanese aircraft would enter a traffic pattern filled with heavy bombers and tiny radio-controlled target planes; multi-colored parachutes would float down with dummies hanging from them.

In the Materiel Command laboratories at the field are thousands of activities: a civilian behind the control room panel of the world's largest high-speed wind tunnel plays with 400-mile-an-hour tornadoes; frost-covered men, bundled up like Eskimos, sit in test chambers that simulate the thin air and 50-below-zero temperatures of 40,000 feet altitude; volunteers sweat under intense artificial heat rays while floating in a small rubber raft on the stirred-up waters of an indoor salt water pool; a woodcraftsman carefully puts the finishing touches on a delicate model of a secret plane; thousands of pounds of lead are piled on the wings of a sleek-looking combat aircraft until ribs and spars crumple and snap; a technician adjusts the fine internal mechanism of a bombsight with a watchmaker's care; a 75 mm cannon blasts a warning note to the enemy.

Test Pilots—Despite years of expert ground and paper engineering, only the test pilot can prove whether the engineering theories behind the airplane design are right or wrong; whether an airplane will or will not fly successfully. Both the manufacturers and the AAF depend greatly on test pilots.

One of the most difficult assignments for test pilots is flying radically different plane types during a single day's routine. A B-29 with 8800 horsepower requires a completely different flying technique than a sensitive P-51 Mustang or a light 95-horsepower liaison plane. Test pilots of the AAF fly any and every type of airplane, including captured Messerschmitts, Junkers, Focke-Wulfs and Zeros.

Test pilots are responsible for obtaining accurate performance data which is indispensable to the development of military aircraft and equipment. Since their findings must be as reliable as engineering formulae, it is essential that their training and their methods be standardized.

Before each flight test, special project officers and engineers prescribe the exact speed, altitude and maneuvers to be executed. Reliability of the test depends on the ability of the test pilot to fly precisely according to instructions—not 345 miles an hour when the instructions say 355, not at 27,000 feet when directions call for 26,500.

Proving Ground—New combat equipment developed and laboratory-tested at Wright Field must be proved for combat. Proving is the job of the Proving Ground Command, which tests the battle fitness of new equipment and ascertains the most efficient ways to use it.

Main base of the Proving Ground Command is Eglin Field, Fla. Covering 600 square miles in the northwestern section of the state, Eglin Field includes 9 airfields, scores of warehouses, laboratories, barracks, vaults, shops, hangars, bombing and gunnery ranges. Under jurisdiction of the command is the cold weather testing station at Ladd Field, Alaska, where equipment is proved under frigid temperature conditions.

Proving at Eglin Field answers 2 questions about equipment: Is it fit for combat use? What's the best way to use it? Fitness for combat is determined by a series of rigorous tests which are designed to foresee, as much as possible, the exigencies of combat. The best methods of using equipment are found by practical demonstrations.

HOW WE KEEP 'EM FLYING

The very virtues of our weapon—speed, mobility and range—also present certain difficulties. Since the airplane cannot take along sufficient reserve supplies and cannot adequately live off the land, its continuing effectiveness depends upon an uninterrupted flow of supplies to its base. Many of these supplies—fuel, ammunition, spare parts—are required in vast quantities and are highly specialized. They must be shipped principally by surface transportation to units that are often more than halfway around the world.

Logistics—which means getting what we need, where we need it, when we need it—is a consideration of critical importance in all aerial strategy. Although a bomber and its crew can be flown from the U. S. to any theater of operations in the world in a few hours, the ground crews and supplies necessary to keep the bomber in operation require weeks or even months to reach the theater by surface transport. For this reason, the planning of supply and transport must be carried on months in advance of major air operations, and an error in calculations or a failure in the supply system may cost a campaign.

In one way or another almost every man in the AAF participates in logistical functions. A combat aircrew, although a tactical unit, must nonetheless check its own limited supplies and even make minor repairs in flight. Similarly, ground crews are concerned with supply and maintenance activities, while a large proportion of the personnel on every base devote their full time to such duties.

The commands which are principally responsible for AAF supply, transport and maintenance are:

1. AIR SERVICE COMMAND (ASC) is the stockroom and garage of the AAF. Operating within the continental U. S., it receives all our aircraft and aircraft equipment and supplies; maintains necessary stocks upon which the using units can draw; sees to it that such stocks are in the right place at the right time; provides for overhaul and heavy repair work; salvages damaged or excess material. ASC schedules the equipment and supplies which will be required by units in this country and by all the overseas air forces so that they may be ordered, delivered and stocked. ASC is organized into 11 subordinate area air service commands, each operating in a designated area of the U. S.

2. AIR FORCE AIR SERVICE COMMANDS perform within the theaters of operations supply and maintenance functions similar to those of the ASC within the continental U. S. While under the command of the air force commander, each air force air service command depends upon the ASC at home for its stocks of supplies and for technical instructions and guidance as to maintenance. In a large theater, the air force air service command may be subdivided into subordinate area air service commands.

3. THE AIR TRANSPORT COMMAND (ATC) provides all air transport for the War Department of cargo, personnel and mail to, from and between theaters of operations and within the continental U. S. Through its ferrying division it ferries planes within the continental U. S. and overseas.

4. AIR FORCE TROOP CARRIER COMMANDS, OR WINGS, among other duties, provide air transportation both for air and ground personnel and for cargo in combat areas.

In addition, the AAF relies heavily upon the Army Service Forces (ASF), with its 7 supply services (see page 180), for materiel common to the entire Army as well as for certain special supplies such as bombs. The Army Transportation Corps, a part of the ASF, is responsible for Army land and water transport and carries the bulk of AAF materiel to overseas destinations.

SUPPLY

During the early months of the war the AAF supply problem was principally one of production. As production has gradually come abreast of requirements, except for certain critical items, the supply-distribution problem has multiplied many times. Most of our supplies are now sent overseas. Supply levels must be maintained in each theater—enough for anticipated needs plus a reserve, but not so much in any one theater as to handicap others.

Types of Required Supply—Supplies required by AAF units may be divided into 4 major groups. First are airplanes themselves. The AAF has received over 100,000 planes of more than 140 different types. The supply of aircraft and their allocation to the different theaters of war are determined in the first instance by the strategic and tactical plans for the air war. In turn, aircraft allocations determine to a large extent the requirements for almost all other types of AAF supply.

The second major category includes aircraft spare parts, maintenance equipment and certain special aviation equipment and supplies. An AAF heavy bomber consists of as many as 12,000 individual parts, any of which may require replacement due to battle damage or wear. Supply requirements demand that Air Service Command have on hand, and located at points around the world where they will be needed, 500,000 different articles, or 10 times the number of items listed in a Sears-Roebuck catalogue. Their variety is infinite: nuts and bolts, flying suits, instruments, propellers, lubricants, engines, maintenance machinery and tools.

Third are the consumable supplies required by combat airplanes: aviation fuel, bombs and other ammunition. A single squadron of 12 B-24s may expend more than 16,000 gallons of aviation gasoline, more than 30 tons of bombs on a typical 5-hour mission. However, in modern aerial warfare, we measure our logistical requirements not in terms of squadrons but in terms of

500 and 1000-plane missions. To equip 1000 heavy bombers for a hypothetical mission over Berlin from British bases might require as much as 2½ million gallons of gasoline, 3000 tons of bombs and 2 million rounds of .50 caliber ammunition. If 1000 fighters were sent along as escort, they would probably require more than ½ million gallons of gas and 2½ million rounds of ammunition.

The 4th category of supply required by AAF units consists of materials procured by the Army Service Forces to fulfill the everyday needs of life: food, clothing, blankets, vehicles, as well as certain special types of supply. The major types of these supplies are:

QUARTERMASTER—*subsistence, clothing, personal equipment, general supplies (beds, blankets, cooking utensils), fuel and oil for vehicles.*

ORDNANCE—*bombs (other than chemical bombs), and other ammunition, weapons and general purpose motor vehicles.*

SIGNAL CORPS—*communication systems (telegraph, telephone, ground and airborne radio, radar, teletype, pigeons).*

MEDICAL CORPS—*medical supplies and equipment.*

CORPS OF ENGINEERS—*construction equipment and supplies (graders, bulldozers, concrete, lumber, landing mats, brick), searchlights, barrage balloons.*

TRANSPORTATION—*rail equipment (railroad cars), floating equipment (boats and barges), pier equipment.*

CHEMICAL WARFARE—*incendiary bombs, smoke bombs, smoke, gas masks, decontamination equipment and supplies.*

Domestic Supply—Near the center of each of the 11 continental Air Service Command areas is an air depot. An air depot is a large wholesale house and warehouse, normally stocked with 2 months' supply of the types of property required in its area. It also performs heavy aircraft maintenance.

Each of the major airbases in the U. S. has a base supply organization which furnishes air supplies to all units located there. Base supply is under the base commander, but works closely with the air depot in the area. It normally carries a 30-day stock.

When a unit stationed at a base requires a part for a plane, it requisitions base supply. Base supply furnishes the part and, when necessary, replenishes its own stock from its air depot, or from one of the ASC specialized depots which maintain central stocks of certain specialized types of equipment. Air depot stocks are maintained by deliveries from manufacturers and from ASC specialized depots. Continuous stock controls are maintained at all these installations, making it possible at short notice to correct shortages that develop in one area by calling on depots in another area and shipping by air.

Overseas Supply—The Air Service Command obtains and issues initial equipment and supplies to units going overseas, and maintains supply levels in each theater with continual replenishments on requisitions from the theaters. Once supplies have been received in the theater, however, direct responsibility for them rests with the air force air service command of that theater.

The set-up for supplying combat units in a theater air force is fundamentally comparable to domestic supply except that the need for mobility and flexibility is more pronounced. During a tactical campaign when air combat units may move rapidly forward, supply units must be prepared to leap-frog from field to field. Fixed bases with permanent facilities are found only in areas well to the rear.

Each theater air force includes at least one air force general depot which provides a wholesale center for AAF technical supplies as well as supplies procured by Army Service Forces; it also renders heavy maintenance (see page 201). Operated in connection with the air force general depot, and also under the command of the air force air service commander, are a number of branch depots which store and issue supplies that require special methods of handling and storage. They include an aviation gas and oil depot, an ordnance ammunition depot and a chemical ammunition depot. In addition, the following branch depots, which provide supplies used by both ground and air forces, are established if suitable ground force depots are not conveniently located: quartermaster class I depot (for consumable supplies such as food), quartermaster class III depot (for motor fuels), engineer depot (for construction and camouflage materials).

The retailers of supplies are the service centers which cor-

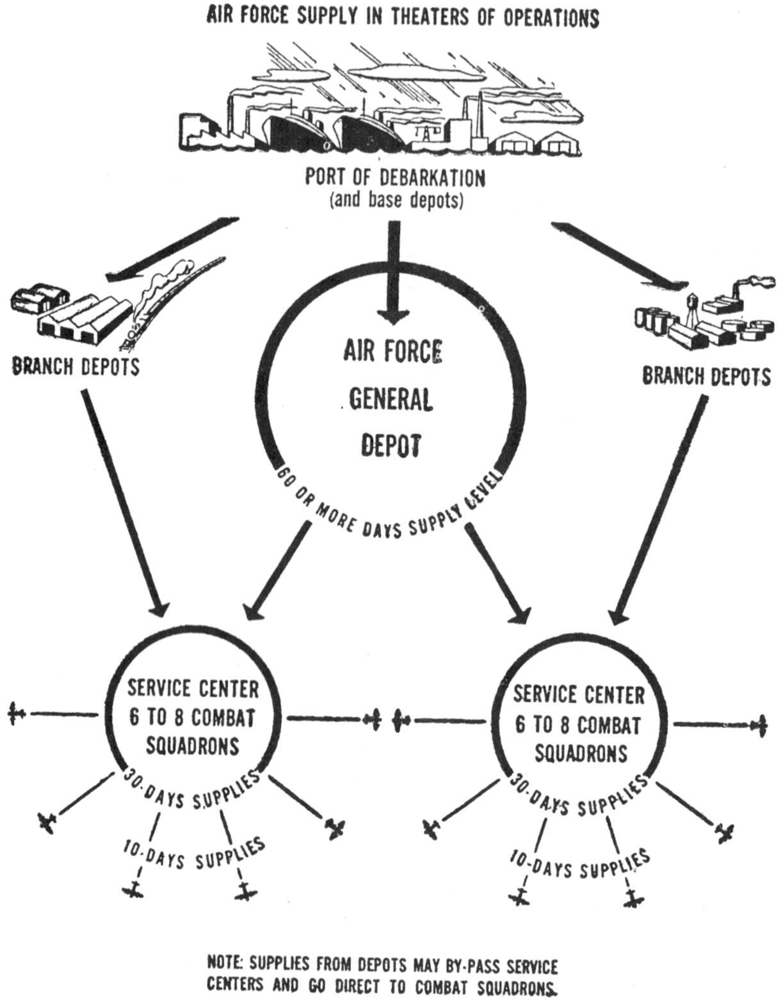

AIR FORCE SUPPLY IN THEATERS OF OPERATIONS

PORT OF DEBARKATION
(and base depots)

BRANCH DEPOTS

AIR FORCE
GENERAL
DEPOT

60 OR MORE DAYS SUPPLY LEVEL

BRANCH DEPOTS

SERVICE CENTER
6 TO 8 COMBAT
SQUADRONS

30-DAYS SUPPLIES

10-DAYS SUPPLIES

SERVICE CENTER
6 TO 8 COMBAT
SQUADRONS

30-DAYS SUPPLIES

10-DAYS SUPPLIES

NOTE: SUPPLIES FROM DEPOTS MAY BY-PASS SERVICE
CENTERS AND GO DIRECT TO COMBAT SQUADRONS.

respond roughly to the continental base supply organizations. Service centers, located closer to the front lines than depots, furnish supplies and provide repair services for all types of equipment. Sections may be separated from the service center and assigned to advanced fields or may work as a unit at the service center. A service center may service as many as 8 combat squadrons. Its supplies are replenished by deliveries from the air force general depot and branch depots.

The general pattern of overseas supply systems is adapted to the peculiar military and geographic features of each theater. In England, service center personnel are merged with the supply and maintenance sections of combat units; air force general depots are not located far to the rear and, indeed, are sometimes in advance of combat units. Service center organizations in the Pacific have been adapted to the island campaigns by splitting into sections for rapid movement to advanced bases.

AAF supply and maintenance organizations contain elements thoroughly familiar with the equipment and supplies procured by the Army Service Forces. The service center provides for supply and maintenance of materiel originally procured by Army Service Forces for AAF use as well as AAF-procured materiel. Likewise, the AAF furnishes the rest of the Army with such aviation supplies as parachutes, liaison airplanes, aerial delivery containers and cargo chutes. In advance areas or in theaters in which no ground establishments exist, the air force air service command is responsible for all duties normally performed by the Army Service Forces.

The Supply System—To the maximum possible extent, AAF supply procedures have been standardized and simplified. On the basis of study and experience, standard tables have been prepared showing what equipment each man, each airplane and each unit requires. Consumption data is constantly analyzed so that rates of consumption may be used in predictions of future requirements. Combat supply tables based upon estimated requirements for units in combat are employed in the initial supply of such units overseas. Through the use of perpetual inventory systems and records, supply agencies are able to maintain their stocks at a safe level.

Due to ever-changing situations in the theaters and to improvements in plan, design and tactics, supply tables and procedures are under constant revision. No table, no matter how perfect, will solve the supply problems faced regularly in combat areas. Unlike the ground forces whose supply moves forward gradually with the attacking army, air force units advance in a series of jumps. Between such jumps supply operations at a base may be reduced to routine, but when a new base is captured the movement of supply forward becomes a feverish activity of highest priority.

Living Off the Land—As far as possible, supply personnel utilize the materiel available within their theater. Such supplies may take the form of food, clothing, raw materials, fuel and even armament and other equipment. Allied countries in which our troops are stationed, such as England and Australia, have provided us millions of dollars' worth of supplies, facilitated by the application of reverse lend-lease. In India and China, native labor has been trained to produce some of our required supplies—even to airplane parts and assemblies.

TRANSPORTATION

In terms of world logistics, the U. S. is an island, separated from every active war theater by thousands of miles of water. Our effectiveness as a fighting air force has rested from the beginning upon the ability of the United Nations' transportation resources to ship our personnel and supplies to the combat areas. All war transportation agencies have united in the unprecedented development of transportation facilities and in their operation against all obstacles the enemy could present. The merchant marine and the shipbuilders are over the hump of early shortages and submarine losses; the American and British navies have overcome the threat of the German underwater fleet; our railroads and other commercial carriers are satisfying the heaviest demands in their history; the Army, through its Transportation Corps, has regulated and coordinated transportation by land and sea for all U. S. Army troops and supplies; and the AAF, through its Air Transport Command, operates the greatest air transport service ever known.

Mediums of Transport—Mediums of transport for the AAF and the characteristics which determine their use are essentially similar to those affecting the civilian traveler carrying on his nor-

mal business. When he is in a big hurry, or in cases where other
means of transport do not exist, he flies. When he is traveling
overland for a relatively short distance, he goes by motor vehicle
—automobile or truck. For long trips overland, he travels by rail.
To go across an ocean, he normally goes by ship.

Military transportation differs from civilian transportation principally because of its tremendous mass movements, the greater
urgency and speed required and the necessity of operating in
little-developed areas of the world under natural obstacles and
those imposed by the enemy. Water transportation, though relatively slow, is economical of manpower and fuel and essential to
move the bulk of our men and materiel overseas (see table).
Rail and truck are equally indispensable for inland transportation, though inland waterways are preferable for the movement of
bulky goods when speed is not a prerequisite.

TURNAROUNDS

Turnaround time is the time required to load a ship, to move it
to destination, unload and reload, and return to home port and
unload, with an allowance for normal repairs. Average turnaround times between U. S. ports and major theaters, based on
AAF experience, are:

	Transport Ship	Cargo Ship
New York-North Africa	49 days	79 days
New York-England	42 "	75 "
San Francisco-Hawaii	30 "	39 "
San Francisco-Australia	70 "	120 "
West Coast, USA-India	120 "	210 "
Seattle-Alaska	30 "	45 "

Fastest of all mediums is air transport. The quantities which
can be handled by individual airplanes are limited and air transport is therefore reserved for movements of the highest urgency—
such as key personnel, emergency supplies and equipment, rapid
evacuation of the sick and wounded, and mail. However, air
transport is vital out of all proportion to the modest capacities of
the cargo airplane. It provides access to regions where surface
transportation is blocked by enemy control, as in Burma; by
natural obstacles, such as the Himalaya mountains; or where

roads and railroads do not exist, as in New Guinea. By the employment of many cargo aircraft, large quantities of supplies can be moved over moderate distances with the greatest speed.

Rough, undeveloped areas call for more primitive means of transport—wagons, beasts of burden, even human carriers. In the Pacific islands, native carriers have played an important part in supplying advanced and otherwise isolated units.

AIR TRANSPORT CARGOES AND DISTANCES

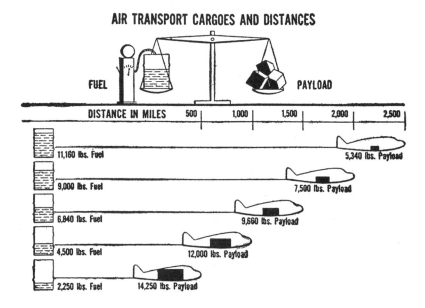

FUEL   **PAYLOAD**

| DISTANCE IN MILES | 500 | 1,000 | 1,500 | 2,000 | 2,500 |

11,160 lbs. Fuel — 5,340 lbs. Payload

9,000 lbs. Fuel — 7,500 lbs. Payload

6,840 lbs. Fuel — 9,660 lbs. Payload

4,500 lbs. Fuel — 12,000 lbs. Payload

2,250 lbs. Fuel — 14,250 lbs. Payload

Moving an AAF Unit—Moving an AAF unit from one base to another means picking up an entire community—its inhabitants, their personal equipment, their industries, their mechanical equipment—and transporting it intact to another locality hundreds or thousands of miles away. Unlike most other military organizations, many air combat units must be split for movement; part of a bomber unit, for example, flies in its own airplanes; the remainder uses other means of transport.

A heavy bomber group consists of about 1790 persons and 48 B-17s or B-24s. Its ground equipment weighs 830 tons of which approximately three-fourths are trucks and other vehicles.

The airplanes themselves will transport all crew members and about 32 tons of equipment. If it is necessary to fly the remainder of the air echelon (see page 19), which consists of 222 persons, 13 cargo airplanes must be provided for this purpose. This leaves about 1100 individuals and about 790 tons of ground equipment to be moved by other means. If the distance is not more than a few hundred miles and roads are available, these probably will travel by motor transport. The group's own vehicles include more than a dozen 2½ ton trucks and a large number of small trucks, trailers and special vehicles, capable of moving supplies and equipment. To these must be added about 30 or more additional 2½ ton trucks from a motor transport pool, making a total procession of over 250 vehicles. Even these will not take care of 8 tractors assigned to the unit, which must be sent by rail, water or special motor carriers.

If the distance is too great for motor transportation or if roads are not available, all of the ground echelon's personnel and equipment may travel by rail. Such a movement would require a total of 173 railroad cars of various types, as follows:

107	40' flat cars
17	50.5' automobile cars
9	40.5' box cars
30	sleeping cars (or 22 coaches)
5	baggage cars
5	kitchen cars

If neither road nor railroad is available, and if it is absolutely essential to fly the unit, it will require about 125 cargo airplane loads in addition to the capacity of the unit's own 48 bombers. (Assuming an average capacity of 6250 pounds, or 27 passengers per cargo airplane.) Even these, however, will not take care of the unit's vehicles, which must be shipped in some other manner or left behind.

Requirements of AAF non-flying service units are even greater than combat units since they have no assigned aircraft. For example, a depot supply squadron of 137 men requires 30 railroad cars to move entirely by rail. If it is flown to its destination, 44 cargo airplanes are required for personnel and equipment other than vehicles. Approximately 100 tons of vehicles then have to be handled in some other way.

Moving an AAF Unit Overseas—When the training of an AAF unit is completed and it is ready for combat operations in one of the theaters, it is processed for movement overseas. In the case of a bombardment unit, heavy or medium, the crews usually fly their planes over while the rest of the unit is shipped by boat. After arrival in the theater, ground and flying personnel reunite at an assigned airbase. Fighter planes and other planes having limited ranges must normally be shipped; air and ground echelons both go by water transport.

The volume of shipping required to move an AAF unit depends upon whether its equipment is dismantled and crated or is shipped uncrated, and this in turn depends upon the facilities available at the destination. Shipments are normally crated to save space if destined for an established area such as England, where facilities for uncrating and assembling equipment are ample. However, equipment bound for a newly captured atoll in the Pacific is generally shipped fully assembled and ready for immediate operation. Vehicles, which comprise the bulk of a unit's equipment, take up about 3 times as much shipping space uncrated as crated. The ground equipment of a heavy bomber group, crated, requires between one-third and one-half the usable capacity of the average liberty ship. In addition, the group's personnel, other than flying crews, require more than half the capacity of an average Army troop transport.

Because of their relatively light weight and bulky shape, airplanes provide a special shipping problem. A method now being successfully employed is the construction of light spar decks several feet above the decks of oil tankers; 20 or more fighters or other small planes can be mounted on these decks. Propellers, wing tips and certain other parts are removed and the surface of the rest of the plane is treated to protect it from moisture. As a result, the long and expensive process of disassembling, crating and reassembling the airplane is avoided, while the fuel-carrying capacity of the tanker is not materially affected, thanks to the light weight of the planes.

Procedure for Overseas Movement—For the purpose of handling, directing and processing the tremendous volume of equipment and numbers of troops enroute overseas theaters, the War Department, through its Transportation Corps, has established 8 large installations known as ports of embarkation which are supplemented by a number of sub-ports. These ports, which are located adjoining key harbors such as New York, New Orleans and San Francisco, are huge installations which include staging areas for troops and large numbers of depots and warehouses for storage of supplies.

All AAF personnel, supplies and equipment not flown to their destination pass through one of these ports enroute their theater destination. Troops are carried by rail or truck to a staging area near a port of embarkation where they are checked and inspected on all such matters as physical condition, inoculations, pay, personnel records, insurance and individual equipment. Only after it is determined that every man meets all Army requirements for shipment does the port commander assign the unit to a specific ship.

Most equipment sent overseas is shipped direct to the port of embarkation by the procuring service. In the case of units bound for the United Kingdom, materiel is pre-shipped, new equipment being assigned to units after they reach the theater. Aviation equipment, parts and spares require special care in handling and packing. Near the major ports of embarkation the Air Service Command operates intransit depots which carry small stocks of AAF technical supplies and where all such supplies are processed and checked before they are shipped.

Procedure for Moving Air Echelons Overseas—The AAF is responsible for processing and monitoring all air shipments to overseas destinations. For this purpose, the Air Transport Command operates 8 ports of aerial embarkation and a number of sub-ports, which perform essentially the same functions as the water ports but on a much smaller scale. Aircrews passing through these ports are checked, processed and then briefed for their overwater hop. At each port of aerial embarkation, the Air Transport Command operates an air freight terminal, which handles, stores and repacks air cargo.

Debarkation—At the end of their journey overseas, troops and supplies leave their ships at theater ports of debarkation, which may be regarded as ports of embarkation in reverse. At a number of such ports of debarkation, air depots, sometimes called ex-transit depots, are maintained by the theater air force air service commands.

Shipment of Supplies and Replacement Equipment—Once the air unit has been moved and established at its theater base, it requires immediate and continuous support in the form of consumable supplies and replacement equipment. As our forces in the theaters grow, these replenishment supplies consume an increasing proportion of total shipping requirements. Except for gasoline and oil, which are usually shipped direct from refineries, such supplies pass through ports of embarkation, water or air, and are handled like original shipments.

Normal supply requirements for units overseas—other than aviation fuel, bombs, ammunition and aircraft—may be roughly averaged at one ship ton per man per month. Thus to keep an air force of 100,000 men supplied with food, clothing, replacement vehicles and their gasoline, parts, and similar items for one month requires about 100,000 ship tons.

Present consumption of aviation fuel by our theater air forces is nearly 150 million gallons per month, or 35 oil tanker loads (assuming average tanker capacity of 100,000 barrels). It is normally shipped by tanker to theater destinations which are equipped with pumping and storage facilities. In the case of newly established bases, however, immediate fuel requirements are met by gasoline shipped in drums in cargo vessels.

Transport Within Theaters—As far as possible, existing transportation lines—railroads and highways—are employed in the movement of supplies and equipment within the theater. However, conditions vary so widely in the different theaters of operations that there is no standard pattern. In Great Britain, distances are relatively short and railroads and highways are well developed. The North African offensive was materially aided by the existence of the railroads skirting the northern and western coasts. The campaigns in the Pacific islands must rely largely upon air and water transport. In India and Burma, where rail and highway facilities are limited, the movement of supply to an advanced post may involve a combination of ship and barge transport, air transport, wagon, pack animal and human carrier.

To a considerable extent the existence of transportation facili-

MOVEMENT OF SUPPLIES TO THE THEATERS OF OPERATIONS

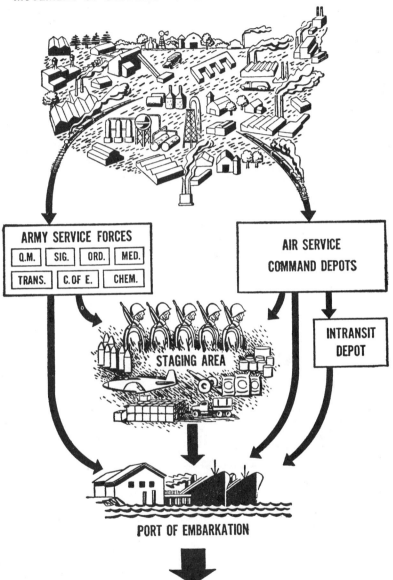

TO THEATER OF OPERATIONS

ties determines the location of depots, service centers and advanced airbases. For a large-scale action it is almost essential that rail or highway lines connect the depot with all its service centers, and that the service centers be located at, or be within a few hours motor distance of, the bases they support. Where such facilities are limited or where distances are great, the importance of air transport within the theater increases. Cargo airplane units are sometimes assigned to the air force air service command to provide fast air freight service between depots and service centers and between service centers and bases.

The amount of transport required to keep combat units in operation may be gauged by the fact that a heavy bomber group averaging 10 missions per month, calls for average daily deliveries

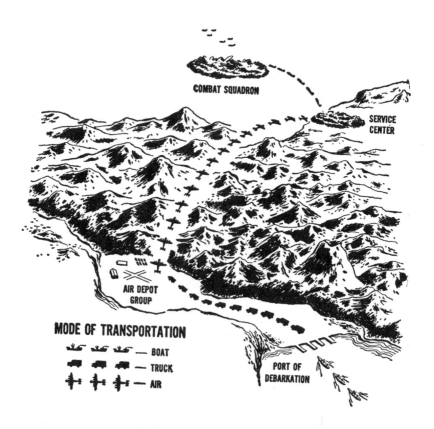

COMBAT SQUADRON

SERVICE CENTER

AIR DEPOT GROUP

MODE OF TRANSPORTATION
— BOAT
— TRUCK
— AIR

PORT OF DEBARKATION

by more than fifty 2½ ton trucks. Estimated transport requirement for one B-17 group to operate one hypothetical mission
with 1000 pound bombs is about 130 loads of 2½ ton trucks
with one-ton trailers. Of this total, about 40 trucks and trailers
are loaded with bombs, about 10 with other ammunition, and
about 80 with aviation gasoline drums.

Ferrying of Aircraft—Principal means of transport for our
major item of supply—the airplane itself—is ferrying it to destination under its own power. Months before Pearl Harbor, we began ferrying lend-lease planes for the British and ferrying our own
planes from factories to domestic bases. Since then, ferrying
operations have grown with the increasing production of aircraft
and with the world-wide development of our theater air forces.
AAF ferry pilots of the Air Transport Command pick up new
planes at the factory and deliver them to domestic bases, to overseas bases, and, in the case of lend-lease aircraft, all the way or
part way to the using nation. In a typical month, ferry deliveries may be as high as 8000, total ferrying miles between 10 and
15 million. In addition to ATC ferrying operations, many combat
planes are flown to their overseas destinations by their combat
crews.

Air Transport—The AAF, through its Air Transport Command, is responsible for all transport by air of cargo and personnel
for the War Department. In addition, it provides air transport
services for other governmental agencies and for governments of
the United Nations. The ATC's principal transport functions are
the operation of air transport services within the U. S., between
the U. S. and all of the theaters of operations, and between different theaters of operations. It operates over air routes in the U. S.
totaling 35,000 miles and overseas air routes totaling more than
95,000 miles. More than 200 bases along these routes have been
established by the AAF as well as a world-wide communications
network and essential weather forecasting units. During December 1943, ATC operations totaled more than 35,000,000 ton
miles of cargo and almost 100,000,000 passenger miles, of which
more than 90% were on foreign routes.

The development of ATC has been materially assisted by the
use of existing civil air carriers. With the need for military air
activity to all parts of the world it was found necessary to mili-

tarize many of the existing commercial airlines extending overseas. A number of civil carriers entered into contracts with the Government under which they operate scheduled transport serv-

ices with planes allotted to them by the AAF. Large numbers of the flight and ground personnel of the air carriers have been absorbed into the AAF, and the carriers also have rendered an important service in the training of military pilots for air transport operations.

ATC operates scheduled flights over AACS routes, but much of its unique importance arises from the speed and mobility with which it can meet emergency demands in combat operations. Air transport can be used to capitalize on the opportunities, avert the threats and minimize the set-backs of battle. For example, when Rommel was making his determined thrust at Cairo, Allied supplies of antitank ammunition were running short. Tons of it were flown to Cairo from the U. S. through exceptionally bad weather and delivered within 3 days. This movement helped turn the tide in the battle for Egypt.

An outstanding operation of the Air Transport Command is the supply of vital materials to the armies and air units operating in China. Since the closing of the Burma Road in April 1942, the only link between China and the other United Nations fighting Japan has been the air route over the hump of the Himalaya mountains. (See page 296.)

Troop Carrier Operations—Air transport of cargo and personnel by troop carrier units has been an important element in combat areas, particularly in the Pacific, Mediterranean and India-Burma theaters. These operations include the carrying of key personnel and troops and rush orders of freight to advanced units, both air and ground. Where other means of

transport are too slow or are blocked, entire units may be carried and supplied by air. Supplies carried to places before landing fields are available are specially packed and dropped from a low altitude, usually by parachute. In Mediterranean operations,

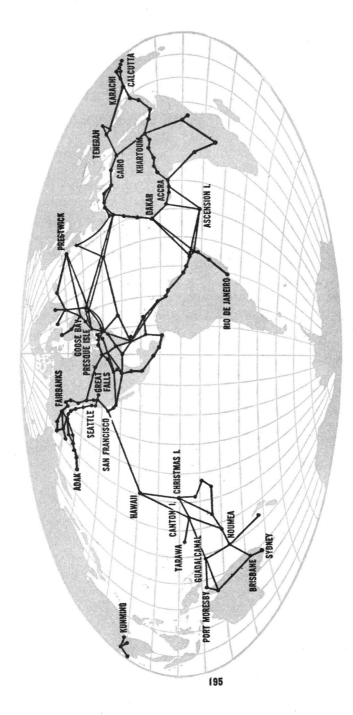

AAF COMMUNICATION ROUTES OVER WHICH AIR TRANSPORT COMMAND OPERATES

troop carrier planes enabled fighter units to leap forward rapidly
to advanced airfields by flying in engineer and maintenance units
first. It was their job to prepare the landing fields and service the
aircraft.

Evacuation of casualties from the front lines is another important function of troop carrier aviation. Medical evacuation
units composed of medical officers and nurses and enlisted men
are trained to take care of casualties while in flight. During 1943
more than 173,000 wounded and sick were evacuated by air by
troop carrier and other AAF units. Air evacuation provides the
greatest possible speed in carrying casualties to hospitals where
they can be properly cared for, and at the same time relieves
vehicular equipment and helps keep the roads clear for tactical
movements overland. Troop carrier units have also flown hospitals
into combat areas.

Air Priorities—Because of limitations in capacity of air transport, a system of air priorities is employed by which space is allo-
cated in accordance with the degree of urgency of each item and
passenger. Air priorities, which apply to domestic as well as overseas air transport, both military and commercial, are divided into
4 classes of relative urgency:

CLASS 1. *Traffic whose movement is required by an urgency so
acute that it should under no circumstances be delayed en route
for collection of additional passengers, mail or cargo.*

CLASS 2. *Traffic whose movement by air is absolutely necessary to
accomplishment of a mission necessary to prosecution of the
war (aircrews to combat theaters on schedule, bomb fuzes necessary for combat operations).*

CLASS 3. *Traffic vital to the war effort and of urgent nature, but
less so than class 2 (personnel necessary for maintenance of
equipment in an active theater; radio tubes).*

CLASS 4. *Traffic of sufficient importance to justify air transport,
but not so urgent as classes 1, 2 or 3; or overseas, specially
needed personnel or materiel moving to destinations accessible
only by air.*

Priorities vary with circumstances. Medical supplies rate a high
priority, and parts for grounded airplanes generally receive class

2 priority. In early 1944, electrically heated gloves and boots for aircrews, essential for high altitude missions, were assigned class 1 priority to meet a critical shortage in the United Kingdom. In one theater, a mimeographing machine, badly needed for preparation of orders, was given higher priority than ammunition because of greater urgency.

Priorities apply also to cargo and passengers carried back from theaters. Serious casualties, urgently requiring special treatment, are flown from the battle line to U. S. hospitals. Critical cases have been speeded from India to Washington, D. C. in 5 days. High priorities are assigned to certain crucial raw materials—mica from India, tungsten from China, platinum from Persia, crude rubber from Brazil.

MAINTENANCE

To keep an airplane operating, even under the best conditions in peacetime, calls for continuous maintenance. In wartime the job is many times multiplied. Few aircraft return from a major combat mission without some battle damage from flak or enemy aircraft. One shell through the fuselage of a heavy bomber may damage the hydraulic system, the gun control mechanism, a number of instruments and wiring systems.

As an illustration of the demands of wartime maintenance, consider one hypothetical daylight bombing attack against a well-defended target by a force of 150 bombers and 75 escort fighters. A fair assumption of losses and damages would be: 10 planes lost over enemy territory; 6 forced to land in locations away from their bases; 25 extensively damaged; 50 moderately damaged; 25 with minor damages; and 109 unscathed. The 6 forced landings would require about 7200 man-hours for maintenance; the 25 extensively damaged would average about 450 man-hours each, making a total of 11,250 man-hours; the 50 moderately damaged, at an average of 300 man-hours, would require 15,000 man-hours;

and the 25 slightly damaged, averaging 150 man-hours, would total 3750 man-hours. The total maintenance required for repairs alone (not service) would be 37,200 man-hours, or a 48-hour work week for 775 men.

AAF maintenance problems are aggravated by purely geographic and climatic conditions in many of our theaters. In Alaska and the Aleutians maintenance is a continuing fight against the cold—against freezing batteries and carburetors, icing on a plane's surface as well as in the controls and mechanisms, frost and snow. Abrasive sand is the chief foe of the maintenance man in the deserts of North Africa and the Near East. Without constant vigilance and care, sand will get into everything—will ruin valves, cylinder walls, and all moving parts; will clog up filters and will pit propellers. In the tropic areas of the South Pacific, maintenance wages its toughest battle against humidity —corrosion of metal surfaces, condensation of moisture within instruments, leakage and short circuiting of wiring and electronic systems. The abrasive effect of dust in the Pacific islands and in India is another major problem for maintenance men.

Echelons of Maintenance—The AAF maintenance system has 2 main objectives: first, retention of maximum mobility for airplane and combat unit; second, economy in the use of specialized personnel and repair equipment. AAF maintenance is divided into echelons, or levels, ranging from repair work done by the aircrew to complete overhaul by an air depot. These echelons may be compared roughly to the maintenance with which the ordinary automobile owner is familiar. As the driver, he is able to make certain repairs himself on the road such as changing a tire (1st echelon); to fix the punctured tire he goes to a service station (2nd echelon); for a major repair job he takes his car to a garage (3rd echelon); and if the engine needs a complete overhaul, it is sent back to the factory (4th echelon).

The maintenance echelon organization is flexible, especially under combat conditions on quickly changing battle fronts. Aircrews sometimes must perform both 1st and 2nd echelon maintenance. Where bases are stable, as in England, ground crews and service center personnel may be integrated and perform all echelons of maintenance except 4th echelon.

Aircrews have done vital maintenance work in flight. Aboard a

Echelons of Maintenance

FIRST ECHELON—Maintenance performed by the air echelon of the combat unit. Responsibilities consist of servicing airplanes (fueling) and equipment; preflight and daily inspections; minor repairs (tightening of nuts and bolts, hose clamps), adjustments and replacements. All essential tools and equipment are transportable by air.

SECOND ECHELON—Maintenance performed by the ground crew of the combat unit, and by airbase squadrons, airways detachments and airdrome squadrons. Responsibilities consist of servicing airplanes and equipment, periodic preventive inspections, and such adjustments, repairs and replacements as may be accomplished with hand tools and mobile equipment authorized for this purpose. Most repair equipment may be transported by air, but certain items necessitate surface transportation. Second echelon maintenance includes checking timing, adjusting valves, engine changes, etc.

THIRD ECHELON—Maintenance performed by the base maintenance organization in the U. S. and the service center in overseas theaters. Responsibilities consist of repairs and replacements requiring mobile machinery and equipment which necessitate ground means of transportation. It includes field repairs and salvage, removal and replacement of major unit assemblies, fabrication of minor parts and minor repairs to aircraft structures. Normally, 3rd echelon maintenance embraces repairs which can be completed within a limited time.

FOURTH ECHELON—Maintenance performed by the air depot. Responsibilities include complete restoration of worn or damaged aircraft, periodic overhaul of assemblies and accessories, fabrication of such parts as may be required to supplement normal supply, accomplishment of technical modifications as directed, and final disposition of reclaimed and salvaged materials.

B-24 on an overwater flight it was discovered that the pump would not transfer gas from the bomb bay tanks to the wing tanks. With only 3 hours of wing tank gas left, the engineer of the aircrew dismantled the pump, found its valves corroded, repaired the pump in 2 hours and got gas into the wing tanks one hour before the plane would have crashed for lack of fuel.

Mobility in Maintenance—Service squadrons, which are a part of the service group, may operate at the service center base, or with the combat squadrons at forward bases in certain instances. In some cases, service center functions may be carried out at permanent installations with hangars and fixed machinery, but under a rapidly-moving combat situation such conditions are the exception. Service center organizations are able to move rapidly and to operate in the field away from their headquarters, sometimes for extended periods. The service squadron includes mobile units which have the function of taking 3rd echelon repair to planes which have crashed or for any other reason can't get back to their base or which operate in advance areas or at dispersed fields. It may consist of one or more of the following: a machine shop to make spare parts and an instrument repair shop, both housed in heavy duty vans; an electric shop; a paint and fabric shop; a propeller shop; a sheet metal shop; and a cabinet shop for woodwork. Most of these shops are housed in tents and can be transported by truck and set up quickly.

Units devised to increase the mobility of aircraft maintenance include the airdrome squadron, which performs 2nd echelon repair in lieu of the ground personnel of the combat unit. It is used in leap-frogging operations to provide immediate service and repair for combat units without waiting for the regular ground crews. It is capable of supporting one to 3 combat squadrons for a week or 10 days.

Maintenance Methods—The importance of rapid and efficient maintenance can be demonstrated easily by an analysis of some hypothetical statistics. Assume that maintenance keeps each plane of a combat group out of commission an average of 45% of the time. If, by improved maintenance methods, this percentage can be reduced to 20%, the effect is equivalent to a 50% increase in the number of effective, flyable planes.

As far as possible, AAF maintenance is systematized according to sound industrial practices. In 1st and 2nd echelons, ground crews are grouped into specialties so that maximum use can be made of specialized training and many can work on each plane at the same time. Thus in servicing, one group may check the spark plugs while another is checking radios, another landing gears, another fuel. Further specialization in both men and equipment occurs in 3rd echelon maintenance, and where possible, 4th echelon maintenance is set up on a production line basis.

In India one air force general depot operates a production line on C-47s. The airplanes run through the shop in reverse of the way they were built; one de-assembly line tears them down; the pieces are reconditioned; and the plane reassembled. Such methods make possible the simplification of jobs so that they may be easily taught to native labor. In the U. S. and in the large theaters of operations the depots are specialized. One will handle the overhaul of engines, or of certain types of engines, while others, will overhaul particular parts or accessories.

Under battle conditions, however, maintenance depends heavily upon the ingenuity and inventiveness of ground personnel who cannot wait for overhaul or replacements. In China a service squadron needing insulators found that carving them out of the base of a water buffalo's horn served the purpose. In New Guinea a 2½ ton truck was needed at a new field but it wouldn't go through the door of a C-47. Maintenance men dismantled it and cut the larger pieces with acetylene torches, loaded them into the plane, and welded them together again after they had been flown to the new field. Gasoline drums are improvised into washing machines, outdoor showers, etching tanks for propeller blades. In North Africa the bomb release on an A-36 would not always free its bombs. A ⅜th inch spring was needed to provide the necessary extra kick. There were no springs in stock but it was discovered that the springs under the saddle of a German motorcycle would do perfectly. Every captured motorcycle was stripped and springs supplied for the A-36 bomb releases.

Preventive Inspection—The basis of the AAF maintenance system is inspection of all parts to prevent accident, damage or part failure before it occurs. For this purpose a detailed and systematic inspection procedure is prescribed, and definite responsibility is fixed for different phases of each inspection. The Maintenance Inspection Record is a complete logbook of each airplane's operations and maintenance. It contains the record of flying time and tells when engines should be changed, when oil is to be changed and similar items. Inspections are made before every flight; daily; after 25, 50 and 100 hours of flight; at time of engine change; 25 hours after engine change; and at special periods as required by the particular model of airplane. These inspections are progressively more detailed and thorough, and by the time a plane has completed 500 hours every part and every accessory has been checked. Upon these inspections depend the lives of the crews, the success of the missions; they are done with the greatest care. A 25-hour inspection of a B-17 requires about 100 man-hours, and a 100-hour inspection may take 400 man-hours.

Technical Instructions—To disseminate adequate, authentic and uniform technical instructions for the operation and maintenance of all AAF equipment throughout the world, the Air Service Command issues a series of publications known as Technical Orders. These range in size from one page to a book; a complete set consists of about 190 volumes. Tech Orders cover every type of plane, every part and accessory. They provide detailed, illustrated instructions of maintenance methods for all the various skills and trades required in aircraft maintenance. Four Tech Orders are issued with each plane as it leaves the manufacturer's assembly line: 1. *Handbook of Operations and Flight Instruction;* 2. *Handbook of Service Instruction;* 3. *Handbook of Overhaul Instruction;* and 4. *Illustrated Parts List.* Tech Orders are being constantly revised and supplemented to keep pace with improved maintenance methods and modifications in aircraft and equipment. Thus, speed is essential in the distribution of Tech Orders; some are microfilmed and flown to their overseas destinations. Tech Orders also are known as TOs.

Manufacturers' Representatives—Aircraft, engine and aircraft accessory manufacturers are under contract to the AAF to furnish technical personnel in the theaters of operations to supervise and instruct in the maintenance and operation of equipment. These men are responsible to the air force air service commander who usually requests them, and to whom they are required to make weekly reports.

Manufacturers' representatives are subject to military law and are lawful belligerents. They are treated as prisoners of war if captured. Their privileges are the same as those of commissioned officers and they wear the same uniforms without insignia of grade, arm or service. At present there are over 800 manufacturers' technicians in the theaters of operations.

Reclamation and Salvage—Due to the value of the military airplane and all its parts, it is important that nothing be thrown away. In fact, in most theaters, a principal source of technical supplies is from planes damaged in action. Wherever possible a wrecked or damaged plane is repaired and put back in the air again. When this is not feasible, the usable parts are stripped off and either used immediately on other planes or are stocked. This is known as reclamation. Whatever is left after a plane has been stripped for parts is returned to the depot where it may be melted down for use in fabrication or sold for its basic materials. This is known as salvage. Reclamation and salvage in some theaters assume such large proportions that organizations are sometimes detailed for the purpose. These units follow the path of war to pick up reclaimable material and glean any parts left.

WHAT WE FIGHT FROM

Just as a boxer demands a solid footing to deliver his blows, we must have airbases from which to initiate our attacks. Because of its global responsibilities and the geographic position of the U. S. in relation to the fighting fronts, the AAF, more than any other air force, is dependent upon a world-wide network of bases.

Airbases are the stepping stones of our offensive. Full-fledged campaigns—involving ground, naval and amphibious forces—are often waged to establish heavy bomber bases within range of the enemy's factories and interior communications.

Our bases at home serve for training and national defense, for the development of planes, and the general support of our air establishment. Intermediate bases between home and front are links in a world-wide chain of airlanes over which we transport vital supplies and ferry combat planes and aircrews to the battle zones.

We had only 200 bases on Dec. 7, 1941. Two years later our airmen were flying from 1400 bases, 800 of them overseas.

Types of Bases—Because an airbase is a military establishment designed for the landing and takeoff of airplanes, its core is necessarily the landing field. This consists of one or more runways and connecting taxiways. A runway is the ground over which a plane begins its takeoff or concludes its landing. A taxiway is the path on the ground which a plane takes in leaving or approaching a runway. The landing field is located on ground as nearly flat and level as it is possible to obtain, in an area free of obstructions in the directions by which airborne planes approach or leave.

AAF airbases vary as to purpose, size, strength and permanence of landing field, and nature and number of installations. For example, a base within the continental U. S. whose prime purpose is training, does not ordinarily possess the dispersed layout, camouflage, antiaircraft and other defense installations characteristic of an overseas base, whose prime purpose usually is combat. Nor does a base built to accommodate transient planes have the same facilities as one calling for the permanent stationing of planes.

Maintenance and repair facilities of a permanent heavy bomber base are far more extensive than those of a staging field, which is a forward base used for assembling and refueling an air striking force whose components are regularly based elsewhere. Again, a base used by Flying Fortresses or Liberators or B-29 Superfortresses has runways much longer and stronger than those of a fighter base, because of the greater weight and takeoff roll of the bombers.

Furthermore, the location of some bases is dictated by the necessity to meet the continuing demands of war and the eventual commercial requirements of peace. Others, the product of the chance geography of battlelines, and short-lived as to usefulness, are located in remote places.

Offensive Base—A completely equipped offensive base for a combat group consists of runways, dispersed parking facilities and connecting taxiways, control and operations buildings, service and maintenance facilities, defense and camouflage installations, housing, and necessary utilities such as water, electric lights and roads. However, an advanced landing strip for liaison flights might contain only a single runway, and that merely a crudely cleared piece of level ground.

In order to avoid presenting an easy bombing target, a combat base, following the principle of dispersal, scatters its airplane parking places (commonly designated as hardstands), its gasoline and bomb storage units, its housing and its runways. If there is only one runway, its direction is that of the prevailing wind. Additional runways follow the directions of the next most frequent winds. Depending on the size of planes using them, runways are from 2000 to 8000 feet long at sea level. Sea level lengths are normally increased by 500 feet for each 1000 feet of elevation, since the thinner air accompanying increased elevation requires greater speeds and consequently longer rolls for a plane to become airborne. Standard minimum width of a runway is 150 feet, although a width of 100 feet has been used successfully in at least one of the active theaters. The runway proper is surrounded by a cleared zone of prepared ground.

The surfacing of a runway may be one of 4 kinds, or a combination: NATURAL. which sometimes calls for breaking up, moistening and rolling the ground for added firmness; STABILIZED SOIL, in which asphalt or cement is mixed with the ground and compacted and rolled; PAVED, which involves a series of earth-moving and earth-treatment operations, plus asphalt or concrete paving; and LANDING MAT, which is an armor of linked metal plates or grids laid over the ground.

When not flying, planes must be parked off the runways. In the U. S., where attack is unlikely, they are often parked in compact array on spaces along the hangar line known as parking aprons. At overseas combat bases, however, planes are parked singly, in pairs, or, at most, in threes, at widely separated spots in dispersal areas adjoining the runway area. The ground or hardstand on which an airplane is so parked is surfaced to the same extent as the runway. Single hardstands are at least 450 feet apart and triple ones at least 600 feet apart. None is within 500 feet of the centerline of a runway.

Dispersed hardstands are additionally protected by concealment—under trees, along hedge lines and occasionally by revetments. A revetment is a breastwork or embankment to protect planes from bomb splinters and strafing. Taxiways, surfaced like runways and hardstands, are at least 30 feet wide, are bordered by cleared zones on each side equal to at least half the wing-spread of the planes using them.

HARDSTAND LOCATION

Maintenance and Control—The principle of dispersal is also followed in laying out an overseas base's servicing and maintenance facilities—repair shops, installations for weather observation and communications, access roads, fuel and bomb storage. Bombs, along with ammunition and chemicals, are stored in the open and protected by revetments where possible. Incendiary bombs, however, are stored under shelters with roofs. Gasoline and oil are usually stored in bulk at permanent and semi-permanent bases, but limited to operating quantities at temporary bases. Drums and cans are used for storage of reserve fuel and oil supplies at advanced or remote airfields or for supply during initial stages in a combat area.

Bulk storage calls for large tanks, either underground or partly dug into the ground and partly revetted, spaced at least 100 feet apart and 150 feet from the nearest plane.

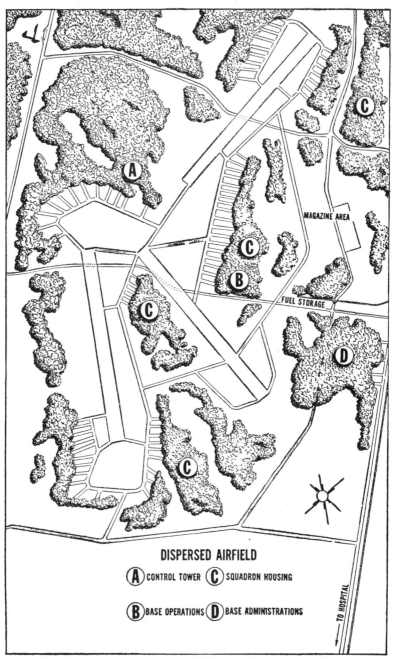

DISPERSED AIRFIELD

Ⓐ CONTROL TOWER   Ⓒ SQUADRON HOUSING

Ⓑ BASE OPERATIONS   Ⓓ BASE ADMINISTRATIONS

TO HOSPITAL

MAGAZINE AREA

FUEL STORAGE

Existing buildings are used when suitable for maintenance facilities; sometimes a hillside is dug out. When a new building is needed in a hurry, the answer is a portable hangar made of canvas and light steel ribs. Two skilled men and 30 unskilled men can erect a portable shelter 80 by 120 feet in 12 hours. Nose hangars, smaller portable canvas-and-steel units, afford enough shelter for working on engines. Housing may vary from shelter under airplane wings to a community of buildings and utility installations which, on a base for a heavy bomber group, accommodates more than 2300 men and women.

Nerve center of the base is the operations building where assistance and control of flying operations are focused. A necessary adjunct to the operations building is the control tower, through which the operations office controls all air traffic in the vicinity by ground-to-air communications. Since traffic direction is visual, the control tower must command a view of the entire landing field.

Access roads are of the utmost importance in keeping a base supplied with necessities. These sometimes run to astonishing proportions. During a peak period, a single heavy bombardment group in North Africa required 174 tons each day of fuel, ordnance, spare parts and rations. Inadequate access routes can cripple an entire base.

A complete base is often surrounded, at varying distances up to several dozen miles, by a number of less complete bases toward which it occupies the position of a parent base. Outlying bases, dependent upon the parent base for advanced maintenance and repair facilities, in turn provide enhanced dispersal and alternate flying facilities in the area of the parent base.

Defense—The defense of an airbase begins long before any attack. The defensive measures fall into 2 categories: active and passive. Active defense is handled in the air by interception fighter planes and the related aircraft warning system (see page 274), and on the ground by ground fighting and such installations as antiaircraft gun emplacements, road blocks and gun positions. The latter command not only the key approaches to key installations but also neighboring areas which the enemy might use for landing airborne troops. Alternate and dummy positions are sometimes prepared. For active defense, the base commander normally has at his disposal an MP company (aviation); antiaircraft artillery; a chemical warfare service detachment; and an aviation engineer maintenance detachment. A sentry system guards against sabotage and sneak attacks and acts as a control factor.

Measures for passive defense (which do not involve fighting) include slit trenches, revetments, underground or mounded-over splinterproof and gasproof shelters, dispersal, camouflage (see page 221), radio silence, smoke screen, barrage balloons and such demolition preparations as mining.

Rehabilitation measures at an airbase include the filling in of bomb craters, removal of debris, replacement of twisted landing mat and patching up of landing surfaces in general.

REVETMENT

AAF Installations—Not all AAF stations are airbases. At the peak of expansion there were more than 1200 AAF stations in the U. S. alone, only about 600 of which were airbases in the sense of this chapter. Others were depots, of which there were more than 300 of various kinds—control, storage, special storage, intransit and subdepots. There were more than 150 college training detachments, more than 50 war service training detachments and well over 100 technical schools covering a wide range of subjects from welding to meteorology. There were 18 modification centers and 8 government-owned assembly plants. At 23 other AAF stations, air depot and service group training was carried on. Besides these there were numerous miscellaneous stations, such as bombing and gunnery ranges, searchlight stations, rest and redistribution centers.

Because of the great variety of these stations, some of which are referred to in other chapters, and because of the changing status of some of them, a more detailed discussion or listing of AAF stations is not possible in this guide.

DEFINITIONS

A LANDING STRIP or LANDING FIELD is a field or strip of ground specially prepared and maintained for landing and takeoff of airplanes.

BASE FACILITIES is a collective term covering fuel and ordnance storage and service facilities; maintenance and repair facilities over and above those provided by airplane tool kits; and weather and communications facilities and living accommodations.

An AIRBASE, in its exact sense, is a field to which a subdepot or service squadron shop has been added.

A SATELLITE FIELD is a field whose base facilities are normally very limited, intended for use in case the unit field or airbase has become unfit for service, or for dispersal and training.

A SUBBASE is an alternate field which has been placed under the jurisdiction of the commanding officer of an airbase.

An AIRBASE AREA is an area of responsibility for administration, supply, maintenance and reclamation, charged to the airbase, and possibly including a number of alternate landing fields.

An AAF AIRWAYS STATION is a military establishment consisting of a landing field and servicing facilities, used primarily as a refueling station for transient aircraft.

OUR AIRBASE PROGRAM

On Aug. 28, 1939, 3 days before Germany set off World War II by invading Poland, the AAF was regularly using 69 airbases.

To appreciate the expansion of the AAF airbase system from this nucleus to more than 1400 bases 50 months later, it must be realized that figures do not tell the whole story. For one thing, all kinds of airbases, from a temporary landing strip in New Guinea to a great permanent base in Hawaii, count equally as one base. For another, today's standards for airbase construction are notably more rigorous than those of 1939.

Increase in weights and landing speeds of planes has necessitated longer, stronger runways. The B-12, our largest plane in tactical use in the 1930's, weighed 16,500 pounds with maximum permissible overload and landed at 69 mph; today's Liberator (B-24D) weighs 56,000 pounds loaded and lands at 105 mph. Another factor affecting runways is the development of blind flying by the AAF since 1939. This now makes it possible for a pilot to land in weather which is nearly zero-zero, and requires longer and wider runways by way of compensation.

Expansion for Defense—Defensive bases were acquired in the U. S. and its possessions before Pearl Harbor.

Domestically, the Civil Aeronautics Administration obtained funds from Congress for the general development of aviation and in 1940 prepared a civil airport expansion program calling for the building or improvement of some 4000 public airports in the U. S., its territories and possessions. Out of this grew 543 airports for defense purposes, of which the AAF regularly uses approximately 200.

Another contributor to domestic airbase growth was the Army

Corps of Engineers which between mid-1940 and the end of 1943 made available some 500 bases to the AAF. Unlike the CAA bases, which were undertaken with an eye to eventual commercial use, these were mostly new establishments constructed solely for military purposes.

Our defensive airbase network was extended to foreign territory in September 1940 by the destroyer-base deal with England by which 50 over-age U. S. destroyers of World War I vintage were traded to Great Britain in return for U. S. rights to air and sea base sites in 8 British possessions in the Western Atlantic, the Caribbean, and South America. The Corps of Engineers at once began construction of airbases in these areas.

Another important addition to our airbases consisted of commercial airports developed by Pan American Airways (PAA) in Latin American countries. Since Pearl Harbor, nearly every South and Central American country in which these fields are located has declared war on the Axis and has made its bases available to the AAF.

Another PAA-built system of defensive airbases came to us as the result of our pre-Pearl Harbor policy of self-defense through aid to Britain. In 1941 negotiations were completed between the British Government, the War Department and PAA for a chain of bases extending across the African interior from Accra on the Gold Coast to Khartoum in Anglo-Egyptian Sudan, thence north to Cairo, with connections to the Middle and Far East. Necessary clearance for flying across French Equatorial Africa was secured by consultation with Free French authorities. Britain made available all existing facilities along the route. In 1942 these bases were militarized.

Offensive—The AAF began to acquire offensive bases in 1942, when the British Air Ministry turned over 77 bases in the United Kingdom to the 8th Bomber Command. Many of these were either complete or in advanced stages of construction. In other cases, sites were released to us and AAF engineers did the building. On Aug. 7, 1942, the invasion of Guadalcanal by the Marines yielded us our first base captured from the enemy—Henderson Field. Since then, many offensive bases have been obtained by force. In this, U. S. Navy, British and Australian units, among others, help us establish and construct bases.

THE BATTLE FOR AIRBASES

AAF offensive combat bases fall into 2 classes, strategic and tactical, corresponding to the 2 major ways in which the AAF uses airpower offensively.

Strategic bombing (see page 256), translated into terms of bases, means that the heavy and very heavy bombers used by the AAF for strategic operations can be effectively based in areas so distant and in so many directions from enemy zones of the interior that the enemy's ability to act offensively and defensively is impaired by division of his forces and his relatively long—and therefore vulnerable—lines of communication.

In tactical operations (see page 257), where the targets are the enemy forces and air and ground installations opposite our lines, as well as enemy naval installations and sea supply routes in the vicinity, range does not play the same part as in strategic operations. And since the enemy, by choice or necessity, is likely to shift the disposition of the targets with changes in the tactical situation, flexibility is essential. Since the AAF goes in the van of surface offensives, there is a constant struggle for forward and flanking airbases from which air supremacy can be most confidently sought.

An advantageously located tactical base cuts down the consumption of gasoline and thus makes for increased firepower and bomb loads. However, all sites with similar advantages of position are not always equally suitable for bases. Other factors affecting their value involve such considerations as prevailing weather, problems of defense and supply, the amount of work, materials and equipment needed for construction.

Although offensive airbases are often won by ground and naval surface forces, these depend on friendly air forces for initial air supremacy. And while supply lines on which air and ground and naval forces mutually depend are chiefly surface lines, no surface force can maintain them without the protection of friendly air forces. This interdependence, calling for 3-way teamwork, has been a continuing relationship in the Allied conduct of the war.

An excellent example of the battle for airbases is the Solomons-New Guinea fighting, which is illustrated on pages 216-17. The

Solomons-New Guinea principle of struggle for airbases has been extended to larger areas. Capture of the Gilbert and Marshall Islands bases, along with those in New Britain and the Admiralty Islands, flanked and isolated the Japanese air and naval bastion of Truk in a pincers-like movement.

The Italian campaign provided us with invaluable airfields, such as Foggia, for a deeper penetration by our strategic bombing forces into Nazi industry. An airbase built in early 1943 by the aviation engineers on the Aleutian island of Amchitka, 70 miles from Kiska, during the Japanese occupation of Kiska, so jeopardized the enemy position by the threat of isolation that he eventually evacuated the island.

HOW WE BUILD AIRBASES

Temporary AAF forward fighter and light bomber bases in combat theaters often have to be built quickly. In the case of an amphibious invasion, for example, airbase construction after a successful landing on a hostile shore ideally conforms to the following schedule:

Within 36 hours of the establishing of a beachhead, landing strips must be available for fighter planes for purposes of refueling and range extension. During the 3 or 5 days between capture and consolidation of the beachhead, landing fields must be provided on which to base fighter and supporting plane units; some of the original temporary strips may be converted to this purpose. Once the advance from the beachhead commences, landing grounds have to be provided for fighters not more than 50 to 75 miles behind the vanguard.

In charge of this construction are aviation engineers who form part of an air task force. There are always heavy demands on beachhead communications routes and a high premium on invasion shipping tonnage, so priorities rarely permit an engineering battalion to begin construction with full equipment. Thus, aviation engineers must employ key equipment resourcefully. Wherever possible captured enemy fields are used. Steel mat may be used for surfacing runways, but since even the lightest type of

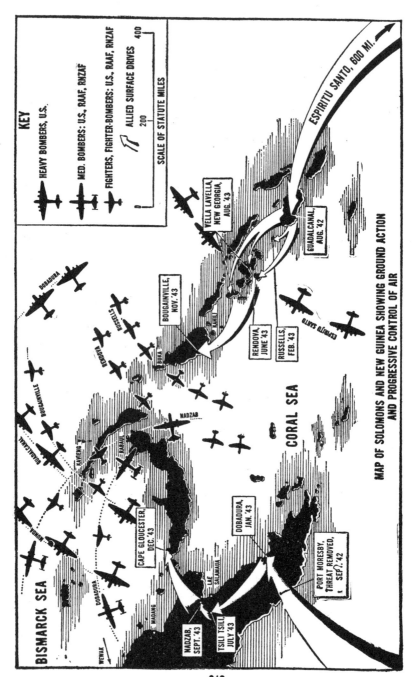

KEY

HEAVY BOMBERS: U.S.

MED. BOMBERS: U.S., RAAF, RNZAF

FIGHTERS, FIGHTER-BOMBERS: U.S., RAAF, RNZAF

ALLIED SURFACE DRIVES

SCALE OF STATUTE MILES

200   400

ESPIRITU SANTO, 600 MI.

VELLA LAVELLA, NEW GEORGIA, AUG. '43

GUADALCANAL, AUG. '42

BOUGAINVILLE, NOV. '43

RENDOVA, JUNE '43

RUSSELLS, FEB. '43

CORAL SEA

BISMARCK SEA

DOBADURA

RUSSELLS

FERGUSA

BOUGAINVILLE

GUADALCANAL

ESPIRITU SANTO

BUKA

KAHILI

NADZAB

KAVIENG

RABAUL

VUNAKANAU

DOBADURA

MADANG

WEWAK

LAE

SALAMAUA

CAPE GLOUCESTER, DEC. '43

DOBADURA, JAN. '43

PORT MORESBY, THREAT REMOVED, SEP. '42

NADZAB, SEPT. '43

TSILI TSILI, JULY '43

MAP OF SOLOMONS AND NEW GUINEA SHOWING GROUND ACTION AND PROGRESSIVE CONTROL OF AIR

216

SOLOMONS-NEW GUINEA BATTLEMAP

Two campaigns are shown up to the end of 1943—one from the east, advancing up the Solomon Islands, the other from the west, moving up New Guinea. Captured bases converge like pincers on Rabaul and Kavieng.

The prime objectives of Allied battle strategy were airbases. Operating from these, Allied land-based planes:

1. Reduced ground fighting, by isolating enemy occupying forces through destruction of communications lines, thus preventing the enemy's reinforcement, supply or evacuation.
2. Cut down the scale of surface offensives, since only small areas needed to be seized and held for bases from which air operations could isolate thousands of the enemy.
3. Enabled the Allies to by-pass Japanese positions.

BISMARCK SEA BATTLEMAP

The triumph of the Bismarck Sea Battle, in which a Japanese convoy of 22 ships carrying an entire division with supplies was virtually destroyed by land-based aircraft, would have been difficult, if not impossible, without the Allied advanced base at Dobadura, New Guinea. The battle was fought March 1-4, 1943. Airstrips at Dobadura, seized by the Allies in January and subsequently improved, served as a staging field for AAF bombers based at Port Moresby, thus nullifying the obstacle of the Owen Stanley Range. Dobadura-based fighters provided effective overhead cover, which enabled our bombers to carry out operations virtually unmolested. Allied planes shot down 50 enemy fighters, lost only one B-17 and 3 P-38s. Allied ground forces had one less Japanese division to fight.

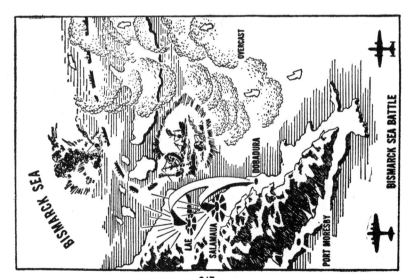

metal runway surfacing for a fighter strip occupies 800 ship tons of space, it is not generally available. Engineers do their best with existing surfaces, taking every possible advantage of the terrain. Minimum standards are the rule.

Because of these limitations, thorough engineering preparations have to be made prior to a landing. The air force engineer, who commands the aviation engineers, and the air force commander must agree on definite standards for all establishments. The air force engineer must study potential sites, using all available information from maps, charts, reconnaissance photographs and intelligence reports. The number of engineering battalions and the essential equipment needed must be determined on the basis of the time it takes one battalion to build one airbase, the number of advanced fighter bases needed for operations and the estimated rate of ground progress.

Once a landing has been made, these factors are reconsidered in the light of actual conditions. Final choice of each site is the joint responsibility of the air force engineer and an experienced AAF operations officer whose opinion as to the best available flying features in both site and landing field layout is consulted. Although aerial reconnaissance may be used to eliminate unsuitable sites, no base is finally approved until it has been surveyed on the ground.

Actual construction commences only after consultation with the ground forces commander (corps or division) in whose area the projected landing field lies, who determines whether the tactical situation permits it. This liaison—calculated to avoid conflict or duplication in the use of communications routes, plans for defense, location and scope of supply dumps—is a continuing factor at every phase of construction.

Once construction of an advance fighter base is to be started the engineering battalion in charge moves up to the site in several echelons, beginning with a headquarters company reconnaissance party to stake out runways and prepare rough plans. Next come intermediate parties with additional equipment, and finally the rest of the unit. Because an advance base is often only temporary, and because of the speed with which it has to be built, it devotes a minimum of construction to storage units for fuel, ordnance and chemicals. Its access roads and defense installations are necessarily hasty, and its camouflage consists largely of a judicious avoidance of the conspicuous. For housing it depends on what is found at the site, what can be brought to it and what can be improvised on the spot.

RUNWAY CONSTRUCTION AND DRAINAGE

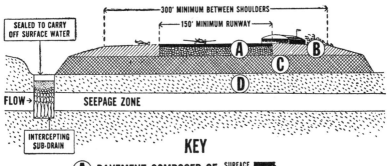

KEY

(A) PAVEMENT COMPOSED OF SURFACE / BASE

(B) SHOULDER: COMPACTED SELECT MATERIAL

(C) STABILIZED SUBGRADE IN 9" COURSES

(D) FOUNDATION OF NATURAL SOIL, GRADED & COMPACTED

NOT DRAWN TO SCALE

Bomber Bases—Considerably more extensive construction is required for medium or heavy bomber bases, some of which have been built in such remote regions as the Aleutians and the jungles of New Guinea. Because of their range, bombers can be based some distance behind the lines. They use the same bases for long periods, so construction is generally on a permanent or semi-permanent basis. Engineers working on bomber bases normally have complete equipment, and sometimes access to special materials. Wherever possible, they hire natives to assist them Compared to engineers working on fighter bases, they have ade. quate time.

Runways on bomber bases cannot be makeshift, must be strong and durable. First step in runway construction consists of soil stability tests which determine the bearing ratio of the ground. This is measured by the weight necessary to force a standard plunger a given distance into the soil. It depends upon the soil's moisture content and compaction—i.e. the degree to which it is packed. Thus mud and dry sand both have low bearing ratios, while sand which has been moistened and packed has a fairly high bearing ratio. Mud and dry sand are unstable; moistened, compacted sand is stable.

Soil stability tests, taken by sampling material at various depths on and around the projected base, enable the engineer to determine what sort of runway he must build. He may have to strip the top soil down to the best available foundation and build the runway from there up. Such a runway consists of a stabilized subgrade and a pavement. The pavement is a smooth, hard, weatherproof surfacing rigid enough to support the weight of a plane as concentrated in the small contact areas of its tires. Since importation of select material even over a short distance involves a tremendous outlay of man-hours and vehicles, soil survey plays a vital part in site reconnaissance.

Landing Mats—The landing mat most widely used by the AAF is pierced steel plank or Marston mat (see accompanying drawing). Though rigid enough to bridge over small surface inequalities of the ground, it is used to best effect on stabilized subgrade. This combination provides an adequate semi-permanent runway, as exemplified by those at Kualoa and Haleiwa in the Hawaiian Islands, which were laid in January 1942 and are still in use.

Although transportable in compact bundles, Marston mat is heavy; enough for a 3000 foot runway 150 feet wide weighs nearly 1200 tons. A runway this size can be put down in 90 hours by 100 unskilled men. As of July 1, 1943, approximately 175,000,000 square feet of mat had been shipped overseas, and 300,000,000 were on order for 1944. Research on magnesium alloy and aluminum mats, designed to weigh less without sacrifice of strength and durability, is currently under way.

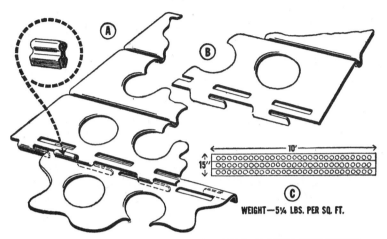

PIERCED PLANK LANDING MAT SHOWING:–A–MANNER OF JOINING WITH LOCKING
SPRING CLIP;–B–DETAIL OF BAYONET HOOK JOINT;–C–COMPLETE PLANK

Camouflage—The object of camouflage is to conceal and deceive. Since man is not naturally equipped to fly, his instincts do not help him to foil aerial observation or attack. Every vestige of human activity on the ground—trampled or tracked earth, scars from digging or fires, the regular outlines or shadows of man-made objects—conspires to betray his presence. Thus a fundamental requisite of camouflage is camouflage discipline, which trains every member of an airbase complement to cover himself and his traces for the safety of the entire establishment.

Plans for camouflage begin with plans for the airbase. The natural outlines of the terrain are left undisturbed or are imitated as well as possible. Existing structures are used to the utmost, as being least subject to suspicion. Since texture differences are more easily discernible from the air than color differences, violent contrasts in texture of terrain are avoided or minimized. Every object alien to the setting—airplanes, tenting and supplies—is concealed in hillsides, under trees, or beneath garnished nets resembling continuation of foliage, grass, sand or other natural surface features.

Deception includes construction of dummy installations or

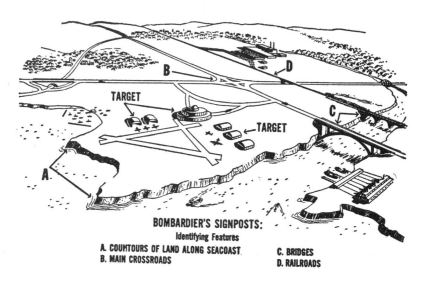

BOMBARDIER'S SIGNPOSTS:
Identifying Features

A. COUNTOURS OF LAND ALONG SEACOAST   C. BRIDGES
B. MAIN CROSSROADS   D. RAILROADS

simulated destruction after an air attack. Such construction must be far enough away for safety but not so far as to arouse suspicion; 3 to 5 miles is about right. Roadways or paths leading to key buildings are continued beyond them in a consistent system known as a track plan.

Camouflage need not be refined in order to succeed. Since other agencies of airbase defense, such as fighter planes and anti-aircraft fire, leave the enemy only seconds to locate the target, momentary confusion or misleading of an enemy bomber usually is sufficient.

Construction Facts and Figures—A full account of the materials, methods and native labor used in building AAF bases all over the world is beyond the scope of this guide. Here are a few sidelights:

IN NEW GUINEA, natives under American engineers build landing fields for cargo airplanes by clearing the high kunai grass, and tramp out runways with their bare feet.

IN NORTH AFRICA, where mud and sand constitute a problem, long, wide strips of sand are moistened and compacted by rollers. French troops and Arabs have helped out short-handed aviation engineers.

IN THE UNITED KINGDOM, heavy bomber bases, costing an average of $3,000,000 each and taking several months to build, have required the importation of AAF aviation engineers because the thorough absorption of civilians in the national war effort has not left enough trained British civilian contractors to do the job.

IN ASSAM, native women working for native contractors hired by the British but supervised by the AAF, mix concrete by hand and carry it in trays on their heads, passing it from one to the next every few yards until it reaches the forms. Supplies and equipment must travel from Calcutta over inadequate railroads of many different gauges.

IN CHINA, as many as 100,000 natives have worked on a single airbase. At a word from Generalissimo Chiang Kai-shek and under the direction of Chinese engineers, who are capable airfield builders, the Chinese will build a huge base in 3 months. Runways are crushed stone bound by mud and are 2 or more feet thick. Rock is quarried by hand pick, crushed by hand hammer and transported in wheelbarrows and baskets. Mud cement is mixed with bare feet. Runways are laid by home-made concrete rollers weighing 3½ to 10 tons and dragged by 150 Chinese.

OUR AVIATION ENGINEERS

The Aviation Engineers, charged with providing airbases for the AAF in theaters of operations, were established in June 1940. The original unit consisted of some 800 officers and men. However, aviation engineers' expansion quickly followed that of the AAF in general, and by Nov. 1, 1943, the organization, although still not up to its authorized strength, totaled about 80,000 troops, of which more than 65,000 were overseas.

Aviation engineer units include airborne construction battalions and companies whose equipment is specially designed for movement by transport plane and glider. The first of these, the 871st Airborne Aviation Engineer Battalion, was activated at Westover Field, Mass., on Sept. 1, 1942. The Troop Carrier Command promptly furnished planes and pilots for the intensive training which followed. Twelve weeks later, 2 airborne companies were in North Africa with the invading Allied troops.

Today, aviation engineers, both regular and airborne, are permanently stationed and trained at AAF bases and constitute an integral part of the AAF.

A regular battalion's equipment consists of 220 pieces and 146 vehicles. Mostly devoted to landing field construction, these include many road-building and agricultural-type machines, ranging in weight up to 32,000 pounds and in capacity to 8 and 12 yards, which handle earth moving, soil treatment and paving. All are power-operated, either by their own engines or by attachment to gasoline or diesel units. Trailer-mounted compressors power a variety of pneumatic tools.

To defend itself and its projects, a regular battalion packs more fire power than a World War I brigade. Its weapons include multiple AA mobile machine guns, .50 caliber antiaircraft machine guns, mortars and bazookas, rifles and carbines.

Airborne equipment, on the other hand, is designed to fit into the C-47 cargo plane and CG-4A glider. This limits the load to 4500 pounds for the plane and 3200 pounds for the glider. The limiting width is 80 inches and the maximum height 60 inches. An airborne battalion is equipped with track-laying (caterpillar) and rubber-tired tractors, scrapers, graders, sheepsfoot rollers, dump trailers, 2½ ton trucks, jeeps, air compressors, electric generating sets, welding sets and a pool of organizational items. It takes 79 C-47 cargo planes to move a battalion and its equipment, or a smaller number if gliders are used. The CG-4A glider carries 15 men or any major piece of equipment; a loaded C-47 can tow 2 loaded CG-4A gliders.

An airborne battalion's bantam equipment is too light for operations on the scale attainable by a regular battalion's heavy and more abundant apparatus. Airborne units are used in special cases only, as weapons of opportunity. They are appropriately employed in situations calling for airbases in areas inaccessible except by air.

Here are a few notable aviation engineer accomplishments, culled from many:

In the Aleutians, in September 1942, a regular battalion built a fighter strip on the sand-and-marsh bottom of a tidal lagoon on Adak Island in 8 days. The lagoon bed, which became a creek bed at low tide, was dried by diverting the creek at its head and building a gate at the seaward end. The landing mat for the runway, 3000 by 100 feet, was put down in 2 days.

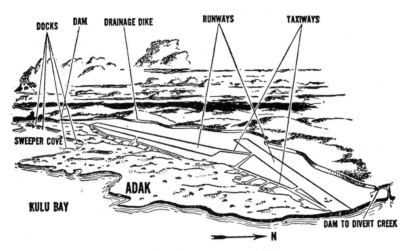

CONSTRUCTION OF ADAK AIRBASE

In 3 weeks, starting July 10, 1943 an airborne battalion at Tsili Tsili, 40 miles from Lae, New Guinea, built a landing field of 2 runways, one 6000 feet long and the other 4500 feet, as well as many hardstands. Between August 17 and 21 this base was used as a staging field for a striking force which destroyed or totally incapacitated 309 Japanese planes at Wewak. One fighter group based at Tsili Tsili provided the same support for operations against Lae as would have required 3 fighter groups based on Port Moresby, the other side of the Owen Stanley Range. The Tsili Tsili site was accessible only by air.

This same battalion moved in mid-September to Nadzab, just outside Lae and behind enemy lines, after its capture by Allied vertical envelopment. It was joined there by another airborne battalion, flown in from Port Moresby. Together these units rehabilitated the former Japanese base, which became a major AAF bomber base.

At Sbeitla, in Tunisia, a regular battalion took only 3 days to build 5 landing fields requested by an AAF commander. Part of this battalion rushed out ahead of our front lines to build a field in no man's land.

During 10 days of September 1943, Baker Island—a tiny Pacific landspot 650 miles west of Tarawa, which was then held by the Japanese—was transformed by a regular aviation engineer battalion into a complete forward bombing base, with a 3700-foot steel mat runway which was subsequently expanded to 5500 feet.

At Ben Arouba, Tunisia, aviation engineers removed 1788 mines from a single runway of a captured German base. The job was done in 8½ hours, with no casualties.

Two days after the 5th Army landed at Salerno, a fighter field was ready on that narrow beachhead.

HOW WE USE OUR COMBAT AIRBASES

Since the ultimate in AAF combat bases is the heavy bomber base, from which the long-range daylight precision attacks fundamental to AAF strategy are carried out, it may be useful to examine a typical base of the 8th Air Force in Great Britain. Such a station bases 48 to 72 Flying Fortresses or Liberators, each a hive of intricate engines, delicate instruments, and thousands of parts which require constant replacement, repair, adjustment or calibration because of the wear and tear of flying and the damage of enemy shells.

The base also houses nearly 1700 officers and men of the bomber group, a base maintenance detachment, a service group and administrative personnel—a total of more than 2300 men and women. At the base they eat, sleep, receive medical care, get their mail and pay, shop at the PX, carry on their religious, social, athletic and recreational activities, and their never-ending training. Airplanes are worked on day and night for repair, overhaul, improved functioning. Mobile repair units visit the base regularly to do specialized work. Men, besides being kept in the best health and spirits possible, are constantly instructed in methods, purposes and results.

In the case of a dawn mission by the 8th Air Force, the participating group will be notified of its role the previous evening, when higher headquarters, having waited on the weather, has decided to stage the mission. Detailed field orders come through around one or two A.M., and during the remainder of the night the tuning up of engines at dispersal places by ground crews envelops the base with a heavy drone. Mechanics apply kill-frost to wings, clean and dry guns. Squadron arming and servicing crews arm and service the planes, obtaining their materials from storage units maintained by specialists.

Aircrews are wakened about 4 A.M., ride to the base messes in vehicles furnished by the base motor pool. Base kitchens hoard their eggs to give the fliers a good breakfast. Diet is watched to avoid foods which cause distention at high altitudes.

Next they draw their personal flying equipment from the supply room, where a personal equipment officer sees that their oxygen units, electrically heated flying suits, Mae Wests and flak vests are in top condition. This is followed by briefing, which consists of an organized presentation of all information bearing on the successful completion of the mission—maps, target charts, analysis of target and reason for its selection, weather information, most recent information on flak and fighter opposition to be expected, procedure orders, and the supplying of communications ciphers on edible rice paper. This information is the joint product of such installations as the group intelligence library, the signal office and the weather office.

The bombardiers obtain their sights from the base bombsight vault. Cameras and films are installed in one of every 4 to 6 planes by the photographic officer. Ready in the planes are parachutes, life rafts, flares, an oxygen system, emergency rations, manual radio equipment and navigation instruments. Responsible for this equipment is a series of base specialist shops charged with maintenance and replenishment.

The great planes trundle out of their parking area and marshal along the taxiways and at the runway ends. A flare from the control tower signals the lead ship into its takeoff and the rest follow at 30-second intervals.

Base area controls now go into effect, implementing plans for escort rendezvous and diversionary missions which have been initiated at scores of base operations offices throughout the base area. Aircraft forced to drop out of formation by flak or fighter damage receive high and medium frequency signals from a series of stations all over the base area, each of which gives a specified signal during a specified time in accordance with the rice paper schedule of ciphers. Planes whose radios are knocked out can get "talked in" on command radio sets from positions near any British base. Crews forced to ditch in the Channel are quickly spotted and picked up by the British air-sea rescue service.

Planes returning from a mission are met by ambulances and fire trucks waiting at the runways with engines turning over. Red flares fired from the incoming planes indicate wounded personnel and give these planes landing priorities. Blood plasma has been warmed at the base hospital; the operating room is ready for immediate surgery.

Motor pool transportation also meets each plane as it rolls to a stop. After the removal of injured crew members, the rest are rushed to the briefing room for all-important interrogation. Red Cross workers supply hot coffee, doughnuts and cigarettes. Then all airplanes are taxied to their dispersed hardstands, except those too seriously damaged, which are moved aside for later transfer to base hangars and major repair or salvage. At the dispersal point the photographic officer removes camera and films from the planes to the base photographic laboratory.

At the interrogation, trained intelligence officers get first hand reports from the aircrews. When the interrogation is over, the films, still damp from processing, are studied in the photo lab. A period of suspense then ends, as these are the unmistakable evidence of the success of the mission.

Immediately following a mission, maintenance and repair of the participating planes is resumed. The crews are encouraged to rest and relax. Already the facilities of the base are concentrated on sending the group on its next mission.

AWARDS AND INSIGNIA

The Military Aviators Badge, recognizing "courage and ability to complete hazardous qualification tests in military aviation" was authorized on May 27, 1913. This first decoration for military airmen was awarded to 14 officers then on aviation duty with the Signal Corps, including General (then Lt.) H. H. Arnold, now Commanding General, AAF.

DECORATIONS—Deeds of high valor, wounds received in action against the enemy, military achievements in action, honorable service over a period of years—all are recognized by the President of the United States who, through the War Department, awards appropriate decorations. Ribbons, representing the medal awarded, are worn on the left breast of the uniform.

Two awards are granted specifically for achievement in aerial flight—the Distinguished Flying Cross and the Air Medal. These are in addition to numerous other War Department awards for which AAF personnel are eligible. The Medal of Honor, highest military decoration of this country, has been awarded to both officers and men of the AAF.

Units, organizations and detachments, as well as the individual soldier, may be cited for outstanding achievement in action, a device being issued to all members of such units. This device is worn on the right breast of the uniform.

None of the decorations authorized is issued more than once to any one person (except a posthumous award of the Purple Heart), but for each succeeding achievement sufficient to justify an award, a bronze oak leaf cluster may be awarded. One silver oak leaf cluster is authorized for wear in place of 5 bronze oak leaf clusters.

FOR HEROISM

MEDAL OF HONOR • *Highest of our military decorations. Established in 1862, it is awarded in the name of Congress to an officer or enlisted man who, in actual conflict with the enemy, distinguishes himself conspicuously by gallantry and intrepidity at the risk of his life above and beyond the call of duty.*

DISTINGUISHED SERVICE CROSS • *For extraordinary heroism in connection with military operations against the enemy.*

SILVER STAR • *For gallantry in action which does not warrant the award of the Distinguished Service Cross.*

DISTINGUISHED FLYING CROSS • *For heroism or extraordinary achievement during aerial flight while serving with the AAF.*

SOLDIER'S MEDAL • *For heroism not involving actual conflict with the enemy. The medal: on a bronze octagon is displayed an eagle standing on a fasces between groups of stars and above a spray of leaves. A shield on the reverse is inscribed "U. S." and supported by sprays*

of laurel and oak leaves. The words "Soldier's Medal, For Valor", and the recipient's name, appear as inscriptions.

AIR MEDAL • *For meritorious achievement while participating in aerial flight, not warranting award of the Distinguished Flying Cross. May be awarded for single actions or sustained operational activities.*

PURPLE HEART • *Originally established in 1782 as the Badge for Military Merit, this award was not issued for many years. Today it is awarded for a wound which necessitates treatment by a medical officer and which is received in action with an enemy of the U. S. The medal: on a purple enameled heart within a bronze border is a profile head of General George Washington in military uniform; above, in green enamel is his coat of arms between 2 sprays of leaves. On the reverse, below a shield and leaves, is a raised bronze heart with the inscription "For Military Merit", and the name of the recipient.*

BRONZE STAR • For heroic or meritorious achievement not involving participation in aerial combat (but not warranting the Silver Star or Legion of Merit) and must have been achieved in combat or in support of combat on the ground. The medal: bronze star in center of which is smaller raised bronze star, the center lines of all rays of both stars coinciding. Reverse: "Heroic or meritorious achievement" and recipient's name inscribed. Ribbon is glory red with vertical blue stripe in center. Both blue stripe and ribbon ends are piped in white.

FOR ACHIEVEMENT

DISTINGUISHED SERVICE MEDAL • For exceptionally meritorious service to the Government in a duty of great responsibility.

LEGION OF MERIT • Like the Purple Heart this decoration stems from the Badge for Military Merit, America's oldest decoration, and is awarded to outstanding officers and enlisted men of the armed forces of the U. S. for exceptionally meritorious conduct in performance of outstanding services. It is also awarded, in several degrees, to personnel of the armed forces of friendly foreign nations.

SERVICE MEDALS

Service awards and current campaign medals denoting theater of service are represented, at present, by ribbons only. Appropriate medals for these awards will be manufactured and distributed after the war.

AMERICAN DEFENSE MEDAL • Issued to military personnel who entered on a tour of duty of 12 months or longer and who, in discharge of such service, served at any time between Sept. 8, 1939, and Dec. 7, 1941.

GOOD CONDUCT MEDAL • Authorized for award to those enlisted men of the U. S. Army who, on or after Dec. 7, 1942, honorably completed one year of active Federal military service and who are recommended for the award by their commanding officers for exemplary behavior, efficiency and fidelity.

THEATER CAMPAIGN MEDALS • For 30 days' consecutive or 60 days' non-consecutive service in the present war in the following theaters: European - African - Middle Eastern; Asiatic-Pacific; American Theater—for service within the American theater outside continental U. S.

For pictures of the above decorations and ribbons (unless described in text), see color plate facing page 237.

SQUADRON INSIGNIA

Squadron insignia were adopted during the last war by the first U. S. airmen to fight for the American flag.

Above are the earliest of these insignia—the Indianhead of the Lafayette Escadrille, famed American volunteer squadron which fought with the French before our entry into World War I; and the Hat-in-the-Ring of Capt. Eddie Rickenbacker's 94th Aero Pursuit Squadron.

Today the tradition is a part of the AAF—a tradition that is being carried to all our global fighting fronts by young men like the aviation cadet shown on the opposite page saluting Old Glory at retreat.

Official insignia have been adopted by more than 800 AAF squadrons. In the U. S. these are widely used on airplanes and equipment. Overseas, supply and tactical considerations limit their use; here identifying insignia may be found on crewmen's flight jackets and stationery, and on plaques hung in messhalls and squadron huts.

Like the coats-of-arms emblazoned on the armor and trappings of olden-day knights, AAF squadron insignia stand for more than identification; they represent a mission and a goal.

For a few samples of AAF combat unit insignia, turn the next page.*

*Insignia appear in color on the four pages following page 338.

718th Bombardment

TYPICAL
SQUADRON
INSIGNIA

532th Bombardment

344th Fighter

338th Bombardment

20th Tact Reconnaisance

529th Fighter Bomber

81st Service

425th Bombardment

714th Bombardment

6th Weather

310th Fighter

487th Fighter

557th Bombardment

77th Troop Carrier

420th Bombardment

25th Liaison

528th Bombardment

SHOULDER PATCHES OF THE AIR FORCES

1st Eastern U.S.

2nd Western U.S.

3rd S. Eastern U.S.

4th Far Western U.S.

5th SW Pacific

6th Canal Zone

7th Central Pacific

8th United Kingdom

9th United Kingdom

10th India-Burma

11th N. Pacific

12th Mediterranean

13th S. Pacific

14th China

15th Italy

Hq. and Commands

UNITED STATES AIRCRAFT MARKING

The present insignia is visible at 60 percent greater range than the previous AAF marking. The red disc was removed to prevent confusion with Japanese marking. Dates show when changes were made.

Jan. 1, 1921   Aug. 18, 1942   June 29, 1943

Sept. 17, 1943

SOLDIER'S MEDAL

PURPLE HEART

GOOD CONDUCT

AMERICAN DEFENSE

MEDAL OF HONOR

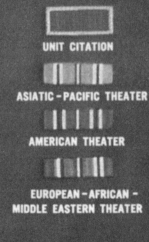

UNIT CITATION

ASIATIC-PACIFIC THEATER

AMERICAN THEATER

**EUROPEAN-AFRICAN-
MIDDLE EASTERN THEATER**

DISTINGUISHED SERVICE CROSS

DISTINGUISHED SERVICE MEDAL

LEGION OF MERIT

SILVER STAR

DISTINGUISHED FLYING CROSS

AIR MEDAL

OUR BATTLEFIELD

The air is our battlefield. It provides not only the field of action but also, in itself, a number of positive hazards. To minimize these we continually enlist the elements of the atmosphere as allies, but the same elements often become formidable enemies.

Our machines are built to withstand the tremendous stresses of the air, but we who fly the machines are accustomed to the natural forces at the earth's surface. Our physiology is designed to work on the ground. Airborne, we are divorced from our natural habitat. Before a mission can be flown or a bomb dropped, the basic problems of air adaptability must be mastered.

The act of flying through the air is a temporary truce with gravity. Man and plane must eventually come down. Ordinarily the landing is deliberate and safe, but sometimes it is unexpectedly abrupt. To the problem of returning safely to earth there frequently is added the problem of survival in areas unnatural to us.

WEATHER

The atmosphere, terrain of the air war, is the most fickle and treacherous of all terrains. If a ground commander were confronted daily with mountains changing height, rivers altering their course, ground moving up and down like an elevator and oceans going dry, his terrain problems would begin to resemble those of an AAF tactician.

TAILWIND

The atmosphere is like an ocean extending nearly 200 miles above the earth's surface; through it move deep masses of air, like currents in the ocean. Cold air masses travel from the polar

ICING

regions, warm air masses from the equatorial belt. The velocity of air movement varies from a gentle breeze to a heavy wind. When warm air and cold air meet, clouds are formed which often result in rain, snow or storm. Within the air masses there is constant motion as heated air rises and cold air drops. Above all this is the intense cold of the upper air.

TURBULENCE

High-velocity winds which push a plane off its set course necessitate constant adjustments in navigation. Greatest wind menace is a headwind blowing directly against the plane's front.

FOG

Bucking such headwinds, a plane sometimes consumes so much fuel that it falls short of its destination. Tailwinds, on the other hand, push the plane more quickly to its goal and make it possible to reduce the fuel load. Updrafts and downdrafts may move at speeds up to 200 miles per hour. In places where an updraft passes a downdraft, a condition called turbulence results. Turbulence can toss a plane about like a cork—even rip its wings off.

Fog lies close to the ground, can reduce visibility to zero, making landings and takeoffs extremely dangerous. Snow and rain can seriously curtail visibility in the air. Hail can blast holes in a plane's wings and fuselage. Ice and frost can sheath a plane in a matter of minutes, reduce its lift and make it unmanageable.

Clouds may be both friend and foe to the flier. From some

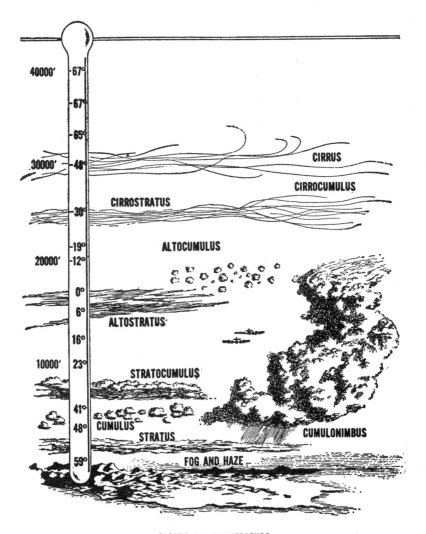

CLOUDS AND TEMPERATURE

clouds he can learn the stability of the air and the direction of approaching storms; he can employ clouds for cover in air battle. Often, however, clouds mean trouble. They affect visibility and stability of the air. On occasion we must combat the dark towering cumulonimbus (thunderhead), most dangerous of clouds, a center of extreme turbulence.

Such is the dynamic terrain of the air battlefield.

Communications Network—All over the world radio navigational aids are provided to AAF and Allied airplanes by the AAF's Army Airways Communications System, whose stations are located in all 48 states and in 52 foreign countries and territories. It is now possible for a plane to fly blind all the way around the world guided entirely by AACS radio navigational aids. In addition to direction beams, AACS sends out signals warning against mountain barriers and enemy aircraft. Weather data supplied by the AAF Weather Service is transmitted by AACS.

Weather Service—Like AACS stations, weather service bases are located in the far reaches of the world, in lonely outposts in the arctic and tropics where weather is born. Reports from these stations are transmitted to Headquarters in Washington, D. C. where weather maps are made and forecasts sent out all over the world. To provide on-the-spot short-range forecasts, weather service units accompany tactical, transport and troop carrier units. Wherever there is an AAF base, there are weather personnel to interpret and forecast climatic conditions. Often the weather stations are mobile; in the landing at Salerno, for instance, a jeep fitted with weather observing equipment was with one of the first units to make a landing. Weather reconnaissance airplanes regularly fly long distances to gather data before fighters, bombers or transports take off.

Foreknowledge of the weather is more than a protective measure. It is a tactical weapon. A typical instance was during an attack on Wewak, New Guinea. The planes which attacked were based at Port Moresby. Between the airbase and the target lay the 16,000-foot Owen Stanley Range. Over the Owen Stanleys there are usually banks of thunderheads rising as high as 40,000 feet. The attack could not be carried out while the thunderheads blocked the way. The weather service was asked to predict a cloudless day. Seven days elapsed before the weather officer decided that proper conditions were on the way. He issued a fore-cast 24 hours in advance, predicting just the type of weather desired. The attack was timed precisely to the forecast and 309 planes which the Japs had thought safe were destroyed.

Sometimes, in combat, bad weather is advantageous. In an attack on Trondheim, Norway, for example, bomber aircraft based in Britain took advantage of a blanket of overcast that extended almost to the edge of the target before it opened. The bombers flew undetected to Trondheim, dropped their bombs on the perfectly visible targets and made their journey home protected by the overcast.

THE BODY IN FLIGHT

On the ground the human body—with the aid of proper food, clothing and shelter—is well adjusted to such natural forces as air pressure, gravity, temperature and inertia. But when man goes up in the air 10,000 feet or more, these same forces may run to extremes far beyond the body's breaking point.

Yet every day air operations are being conducted at altitudes far above 10,000 feet. The answer is that aviation medicine has made discoveries that compensate for the strains of high alti-tude—discoveries that adjust earth-accustomed physiology to aerial activity.

Anoxia—The air we breathe is 78% nitrogen, 21% oxygen and 1% other gases. Oxygen is necessary to sustain human life. When air is inhaled into the lungs, oxygen is picked up by the blood stream and delivered to all parts of the body. Carbon dioxide, a waste product, is transported back to the lungs, ex-haled along with the other unused gases of the air.

The amount of oxygen which can be absorbed by the blood-stream depends on the quantity of air present in the lungs; this is determined by the outside atmospheric pressure. As the

altitude increases, the pressure falls and the atmosphere becomes more and more rarefied. As the air content of the lungs
becomes progressively smaller, so does the oxygen content. This
condition is primarily responsible for the oxygen want which
develops with increasing altitude.

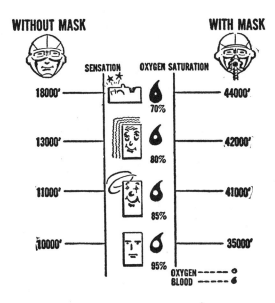

The medical name for oxygen-want is anoxia. To combat
anoxia, we rely on the oxygen system, which increases the oxygen
content of the air that the flier breathes at high altitudes. At
18,000 feet, for example, the oxygen content of the lungs has
fallen to one-half its ground level value. At this altitude the
oxygen system raises the percentage of oxygen in the air breathed
by fliers from 21% to 42%, thus raising the oxygen content of
the lungs to its normal ground level value. At 34,000 feet, 100%
oxygen must be breathed; above 34,000 feet, even 100% oxygen
does not provide a sufficient quantity of oxygen, although the
deficiency does not become critical until an altitude of 40,000
feet. Above this altitude, the pressure is so low that even pure
oxygen will permit consciousness only for short periods.

All aircrew members are instructed to wear oxygen masks when flying above 10,000 feet. Masks are fitted to the contours of the flier's face and have a small built-in microphone to facilitate interphone and radio communication. The masks are connected by hose to a central oxygen system. There are 2 types of oxygen systems in use by the AAF: the demand system and the continuous flow system. In the demand type, an automatic mixer steadily increases the oxygen content of the air as the airplane gains altitude in order to maintain the quantity of oxygen equal to that present at ground level. This system is fully automatic, saves oxygen by functioning only when a man is actually inhaling, and adjusts itself to the speed of breathing; it supplies all the oxygen needed when exertion causes faster breathing. The continuous flow oxygen system is an older type and is not regulated automatically. The flier himself adjusts a valve that governs the amount of oxygen flowing into the mask. This system has largely been replaced by the demand type.

In bombers it is often necessary for men to walk around inside the airplane while performing their duties. In planes equipped with demand systems, the flier disconnects his mask hose from its fixed oxygen outlet and plugs it into a walk-around bottle which can be refilled from the main lines. A small type bottle lasts about 5 minutes under average conditions, while a new and larger type lasts between a half hour and an hour. When a plane has a continuous flow system, the walk-around bottle contains an hour's supply and is non-refillable.

For parachute jumps from high altitudes, bailout bottles are provided. They are usually strapped to the legs, and contain a 10 minutes' supply of oxygen, sufficient to allow a parachutist to descend safely through the upper air. In an older type bottle, the oxygen is sucked through a pipestem, while in a newer type it is delivered into the mask.

In night operations, fliers do not wait until they reach 10,000 feet to put on their oxygen masks. They wear them from the time they take off, for the first effect of anoxia, even slight anoxia, lessens the ability to see in the dark.

Aeroembolism—When a bottle of soda pop is uncapped, the gas which has been imprisoned in the liquid under pressure escapes rapidly in the form of bubbles. The same type of thing can happen within the body fluids in the upper air. Nitrogen gas (and small quantities of oxygen, carbon dioxide and water vapor) is normally found dissolved in the blood and other body fluids. These gases are kept in solution by the pressure of the atmosphere. At high altitudes the nitrogen pressure within the body may exceed the nitrogen pressure in the air outside. The gas in the blood, seeking exit, forms bubbles in the joints and fat tissues and sometimes in other parts of the body. The result is a very painful condition called aeroembolism, known as the bends to deep sea divers and sandhogs.

The occurrence of aeroembolism is infrequent. It usually happens at 30,000 feet and above, and the majority of fliers are not susceptible to it even at those altitudes. A flier who has had trouble can guard against recurrence by breathing pure oxygen for 45 minutes before taking off and then continuing to breathe 100% oxygen from the ground up. This method, called denitrogenation, reduces the pressure of nitrogen in the lungs to zero and allows a large part of the gas in the body to escape painlessly. When an airman is stricken with aeroembolism, he normally can obtain relief by descending immediately to 25,000 feet or lower. Descent to a level of higher pressure will prevent serious injury to a flier in all cases if it is done in time.

Blackouts and Redouts—The symbol 1G represents the force which is exerted on an object by the pull of gravity. When the body is subjected to a prolonged pull greater than the force of gravity, it may not function properly. Such a prolonged pull is measured in terms of numbers of G's, such as 2G's, 3G's, 4G's, and up, depending upon the degree of force exerted.

Centrifugal force, the force that throws an object outward when it moves in an arc, may be greater than 1G. When a flier loops, or pulls out of a dive or climb, centrifugal force affects the body. Inside looping or pulling out of a dive (see diagram) forces the blood toward the lower part of the body. The blood, forced away from the head, leaves the brain without sufficient oxygen. The first effect is gray vision. An increase in force results in a blackout. Usually the flier does not become unconscious during blackouts, but he may if the force continues.

During outside looping or termination of a climb, the blood rushes in the opposite direction—toward the head. If the force is strong enough, the head throbs with pain, the eyes feel as though they are bulging and vision becomes red. Blackouts and redouts are of short duration, rarely have lasting effects and occur only under highly accelerated gravity pulls. To reduce the danger of blackouts and redouts, fliers learn to level off gradually from dives and climbs. Another aid is tensing the muscles and yelling to help slow the flow of blood.

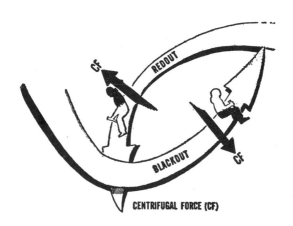

CENTRIFUGAL FORCE (CF)

Cold—Normal temperatures at altitudes of 25,000 to 30,000 feet range from 30 to 50 degrees below zero. Consequently, body warmth ranks next to oxygen supply as the most important need of the airman for efficiency at high altitude. A hand exposed to 40-below temperature becomes frostbitten within a few minutes, and a severe frostbite of one finger is sufficient to ground a gunner for days and sometimes weeks.

The AAF's fleece-lined leather flying suit and the improved alpaca type flying suit have been designed to provide the airman the maximum protection from cold with the minimum restriction of movement. The winter flying suit includes felt boots and leather gloves, both of which can be worn over additional layers of wool, fleece or rayon in any desired combination. Tight fitting clothing is avoided, because adequate circulation is also essential to keep the hands and feet warm. However, measures which merely insulate the body against loss of heat are insufficient for long exposure to extreme cold. The ideal solution is cabin heating, which is effective in fighter planes and the closed compartments of bombers, but not feasible in the exposed portions of the fuselage. Electrically heated suits, gloves and boots are necessary to protect tail, waist and turret gunners.

Night Vision—The retina, an area at the back of the eye which does the actual "seeing," is made up of tiny cells called rods and cones. The cones, which distinguish colors and structural detail, are used when bright light is available. Since they are principally grouped in the center of the retina, an object is best seen when we look directly at it. However, the cones are unable to participate in vision at night when the light is very dim. We are then dependent on the rods, which enable us to see the general form of objects in various shades of gray. Since the rods are distributed around the outer surfaces of the retina, objects are best seen on a dark night by looking at them a little off center. To do this accurately requires constant practice.

Ability to see in the dark can be lost quickly if the eyes are exposed to a bright light. A period of protection from bright light is required to adjust the eyes to night vision. Adapting the eyes to the dark can be accomplished by spending 30 minutes in a darkened room before a flight or by wearing red goggles for the same period. Red goggles shut out all colors but red, which least affects night vision.

Pilots read their instrument boards rapidly during night flight, thus exposing their eyes to the lighted panel for the shortest period possible. To further minimize the period of adjustment back to darkness after reading an instrument board, panel lights are kept as dim as practicable. Fluorescent lighted instruments reduce eye fatigue, help night vision.

A normal supply of Vitamin A, found in all green and yellow foods, is essential to night vision. When airmen are unable to get sufficient Vitamin A in their diet, a concentrate is given.

Diet—The gas in an airman's intestinal tract expands as the altitude increases. Effects may be painful, but ordinarily may be quickly relieved by passage of excess gas. Some men are sensitive to foods which produce excessive amounts of gas. Onions, cucumbers, radishes, cabbage, soda pop, dried beans, apples, melon, cauliflower and fat or rich foods are taboo for such men while on flying duty.

Fatigue—Flying fatigue is a double problem: immediate fatigue is induced by the hard work, extreme cold, possible accidental anoxia, constant alertness and emotional strain of a single mission; chronic fatigue, or staleness, is brought on by the accumulated nerve-wear of a series of missions.

For the fatigue of a single mission a good night's sleep, a little diversion and a satisfying meal are usually cure enough. The intensity of such fatigue is reduced by comfortable seating, proper oxygen and cold weather equipment, adequate rest between operations.

Chronic fatigue is mainly a mental condition. When it occurs, it is best treated by complete rest, freedom from strain, a change of scene and relief from arduous duties. AAF surgeons have been able to reduce the occurrence of chronic fatigue by a program of preventive measures: 24 hours' rest between missions when possible, a period of leave and alternate duty after a certain number of hours of flying, and athletics and recreation.

Aviation Medicine—The peculiar medical problems of aviation have given rise to the special science of aviation medicine. Since World War I the AAF has studied and experimented with the physiological difficulties resulting from flight. Today the office of the Air Surgeon supervises all medical activities in the AAF. Every medical officer who wears the golden wings of a flight surgeon has studied at the AAF's School of Aviation Medicine, has worked with flying personnel, and has had many hours of flying time in which to familiarize himself with the air.

A flight surgeon is assigned to every flying squadron. He watches over the daily health of the men and determines when they are fit to fly. He may ground a man with a slight cold because a cold which would cause little trouble on the ground might have serious consequences in the upper air where the ears and sinuses are under extra stresses. The flight surgeon prescribes all medication. Simple drugs like aspirin can have undesirable effects at high altitudes. A personal equipment officer is also assigned to each squadron. With the flight surgeon he checks oxygen equipment, instructs crews in its use and conducts an educational program in first aid in flight.

All flying personnel are kept in top physical condition at all times. A healthy body is the best safeguard against the air's physiological hazards.

EMERGENCY LANDING

No matter what we have done in the way of equipment and education to reduce the hazards of activity in our battlefield, there is always the chance that a plane will be forced out of the sky either by enemy action, mechanical failure or human failure. Proper precautions must be taken. Our planes are equipped for all eventualities and every man who flies is trained in the procedures of emergency evacuation and the techniques of survival anywhere on earth.

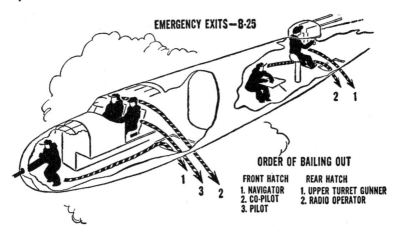

EMERGENCY EXITS—B-25

ORDER OF BAILING OUT

FRONT HATCH	REAR HATCH
1. NAVIGATOR	1. UPPER TURRET GUNNER
2. CO-PILOT	2. RADIO OPERATOR
3. PILOT	

Bailing Out—When it becomes necessary to bail out, the ideal way is to set the plane on a level course and slow its air speed. In a bomber crew, members use bailout exits located in easily accessible sections of the airplane. Fighter pilots turn their planes over if possible, dump the cockpit canopy, release safety belt and thrust themselves out with their feet.

If there is danger of enemy fire, the airman employs a long, free fall—that is, he opens his parachute only after he has fallen well below the level of enemy planes. At high altitudes the free fall also is advisable because it speeds the airman's descent through the intense cold and rarity of the upper air. A bailout oxygen bottle (see page 244) is provided for high altitude jumps. In a jump from a medium altitude where there is no enemy fire, the airman waits 2 to 6 seconds before pulling his ripcord. The delay minimizes danger of fouling the parachute with the airplane and serves to slow the parachutist's downward speed, thus reducing the shock when the parachute billows open.

After the parachute opens, the airman descends feet down, relaxed and, if possible, with his face in the direction he is drifting. He lands with flexed legs and attempts to run forward with the wind behind him, while pulling the shrouds to help collapse his parachute. Should the parachutist land in a tree, he crosses his arms in front of his head, burying face in forearm; feet and knees are held together. If an airman lands in water, he releases his parachute harness just before his feet touch the surface and quickly inflates his Mae West life vest. Pilots of single-place aircraft are usually equipped with one-man life rafts containing emergency rations and equipment. Both life rafts and Mae Wests can be instantly inflated by attached carbon dioxide cylinders.

Ditching—If a bomber pilot decides his plane must be ditched —landed on water—the crew immediately takes preparatory measures. All loose equipment like guns, ammunition (or anything that adds weight) is thrown out. Bombs and depth charges are jettisoned or disarmed. Emergency equipment (including a radio set) and supplies are placed near the escape hatches. Bomb bay doors are closed to prevent an inrush of water upon landing. The radio operator sends out a steady distress signal.

The pilot brings the plane down under power if possible rather than in a glide with the engines off. When the plane comes to rest, the men exit rapidly through their assigned ditching hatches, carrying equipment with them. There are different ditching procedures for each type of aircraft, but in all cases every man has his specific job, a specific exit. Rubber rafts are released from the fuselage and pop out on to the wings. The rafts are loaded, the crew boards them and they shove off. The rafts are tied together in the water.

DITCHING

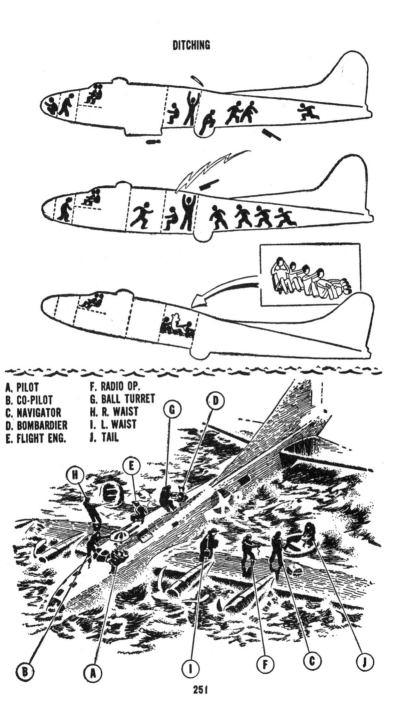

A. PILOT
B. CO-PILOT
C. NAVIGATOR
D. BOMBARDIER
E. FLIGHT ENG.

F. RADIO OP.
G. BALL TURRET
H. R. WAIST
I. L. WAIST
J. TAIL

As long as the plane stays afloat, the rafts stick near it, for a plane on the water can more easily be spotted by rescue aircraft. When the plane sinks, the crew strikes out in a direction that has been determined after calculation by the navigator. The pilot is in command. He plans a course of rationing for the food and water stores. It is desirable to remain clothed to avoid sunburn and excessive exposure.

Rafts are equipped with rations, fishing tackle, first-aid kit, Very (flare) pistols, an apparatus for making sea water drinkable, and a sea marker—a chemical which forms a large yellowish-green spot on the water making the raft's position visible to a rescue plane. There are 3 types of rafts in use: 2500-pound capacity, 1000-pound capacity and one-man raft.

Stories of raft survival have become commonplace. Life on a raft in the open sea is not pleasant, but it is possible to exist if the men use their equipment and provisions as they have been trained to use them. Hope of rescue, probably the greatest sustaining force for men adrift, need never be given up. Emergency rescue units, devoted solely to searching for and rescuing lost personnel, keep looking for men as long as there is even faint hope that they can be found. Boats, long-range amphibian planes and land planes equipped with floats are used for sea rescue. In theaters of operation air-sea rescue is abetted by the work of the Navy and Allied naval and air forces. Search operations are also conducted for men forced down in jungle, desert or arctic.

Forced Landing—When in distress over jungle, desert or arctic, it is usually better to try to crash-land an airplane than to bail out. The outline of a grounded plane can be spotted from the air, and the airplane itself provides shelter, fuel and material for fashioning improvised weapons and signaling devices.

The AAF has long studied the problems of survival in jungle, desert and arctic. The results of the studies are imparted to aircrew members during their training and in combat zones. An Arctic, Desert and Tropic Information Center, set up in the AAF, is constantly accumulating and disseminating new survival information. Available to all aircrew members are concise, fully illustrated easy-to-carry manuals crammed with information for emergencies. The manuals tell how to signal for help, how to build shelter, what foods to eat and which to avoid, how to treat ailments and safeguard health, how to deal with natives, how to travel over difficult terrain and scores of other useful items.

Crewmen are equipped with all-purpose emergency kits containing sun glasses, jackknife, needle and thread, fishing tackle, first-aid supplies, water and food rations, and various tools and implements. The kit is in the form of a seat cushion and is wrapped in a zipper-fastened canvas cover. A smaller kit fits snugly around the body like a jacket. A quilt, olive drab on one side and blue on the other may serve as a sleeping bag, a hammock, a raincoat, a pup tent or a signaling device.

CRASH LANDING

OUR AIR FORCES IN ACTION

HOW WE FIGHT

Combat operations bring into concerted action the various AAF elements—personnel and equipment, organization and training, supply, maintenance and bases. All are welded together in a united effort against the enemy. Because our weapon can be employed effectively in many ways, our combat operations are fairly complex. The following basic definitions may lead to a better understanding of how we fight.

Strategy involves long-range planning, determines the manner in which a war is to be fought. All our actions are conditioned by the strategy governing our nation's conduct of the war.

Tactics are the methods we employ in our operations against the enemy; they constitute the means by which we implement existing strategy and apply it locally to achieve victory in a battle. Strategy may best be thought of in terms of a war, tactics in terms of a battle.

Just as tactics are subordinate to strategy, so is technique subordinate to tactics. Technique consists of the manner in which tactics are performed.

An air force employs strategy; a formation of aircraft executes tactics; individual aircraft use technique.

STRATEGIC AND TACTICAL OPERATIONS

Our combat operations fall into 2 major categories—strategic and tactical—both of which can be identified with the terms from which they were derived. Strategic operations, based on long-range planning, are designed to prevent the enemy from obtaining the weapons he must have to make war, and to destroy his will to fight. Main objectives of AAF tactical operations are to achieve and maintain air supremacy, to destroy or disrupt enemy supply and communication lines, and to participate in a combined effort of the air, ground and sea forces on the immediate battlefront or adjacent to it. However, strategic operations may

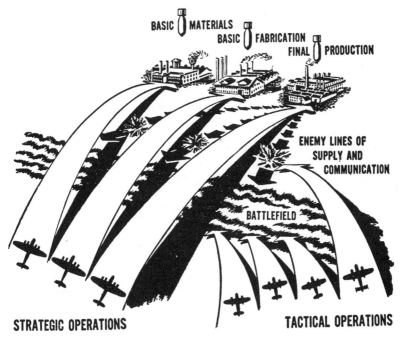

BASIC MATERIALS
BASIC FABRICATION
FINAL PRODUCTION

ENEMY LINES OF
SUPPLY AND
COMMUNICATION

BATTLEFIELD

STRATEGIC OPERATIONS   TACTICAL OPERATIONS

entail the destruction or neutralization of the enemy's airpower as a prerequisite to the primary strategic objectives.

Strategic Targets—The targets of strategic operations are the sources of production and maintenance of the enemy's war machine. They include rear bases and supply lines out of reach of tactical air units; key industries engaged in producing aircraft, other machines of war, ammunition and critical raw materials; electric power, transportation and fuel systems. They are selected only after careful, expert analysis which takes every conceivable factor into consideration. For example: How vitally will the destruction of a given plant affect the enemy's front line fighting ability? Which plants should be selected as involving, in the

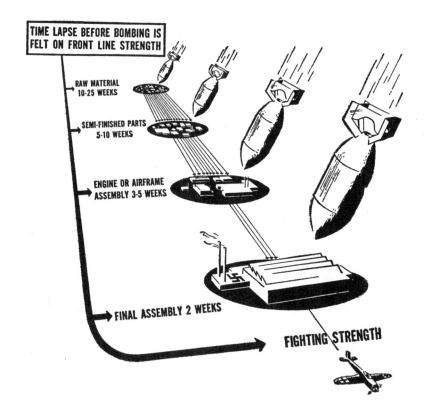

event of their destruction, the shortest time-lag in making their destruction felt?

Another important consideration is the selection of targets most likely to be disrupted by bomb damage. Factories producing material for which no ready substitute can be developed serve as an example. Strategy may call for concentration on one phase of enemy manufacture—aircraft production, for instance. But sometimes effective bombing directed at a single vital item, such as ball bearings, does more harm to enemy aircraft production than destruction of factories making the planes themselves.

Tactical Targets—Tactical targets consist mainly of enemy forces and supplies. Rapidly changing situations may cause these targets to change from day to day. On land, they include communications, aircraft and airfields, troops, transportation and battle emplacements. If the battle area is at sea, they include shipping and naval surface craft. In the air—over land and sea—the targets are enemy aircraft. But the prerequisite of tactical operations is to establish and maintain air superiority.

Basic Weapons—Because strategic air operations are characterized by long-range and sustained mass attack, the basic weapon is the heavy and very heavy bombardment airplane. Such operations, however, also usually involve long-range reconnaissance aircraft and escort fighters. Strategic operations place great emphasis on complete intelligence of the activities of an enemy nation; they are further characterized by the need for long-range weather forecasting, and by relative freedom from enemy attack on its bases of operation.

Tactical air operations demand a high degree of mobility and the employment of specific types of aircraft for striking at the enemy's front line strength, such as supply and communications, and for actual contact on the battlefield. These operations may involve the following components: medium bombardment aircraft, light bombardment aircraft, fighter and fighter-bomber aircraft, reconnaissance and photographic aircraft, antiaircraft artillery and aircraft warning services.

Most types of aircraft can perform both strategic and tactical operations; and, as military necessity dictates, tactical and strategic air units may be operated against the same objectives. Strategic air forces are combat components of the AAF organized, trained and equipped for the primary mission of performing separate air operations against strategic targets. Tactical air forces are organized, trained and equipped to operate more efficiently against tactical targets. When a single air force has both components, they generally are designated as a strategic command and a tactical command, respectively.

BOMBARDMENT

Our combat operations are dependent upon the employment of land-based aircraft which, because they are not limited as to takeoff and landing facilities, can carry heavier bomb loads and operate at longer ranges than carrier-based aircraft; they also can operate more efficiently than amphibious aircraft.

Bombardment units are classified, according to the kind of aircraft with which they are equipped, as very heavy, heavy, medium, light, or attack.

Very heavy and heavy bombers are long-range aircraft; medium bombers are intermediate range aircraft. Designation of heavy or medium is determined by bomb load and fuel capacity. In general, light bombardment planes are smaller, more maneuverable, and have a shorter operating radius and less bomb-carrying capacity than medium bombers. Light bombardment units are designed and equipped for low and minimum altitude operations.

Tactics in any attack are determined by the target and by enemy defenses enroute and at the target. In this latter connection, 2 factors are involved: the strength, effectiveness, number and disposition of ground defenses; and the strength and location of enemy fighter aircraft.

The size and shape of the target itself may determine whether a concentration or dispersal of bombs in the target area is required. Care must be taken to select the correct type of bomb in regard to its weight, fuzing and content. (See page 150.) Attacks cannot follow any set formula, since they may be delivered at high or low altitudes, during daylight or at night, by means of precision or area bombing, and may be opposed or unopposed by the enemy.

BOMBING ALTITUDES

MINIMUM	up to 1000 feet
LOW	1000 to 7500
MEDIUM	7500 to 15,000
HIGH	15,000 and up.

Bombing Problem—A target which includes many structures may sometimes be divided and so assigned to attacking aircraft that if each structure is hit by one bomb of proper size the entire target will be destroyed. Still other targets may require a uniform pattern of hits over a given area.

An important consideration in bombing is the size of the force which a mission must employ to assure a reasonable chance of obtaining the required number of hits. While economy dictates the use of the smallest practical number of planes and crews, the chance of success increases with the size of the force. These 2 factors plus the estimated enemy opposition to any particular mission must be weighed for final determination of the number of planes to be used.

Day and Night Bombing Operations—Daylight bombing constitutes the core of AAF combat operations. Its effectiveness lies in the ability to sight the target, and thus employ the synchronous bombsight. This permits high altitude precision bombing; also, daylight operations allow us to take advantage of formation flying. Night operations, in which AAF men also are trained, involve such problems as locating the target, more complicated navigation; greater operational hazards and the impracticability of formation flying.

Formations—Flying in a prescribed pattern, or formation, increases offensive and defensive strength. Arrangement of a formation is usually based upon the strength, disposition and employment of the individual combat unit. As a rule, all planes in a given formation are of the same type or have similar performance characteristics in order to maintain the formation pattern. There are no prescribed types of bomber formations which must be rigidly followed. Each formation must meet the requirements of the specific situation presented, must be sufficiently flexible to adapt itself during flight to changing situations. The possible types of formations are many.

COMPONENTS OF FORMATIONS

ELEMENT . . . . 2 to 4 aircraft
FLIGHT . . . . 2 or more elements
COMBAT BOX (OR GROUP) . . . . 2 or more flights
COMBAT WING . . . . 2 or more groups

Bombardment Attack—Targets generally are classified as fixed, transient or fleeting. Fixed targets are immobile—factories, dams, dock installations. Transient targets are those capable of being moved—supplies, ammunition dumps, concentrations of motor equipment. Fleeting targets are those in motion—shipping, navy craft, tanks, motor transport.

Heavy Bomber—The ability of heavy bombers to drop bombs with accuracy from altitudes in excess of 30,000 feet is directly attributable to precision bombsights and Automatic Flight Control Equipment—a device which actually flies the plane during the bombing run (see page 171). Together they solve extremely difficult and complex bombing problems in a matter of seconds. The bombardier, who is a specialist doing his calculations in split seconds, must deal with such problems as the speed of the plane, correct altitude, direction of the wind in relation to the aircraft, identification of the target at extreme altitudes, the inevitable discomfort due to cold and the use of oxygen, and the fact that the bomber may be under enemy attack.

Although low level bombing is seldom performed by AAF heavy bombers, they have been used on occasion in low level attacks when little ground opposition was expected, or in the interest of complete surprise. Because of their size and relative lack of maneuverability and speed, heavy bombers are exceedingly vulnerable at low levels.

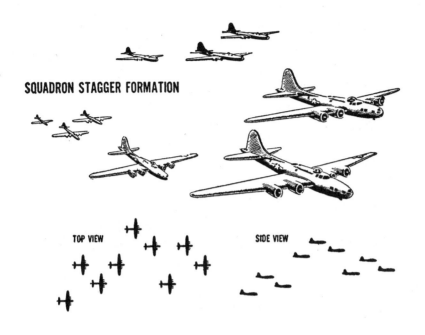

SQUADRON STAGGER FORMATION

TOP VIEW

SIDE VIEW

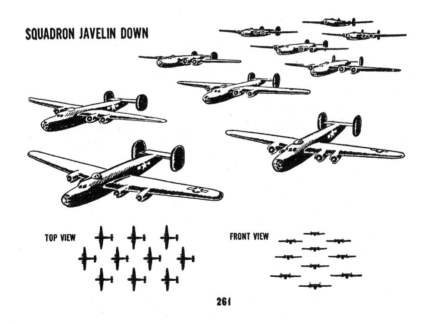

SQUADRON JAVELIN DOWN

TOP VIEW

FRONT VIEW

AB is BOMBING RUN. B is the point of bomb release. C is the position of the airplane at the time the bomb strikes the target. RANGE ANGLE, which determines proper release point, is established by altitude and distance from target. In calculating for bombing, wind, which affects the path of the plane and therefore the trajectory of the bomb, must be taken into consideration.

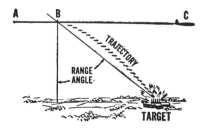

Bombsight—As new models of our bombers have attained higher altitudes and greater speeds, the problems of precise bombing have become more complex. Improvements in bombing equipment and accessories have been necessary to keep pace with engineering achievements which have made possible altitudes of more than 7 miles, speeds greater than 300 miles per hour, bomb loads over 8000 pounds.

The synchronous bombsight, an instrument not much larger than a typewriter, makes possible the placement of bombs in the most vital areas of a target. As a result, difficult targets requiring a concentration of hits in a small area can be bombed effectively. In general, the tactics employed in horizontal bombardment rely on the increasingly efficient use of this bombsight.

The bombsight, with data computed by the bombardier set into the mechanism, determines the correct point in space at which a specific type of bomb must be released to strike a selected target. The fundamental data set into the bombsight is determined by the altitude of the plane above the target, its rate of speed relative to the ground, and the type of bomb to be used. This data is figured by the bombardier before the plane reaches the target area. Once the bombing run is begun, the bombardier's technique determines whether or not the bomb will reach its objective.

Through its telescopic mechanism the bombsight establishes an angle between the position of the plane and the target. This angle, varying with the altitude, determines the distance from the target at which the bomb must be released. The computing of this distance is called range. Errors in such computation will cause the bomb to fall short of, or go beyond, the target.

The second problem solved by the bombsight is deflection. An error in calculating deflection will cause the bomb to fall to the right or left of the target. The bombardier, looking through the telescope of the bombsight, can detect the direction that the plane is drifting. The aircraft is lined up with the target by means of Automatic Flight Control Equipment, or by a device which enables the pilot to fly by directions received from the bombardier. When these 2 operations are performed, that is, when the correct range has been established, and deflection error has been eliminated, the bombsight is said to be synchronized. The bombs will then be released automatically when the aircraft reaches the bomb release point as calculated by the bombsight.

Automatic release of the bombs, individually or in any number, is done by the intervalometer. This device, when set by the bombardier, releases the bombs as desired. Bombs may be released to fall every 25 feet, 50 feet, or at whatever interval the target may require. In an emergency, either the bombardier or pilot can release all the bombs manually. This operation is called the salvo. Bombs can also be released "safe" (so they will not explode on impact) in case they have to be jettisoned over friendly territory or in non-combatant areas.

Area Bombing—Area bombing is employed when the objective

BOMBSIGHT TELESCOPE

Target is sighted.

Bombardier observes aircraft is drifting as indicated by target "moving" across vertical cross-hair.

Course to the target is established and the bombsight telescope begins TRACKING the target. This is DEFLECTION.

The horizontal cross-hair is placed on the target and proper RATE of telescope movement is established to determine RANGE.

When the target remains in the intersection of the vertical and horizontal cross-hair, the bombsight is SYNCHRONIZED. When the aircraft reaches the release point, the bombs will be released automatically.

is large and contains a multiplicity of targets. The attacking formation remains intact, forming the pattern desired for bomb coverage. Usually the lead plane will use the synchronous bombsight—the bombardiers of other planes releasing their bombs upon visual observation that the lead plane has dropped its bombs.

Overcast Bombing—A special method of bombing is employed to overcome complete cloud coverage when no visibility of the ground exists. Bombs are dropped on the target by means of electronic devices which locate both the main objective and the specific target. Accurate high level bombing has been accomplished by this means through more than 25,000 feet of overcast.

Defensive Action—Enemy opposition to our bombing operations is concentrated chiefly in fighter aircraft and antiaircraft fire. The AAF continually develops tactics to lessen the effectiveness of such enemy defenses. The great concentration of firepower on our heavy bombers has been developed solely for their protection during the performance of their mission. A bomber never initiates an attack in the air, and will avoid an engagement with enemy fighters if possible. Enemy fighters are attacked by a bomber only as a by-product of the bomber's defense of itself.

The best bomber defense against attack from enemy fighters is close formation flying. By remaining in formation the fire power of all the planes may be concentrated to meet attackers from any direction. If, during an attack on a target, the enemy fighters disengage and antiaircraft fire begins, the bombers may loosen up their formation. Should the fighters return, the bombers must close their formation.

Use by the enemy of rocket projectiles and air-to-air bombing calls for evasive tactics—varying altitude and speed, weaves, turns and dives. Rocket tubes installed on the wings of enemy fighters permit them to remain out of range of the bomber's guns but by the same token make it difficult for the fighters to fire accurately. Rocket projectiles must explode close to a bomber to be effective. Similarly, air-to-air bombing from above a formation of bombers requires a precision difficult to obtain in view of the high speeds of both the attacking enemy fighters and the bombers.

High altitude flying is our basic defensive measure against

antiaircraft fire; the greater the altitude, the less effective the ground defenses. Most antiaircraft fire (commonly called flak) is controlled on the ground by a predictor system. It consists of devices which determine the altitude and speed of attacking bombers and attempt to predict the point in space where projectile and plane will meet.

AAF aircraft employ evasive action to confuse the calculations of antiaircraft gunners. The most critical period for bombers is during the bomb run, when the aircraft must be flown straight, level and at constant speed.

In attempting to stop a large attacking formation of bombers enemy antiaircraft batteries may fire flak barrages, forming a concentration of fire just in front of the bomb release line. This method of fire is much more inaccurate than predicted fire but is used as an attempt to impair the accuracy of bombing as well as destroy the attacking bombers.

Medium Bomber—The medium bomber is the main component of tactical operations. Highly flexible, it operates from medium, low or minimum altitudes, and can release torpedoes as well as bombs. It is well armed for defense against enemy fighters. Its speed and maneuverability add to its security in flight. Because of the variety of tactics employed in its use, modifications and developments adding to its effectiveness have been frequent.

Medium Altitude Attack—In medium altitude attack, for the most part, the medium bomber uses the same tactics as the heavy bomber. During the release of bombs the plane is vulnerable to fire from automatic weapons and light antiaircraft guns. The greater speed and maneuverability of the medium bomber govern its tactics in attack.

Low Level Bombing—Low level bombing is one of the most effective uses of the medium bomber. The element of surprise is very great. Using the cover of trees and hills, attacking planes often reach the target and release their bombs before they are detected by the enemy. Even electronic warning devices are fallible in trying to pick up planes flying at low altitudes. During the bombing run the heavy armament of the medium bomber is used both to damage the target and to prevent enemy ground defenses from going into action. Though very effective, low level bombing requires tactical precision in operations, because the planes are extremely vulnerable to ground defenses if such defenses are able to open fire. Generally, bombers must fly through a cross-fire set up by the enemy. However, antiaircraft guns in

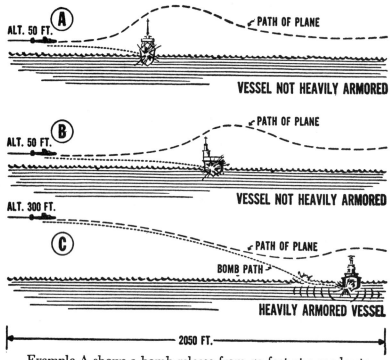

Example A shows a bomb release from 50 feet at a moderate speed. In Example B the airplane is traveling at a higher speed; here the bomb must be released farther from the ship. Example C shows how, when attacking a heavily armored vessel, the aircraft must be at a higher altitude so the bomb will submerge and detonate beneath the water.

---

most cases cannot be directed effectively against bombers flying at extremely low altitudes.

Minimum Altitude Attack—Employed both on land and sea, the attack is usually made from as low a level as possible, with a pull up to the necessary bombing altitude as the target is reached. Delayed action bombs enable the airplane to escape the danger area of bomb bursts. Minimum altitude attack requires a high degree of skill and technique, in aiming the bombs and in flying. The planes used for this type of attack usually have a great concentration of forward fire power to destroy targets and minimize ground defenses.

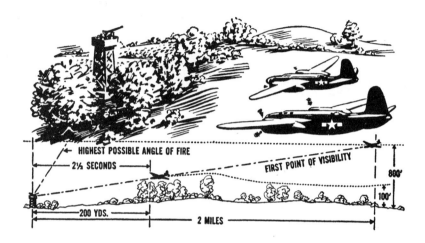

Since the bomb is released so close to the target, great accuracy results. The bomb assumes the flight path of the plane and therefore the direction of the wind is important because drift can cause the bomb to miss its mark. The distance from the target at which the bomb is released is a prime factor. Accurate judgment of the required distance can be accomplished only after much practice and training. As a variation, bombs are often aimed so as to skip on the surface and thus into the target.

Light Bomber—The light bomber supplements the medium bomber, and attacks such targets as enemy personnel, enemy aircraft, motor transport, tanks, railway equipment and rolling stock, and other objectives requiring precision attack and which are susceptible to destruction by small bombs. Heavily armed, the light bomber can strafe the enemy as it makes its bombing run. Usually parafrags and delayed action demolition bombs are employed to obtain a scattering of fire which allows the air-

MINIMUM ALTITUDE BOMBING

craft to escape concussion. This strafe-bombing tactic has been highly successful against enemy airfields in the Southwest Pacific.

Fighter-Bomber—The fighter-bomber performs the same general function as the light bomber. In the AAF all fighter aircraft can carry bombs; some are capable of carrying a bomb load of 2000 pounds or more. The size and weight of the bombs

carried vary with the type of aircraft. When carrying bombs, the fighter is less maneuverable and for protection may be escorted by other fighters.

FIGHTER AIRCRAFT

Fighter aircraft are today an important component of AAF offensive power. Developments in both armament and performance have enabled fighters to perform added duties.

High speed, superior rate of climb and maneuverability are essential factors; the flexibility of fighter aviation is perhaps greater than in any other type of air combat.

The unit possessing superior airplanes and equipment can, within limits, choose the time and place for initiating a fight—a distinct advantage. The relative maneuverability of aircraft materially influences the tactics employed in air fighting. In fighter planes, equipped only with fixed guns, maneuverability is of extreme importance as it governs the ease and speed with which the guns can be aligned and held on the target; it also makes evasive tactics possible.

Accuracy of fire is dependent primarily on the following: (1) The shorter the range, the more nearly will the projectiles conform to their mean trajectory and hit at the point indicated by direct sighting. (2) The shorter the range the greater the accuracy of fire, since if the target is maneuvering it may move out of the cone of fire while the projectiles are in flight. (3) The greater the individual skill the more successful the air fighting, since correct estimation of range, accurate aiming, and, for fixed gun installation, skillful piloting are essential.

Tactics—Tactics employed by fighter aircraft vary with the combat theater in which the fighters are operating, with the design and characteristics of the particular aircraft used, and with the tactics of the enemy. Because the tactical situation and the geographical location of our forces vary, different demands are imposed on our fighter aircraft. Basically, the fighter is exceedingly adaptable, and with a minimum amount of modification can be adapted for use in a specific locality.

Unlike combat aviation in World War I, the glory of individual combat has little place in today's air war. No longer does a single plane go out seeking to engage an opponent. Fighter planes are organized into units trained to fight as teams. There may be 2, 4, 6, 8 or any number, but always more than one (except in night fighting).

By remaining in formations, or by flying in pairs, the entire component can train its combined fire power on the enemy. Also, it can more easily maneuver the enemy into effective range. Fighting in units rather than singly enables each pilot to cover the other, and provides more eyes to search the sky for enemy fighters.

Weather conditions and the presence and location of the sun have considerable influence on air fighting, both as advantages and disadvantages. Small units of fighters approaching an objective from the direction of the sun are sometimes able to launch a surprise attack. In timing an attack immediately after sunset or immediately before sunrise, the advantage of approaching a silhouetted target is gained.

The factor of visibility plays contrasting roles in offensive and defensive operations. High visibility favors fighter pilots in locating targets for attack. Low visibility aids defensive formations, or small units, in evading fighter interception.

Clouds afford an excellent place for concealment from which surprise attacks may be launched against enemy planes and provide effective cover enroute to and from an objective.

Fighter Formations—Fighter formations call for a sufficient degree of flexibility to permit sudden rearrangement to meet rapidly changing conditions. Maneuverability is important in order that the planes of a formation may retain the advantage of position in offensive air fighting, and at the same time be able to interpose elements between an attacker and the formation itself. Fighter formations must be readily controllable. This requirement is effected by indoctrination, visual signals, or radio.

There are 2 types of basic fighter formations: close or normal formation, and search or extended formation. In close formation, aircraft are spaced only far enough apart to allow freedom of maneuver while remaining within close supporting distance of each other. This formation is used in combat.

In extended formation, the sub-units are beyond support of each other but are still under tactical control. Adjacent units

A FIGHTER FORMATION

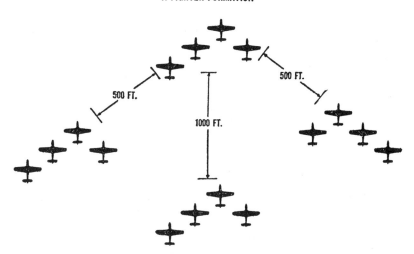

500 FT.

500 FT.

1000 FT.

maintain visual contact at all times. This type of formation is used for patrols and search missions.

Combat Operations—Fighter combat operations have 3 phases: approach to combat, the combat, and withdrawal. The approach to combat phase has a greater influence on the result than any other phase of fighter operations. Approach toward the most vulnerable or blind sector of the hostile formation confuses the enemy and delays proper counteraction. Fighter pilots must be thoroughly familiar with the characteristics and the most vulnerable sectors of enemy aircraft and formations. When the enemy

is sighted, the attack or maneuver-for-attack position should be
initiated without delay.

The first blow is very important. Sustained fire begins as soon
as the enemy planes are within range. Every effort is made to
maintain the pattern of the attacking force and prevent a melee
of individual engagements.

The withdrawal phase involves a determined effort to take
advantage of any confusion and dispersion of the enemy force
which may result from the initial attack. If the attack has been
indecisive or unfavorable, a withdrawal is effected utilizing speed
and evasive tactics to minimize losses. An attempt is then made
to regain advantage by regrouping.

Fighter Escort—Range is the determining factor in the employment of fighter planes as escort for bombers or fighter-
bombers. Fighters may escort bomber formations through all or
part of a mission, furnishing a screen against enemy attack and
augmenting defensive fire power.

To be most effective, fighter escort must be able to concentrate fire in any direction. Relative speeds, escort strength and
visibility conditions predicate the distance from which fighters
normally cover bomber formations. Escorting aircraft counterattack only when hostile fighters make direct attacks on a formation.

FIGHTER ESCORT

In escorting bombers on long-range missions over heavily defended territory, as many as 6 or 8 separate fighter missions may be employed, involving a complex system of precision timing. Air speeds, fuel consumption, weather conditions (especially cloud formations) and enemy opposition must be taken into consideration.

An attack on a target 500 miles away normally requires at least 4 separate fighter escort missions. Fighter escorts rendezvous with the bomber formations at predetermined points. Since fighters cannot hold down their speed to that of bombers, they must weave back and forth or circle, thus using fuel and cutting down their range. One relay of fighters escorts the bombers for the first leg, another replaces it, and finally the longest range fighters furnish escort to the target and for the first leg of the return trip. If fighter fuel supplies are dwindling on the way back, the long-range fighters may be relieved by another long-range fighter escort which accompanies the bombers to a point where short-range fighters meet the formation, escort it back to home territory.

Fighter Sweeps—Fighter diversionary sweeps frequently are flown over enemy airbases prior to a bombing mission to act as decoys. This action brings up enemy fighters and exhausts their fuel, enabling the bombers to strike with less opposition. In this type of mission fighter aircraft have complete freedom of action and normally engage any enemy aircraft encountered. The effectiveness of fighter sweeps has increased through the use of fighter-bombers. Even though the enemy knows that the sweep is diversionary, he cannot ignore the threat of fighters armed with bombs. He is therefore compelled to intercept. These missions are generally flown at high altitudes. Fighter sweeps also are flown at other altitudes to clear the air of enemy aircraft and to cover ground forces in battle.

Intruder Raids—Intruder raids usually are flown at night by individual night aircraft to harass the enemy. The intruder may join an enemy formation and, undetected, fly to an enemy airfield, strafing or bombing it. The intruder also may penetrate deep into enemy territory undetected, and bomb or strafe targets of opportunity.

Night Fighters—The night fighter is a short-range, heavily armed, and high-performance fighter. For operations in a localized area, special GCI radar equipment is used. Enemy planes, first detected on long-range sets, are reported to a ground station where night fighters are alerted. Controllers at the station give AAF night fighters a series of vectors, or directions, to follow which will bring the night fighters to positions fairly close to the enemy bombers—preferably behind them. The radar operators in the night fighters then switch on their airborne-intercept equipment which spots enemy planes at fairly close range. The operators keep the pilots advised over interphones until it is time to fire. Day fighters may be used at night to attack enemy planes if the attacking aircraft are within range of searchlight batteries.

WARNING AND CONTROL—The development of aircraft warning and control systems has greatly changed the AAF's use of fighter forces by providing ground control of all friendly aircraft in a given vicinity, not only for defense but in practically all tactical air actions. Such operations may be explained as follows:

DETECTION. There are various means of obtaining information of enemy aerial activity. Long-range radar sweeps the skies for a radius of over 100 miles and usually gives the first warning of approaching aircraft. In some areas this information is supplied by reports radioed from ground observers stationed far beyond radio detection range and sometimes behind enemy lines. Often a report comes as soon as an enemy flight has left its own airfield.

EVALUATION AND DISPLAY. Reports received from many detecting sources within an area must be plotted and filtered by trained plotting troops in filter centers. The results are passed on to a central information center. All flights detected are plotted, displayed on operations boards and identified as friendly or hostile. In the case of a hostile flight, the controller orders fighter squadrons into the air to intercept the enemy planes before they reach their target. Ideally, fighters are ordered to "scramble" 60 to 90 seconds after enemy planes have been detected.

CONTROL. Any flight control must have (1) direction-finding radio equipment by which the exact location of our own aircraft can be established, and (2) effective ground-to-air radio communications. Through the latter the intercept officer directs a flight leader to intercept an enemy formation, to join our bombers, or to attack a specific target.

Fighter Control in Tactical Operations—Each tactical air division has a tactical control center which in a given area directs the fighter, fighter-bomber, and reconnaissance operations by direct radio communications. Such centers are hubs of wire and radio networks connected to airbases, military ground observers, radars, direction-finding stations, air-parties operating with ground troops, higher headquarters and other military, naval and civil agencies. The centers are furnished with map displays which summarize the air picture minute-by-minute. Intelligence flows in over high-speed networks.

Fighter Control in Strategic Operations—Aircraft warning and communication elements serve to warn AAF pilots of hostile air activity which our bombers may encounter while proceeding to a target.

Ground control of fighter escorts is another helpful factor. For example, 2 bombing missions, both escorted with fighter aircraft, head for different targets. One mission reports no aerial interceptions. The other reports it has run into more enemy fighters than were expected. The fighter controller, acting from the ground, diverts some of the fighters from one flight to the other.

Air Defense—Air defense constitutes those measures necessary to prevent, to interfere with, or to reduce the effectiveness of hostile air action after hostile aircraft have left their own airfields or carriers.

The most effective measure is to send fighter aircraft to intercept enemy planes and knock them down or drive them off before they reach their target. Antiaircraft artillery, automatic weapons, barrage balloons and an aircraft warning service are other defenses against air attack.

Active air defense comprises all measures which aim to destroy, or threaten destruction of, hostile aircraft and their crews in the air.

Passive air defense comprises other defense measures undertaken to make our surface objectives less susceptible to observation and bombing—air raid precautionary measures, dispersion, blackouts, suppression of aids to the enemy, camouflage and concealment.

Air defense situations are never exactly alike. The object to be defended may be a recently captured airfield in enemy territory, a harbor where our supplies are being unloaded, important battle positions, communications lines, an island base, the Panama Canal, or one of a score of other areas or installations.

Two systems, with many variations within each, have been evolved to meet different military situations. These systems are known as fixed or mobile, characterizing respectively the type of aircraft warning and control equipment used.

INTERCEPTOR ATTACK ON BOMBERS

A fixed air defense system is one used for the strategic air defense of a specific area; it is custom-built to defend one particular locality and no other. The warning equipment used is more or less permanent. Fixed defense systems are used for defending the United States, Panama Canal, Iceland and Alaska, and areas removed from the actual front line fighting.

Mobile and air-transportable defense systems are established and operated by a tactical air force and used in forward battle areas. Both of these are extremely flexible and can be sent immediately to any forward areas into which our troops and supplies may be moved. Whichever type is used, the mission of air defense systems is the same: to deny the enemy the use of the air.

AIRBORNE WARFARE—Airborne forces are Army Ground Force units specially organized, trained and equipped to utilize air transportation for entry into combat. Included in these units are parachute and glider-borne elements.

Troop carrier forces are AAF units specially organized, trained and equipped to transport airborne troops and equipment into combat. Troop carrier units should not be confused with the Air Transport Command whose primary mission is transporting personnel, supplies and mail between theaters.

Employment—Airborne troops ordinarily are employed as part of a combined effort undertaken in close coordination with other military and naval forces. Trained and equipped to accomplish specific missions, they are employed only on missions that cannot be performed more expeditiously and economically by other forces. The geographical inaccessibility of an object to a ground force is a major factor in considering the employment of airborne forces. These troops normally are not employed unless they can be supported in a very short time or unless they can be withdrawn after their mission has been accomplished.

Airborne troops are employed in mass and landed rapidly in as small an area as practicable. Since air superiority is a prerequisite for successful airborne operations, the degree of air superiority and the amount of small arms fire to be expected from the landing area are factors in determining whether airborne operations should be initiated during daylight or at night.

Instead of avoiding antiaircraft fire by altitude or evasive action, routes are selected which avoid it entirely. Pathfinder aircraft with highly trained crews are employed to precede the leading troop carrier flight to the dropping or landing area.

In order to prevent early detection, the initial approach to hostile positions is made at low altitude. In the selection of landing areas, usually one close to the objective is chosen to insure surprise. Cover near the landing area is important. Suitable terrain for defense is required.

All land, sea and air forces in the areas involved must be informed of scheduled airborne operations. Complete coordination and mutual understanding are imperative; airborne troops must be advised of the identification means used by the ground troops with whom they may operate. The objectives of airborne forces are: to seize, hold or otherwise exploit important tactical localities such as airdromes, bridges, high ground and crossroads, in conjunction with or pending arrival of other military or naval forces; and to seize areas which are not strongly held and which the enemy cannot readily reinforce.

AUXILIARY OPERATIONS

Reconnaissance Aviation—The mission of reconnaissance aviation is the securing of enemy information from the air. Both photographic and visual means are used. Two types of reconnaissance are provided for the procurement of such information. One is photographic reconnaissance which operates normally at high altitude and at long-range in cooperation with organizations operating strategically. The second is tactical reconnaissance which normally operates at medium or extremely low altitude in cooperation with organizations operating tactically. Reconnaissance should precede operations of striking units to secure information necessary for planning the employment of a striking force, thus supplementing other intelligence agencies.

Navigation—Air navigation is the art of determining geographical position and maintaining desired direction of aircraft relative to the earth's surface by means of pilotage, dead reckoning, celestial observations or radio aids.

Pilotage is the method of conducting aircraft from one point to another by observation of landmarks either previously known or recognized from a map. This form of navigation is used when the pilot or navigator has good visibility and the terrain features are such that recognition of objects can be made from the altitude flown.

Dead reckoning is the method of determining geographical position of aircraft by applying rate of speed to the flight path of the aircraft as estimated or calculated over a certain period of time from point of departure, or from last known position. It is employed when flying overwater in the daytime, or when poor visibility makes pilotage impossible.

Celestial navigation makes use of the sun, stars, planets and moon to determine geographical position. Celestial navigation is not an independent form of air navigation but is employed to verify or correct the other forms.

Radio navigation makes use of the direction from which radio waves are received to determine, by means of a loop antenna, the direction of the transmitting station. The loop antenna is so constructed that when coupled with a suitable receiver, bearings may be taken on a distant radio station by rotating the loop until the signal is of minimum strength. At this point the plane of the loop is perpendicular to the direction of the transmitting station. Knowing the location of the transmitting station, the aerial navigator is enabled to calculate his position in relation to that station. The plane may also fly in on the beam direct to the station.

Intelligence—Combat intelligence provides material for briefing aircrews—an action in which the aircrews receive pertinent information from officers in charge of many phases of operations. Briefing takes place immediately prior to an aircrew's takeoff for a mission. It deals with target information, enemy opposition that may be encountered both in the air and from ground defenses, what to do in the event of capture, importance of the target to the enemy.

Upon return from the mission the interrogation of the aircrews takes place. From this is learned what tactics the enemy employed, how many enemy fighters were destroyed, extent of direct hits on target and estimate of damage, observations made of troop movements or concentrations in enemy territory, location of enemy ground defenses and strength, and any other information concerning the enemy.

Photographic intelligence is derived from the interpretation of aerial photographs taken primarily by reconnaissance aircraft, and secondarily by cameras on bombing aircraft during bombing missions. Highly trained photo-interpreters analyze the photographs to prepare factual reports on damage assessment, industry, transportation, airfield activity, ground and coast defenses, camouflage, dummys and decoys, communications, ground force activity, shipping and ship building. Most important information is obtained by comparison of recent photographs with previously obtained photographs of the same area. Great advances have been made in the field of aerial photography in its military application through the development of various types of cameras for specialized jobs including high altitude, low altitude, high-speed, infra-red, mapping, color and night photography. Photographic reconnaissance contributes the largest portion of intelligence upon which military decisions can be based. Intelligence is also obtained from captured enemy personnel and equipment.

Communications—The various communication devices and systems developed by the AAF have contributed greatly to its effectiveness. Without communications, coordination would be impossible.

Interphone communications enable every crew member to be in constant contact with others in the same aircraft. It is essential during an attack that the pilot be informed of the location of enemy aircraft, antiaircraft fire, and the position of other friendly aircraft in the formation, so that he can maneuver the plane for more effective fire power.

Air communications enable planes in flight to communicate with each other. The formation leader can talk with other aircraft, and they in turn with each other. However, enroute to the target radio silence is the rule.

Air-ground communications are essential to all types of planes. By means of this system planes are cleared for takeoff and instructed in landing, weather information is given to pilots, and fighter aircraft are directed to areas where enemy attackers are operating. Normally, aircraft are in constant touch with ground stations.

Gunnery—The success of a mission and the lives of a crew are in a large measure dependent on the accuracy and effectiveness of the gunner.

Downing one airplane by another with gunfire is complicated by the problem of keeping a fast-moving target in range. In one sense the quality of the equipment provided the gunner can be considered a potential of his fire power. The ballistic behavior induced when a projectile is fired from an airplane, the human element, and the speed and maneuverability of the airplane target make aerial gunnery a complicated procedure.

Gunfire from an airplane differs from ground fire principally in relation to the speed of the plane and its altitude. The trajectory of a bullet is affected by the speed of an airplane. Altitude increases the speed of a bullet because thin air offers less resistance to a projectile on its course. These factors have brought about a new set of gunsighting rules.

Nevertheless, the gunsight doesn't do it all. Tracking and rang·
ing, the 2 main factors in aerial gunnery that determine the accu·
racy of gunfire after computation, must be calculated by the
gunner himself. Unless he tracks smoothly and ranges precisely,
the computing gunsight will absorb inaccurate data on which to
base its calculations. Tracking involves keeping the gunsight pre·
cisely on the target without deviation, while ranging involves
manipulation of the sight's range-measuring mechanism to keep
the correct range constantly in the computer. Both are done by
wrist or foot movements.

Just as guns on the ground must be elevated to compensate
for the trajectoral curve of the projectile, so guns on aircraft also
must be tilted upward—since after the projectile leaves the muz·
zle of the gun the bullet follows the same relative curve at an
elevation of 40,000 feet as it does at 1000 feet. This explains the
slight elevation of fixed forward firing guns on both fighters and
bombers. Conversely, attack planes, designed specifically for
ground strafing, have their fixed guns aimed slightly downward.

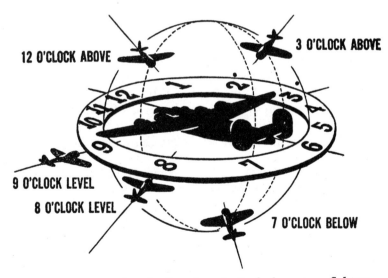

Clock System used to fix direction of attacks by enemy fighters.
12 o'clock is nose of bomber, 6 o'clock tail.

THE COMBAT AIR FORCES

Our strategy, tactics and techniques are translated into results through the operations of strategically located combat air forces which blanket the battle areas of the world.

The accomplishments of these organizations must be examined in perspective. Military necessity gives priority to certain enemy objectives at the expense of others; our air strength has been apportioned accordingly. Its achievements must be judged on the basis of planes and men available in a given area at a given time.

In the early months of the war it was a taxing feat for the AAF's lone heavy bombardment unit in the Southwest Pacific to fly a mission with the strength of half a squadron. Today, in at least one theater of operations, squadrons tend to lose their identity, become swallowed up in groups; groups are massed in wings and wings in air divisions. The Aleutian island of Kiska was retaken from the Japanese only after the 11th Air Force, in several thousand sorties flown over a period of 14 months, had dropped some 3000 tons of bombs on the target. Great as this accomplishment was, the same tonnage of bombs is dropped today in a single 8-hour mission over Europe. In turn, a full-fledged military campaign elsewhere in the world may not equal in strategic importance a single massed air attack on Germany.

AAF SUMMARY OF OPERATIONS—TOTAL OF ALL THEATERS—
December 1941 to March 1, 1944

SORTIES FLOWN	TONS OF BOMBS DROPPED	—PLANES LOST IN AERIAL COMBAT—	
		ENEMY	AAF
525,954	285,350	12,656 *	4217

* Also destroyed: a verified total of 1873 enemy planes on the ground.

Following are brief introductions to the combat air forces and to a few significant complementary organizations.

8TH AIR FORCE

ESTABLISHED: Jan. 28, 1942.

AREA OF OPERATIONS: Germany and the occupied countries of Europe.

COMMAND: Lt. Gen. Carl Spaatz, May 2, 1942 to Nov. 28, 1942; Lt. Gen. Ira C. Eaker, Dec. 1, 1942 to Jan. 1, 1944; Lt. Gen. James H. Doolittle, Jan. 1, 1944 to date.*

* Military ranks throughout this section are as of May 1, 1944.

SUMMARY OF OPERATIONS—*August 1942 to March 1, 1944* †

SORTIES FLOWN	TONS OF BOMBS DROPPED	—PLANES LOST IN AERIAL COMBAT—	
		ENEMY	AAF
107,001	92,468	5304	1509

† Includes 9th Air Force, beginning October 1943.

PRINCIPAL OPERATIONS: The 8th Air Force is the daylight stra tegic bombing force of a combined British-based air offensive against Germany. In cooperation with the Italian-based 15th Air Force, and the night bombing Royal Air Force, its objective is the destruction of the German war machine and of the German will to fight.

In its first mission against the enemy in Occupied France on Aug. 17, 1942, the 8th's striking force consisted of 12 B-17s. By early spring of 1944, its air divisions, hammering deep into Germany, represented an increase of nearly a hundred-fold.

In the intervening months, the 8th had achieved the size demanded for its task; acquired the ability to deliver repeated mass attacks; surmounted the most formidable aerial and antiaircraft opposition encountered in any theater; with the help of the 9th Air Force, built up the fighter escort required; and perfected its tactical employment for continued deep penetrations against priority targets.

The time required to mount these massive attacks was subject to military necessity. The experimental phase of operations against targets in Occupied France was hardly begun before the demands of the African invasion gave the latter first priority to the products of our aircraft factories. Moreover, the heavy loss of shipping to submarine attack made U-boat manufacturing and docking and repair facilities, rather than the German industrial system, the primary 8th Air Force objective through late 1942 and early 1943.

While the Casablanca directive of January 1943 assigned that industrial system as the objective for the strategic air offensive, months were to elapse before means would be available for the required deep daylight penetrations. Meanwhile, in 1943, the July attacks on the Heroya magnesium plant in Norway and the mid-August attacks on Regensburg and Schweinfurt, Germany, established the destructive potential of daylight precision bombing. Virtually each attack became a major air battle. Early in August, 8th Air Force B-24s and crews joined those of the 9th Air Force in an attack from the Middle East on Axis oil refineries at Ploesti, Rumania.

Late September saw the first use of instruments permitting bombing through cloud cover. Soon a significant change appeared in the choice of targets: after the Oct. 4, 1943 assault on Frankfurt, targets in Germany proper became the rule rather than the exception. At the same time, the bombing pace was stepped up: planes dispatched on missions in November showed a 58% increase over October; December exceeded November by another 53%; and in January, despite normal bad weather, the December gain was not only maintained but exceeded by 7%.

By late January 1944 the combined 8th Air Force-RAF bombing offensive was in full swing. On the night of Jan. 28 the RAF attacked Berlin; the next day the 8th Air Force hit Frankfurt with 806 bombers escorted by 634 fighters. On Jan. 30 Brunswick and Hanover were attacked in strength.

These operations heralded a plan of attack, on a scale long projected but hitherto beyond our capacity, directed toward the No. 1 objective—the German Air Force and its industrial means of survival. Between Feb. 20-25, while the RAF struck German factories and defenses with night assaults, the 8th Air Force delivered major blows against more than a dozen airplane factories in Germany. Simultaneously, another arm of the AAF aerial pincers reached up from Italy for the first time as the 15th Air Force sent bombers against Regensburg.

Clear warning of things to come was given to Germany early in March when the 8th Air Force invaded Berlin in repeated daylight attacks. All through March the assault on Germany continued, in good weather and bad. Even greater assaults were in the making.

15TH AIR FORCE

ESTABLISHED: Nov. 1, 1943.

AREA OF OPERATIONS: Germany and Austria, the Balkans, Northern Italy and the Mediterranean Coast of France.

COMMAND: Lt. Gen. James H. Doolittle, Nov. 1, 1943 to Jan. 1, 1944; Maj. Gen. Nathan F. Twining, Jan. 1, 1944 to date.

SUMMARY OF OPERATIONS—*November 1943 to March 1944*

Operations are included in total for 12th Air Force.

PRINCIPAL OPERATIONS: With the occupation of the southern portion of the Italian peninsula and especially the airbase at Foggia, the 15th Air Force was activated as the strategic element of the Mediterranean Allied Air Forces to cooperate with British-based air units. Its place in the overall strategy of air attack against Germany finally became integrated in late February when it took its turn with the 8th Air Force in attacks on aircraft factories in Regensburg, Steyr and Obertraublung. The program began with the 15th's maiden mission against the Messerschmitt factory at Wiener Neustadt, Austria on Nov. 2, 1943; subsequent missions were directed against aircraft factories in Augsburg and Klagenfurt, and ball bearing factories in Turin and Villa Perosa, Italy. Most of the 15th's efforts during the winter of 1943–44, however, were devoted to facilitating the ground campaign in Italy. To this end it made repeated attacks on marshaling yards throughout the peninsula and on the bases of German air operations. For special missions, it also ranged to Toulon and Marseilles, France, to Sofia, Bulgaria, and repeatedly to airfields in the Athens area. On March 15, in the effort to eliminate German ground resistance in Cassino, planes of the 15th Air Force joined by those of the 12th, dropped hundreds of tons of bombs in that area. In the early months of 1944, the 15th was the fastest growing air force in the AAF.

12TH AIR FORCE

ESTABLISHED: Aug. 20, 1942.
AREA OF OPERATIONS: Italy; formerly North Africa, the Western Mediterranean and Sicily.
COMMAND: Lt. Gen. James H. Doolittle, Sept. 23, 1942 to Feb.

23, 1943; Lt. Gen. Carl Spaatz, Feb. 18, 1943 to Jan. 1, 1944; Maj. Gen. John K. Cannon, Jan. 26, 1944 to date.

SUMMARY OF OPERATIONS—*November 1942 to March 1, 1944* *

SORTIES FLOWN	TONS OF BOMBS DROPPED	—PLANES LOST IN AERIAL COMBAT— ENEMY	AAF
199,179	106,567	2959	1473

* Includes operations of 15th Air Force since November, 1943.

PRINCIPAL OPERATIONS: Ever since the first landing of American troops on North African soil, the 12th Air Force has coordinated its primary activities with the movement of Allied ground forces in North Africa, Sicily and more recently in Italy.

In its initial encounters with the German air force over Tunisia in late 1942, fighters and bombers of the 12th repeatedly achieved destruction many times that of their own losses on the ground and in the air. In a 3-month period the 12th accounted for more than 400 enemy planes. On Feb. 18, 1943, to achieve the maximum utility of air strength, the 12th merged with other Allied air units to form the Northwest African Air Forces (see page 24). Four days later it contributed to a heavy concentration of airpower that relieved a dangerous situation at Kasserine Pass for ground units moving toward the coast. Mounting concentrations of air strength were utilized for the March 1943 break-through at the Mareth Line and for the final assaults on Tunis and Bizerte.

The striking power built up for the African campaign was used to reduce resistance on the Italian island of Pantelleria, which surrendered after 12 days of relentless attack by aircraft of the 12th and 9th Air Forces and the RAF. When our armies moved across the Mediterranean to invade Sicily, and throughout the ensuing campaign, the 12th maintained almost unchallenged air superiority. In early September, when a large ground force was in jeopardy on the Salerno beachhead, aircraft of the 12th were instrumental in the air action that made the beachhead secure for continued ground movement northward in Italy. The 12th has maintained air supremacy over most of the Italian peninsula and has attacked the enemy's supplies, communications and troops in the battle zones.

9TH AIR FORCE

ESTABLISHED: April 8, 1942.

AREA OF OPERATIONS: The occupied countries of France, Holland and Belgium; formerly the Middle East.

COMMAND: Lt. Gen. Lewis H. Brereton, June 28, 1942, to date.

SUMMARY OF OPERATIONS—*November 1942 to October 1, 1943* *

SORTIES FLOWN	TONS OF BOMBS DROPPED	—PLANES LOST IN AERIAL COMBAT—	
		ENEMY	AAF
27,080	20,127	610	227

* Later operations are included with those of 8th Air Force.

PRINCIPAL OPERATIONS: As the tactical force of the AAF based in England, the 9th Air Force by early 1944 was engaged in a campaign against enemy fortifications on the Channel coast and against airbases and other military installations in the occupied areas. For most of these operations it employs medium bombardment. The 9th also provides fighter aircraft for long escort missions with the 8th Air Force, missions which have extended deep into Germany.

In the preceding Mediterranean phase of its activities, from June 1942 to the Fall of 1943, the 9th prevented supplies and reinforcements from reaching the African air and ground forces of the Axis by attacks on docks, ports and shipping. For 4 months prior to the break-through at El Alamein, when it rarely had more than 25 planes in the air together, the 9th attacked targets in the harbors of Tobruk and Benghazi, Navarrino Bay (Greece), and on the Mediterranean; it destroyed some 60% of the fuel, food and ammunition sent to the Axis forces. In the same period, its medium bombers and fighters supported the 8th Army in the Battle of El Alamein, while its troop carrier unit transported ammunition, gasoline and supplies to the forward battle area. In the course of the destruction of enemy resistance in Tripoli, Tunisia and Sicily, the arc of the 9th Air Force attack widened to include Italian points such as Naples, Palermo and Messina. Coordinated attacks by the 9th and 12th Air Forces brought about the surrender of Pantelleria.

On July 19, 1943, B-24s attached to the 9th Air Force made the first assault of the war on military targets in Rome and vicinity. On Aug. 1, reinforced by B-24s of the 8th Air Force, the 9th executed the Ploesti attack, and on Aug. 13, similarly reinforced, it struck at the strategically important Messerschmitt plant at Wiener Neustadt, Austria.

Its mission completed with the successful conclusion of the African Campaign, the 9th Air Force was relocated in Great Britain and heavily reinforced for its present tactical duties.

5TH AIR FORCE

ESTABLISHED: Sept. 20, 1941 as Philippine Department Air Force; Oct. 28, 1941 as Far East Air Force; Feb. 5, 1942 as 5th Air Force.

AREA OF OPERATIONS: Southwest Pacific.

COMMAND: Lt. Gen. Lewis H. Brereton, Dec. 7, 1941 to Jan. 18, 1942; Lt. Gen. George H. Brett, Feb. 23, 1942 to Aug. 4, 1942; Lt. Gen. George C. Kenney, Sept. 3, 1942 to date.

SUMMARY OF OPERATIONS—*December 1941 to March 1, 1944*

SORTIES FLOWN	TONS OF BOMBS DROPPED	—PLANES LOST IN AERIAL COMBAT—	
		ENEMY	AAF
117,076	34,249	2172	524

PRINCIPAL OPERATIONS: The 5th Air Force was formed by officers and men who had been forced to retreat from the Philippines and the East Indies and by the first U. S. air reinforcements to arrive in the Southwest Pacific. Its initial operations were from Australian bases.

When the defense of Australia was assured, the 5th initiated a struggle for air superiority against Japanese units based to the north. In August 1942 it supported surface forces in the initial landings on Guadalcanal. Despite lack of aircraft and supply problems, it gradually widened its arc of operations, served as a spearhead for surface offensives northward, helped prevent the supply and reinforcement of enemy bases.

Tactical achievements of the 5th include a refinement of low-level, strafe-bombing attacks, and the successful employment—over water—of mast-head and skip-bombing. In the destruction of parked aircraft and airbase installations, the 5th has specialized in the pinning down of ground defenses with massed forward fire followed by delayed-action and parachute bombs. This has resulted in the destruction of hundreds of enemy aircraft.

On Nov. 4, 1942 the 5th began sustained action against Jap invaders in the Papuan territory of New Guinea. Units of the 5th transported an Allied ground force by air from Australia to the battle area in New Guinea, subsequently combining with the ground forces to drive back the Japanese. On repeated hazardous hops over the 14,000 foot Owen Stanley Range, the 5th transported to forward areas 2 U. S. regiments and an Australian company along with their equipment. It protected these with fighter cover, kept them completely supplied from the air, eventually evacuated their wounded. Thanks to coordinated air-ground action, 14,000 enemy troops were annihilated.

In early March 1943 elements of the 5th sighted a 22-ship enemy convoy enroute from Rabaul to reinforce Jap troops in the Lae-Salamaua area of New Guinea. After some 20 missions employing 174 planes the 5th, with some RAAF support, virtually wiped out the convoy with its 15,000 troops and many tons of equipment at the cost of only one B-17 and 3 P-38s. Throughout 1942–43 the 5th Air Force continually blasted the enemy's supply base at Rabaul.

Heavy pressure maintained by the 5th on Jap bases on New

Guinea and New Britain has enabled Allied ground forces to advance northward. By early 1944 the 5th's striking power had been instrumental in the success of amphibious landings and the resulting occupation of strategic points on Cape Gloucester and in the Admiralty Islands. Its planes had also struck far over-water to Java, Borneo and Truk.

13TH AIR FORCE

ESTABLISHED: Jan. 13, 1943.

AREA OF OPERATIONS: Solomon Islands and Bismarck Archipelago.

COMMAND: Maj. Gen. Nathan F. Twining, Jan. 13, 1943 to Dec. 28, 1943; Maj. Gen. Hubert R. Harmon, Jan. 7, 1944 to date.

SUMMARY OF OPERATIONS—*January 1943 to March 1, 1944* *

SORTIES FLOWN	TONS OF BOMBS DROPPED	—PLANES LOST IN AERIAL COMBAT—	
		ENEMY	AAF
33,085	11,638	739	198

* Includes operations of AAF units in S. Pacific prior to January 1943.

PRINCIPAL OPERATIONS: Throughout 1942 several AAF units operated in guerrilla fashion from islands northeast of Australia. Although numerically weak and functioning under separate base commanders, their B-17s were on constant patrol guarding American supply routes in the South Pacific.

Satisfying the obvious need for centralized command, these separate units were combined in January 1943, with activation of the 13th Air Force. Headquarters was established on Espiritu Santo and reinforcements were brought in. Soon the 13th moved its headquarters to New Caledonia. By this time shipping lanes were secure from attack, and a large part of Guadalcanal was in Allied hands.

Initial objectives of the 13th were to gain air superiority and to support land and sea offensives in the Central Solomons, destroy enemy supply lines in the Northern Solomons. Though organized resistance to ground forces on Guadalcanal ended in early February, the Japanese continued to operate offensively against it from the air. A decisive blow to end this threat was struck in June when in a single day airmen of the 13th, together with Navy and Marine fliers, intercepted an enemy striking force of 120 planes and shot down approximately 75 of them.

In July the 13th moved its headquarters to Henderson Field, Guadalcanal. With the combined Allied offensive gaining strength, the 13th began to neutralize enemy airfields and other installations on Bougainville; support and protect amphibious operations in the Northern Solomons. In December the entire campaign was intensified.

Early 1944 found the 13th part of an offensive force combining aircraft of the Army, Navy, Marine and Royal New Zealand Air Force. The main objective was Rabaul, the enemy's supply depot for channeling reinforcements to Jap bases in the Bismarck and Solomon Island groups. Rabaul had been an established target of the AAF. Planes of the old 19th Bombardment Group attacked it as early as Jan. 25, 1942; throughout 1942–43 it had been hit continually by bombers of the 5th Air Force. By the end of 1943, bases were established close enough to Rabaul to permit fighter escort; the 5th had transferred its operations to the west; Rabaul was left to the 13th.

The 13th concentrated on this target, meanwhile serving as a spearhead for surface forces which took islands and parts of islands, built airfields on them, moved up planes and shipping, took more islands, moved up again, cut off the Japs from supplies and support. When Green Island was taken, the first half of the flanking movement on Rabaul was accomplished. In March, occupation of principal airbases in the Admiralty Islands, northeast of Rabaul, under cover of 5th Air Force planes, completed the encirclement. Strategically, Rabaul ceased to exist as an enemy base. Rabaul and Jap units in the Solomons were left to suffer military starvation.

7TH AIR FORCE

ESTABLISHED: Nov. 1, 1940 as Hawaiian Air Force; Feb. 5, 1942 as 7th Air Force.

AREA OF OPERATIONS: Central Pacific, north of the Equator.

COMMAND: Maj. Gen. Frederick L. Martin, Nov. 2, 1940 to Dec. 18, 1941; Maj. Gen. Clarence L. Tinker, Dec. 18, 1941 to June 7, 1942; Maj. Gen. Howard C. Davidson, June 7, 1942 to June 20, 1942; Maj. Gen. Willis H. Hale, June 20, 1942 to date.

SUMMARY OF OPERATIONS—*December 1941 to March 1, 1944*

SORTIES FLOWN	TONS OF BOMBS DROPPED	—PLANES LOST IN AERIAL COMBAT—	
		ENEMY	AAF
4142	3326	110	60

PRINCIPAL OPERATIONS: The aerial striking force across the Central Pacific to Japan is the 7th Air Force. Its trans-oceanic search missions keep the enemy under constant vigilance; long-range heavy bomber attacks soften up strategic islands for amphibious invasion; medium bombers and fighters move up to bring greater weight against the perimeter defenses of the Japanese; gains are consolidated, and the procedure is repeated from newly won bases. The air action involves pin-point targets and some of the longest overwater operational flights in the AAF.

The 7th felt the first blow of the Japanese at Pearl Harbor, suffered several hundred casualties and the loss of many aircraft. The remaining fighters and bombers were quickly marshaled for the air defense of Hawaii.

Its first offensive opportunity came in June 1942 when an enemy invasion fleet ventured within land-based bomber range of Midway Island. B-17s of the 7th attacked the convoy and aided Marine and Navy aircraft in routing it with heavy losses.

Bombers of the 7th attacked Wake Island in July, and again in December of 1942. In early 1943 they struck Jap bases at Nauru and Tarawa in the Gilbert Island chain, but it was not until Fall of that year, with the construction of advance bases far out in the Central Pacific, that systematic operations against the Gilberts could be undertaken and their invasion accomplished. After heavy aerial attacks on the Marshall Islands from late November 1943 through January 1944, surface action against these positions was begun, thus furnishing more advanced bases for deeper penetration into the system of Japanese island defenses.

10TH AIR FORCE

ESTABLISHED: Feb. 12, 1942.

AREA OF OPERATIONS: India, Burma, Thailand and the Bay of Bengal.

COMMAND: Lt. Gen. Lewis H. Brereton, Feb. 25, 1942 to June 23, 1942; Maj. Gen. Clayton L. Bissell, Aug. 18, 1942 to Aug. 19, 1943; Maj. Gen. Howard C. Davidson, Aug. 19, 1943 to date.

SUMMARY OF OPERATIONS—*April 1942 to March 1, 1944*

SORTIES FLOWN	TONS OF BOMBS DROPPED	—PLANES LOST IN AERIAL COMBAT—	
		ENEMY	AAF
21,233	11,407	210	75

PRINCIPAL OPERATIONS: Offensive operations against Japanese supply ports and transportation facilities in Burma have been the chief concern of the 10th Air Force. As part of the larger strategy to defend India and maintain the aerial supply route to China, this program has been pushed despite handicaps of supply and difficult flying during the monsoon season. Targets of the 10th have included dock and shipping facilities at Rangoon, Moulmein and Akyab; storage facilities at Lashio and Henzada; rail junctions at Rangoon, Mandalay and Sagaing. It has attacked nearly 150 enemy targets, has prevented the enemy's use of much of the rail facilities in Burma, and has sunk an appreciable amount of shipping. The air route of supply over the Himalayas to China was first flown under direction of the 10th Air Force. When this operation was taken over by the Air Transport Command, the 10th and 14th Air Forces shared responsibility for protecting the route. Other achievements of the 10th include extremely long-range attacks on objectives in Thailand. By early spring of 1944 the 10th was cooperating closely with Allied ground forces in Burma.

14TH AIR FORCE

ESTABLISHED: March 10, 1943.

AREA OF OPERATIONS: Southeast and Central China, the South China Sea, Hainan, Formosa, North Burma and Thailand.

COMMAND: Maj. Gen. Claire L. Chennault, March 10, 1943 to date.

SUMMARY OF OPERATIONS—*February 1943 to March 1, 1944*

SORTIES FLOWN	TONS OF BOMBS DROPPED	—PLANES LOST IN AERIAL COMBAT—	
		ENEMY	AAF
10,186	2026	477	126

PRINCIPAL OPERATIONS: Our China-based air force which wears the insignia of the Flying Tiger grew out of the China Air Task Force which in turn originated in the Flying Tigers of the American Volunteer Group. The latter, made up of former AAF, Navy and Marine pilots, had been at war against the Japanese for some 5 months before Pearl Harbor.

In preserving Chinese territory as a base for our future attacks on Japan itself, the 14th Air Force has worked closely with the Chinese army and has engaged the Japanese Air Force for control of the air in Central China. Its activities have persisted despite its meager strength and despite the fact that everything it utilizes —men, materials, fuel and ammunition—has to be brought into China by air (see page 194).

Long composed almost entirely of fighter aircraft, the 14th gradually added medium and heavy bombers. These have attacked Hankow airdrome, the Hong Kong harbor area and Jap bases on the island of Hainan and Formosa. The initial attack on strongly-defended Formosa, trans-shipment base for the enemy's Burma and Pacific bases, was an example of perfect timing and execution. With a force of only 14 B-25s and 15 escorting fighters, the 14th destroyed 42 enemy aircraft and probably destroyed or seriously damaged 12 more. The attack was conducted without loss to the 14th. As a result of its steady attrition of Jap shipping off the South China Coast (274,939 tons in a year), traffic has been forced away from the coastal waters to regions where it is much more accessible to our submarines. An innovation of the 14th is its Chinese-American Composite Wing composed of Chinese airmen trained in the U. S. who fly our B-25s and P-40s. In its early actions the wing successfully bombed and strafed enemy ground troops, supply installations and shipping.

11TH AIR FORCE

ESTABLISHED: Jan. 15, 1942 as Alaskan Air Force; Feb. 5, 1942 as 11th Air Force.

AREA OF OPERATIONS: North Pacific from the Aleutians to the Kurile Islands.

COMMAND: Col. Lionel H. Dunlap, Feb. 17, 1942 to March 8, 1942; Maj. Gen. William O. Butler, March 8, 1942 to Sept. 6, 1943; Maj. Gen. Davenport Johnson, Sept. 6, 1943 to date.

SUMMARY OF OPERATIONS—*December 1941 to March 1, 1944*

SORTIES FLOWN	TONS OF BOMBS DROPPED	—PLANES LOST IN AERIAL COMBAT—	
		ENEMY	AAF
5971[1]	3542[2]	75	35

PRINCIPAL OPERATIONS: When a Japanese invading force struck at Dutch Harbor in early June 1942, in the war's first threat to the North American continent, it expected little or no opposition from land-based aircraft. The invaders were turned back after continuous attacks by fighters and medium bombers of the 11th Air Force operating from secret, advance bases.

When the enemy had established positions out on the Aleutian Island chain the 11th moved after him, making its first attack on the enemy's main base at Kiska on June 11. The last attack came 14 months later, after strikes and sorties conducted in some of the worst weather in the world. So effectively did the 11th persist in its attack on Jap bases that the enemy rarely had a score of planes operative at one time. Construction of advance bases on Adak and Amchitka permitted action at closer range and made possible air assistance to our surface forces when they occupied

Attu in May 1943. After feeling the effects of 3000 tons of bombs, dropped by the 11th in 3609 sorties up to July 29, 1943, and after their supply lines had been cut by the occupation of Attu, the enemy evacuated Kiska without a struggle.

Elimination of the enemy from the Aleutians enabled the 11th to consolidate its hard-won gains, build up new bases, strengthen others and improve its supply lines. Operating principally from Attu, heavy bombers of the 11th began long range attacks on the enemy's bases in the Kurile Islands. By early 1944, despite unfavorable weather conditions, these attacks against the outer fringe of the enemy's homeland were increasing in intensity.

6TH AIR FORCE

ESTABLISHED: Oct. 20, 1940 as Panama Canal Air Force; Aug. 5, 1941 as Caribbean Air Force; Feb. 5, 1942 as 6th Air Force.

AREA OF OPERATIONS: Panama Canal Zone, Caribbean; adjacent areas of Central and South America.

COMMAND: Maj. Gen. Davenport Johnson, Sept. 19, 1941 to Nov. 23, 1942; Maj. Gen. Hubert R. Harmon, Nov. 23, 1942 to Oct. 27, 1943; Brig. Gen. Ralph H. Wooten, Oct. 31, 1943 to date.

PRINCIPAL OPERATIONS: Responsibility for defense of the Panama Canal, our most strategic military possession in the Western Hemisphere, has kept the planes of the 6th Air Force on a round-the-clock alert since the war started, and for months before. Thousands of operational hours and hundreds of thousands of patrol miles have been flown by 6th Air Force fliers in their watch over the Canal. During the crucial period of the U-boat threat they participated in antisubmarine search and attack missions in cooperation with the Antisubmarine Command and the Antilles Air Command. The 6th is responsible for protecting the southern air transport route, which is in itself a year-round task. Hundreds of reconnaissance and photographic missions have been flown by the 6th incidental to the establishment of our chain of new bases in Central America and through the Caribbean islands. More than a score of bases, and a number of auxiliary airfields are utilized by the 6th Air Force. In a typical month, February 1944, nearly 1000 sorties were flown as part of their operational program. A number of squadrons now serving in overseas theaters have had operational training as part of the 6th Air Force, which also schools fliers of other countries of the United Nations.

ANTILLES AIR COMMAND

ESTABLISHED: June 1, 1943.

AREA OF OPERATIONS: Caribbean Sea and Antilles Island chain from Florida to the South American coast.

COMMAND: Brig. Gen. Edwin B. Lyon, May 27, 1943 to May 31, 1943; Brig. Gen. W. P. Hayes, May 31, 1943 to date.

PRINCIPAL OPERATIONS: Aerial protection to the arc of islands known as the Antilles, which form the outward defense to the Panama Canal, has been provided by the Antilles Air Command. Operating under the Antilles Department, which is a component of the Caribbean Defense Command, it is separate from the 6th Air Force although its objectives are largely the same. Operations of the Antilles Air Command have involved 2 areas: the Trinidad Sector, which covers Trinidad, Aruba, Curaçao and Santa Lucia Islands; and the Puerto Rico Sector, covering Puerto Rico, Jamaica and Antigua. Most important function of the Antilles Air Command has been its antisubmarine activity. Although the U-boat no longer is a serious menace in the area, for the first 18 months of war it was an ever-present threat to shipping through the Caribbean. Bombardment squadrons of the command, usually confined to the use of obsolete B-18 aircraft, flew continuous missions against U-boats.

ANTISUBMARINE COMMAND

ESTABLISHED: Oct. 15, 1942; inactivated Aug. 24, 1943.

AREA OF OPERATIONS: North and Middle Atlantic Ocean, from Newfoundland to Trinidad; Bay of Biscay and the approaches to North Africa.

COMMAND: Maj. Gen. Westside T. Larson, Oct. 15, 1942 to Aug. 24, 1943.

SUMMARY OF OPERATIONS—*October 15, 1942 to August 24, 1943*

HOURS FLOWN	SUBMARINES ATTACKED	SUBMARINES DESTROYED (Inc. Probables)	SUBMARINES DAMAGED
142,842	52	10	13

PRINCIPAL OPERATIONS: The only unit of the AAF based within the continental U. S. to have a major operational mission has been the Antisubmarine Command. In its 10 months of existence it operated from 4 continents in an expansion of functions formerly performed by the 1st Bomber Command.

When the Antisubmarine Command was activated, the curve of Allied shipping losses by U-boat action was rising dangerously; it reached a high level of 700,000 tons of shipping in December 1942. By the fall of 1943 U-boat losses were down to a tenth of that tonnage; the command had contributed materially to the decrease. During the period of its operations, the percentage of U-boats sunk by air action rose from 10% to 50% of all U-boats sunk in that time.

The Antisubmarine Command used B-17 and B-24 heavy bombers, B-25, B-18 and B-34 medium bombers, and A-20 and A-29 light bombers. Its principal weapon was the B-24, specially equipped with detection instruments, capable of seeking out and attacking submarines 1000 miles at sea. The tedious patrol work, conducted for long hours, with occasional short bursts of action, called for special training and the development of special techniques of air warfare. In August 1943, with the main U-boat threat over, further AAF antisubmarine activities were returned to the 1st Bomber Command, and the Navy increased its operations against the U-boat.

"THE NO. 1 JOB of an air force is bombardment. We must have long range bombers which can hit the enemy before he hits us; in short, the best defense is attack . . ."—Gen. H. H. Arnold.

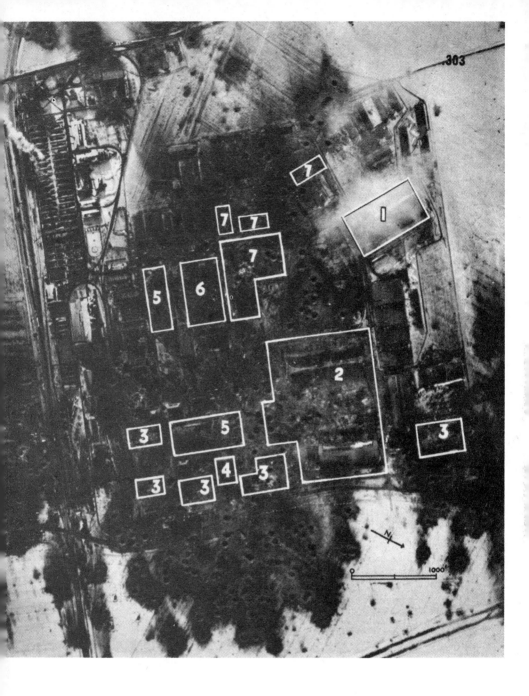

IN THE relentless battle against the Luftwaffe the centers of Nazi aircraft
production are under steady attack. Photographs left (during attack)
and above (after attack) show results of Feb. 20, 1944 smash at Leipzig
plant. Erecting shop (1) still burns; assembly buildings (2) and work-
shops (3) are nearly flattened; powerhouse (4), machine shops (5),
boiler house (6) and other buildings (7) are badly damaged.

ROCKET under wing of Nazi FW-190 is hit and detonated by P-47 fire. Nazis use rocket-bearing planes against bomber formations.

BLAZING Jap bomber below is part of large toll of parked enemy planes taken by low-flying AAF aircraft in the Southwest Pacific.

HITLER'S NO. 1 oil source, Ploesti, Rumania, was bombed Aug. 1, 1943, by a large force of B-24s which came in at smokestack level, braved oil and bombs exploding close beneath them to hit refineries, tanks, cracking plants. B-24s flew a 2000 mile round trip.

DAMAGE of 2 smashes at Jap rail bridge in Burma is shown in these pictures, taken during second attack. Top: south span (A) and parallel bridge (C) still useless after first raid, but bridge largely rebuilt by pontoons (B). Center: bridge hit again. Bottom: results.

IN dropping paratroopers, C-47s usually come in low to take advantage of smoke screen and shorten vulnerable descent of troops.

PHOSPHORUS bombs which scatter incendiary fragments upon impact are used in Pacific against ack-ack positions, parked planes.

DURING the Tunisian campaign Nazis tried to shuttle personnel in huge 6-engine transports. Many suffered fate of the one above.

AT LEAST 42 planes, most of them parked, were destroyed when AAF airmen, including some Chinese, surprised Japs in war's first raid on Formosa.

PRIORITY TARGETS for bombers over Europe are enemy manufacturing centers and supply arteries. The Renault plant outside of Paris (above) produced trucks and tanks for Nazis. Foggia (below) was a hub for German railroad traffic moving into southern Italy.

STRIKING OUT in advance of ground and naval forces, AAF bombers are keeping the Japs off balance in the Pacific, opening the way for new offensives with almost daily bombings of enemy island outposts like Nauru (above) and endless attacks on Jap shipping (below).

MANY airmen owe their lives to the sturdiness of our planes, built to take the worst that the enemy has to offer. Even a mid-air collision with a Nazi fighter failed to down B-17 above; the P-47 below flew back to base with a big chunk of one wing shot away.

CLASSIC precision bombing featured this attack by 100 B-17s on a Focke-Wulf assembly plant at Marienburg on Oct. 9, 1943. Results (above): two assembly buildings (1) gutted; another (2) damaged; hangars (3) gutted; stores and buildings (4) and boiler house (5) destroyed; other buildings (6) damaged. Cost to AAF: 2 B-17s. Pictures at left show target before (top) and during attack (bottom).

IDEAL condition for precision bombing is perfectly clear weather (above) through which every detail of target can be seen. Overcast, however, no longer protects the enemy. Electronic devices now make it possible to bomb through overcast (below) with good accuracy.

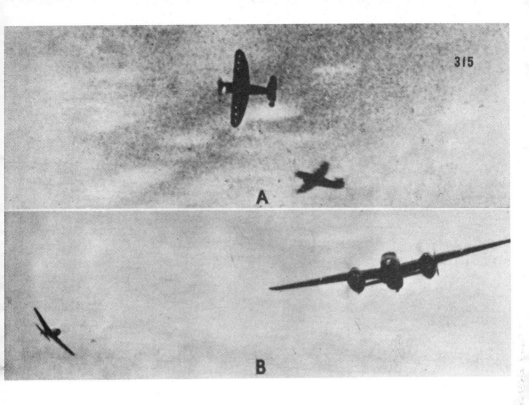

315

(A) P-47 chases Nazi FW-190. Germans try to avoid combat with our fighters, go for bombers. (B) Jap fighter begins futile pass at B-25.

FIGHTERS protect bomber formations at high altitudes where thin, freezing air makes vapor trails like these left by P-47s.

BERLIN in early 1944 was added to the list of AAF heavy bombers' daylight targets. Emphasis was on factories producing for the German air
force. Erkner ball-bearing plant (above), making half the Luftwaffe's
bearing needs, got this treatment on March 8, 1944.

BATTLE HONORS

Our combat air forces are no stronger than their component parts. Their effectiveness against the enemy can be measured in terms of unit strength, unit pride, unit solidarity. The result is greater battle efficiency, greater daring, greater success.

Battle honors, or unit citations, are awarded "in the name of the President as public evidence of deserved honor and distinction." You can distinguish members of cited units by the blue ribbons framed in gold over their right breast pockets; a bronze oak leaf cluster is awarded for each citation in addition to the first.

As of March 1, 1944, World War II battle honors had been awarded to 15 different AAF units and to 3 other military organizations in which AAF units were included. A report on AAF unit citations follows:

THE 5TH INTERCEPTOR COMMAND, part of the Far East Air Force which had been heavily damaged by the Japanese surprise air attacks on Clark and Nichols Fields in December, 1941, helped prolong the defense of Bataan and Corregidor against an enemy superior in numbers and resources. The 5th withdrew to Bataan for a stand with other U. S. and Philippine forces in early January, 1942. There, beyond reinforcement and supply, it operated from inadequately defended airfields, between Jan. 6 and March 8, 1942, repeatedly carrying out perilous reconnaissance missions. Time and again it executed surprise attacks against the enemy's ground, air and naval elements.

THE 19TH BOMBARDMENT GROUP (heavy) has been twice cited, once for its performance from Jan. 1 to March 1, 1942, and again for the period Aug. 7–12, 1942. During the first period the 19th opposed the numerically superior Japanese during the enemy drive through the Philippines and Netherlands East Indies to Java, employed all available aircraft to strike wherever the enemy could be found. Despite adverse weather and lack of adequate maintenance personnel, the 19th daily inflicted great damage upon the enemy. The second citation recognizes the accomplishment of repeated long-range bombing attacks on heavily defended Japanese ground, air and naval elements near Rabaul, New Britain. In the face of hazardous weather, interception by superior numbers of enemy fighters, and intense antiaircraft fire on practically every mission, damage to enemy targets was extensive. (Also cited twice as a unit of 2 organizations engaged in defense of the Philippines, and again as a unit of U. S. Papuan Forces.)

 THE 17TH PURSUIT SQUADRON (provisional) in the defense of Java and other South Pacific islands from Jan. 14 to March 1, 1942, took part in combined operations that checked the Japanese and saved the Allied fleet at Soerebaja. While escorting A-24 dive bombers, the 17th repeatedly entered into combat against a numerically stronger enemy. In less than one month the squadron, under great difficulties, destroyed 38 enemy planes. (Also cited twice as a unit of 2 organizations engaged in the defense of the Philippines.)

 THE 7TH BOMBARDMENT GROUP (heavy) from Jan. 14 to March 1, 1942, threw all available aircraft against outnumbering Jap forces, hit. the enemy wherever and whenever possible during his drive through the Philippines and the Netherlands East Indies to Java. Outstanding performance was achieved despite unfavorable weather, hazardous landing field conditions and persistent fatigue on the part of combat crews exhausted by unremitting operations. Handicapped by shortages of manpower and supplies, ground units, working under enemy fire, successfully handled an excessive maintenance and repair burden.

THE 49TH FIGHTER GROUP defended the area of Darwin, in northwestern Australia, during the time of greatest threat to that vital port. In March 1942 Darwin lay directly in the path of the Japanese as they swept down the Netherlands East Indies. From March 14 to Aug. 25 the 49th intercepted the enemy on every attempted attack. Although greatly outnumbered by the attackers, the 49th exacted a toll from the foe far out of proportion to its own losses. Its combat record and the number of airplanes it kept in action under difficult field conditions were major factors in the successful defense of Darwin. (Also cited as a unit of U. S. Papuan Forces.)

THE 435TH BOMBARDMENT SQUADRON (heavy), a unit of
the 19th Bombardment Group (heavy), between
Sept. 10 and Oct. 10, 1942, fulfilled frequent reconnaissance and photographic missions with unescorted
Flying Fortresses, inflicted severe damage on the
enemy over a wide area including New Guinea, New Britain,
New Ireland and the Solomon Islands. Hampered by adverse
weather which necessitated low flying for observation, and by
hostile antiaircraft fire and fighter attacks, the 435th secured and
transmitted accurate information on enemy shipping, made valuable photographs of important enemy-held bases and areas, and
damaged enemy aircraft, ground installations and shipping. Not-
withstanding many hours of flight and repeated combat damage,
the ground echelon maintained 80% of the aircraft in combat
condition at all times. (The 435th was also cited as a unit of the
19th Group for action Aug. 7-12, 1942, and as a unit of the
U. S. Papuan Forces.)

THE 11TH BOMBARDMENT GROUP (heavy) from July 31 to
Nov. 30, 1942, continually attacked superior Japanese
air units during the enemy attempt to gain a stronger
foothold in the Solomon Islands. It inflicted heavy
damage upon enemy airfields, storage and supply
areas, seaplane bases, troop positions and other installations; sank
4 Japanese ships, damaged 15 more and probably damaged 9
others. Throughout these operations, the 11th faced and solved
extremely difficult problems of logistics and made long, hazardous
overwater flights to reach enemy objectives which frequently
were located at the extreme flying range of its airplanes.

THE 374TH TROOP CARRIER GROUP, taking part in the Papuan campaign, New Guinea, from Sept. 19 to Dec. 22, 1942, flew an average of 100 tons of supplies daily to troops in forward areas and
daily evacuated casualties. Using various types of unarmed aircraft, the 374th successfully accomplished its assigned mission in
the face of attack by Japanese warplanes, including the transport
to battle areas of several thousand troops. (Also cited as a unit of
U. S. Papuan Forces.)

THE 44TH, 93RD, 98TH, 376TH AND 389TH BOMBARDMENT GROUPS
(heavy) carried out the mass low-level attack on the Axis oil refineries at Ploesti, Rumania, on Aug. 1, 1943. Flying from Middle
East Theater bases without fighter escort, they covered a round-
trip distance of more than 2400 miles over the Mediterranean
and defended enemy territory. The planes were prepared by the

ground echelons of the 5 groups, including 3 which arrived in the theater with insufficient service and maintenance personnel. Confronted with an innovation in aerial combat, the air echelons trained untiringly for this hazardous and experimental mission, committing to memory minute details as to their assigned targets, expected enemy defenses and the landmarks of their long flight.

THE 480TH ANTISUBMARINE GROUP, pioneer AAF organization for offensive antisubmarine operations in the Eastern Hemisphere, from Nov. 10, 1942 to Oct. 28, 1943, played a significant part in winning the battle of the Atlantic and in United Nations' operations in North Africa, Sicily and Italy. Operating from bases in the European and North African theaters, it covered Atlantic shipping lanes with missions extending as far as 1250 miles from base and lasting as long as 17 hours. Flying alone, airplanes of the 480th attacked and defeated Ju-88s and FW-200s, and although outnumbered in an average ratio of 1 to 3, destroyed 2 enemy airplanes for every one lost. The unit's killed and missing numbered 101 officers and men, nearly 50% of its strength of 240.

THE INDIA-CHINA WING, Air Transport Command, during December 1943, substantially exceeded the tonnage quota set for transportation of vital supplies to China by air, a quota which itself exceeded the tonnage of lend-lease cargo moved in a month over the Burma Road before its closing by the Japanese in April, 1942. The wing made this record by flying continuously at altitudes of from 18,000 to 22,000 feet, under treacherous weather conditions, through territory patrolled by enemy fighter aircraft.

MEDAL OF HONOR

The massed power of our air forces and the fighting strength of their units are built upon the accomplishments of individual AAF crewmen. Although virtually every move in combat is related to the operation of a machine, our machines are useless without men to run them—men who are willing to put their lives on the line when the situation demands.

Heroism cannot be measured solely in terms of official recognition. Such phrases as "conspicuous gallantry," "undaunted bravery," and "complete contempt for personal danger," all common to the citations, are not wholly adequate. Each heroic deed speaks for itself; sooner or later its impact is felt by every American.

The nation's highest military decoration, the Medal of Honor, is bestowed by the President of the United States in the name of Congress for deeds of surpassing valor, of devotion far above the call of duty.

Up to March 1, 1944, the following AAF officers and men had received the Medal of Honor in this war:

LT. GEN. JAMES H. DOOLITTLE

GEN. DOOLITTLE

APRIL 18, 1942: For 3 months before they took off from the deck of the aircraft carrier, Lt. Gen. (then Lt. Col.) James H. Doolittle trained his 16 volunteer aircrews at domestic bases. Day after day they had lifted their B-25s from runways the size of a carrier deck, had bombed dummy Jap cities. By the time they were on the carrier *Hornet* steaming toward Japan, they knew their targets as well as the palms of their hands.

The plan was to take off about 400 miles from Tokyo. About 800 miles away the *Hornet* encountered a Jap trawler. The carrier's guns sank the boat, but there was no way of knowing whether a radio signal had been flashed to the mainland. An instant decision was made: Gen. Doolittle and his raiders left the carrier 400 miles ahead of schedule.

They came in over Japan by daylight at a few hundred feet. The Japs were caught flatfooted. They scurried wildly through the streets as the B-25s laid the first bombs of the war on the Japanese mainland. Gen. Doolittle's painstaking organization and daring leadership had paid off.

On leaving the targets, the planes ran into strong headwinds and storms which exhausted their gas supply. All were forced to make crash or parachute landings. Although most of the crews came down in friendly territory and eventually made their way to safety, a few of the crewmen were forced down behind enemy lines. Among these latter were the AAF airmen who were executed by the Japanese.

CAPT. PEASE

CAPT. HARL PEASE, JR.
(reported missing in this action)

AUG. 6-7, 1942: There were good reasons why Capt. Harl Pease, Jr., might not have participated in the Rabaul mission: he was not scheduled to go; he had just returned from a grueling attack on a Jap New Guinea base; his own plane was not fit to fly and the best replacement he could find for it had been declared unserviceable for combat.

Capt. Pease took off from Australia and joined his group at Port Moresby, New Guinea, starting point of the Rabaul mission. He had been flying continuously for almost a full day. Before they left, he snatched 3 hours' sleep.

Near Rabaul about 30 Zeros hopped his formation. For 25 minutes a violent battle was fought. Capt. Pease's airplane—the same that had been called unserviceable for combat the day before—was one of those which bore the brunt of Jap attack. Capt. Pease got through to the target (his gunners knocked down several Japs) and dropped his bombs.

On the way home his crippled airplane fell behind. Zeros were waiting for stragglers. When last seen, Capt. Pease's plane was dropping a flaming gas tank; the Japs were closing in.

GEN. WALKER

BRIG. GEN. KENNETH N. WALKER
(reported missing in this action)

SEPT. 5, 1942—JAN. 5, 1943: During the months he was chief of the 5th Bomber Command, Brig. Gen. Kenneth N. Walker habitually accompanied his fliers on missions deep into enemy territory. From personal combat experience he developed a highly efficient technique of bombing in the face of enemy fighters and antiaircraft fire.

On Jan. 5, 1943, Gen. Walker led a daylight bombing attack on Rabaul. In spite of swarms of Jap interceptors which rose over the harbor to meet them, Gen. Walker's bombers shouldered their way through to the target, planted their bombs squarely on 9 enemy ships.

The Japs turned the full force of their attack on Gen. Walker's airplane. They were too many. His plane went crashing down.

COL. DEMAS T. CRAW
(posthumous: killed in this action)

COL. PIERPONT M. HAMILTON

COL. CRAW

NOV. 8, 1942: The troopship stood offshore at Port Lyautey, French Morocco. Col. Demas T. Craw asked permission to land with the first assault boats. He wanted to try to penetrate the French lines, reach the French commander and persuade him to cease hostilities. Col. Craw was told that it was too dangerous, but he insisted he could do it. Permission was finally granted.

Col. (then Major) Pierpont M. Hamilton volunteered to accompany Col. Craw. They neared the shore in the first wave of assault boats. French batteries bracketed their landing craft with shells. The boat was forced to withdraw, attempt a landing at another beach. Here they made shore in spite of unbroken strafing by 3 enemy airplanes.

COL. HAMILTON

Col. Craw and Col. Hamilton got into a bantam truck and proceeded toward Port Lyautey. As they approached, a concealed machine gun nest opened fire at them from point blank range.

Col. Craw was instantly killed. Col. Hamilton was captured but managed to complete the mission.

LT. JACK W. MATHIS
(posthumous: killed in this action)

LT. MATHIS

MARCH 18, 1943: The bombing accuracy of the entire squadron depended on Lt. Jack W. Mathis. As bombardier of the lead plane in an attack on Vegesack, Germany, his job was to make the calculations for the first run over the target. The rest of the planes in the squadron would bomb according to his sighting.

As Lt. Mathis was beginning to make his run, he was hit by a German ack-ack shell. His right arm was shattered above the elbow, a large wound was torn in his side and abdomen, and he was knocked from his bombsight to the rear of the bombardier's compartment.

Although Lt. Mathis was mortally wounded, he crawled back to the bombsight, released the bombs directly on the target. Following his lead, other bombardiers scored hits. Lt. Mathis died slumped over his bombsight.

S/SGT. MAYNARD H. SMITH

SGT. SMITH

MAY 1, 1943: On the way home from Sgt. Maynard H. Smith's first mission over Europe his B-17 ran into a hotbox of German flak and fighter planes. Antiaircraft and fighter cannon shells ripped through the Fortress. Two crew members were badly wounded, the oxygen system was shot out, several vital control cables were severed and fires broke out simultaneously in the waist section and radio compartment. Three crewmen bailed out into the comparative safety of the sea.

Sgt. Smith went into action. He rushed from his waist guns to fight the flames, to administer first aid to the wounded tail gunner, then back to his guns to drive off enemy fighters zooming in for the kill. The escaping oxygen fanned the fire to such intense heat that the radio, gun mount and camera melted. Ammunition stored in the fuselage began to explode.

Sgt. Smith threw ammunition overboard, fought the fires until all fire-extinguishing aids were exhausted. He gave further first aid to the tail gunner. He manned the workable guns until the Nazi fighters gave up pursuit. Then he wrapped himself in a protecting cloth and batted out the fire with his hands.

The plane got home.

MAJ. JAY ZEAMER, JR.

LT. JOSEPH R. SARNOSKI
(posthumous: killed in this action)

MAJ. ZEAMER

JUNE 16, 1943: Every crewman in the bomber which flew the photographic mission over Buka in the Solomon Islands had volunteered. They were told it was going to be tough.

The bombers flew back and forth over the Jap base taking pictures. When they were almost finished, 20 enemy airplanes took off to attack them. The pilot, Maj. (then Capt.) Jay Zeamer, Jr., continued with the mapping run.

As the first Japs closed in, Lt. Joseph R. Sarnoski, the bombardier, fought them off with bursts from his nose guns, making it possible for the mapping to be completed. Then a coordinated frontal attack by the Japs blasted holes in the bomber, wounded Lt. Sarnoski, Maj. Zeamer and 5 crew members.

Lt. Sarnoski continued firing. Two Jap planes fell to his guns. A 20 mm. shell exploded in the bombardier's compartment. Lt. Sarnoski was hurled out onto the catwalk below the cockpit. Mortally wounded, he crawled back to his guns and fired until he was dead.

The battle blazed on. Maj. Zeamer was shot in both arms and legs. One leg was broken. But he stayed at the controls, steadfastly refusing medical aid. He maneuvered the plane to

LT. SARNOSKI

help his crewmen shoot down at least 4 enemy fighters. Maj. Zeamer got one himself.

Not until the Japs broke combat did Maj. Zeamer relinquish the controls. Even then he continued to exercise command. The 580-mile journey home was made under his direction.

2ND LT. JOHN C. MORGAN

JULY 28, 1943: Continent bound, a B-17 formation was nearing the German coast. The Fortress in which 2nd Lt. (then Flight Officer) John C. Morgan was flying as copilot was beset by a swarm of Nazi fighters. German guns knocked out the oxygen system that supplied the tail, waist and radio gun positions. Cannon shells smashed into the cockpit. The pilot's skull was split open. He fell over his steering wheel, grasped it tightly. The plane began to waver.

LT. MORGAN

Lt. Morgan seized the controls on his side and by sheer strength pulled the plane back into formation. The pilot, not conscious of what he was doing, tried to wrest the controls away from Lt. Morgan. A shattered interphone made it impossible to call for help.

Meanwhile the top turret gunner, severely wounded, fell from his position. The waist, tail and radio gunners were unconscious from lack of oxygen.

Lt. Morgan had to decide whether to turn back immediately and risk getting through the enemy fighters alone or to try to fly all the way to the target and back within the protection of the formation. In spite of the wild efforts of the fatally wounded pilot to take over the controls, Lt. Morgan chose to make the long flight with the formation.

For 2 hours he held his position—flying with one hand, fighting off the pilot with the other. At length the navigator entered the compartment and relieved the situation. Lt. Morgan's airplane got through to the target, dropped its bombs and flew safely home.

GEN. JOHNSON

BRIG. GEN. LEON W. JOHNSON

COL. JOHN R. KANE

MAJ. JOHN J. JERSTAD
(reported missing in this action)

2ND LT. LLOYD H. HUGHES
(posthumous: killed in this action)

LT. COL. ADDISON E. BAKER
(reported missing in this action)

AUG. 1, 1943: Every man and every group that participated in the mission to Ploesti, Rumania, was cited for gallantry. Of all the feats of valor that day, 5 merited awarding of the nation's highest award:

Brig. Gen. (then Col.) Leon W. Johnson and Col. John R. Kane both led B-24 formations that were delayed by weather on the way to Ploesti; both arrived late and found that their objectives had already been hit by other airplanes; both were denied the element of surprise that is vital to a low-level unescorted attack.

COL. KANE

Nazi flak was ready and Nazi fighters were in the air when Gen. Johnson and Col. Kane reached their respective targets. The refineries and tanks which they were to bomb from minimum altitude were blazing and exploding from previous attacks. Delayed action bombs, likely to explode at any moment, lay scattered through the burning rubble. Over all hung a pall of dense black smoke.

Gen. Johnson and Col. Kane attacked. Down they led their flights until flames licked at the bellies of their airplanes. Flak and fighter plane bursts whistled around them; their planes were rocked by oil exploding close below. They dropped their bombs into the inferno.

Maj. John J. Jerstad was due for a leave after completing more than his share of missions and he was no longer connected with the group scheduled to make the attack. But he believed that his long experience would be helpful. When the crews were being picked for the Ploesti mission, he volunteered.

MAJ. JERSTAD

A burst of flak caught his plane 3 miles from the target. It began to burn immediately. Rather than jeopardize the formation he was leading by dropping out, Maj. Jerstad ignored the level landing ground below, stayed on his course. The flames in his plane spread but he managed to get his bombs away accurately. Then his plane plummeted, blazing, into the target area.

Second Lt. Lloyd H. Hughes was in the last formation to hit the target. By the time he was ready to make his run, the Nazis had all their antiaircraft in action and the target was a seething mass of flames. Lt. Hughes came in low, dodged skillfully through barrage balloons. Then ack-ack hit his plane. Sheets of gasoline streamed from the bomb bay and left wing.

LT. HUGHES

Between Lt. Hughes' airplane and the target lay acres of table-top meadow. He had plenty of room and ample time to land safely. But he chose to make the run.

Into the flames he piloted his Liberator, gasoline washing from its sides. When the plane came out, the left wing was ablaze. Only then did he try to land; it was too late. The airplane crashed and burned.

Lt. Col. Addison E. Baker's B-24 was set afire by antiaircraft bursts 3 miles away from his objective. He could have dropped out of the formation he led and have landed in the flat country below, but he refused to place the other planes in danger by breaking formation.

COL. BAKER

With the wind-fanned flames spreading rapidly over his plane, Col. Baker led his flight into the target. His bombs hit true. When he tried to climb up so that his crew could bail out, the fire-ravaged plane would not respond. Skillfully, with what was left of the controls, he took his plane out of the path of the rest of the formation.

Then the plane crashed in flames.

MAJ. CHELI

MAJ. RALPH CHELI
(reported missing in this action)

AUG. 18, 1943: With Maj. Ralph Cheli in the lead plane, the formation of B-25s nosed down and began their dive on the Jap base at Wewak, New Guinea. Enemy fighters swooped in, centered their fire on Maj. Cheli's plane, which burst into flames.

The target was still 2 miles away. Maj. Cheli could have pulled out of the formation and gained enough altitude to parachute to safety. But he knew a broken formation would give the Japs a great advantage. He stayed.

With flames streaming from his airplane, he led the low-level bombing and strafing attack. When the mission was completed, he told his wing man to take over as formation leader. Then he crashed into the sea.

COL. KEARBY

COL. NEEL E. KEARBY

OCT. 11, 1943: Col. Neel E. Kearby's mission was completed. He had led a flight of 4 P-47s to reconnoiter the heavily defended Jap base at Wewak, New Guinea. Fuel was running low, and they were on their way home. Suddenly Col. Kearby saw an enemy fighter below him. He dived. The Jap went down burning.

Then the 4 plane formation sighted 12 enemy bombers escorted by 36 fighters. Col. Kearby ordered an attack. Leading the way, he dove into the midst of the Japs, shot down 3 in quick succession. He knocked down another 2 who were on the tail of one of his comrades.

The Japs broke formation to make a multiple attack on Col. Kearby's airplane. He made one more pass before seeking cloud protection. Back in the clear, he called his flight together and led them to a friendly base.

WAR CALENDAR

A Chronological Report on the AAF Since Pearl Harbor

(For a chronological report on military aeronautics from April 19, 1861, to Dec. 7, 1941, see *Historical Highlights*, page 339.)

1941: DEC. 7. Japanese attack Pearl Harbor with about 105 carrier-based planes, strike Hickam and Wheeler Fields, Hawaii, destroy 97 U. S. planes including 23 AAF bombers and 66 fighters; 226 officers and enlisted men are killed or later die of wounds; 396 more are wounded. AAF fighter pilots shoot down more than 20 Jap planes.

DEC. 7-8. Japanese land and carrier-based planes in heavy force attack Army installations and aircraft at Clark and Nichols Fields, P. I. and the P-40 base at Iba, P. I., destroying all but 72 of approximately 290 planes in the Islands.

DEC. 8. First duel of war between U. S.-manned heavy bomber and enemy fighter reported during Jap attack on Clark Field, P. I.

DEC. 9. First U. S. bombing mission of war is flown when B-17s of 19th Gp attack enemy ships off the east coast of Vigan, Luzon, P. I. Several hits are scored; one ship believed sunk.

DEC. 9. A B-17 of the 19th Gp scores hits on a 29,000-ton Japanese battleship of Haruna class; pilot, Capt. Colin P. Kelly.

DEC. 10. 16 B-17s of 19th Gp constitute entire bombardment striking force of AAF in the Far East. About 30 fighters remain in the Philippines.

DEC. 11. Western Defense Command designated a Theater of Operations, assigned the 2nd and 4th Air Forces.

DEC. 15. AAF submits "An Estimate of the Situation and Recommendations for the Conduct of the War" to the War Department.

DEC. 17. Lt. Gen. D. C. Emmons replaces Lt. Gen. Walter G. Short as commander of Hawaiian Department.

DEC. 18. Maj. Gen. C. L. Tinker assumes command of the Hawaiian Air Force.

DEC. 20. At least 4 Japanese bombers are downed near Kunming, China, in first action of American Volunteer Group (AVG).

DEC. 22. First U. S. bombing mission from Australia flown by B-17s attacking ships in Lingayen Bay and off Davao, P. I. Distance: 4000 miles.

DEC. 24. 4th Air Force bomber reports sinking of U-boat off California.

DEC. 24. Eastern Theater of Operations created and assigned the 1st and 3rd Air Forces.

DEC. 31. AAF casualties in Philippines for month of December: 122 officers and men dead, 162 wounded. Enemy air losses: 40 planes destroyed.

1942: JAN. 1. AAF strength: 360,216 officers and men.

JAN. 13. Sikorsky XR-4, single rotary wing, 2-man helicopter, makes first successful flight.

JAN. 15. Hq and Hq Sq, Alaskan Air Force, activated at Elmendorf Field, Alaska.

JAN. 23. Flying Training Command established under the Chief of Air Corps.

JAN. 23-25. AAF B-17s and other Allied bombers join with U. S. naval units to sink 8 to 12 ships in Battle of Macassar Strait.

JAN. 28. Hq and Hq Sq, 8th Air Force, activated at Savannah, Ga.

FEB. 3. First operation of P-40s in Netherlands East Indies: 1 Jap bomber and 1 fighter downed.

FEB. 5. Alaskan Air Force redesignated 11th Air Force; Caribbean Air Force redesignated 6th Air Force; Hawaiian Air Force redesignated 7th Air Force; Far East Air Force is redesignated 5th Air Force.

FEB. 9. 101st aerial victory reported by AVGs.

FEB. 12. About this date tail guns (.50 cal.) are first used by B-17s in SW Pacific.

FEB. 12. 10th Air Force activated at Patterson Field, Ohio.

FEB. 23. Air Corps Officer Candidate School established at Miami Beach, Fla.

FEB. 25. Maj. Gen. L. H. Brereton assumes command of newly formed 10th Air Force at New Delhi, India.

MAR. First 4-engine C-54 (Douglas) troop and cargo transport is delivered to the AAF.

MAR. 10th Air Force begins to cooperate with Allies in evacuation of Burma.

MAR. 8. Col. W. O. Butler assumes command of 11th Air Force, Alaska.

MAR. 9. In a reorganization of the War Department, the Army Air Forces, Army Ground Forces, and the Services of Supply are established on a coordinate footing. The reorganized General Staff is composed of approximately 50% Air Corps officers. Functions of the Commanding General, Air Force Combat Command and Chief of Air Corps are vested in Lt. Gen. H. H. Arnold, Commanding General, AAF.

MAR. 20. Eastern Theater of Operations redesignated Eastern Defense Command.

APR. 2. Andaman Islands attacked by B-17s in first mission of 7th Bomb Gp from India.

APR. 4. New plan permits college men to enlist in the Air Corps Enlisted Reserve on deferred basis and continue college course until graduation unless previously called by Secretary of War.

APR. 8. 10th Air Force begins flying supplies over the Himalayas to Yunnan Province, China.

APR. 13-14. 3 Australian-based B-17s and 10 B-25s, Brig. Gen. R. Royce commanding, attack Japanese installations and shipping off Philippines.

APR. 18. Tokyo, Nagoya, Kobe and Yokohama attacked by 16 B-25s from USN Carrier *Hornet*, Lt. Col. J. H. Doolittle commanding.

APR. 23. Brig. Gen. I. C. Eaker appointed Chief, U. S. Army Bomber Command in Europe.

APR. 24. Operations of the 1st Ferrying Gp, known as the Trans-India and the Assam-Burma-China Ferrying Commands, reported under way.

APR. 28. 22 Jap planes reported downed over Lashio by AVGs.

MAY 2. Maj. Gen. C. Spaatz assigned command of 8th Air Force.

MAY 4-9. Allied air units in Australia including U. S. planes participate in Battle of Coral Sea.

MAY 12. Units of 8th Air Force arrive in England.

MAY 26. Gulf Task Force, 1st Bomber Command, begins active antisubmarine warfare.

JUNE 3. Flight training for West Point cadets begins, first major elective in the history of the Academy. Training is given at Stewart Field, 12 miles north of West Point, with first class numbering more than 200.

JUNE 3 & 5. Bombers, torpedo planes and fighters of the 11th Air Force help turn back Japanese task force from Dutch Harbor in Jap assault on Aleutians.

JUNE 3-7. Seventh Air Force B-17s and torpedo-armed B-26s aid in repulsing Jap invasion fleet during battle of Midway.

JUNE 11. Eleventh Air Force bombers make first attack on Kiska, main Jap Aleutian base.

JUNE 12. Twelve AAF B-24s attack oil fields at Ploesti, Rumania.

JUNE 20. Ferrying Command is reconstituted and redesignated Air Transport Command with 2 divisions: Ferrying and Air Transportation. Original Air Transport Command is redesignated Troop Carrier Command.

JUNE 28. Maj. Gen. L. H. Brereton arrives in Cairo from India and assumes command of U. S. Army Middle East Air Force.

JULY 1. Hq AAF Foreign Service Concentration Command established.

JULY 1. Brig. Gen. Claire L. Chennault assumes command of newly formed China Air Task Force which makes its first operation on this date.

JULY 4. First U. S.-shared attack is made on German occupied territory in Europe; 12 RAF Bostons, 6 manned by AAF airmen, drop bombs on airdromes in Holland.

JULY 4. 23rd Fighter Gp, 10th Air Force, takes over AVG (Flying Tigers).

JULY 8. Flight Officer Act authorizes title of flight officer.

JULY 10. First plane of ATC lands at Ascension Island on new S. Atlantic route.

JULY 10. Maj. Gen. C. Spaatz appointed Chief, U. S. Army Air Forces in Europe.

JULY 12. Activation of following ATC wings: North Atlantic, South Atlantic, Pacific, Africa-Middle East, Caribbean.

JULY 23. First B-24s of the 98th Gp arrive in Middle East Theater under command of U. S. Middle East Air Force.

AUG. 3. In their first combat action 11th Air Force P-38s down 2 Jap flying boats.

AUG. 4. Maj. Gen. G. C. Kenney succeeds Lt. Gen. G. H. Brett as commander, Allied Air Forces, SW Pacific area.

AUG. 14. First German aircraft destroyed in combat in Iceland area by the AAF is a FW-Kurier shot down by a P-39.

AUG. 14. Foreign Service Concentration Command becomes the AAF 1st Concentration Command (ceases operations Dec. 5, 1942).

AUG. 17. Railway yards and shops at Rouen, France, attacked in first mission flown by 8th Air Force in their own aircraft; 18 planes participated, 12 over the target, 6 in a diversionary sweep along French coast.

AUG. 18. Brig. Gen. Clayton Bissell assumes command of 10th Air Force.

AUG. 19. First German aircraft to be shot down over Europe by a U. S. fighter pilot is destroyed over Dieppe.

AUG. 20. Hq and Hq Sq, 12th Air Force activated at Bolling Field, D. C.

AUG. 25. AAF Cold Weather Testing Detachment activated at Ladd Field, Alaska.

SEPT. 1. Joint AAF-RAF fighter sweep over North French coast marks first operational flight for P-38s in European theater.

SEPT. 1. First airborne engineering unit activated at Westover Field, Mass.

SEPT. 3. U. S. units of Allied Air Forces in Australia become 5th Air Force. Lt. Gen. G. C. Kenney assumes command.

SEPT. 12. First use of parafrags (parachute fragmentation bombs) by 5th Air Force against Buna airbase; force of heavy, medium and attack bombers with fighter escort destroys 17 Jap planes on ground.

SEPT. 20. About this date B-17s are fitted with external wing bomb racks.

SEPT. 23. Brig. Gen. J. H. Doolittle assumes command of the newly formed 12th Air Force in England.

OCT. 2. DSM awarded Lt. Gen. H. H. Arnold, Commanding General, AAF, for conspicuous demonstration of leadership upon completion of flight from Brisbane, Australia to Bolling Field, D. C.

OCT. 9. In heaviest U. S. daylight attack to date, industrial plants at Lille, France, attacked by 8th Air Force heavy bombers.

OCT. 15. Antisubmarine Command activated at Mitchel Field, N. Y., with Brig. Gen. W. T. Larson commanding.

OCT. 17. Alaskan Wing of ATC activated.

NOV. 7. North African campaign opens. For landing operations of U. S. troops in North Africa, paratroopers are flown to scene in 47 AAF transports on 1400-mile trip from bases in England.

NOV. 8. Maj. Gen. J. H. Doolittle announced as Commander, 12th Air Force in North Africa; Lt. Gen. Frank M. Andrews, as Commander, U. S. Army Forces, Middle East; Maj. Gen. L. H. Brereton commanding Middle East Air Force. Lt. Gen. G. H. Brett replaces Lt. Gen. Andrews as Chief of Caribbean Defense Command.

NOV. 12. Middle East Air Force, redesignated 9th Air Force.

NOV. 17. AAF School of Applied Tactics established at Orlando, Fla.

NOV. 22. Japanese-held rail center at Mandalay, Burma, attacked by largest formation of U. S. bombers to operate from airbases in India.

NOV. 26. Attack on Japanese-held Thailand made by nine 10th Air Force B-24s. Distance: more than 2000 miles to Bangkok and return.

NOV. 30. About this date Lt. Gen. C. Spaatz arrives in North Africa from London to reorganize Allied Air Forces.

DEC. 1. Maj. Gen. I. C. Eaker assumes command of 8th Air Force in England.

DEC. 1. Air Transport Command takes over operation of ferrying and supply to China.

DEC. 4. In first U. S. attack on Italian mainland, twenty four 9th Air Force B-24s attack Naples and harbor.

DEC. 7. P-40s go into action for the first time in Tunisia.

DEC. 22. In longest offensive massed flight made to date, 26 B-24s of the 7th Air Force stage midnight surprise attack on Wake Island. Distance: 4300 nautical miles, with only stopping point being Midway.

DEC. 25. First Air Evacuation Transport Squadron leaves for North Africa.

DEC. 28. P-38s make debut in New Guinea.

DEC. 30. U-boat pens at Lorient, France, attacked by 8th Air Force bombers; 29 enemy fighters downed.

1943: JAN. 13. Brig. Gen. N. F. Twining assumes command of the newly formed 13th Air Force in South Pacific area.

JAN. 14. European Wing of ATC activated.

JAN. 27. In first U. S. bomber attack on Germany, 53 B-17s of 8th Air Force strike Wilhelmshaven: 2 B-17s hit Emden, and 23 B-24s bomb area near Zuider Zee.

FEB. 4. Lt. Gen. Frank M. Andrews becomes Commanding General, European Theater of Operations.

FEB. 18. 12th Air Force and RAF units in North Africa merge as Northwest African Air Forces (NWAAF), Lt. Gen. C. Spaatz commanding—Maj. Gen. J. H. Doolittle commands Strategic Air Force; Air Vice Marshal Sir Arthur Coningham, RAF, commands Tactical Air Force.

MAR. 1. First group of students begin pre-aviation cadet training under the AAF College Training Program.

MAR. 1-4. In Bismarck Sea action, 174 planes of 5th Air Force and RAAF drop 213 tons of bombs, wiping out virtually an entire convoy and its supplies as well as nearly a division of troops, proceeding from Rabaul to Lae.

MAR. 10. P-47s of 8th Air Force, in their initial combat employment, engage in a sweep off Walcheren Islands, Netherlands.

MAR. 10. Hq and Hq Sq of 14th Air Force activated at Kunming, China, replacing the China Air Task Force operating under 10th Air Force; Brig. Gen. Claire L. Chennault continues in command.

MAR. 18. Automatic flight control equipment linked to Norden bombsight proves combat merit in 8th Air Force operation by 73 B-17s and 24 B-24s over Vegesack, Germany. One submarine capsized, 6 damaged; 52 enemy planes shot down, 20 probables, 23 damaged.

MAR. 19. Lt. Gen. H. H. Arnold, Commanding General, AAF, nominated by Pres. Roosevelt for promotion to full general; he becomes first airman to win this rank.

MAR. 26. Test of first B-25 armed with 75 mm cannon is completed by AAF Proving Ground Command.

MAR. 29. In AAF reorganization, Hq directorates abolished, their functions being assigned to Commands and Assistant Chiefs of Air Staff.

MAR. 29. Flight Control Command established.

APR. 4. Renault Works at Billancourt, France, attacked by 85 B-17s of 8th Air Force.

APR. 17. Focke-Wulf aircraft works near Bremen attacked by over 100 B-17s of 8th Air Force dropping 265 tons of bombs; 63 enemy planes shot down, 15 probables, 17 damaged.

APR. 18. Catania Harbor in Sicily bombed by 12 B-24s and by 48 P-40s of 9th Air Force; 74 German transports and escorting fighters destroyed, 21 enemy planes damaged.

APR. 29. Civil Air Patrol made an auxiliary of the AAF.

MAY 1. B-24s, B-25s, P-38s and P-40s make 104 sorties to Kiska and Attu.

MAY 3. Lt. Gen. Frank M. Andrews killed in plane crash, Iceland.

MAY 7. With aid of heavy supporting aerial barrage, Allied troops enter Tunis and Bizerte.

MAY 14. A heavy blow struck by 4 simultaneous missions of U. S. bombers attacking military objectives at Kiel, Germany; Antwerp and Courtrai, Belgium; and Ijmuiden, Holland.

JUNE 2. Chinese forces, aided by 14th Air Force, check Jap advance into Yangtze River Valley and dislodge Japs from part of Hunan.

JUNE 6. Pantelleria, Mediterranean island stronghold of Italy, bombed by AAF since early May, receives heavy attack by 12th Air Force.

JUNE 11. Heavy and medium bombardment by 12th and 9th Air Forces, with fighters participating, compels surrender of Pantelleria; 10,000 prisoners are taken by occupation forces.

JUNE 16. Japanese air task force over Guadalcanal area intercepted and routed; 32 enemy bombers and 45 Zeros destroyed or damaged.

JUNE 22. AAF awarded National Safety Council Medal for distinguished services.

JUNE 28. Messina, Sicily, attacked in heaviest single operation of Mediterranean war to date by over 100 B-17s of 12th Air Force.

JUNE 30. AAF strength: 2,186,603 officers and enlisted men.

JULY 1. Jacqueline Cochran appointed Director of AAF women pilots' program.

JULY 7. AAF Training Command established, combining functions of Flying Training Command and Technical Training Command; Hq., Ft. Worth, Tex.; Maj. Gen. B. K. Yount, commanding.

JULY 9. American-built 15-place gliders (CG-4) first employed in Sicily about this date.

JULY 10. Eight 11th Air Force B-25s from bases on Attu bomb Paramushiru, Kurile Islands, in Japanese home waters.

JULY 19. Military targets in Rome attacked by 122 B-24s of 9th Air Force.

JULY 22. Longest bombing mission in SW Pacific to date flown by 6 B-24s of 5th Air Force to Soerebaja, Java. Distance flown: 2400 miles.

JULY 24. Heroya and Trondheim, Norway, attacked by 208 B-17s of 8th Air Force flying without escort.

JULY 28. Auxiliary fuel tanks for increased range employed by supporting P-47s on mission of 95 8th Air Force B-17s against Kassel, Germany.

AUG. 1. Ploesti, Rumania, oil refineries, most important source for Axis petroleum products, attacked at low-level by 162 Libyan-based B-24s of 9th Air Force, reinforced by 8th Air Force aircraft and crews. Distance: 2400 miles.

AUG. 7. Hq., AAF Redistribution Center, established at Atlantic City, N. J., with stations at Atlantic City and Miami Beach, Fla., and rest camps at Lake Lure, N. C., Camp Mystic, Tex., and Castle Hot Springs, Ariz.; redistribution program will classify and assign AAF personnel from overseas.

AUG. 13. 61 B-24s of 9th Air Force attack Wiener Neustadt in German-held Austria in 1200-mile flight.

AUG. 15. U. S. and Canadian troops complete occupation of Kiska, abandoned by Japs after long aerial campaign by 11th Air Force.

AUG. 17. Attack on Regensburg, South Bavaria, by 126 B-17s of 8th Air Force with P-47 escort is first notable example by AAF of shuttle bombing, with planes crossing Europe and landing at N. African bases.

AUG. 17. Schweinfurt attacked by over 180 B-17s of 8th Air Force, which drop 485 tons of high explosives and 88 tons of incendiaries on German ball-bearing plants.

AUG. 24. Of 85 B-17s dispatched from among those participating in the Regensburg, South Bavaria, shuttle attack of Aug. 17, 57 bomb Focke-Wulf plant at Bordeaux, France, on return from N. Africa to England.

AUG. 24. Antisubmarine Command redesignated 1st Bomber Command and assigned to 1st Air Force.

SEPT. 5. Maj. Gen. D. Johnson appointed Commanding General, 11th Air Force.

SEPT. 5-8. Heavy and medium bombers of Northwest African Air Force bomb Italian airbases and transportation facilities south of Naples.

SEPT. 9. P-38s and A-36s cover landing of U. S. units at Salerno, Italy.

SEPT. 10. 1st and 4th Air Forces separated from Eastern and Western Defense Commands respectively and placed directly under Commanding General, AAF.

SEPT. 11. 11th Air Force B-24s and B-25s from Aleutian bases attack Paramushiru and Shimushu Islands.

SEPT. 12. Air Transport Command C-87 begins round trip flight from Patterson Field, Ohio, to India, establishing emergency shipment air freight line. Distance: 28,000 miles. Elapsed time: 12 days.

SEPT. 14-15. Troop Carrier Command of Northwest African Air Force moves 2500 paratroopers into battle area in total of 172 sorties.

SEPT. 13-16. All resources of AAF in Mediterranean concentrated on battle area as Germans counterattack strongly around Salerno. P-38s and A-36s strafe and bomb strong points; B-17s, B-24s, B-25s, B-26s destroy road junctions and supply depots to halt reinforcements; P-40s, P-51s and C-47s also participated. On Sept. 14, AAF flies 1294 sorties in Salerno area.

SEPT. 15. 8th Air Force stages large scale night attack against Romilly-Sur-Seine, Caudron and Citroen Works, Paris, Renault Motor Vehicle Works at Billancourt, and Chartres Airfield.

SEPT. 18-19. More than 200 sorties carried out during night of 18th and throughout a good part of day on the 19th, by 7th Air Force and Navy bombers on Tarawa, Makin, Apamama and Nauru Islands.

SEPT. 22. Large force of Northwest African Air Forces B-25s and B-26s shift attack to German positions east of Naples after Salerno beachhead is made secure.

SEPT. 27. 8th Air Force overcast bombing attack on Emden marks deepest penetration into Germany of P-47s equipped with long-range tanks.

OCT. 9. 8th Air Force B-17s and B-24s attack Arado airframe plant, Anklam; Focke-Wulf 190 plant, Marienburg, Germany; Danzig, and entrance harbor, Gdynia, Poland.

OCT. 12. Various units of 5th Air Force strike Rabaul, Rapopo and Tobera.

OCT. 14. Schweinfurt attacked by 228 B-17s of 8th Air Force.

OCT. 24. Bombing of Wiener Neustadt factory by 12th Air Force B-17s and B-24s marks first attack on German-held Austria from Italian bases.

OCT. 28. AAF Tactical Center established at Orlando, Fla.

NOV. 1. Hq and Hq Sq, 15th Air Force, activated in Mediterranean area.

NOV. 1. Maj. Gen. J. H. Doolittle relieved of duty as Commanding General, 12th Bomber Command, and assigned as Commanding General of newly formed 15th Air Force in Mediterranean area.

NOV. 2. Attack on aircraft assembly center at Wiener Neustadt marks initial operation of 15th Air Force.

NOV. 2. In attack on enemy shipping in Simpson Harbor, Rabaul, 75 medium bombers of 5th Air Force sink 3 destroyers, 6 merchant vessels, 2 freighters, 4 luggers; seriously damage 2 heavy cruisers, 2 destroyers, 7 merchant vessels, 2 tankers; 20 enemy aircraft destroyed on ground. Of intercepting enemy aircraft, 67 destroyed.

NOV. 8. Turin, Italy, ball-bearing plant attacked by 81 B-17s of 15th Air Force.

NOV. 14. Attack on Sofia by 91 B-25s of 12th Air Force marks first air attack on Bulgaria from this theater.

NOV. 15. Mili and Makin Atolls attacked by 8 B-24s of 7th Air Force.

NOV. 15. Nation-wide network of flight control centers completed, using communication facilities of CAA, to provide Army fliers with pilots' advisory service.

NOV. 16. Announcement made that assembly line for P-39s has been set up near Persian Gulf to expedite delivery to USSR.

NOV. 16. Rjukan and Knaben, Norway, attacked by 306 heavies of 8th Air Force.

NOV. 24. Toulon, France, and Sofia, Bulgaria, attacked by bombers of the 15th Air Force.

NOV. 29. Bremen attacked by 154 B-17s of 8th Air Force.

DEC. 13. In a record single day's bombing, 1613 tons of bombs dropped on Bremen, Kiel and Hamburg by more than 600 bombers of 8th Air Force.

DEC. 15. N. African Wing of Air Transport Command activated.

DEC. 17. Collier Trophy for 1942 awarded Gen. H. H. Arnold, Commanding General, AAF.

DEC. 24. German military installations on French coast attacked by over 650 heavy bombers with fighter escort—record number of aircraft dispatched by 8th Air Force to date.

DEC. 30. 1393 tons of bombs dropped on Ludwigshaven through overcast by heavy bombers of 8th Air Force with fighter escort of more than 600, largest number of fighters dispatched in single day to date.

DEC. 31. 14th Air Force Hq announces 125,000 tons of Jap shipping sunk since September.

DEC. 31. More than 1200 tons of bombs dropped on Bordeaux and Paris areas by over 450 heavy bombers of 8th Air Force.

DEC. 31. Announcement made that during December British-based AAF planes have flown approximately 13,-876 sorties from Britain and dropped 14,118 tons of bombs.

1944: JAN. 1. Lt. Gen. C. Spaatz assumes command of U. S. Strategic Air Forces in Europe with Hq in U. K.

JAN. 1. Maj. Gen. J. H. Doolittle assigned to command 8th Air Force, replacing Lt. Gen. I. C. Eaker who is announced as commander of Allied air forces in Mediterranean.

JAN. 4. AAF personnel strength: 2,-385,000 officers and men.

JAN. 7. 1000 tons of bombs dropped on Ludwigshaven through overcast by heavy bombers of 8th Air Force.

JAN. 7-13. About 665 tons of bombs dropped on Jap installations and communications at Madang, Alexishafen and Bogadjim area, New Guinea, by bombers of 5th Air Force.

JAN. 10. Largest B-17 mission yet flown from Italian bases dispatched to attack Sofia, Bulgaria: heavy bombers drop 418 tons of bombs on railyards.

JAN. 11. 1258 tons of bombs dropped on JU-88 factory at Halberstadt, ME-110 assembly plants at Brunswick, and Focke-Wulf factory at Oschersleben, Germany, by heavy bombers of 8th Air Force.

JAN. 21. 1142 tons of bombs dropped over the Calais area by more than 350 heavy bombers of 8th Air Force.

JAN. 28. Reports released of Japanese atrocities against AAF and other U. S. military personnel captured at Bataan and Corregidor as related by the late Lt. Col. W. E. Dyess, Air Corps, and other escaped prisoners of war.

JAN. 29. In largest U. S. operation to date, 1886 tons of bombs dropped through overcast on Frankfurt, Germany, by over 800 bombers of 8th Air Force.

JAN. 30. 1748 tons of bombs dropped through overcast on Brunswick and Hanover, Germany, by AAF bombers of 8th Air Force.

JAN. 30-31. More than 400 heavy bombers with 246 fighter escorts drop 905 tons of bombs on enemy airbases in Villaorba area, Italy.

FEB. 3. Approximately 1190 tons of bombs dropped on Wilhelmshaven, Germany, through overcast by over 500 heavy bombers of 8th Air Force.

FEB. 4. 939 tons of bombs dropped on Frankfurt, Germany, through overcast by over 350 heavy bombers of 8th Air Force.

FEB. 10. 350 tons of bombs dropped on Brunswick, Germany, by over 130 B-17s of 8th Air Force with P-38, P-47 and P-51 escort.

FEB. 10. 140 tons of bombs dropped on Boram Airfield, Wewak, New Guinea, by B-24s of 5th Air Force.

FEB. 11. 388 tons of bombs dropped on Frankfurt, Germany area by over 150 heavy bombers of 8th Air Force with escorting P-38s, P-47s and P-51s.

FEB. 18. Announcement made of transfer of 9th Air Force from Africa to England, which strengthens AAF tactical component of the Allied Command in Europe. British-based 8th and Italian-based 15th Air Forces now form strategic arm. British-based 9th (AAF) and 2nd (RAF) Air Forces form tactical arm.

FEB. 20. In a single daylight operation AAF bombers drop 2218 tons of bombs on industrial centers at Leipzig, Gotha, Brunswick, Tutow, Oschersleben, Rostock and Bernburg, Germany.

FEB. 22. 8th Air Force units based in Britain and 15th Air Force units based in Italy make coordinated attacks on Halberstadt, Oschersleben, Bernburg, Regensburg, and other German targets of opportunity.

FEB. 24. Approximately 1750 tons of bombs dropped by 747 heavy bombers of 8th Air Force on aircraft and aircraft component production centers at Gotha, Schweinfurt, Rostock and Eisenach, Germany.

FEB. 25. 1667 tons of bombs dropped by more than 650 heavy bombers of 8th Air Force with fighter escort on aircraft assembly, component and aircraft engine centers at Regensburg, Stuttgart, Augsburg and Furth, Germany, and 560 tons dropped by more than 350 heavy bombers of 15th Air Force in coordinated attacks.

FEB. 29. 450 tons of bombs dropped on Brunswick, Germany, through overcast by approximately 200 B-17s of 8th Air Force.

MAR. 2. "Battle Honors" awarded India-China Wing, Air Transport Command, for outstanding performance of duty.

MAR. 2. Over 750 tons of bombs dropped on Frankfurt, Ludwigshaven, Offenbach, and other German targets by heavy bombers of 8th Air Force.

MAR. 3. 198 escorted 15th Air Force heavy bombers attack airdromes and rail yards in Rome area, dropping over 350 tons of bombs.

MAR. 3. First U. S. fighter mission over Berlin accomplished when 2 groups of P-38s fly to a rendezvous point south of Berlin, then sweep over outskirts.

MAR. 4. First AAF bomber attack on Berlin made by 30 B-17s of 8th Air Force with Allied escort. Attacks also made on Dusseldorf, Cologne and Frankfurt, Germany.

MAR. 6. Heavy bombers of 8th Air Force attack Berlin in strength, 672 B-17s dropping more than 1600 tons of bombs.

MAR. 6. Over 60 tons of bombs dropped on Kavieng-Panapai, New Ireland, by 12 B-24s of 13th Air Force.

MAR. 7. Harbor and submarine base at Toulon, France, attacked by 48 escorted B-17s dropping over 140 tons of bombs.

MAR. 8. More than 1000 tons of bombs dropped on Berlin area by 539 heavily escorted bombers of 8th Air Force.

MAR. 9. Over 1200 tons of bombs dropped on Berlin, Hanover, Brunswick and Nauen by 489 8th Air Force heavy bombers.

MAR. 11. Over 250 tons of bombs dropped on Toulon, France, installations and shipping by 122 escorted B-24s of 15th Air Force.

MAR. 11. Northwest marshaling yards, Florence, Italy, attacked by 35 B-26s of 15th Air Force in first attack on the city during this war.

MAR. 11. Over 350 tons of bombs dropped on Munster, Germany, and on enemy installations of Pas-de-Calais, France, by coordinated missions of 155 escorted heavy bombers of 8th Air Force.

MAR. 11. Wake Island attacked by 22 heavy bombers of 7th Air Force dropping approximately 50 tons of bombs.

MAR. 11-15. Targets in New Guinea area attacked by 300 heavy and medium bombers dropping 571 tons of bombs, during the week ending Mar. 15. In these operations, 5th Air Force destroyed 59 enemy aircraft; 24 probably destroyed.

MAR. 12. Announcement made of special trans-Atlantic aerial freight line inaugurated by 8th Air Force Service Command in England to supplement regular Air Transport Command shipments.

MAR. 15. Over 1200 tons of bombs dropped on Cassino, Italy, during attack by both AAF strategic and tactical air force units in Mediterranean.

MAR. 15. 8th Air Force renews attacks on targets in Germany; 185 B-17s and 143 B-24s drop over 700 tons of bombs on Brunswick.

NOTE: Information in the War Calendar was derived from the best source material available at the time of preparation. Where original records were not available for verification, it is subject to revision based on further research. For a chronological report on military aeronautics from June 1861, to Dec. 7, 1941, see the next chapter, *Historical Highlights*.

718th Bombardment

TYPICAL
SQUADRON
INSIGNIA

532th Bombardment

344th Fighter

338th Bombardment

20th Tact Reconnaisance

529th Fighter Bomber

81st Service

425th Bombardment

714th Bombardment

6th Weather

310th Fighter

487th Fighter

557th Bombardment

77th Troop Carrier

420th Bombardment

25th Liaison

528th Bombardment

SHOULDER PATCHES OF THE AIR FORCES

1st Eastern U. S.

2nd Western U. S.

3rd S. Eastern U. S.

4th Far Western U. S.

5th SW Pacific

6th Canal Zone

7th Central Pacific

8th United Kingdom

9th United Kingdom

10th India-Burma

11th N. Pacific

12th Mediterranean

13th S. Pacific

14th China

15th Italy

Hq. and Commands

UNITED STATES AIRCRAFT MARKING

The present insignia is visible at 60 percent greater range than the previous AAF marking. The red disc was removed to prevent confusion with Japanese marking. Dates show when changes were made.

Jan. 1, 1921 Aug. 18, 1942 June 29, 1943

Sept. 17, 1943

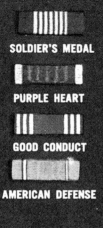

SOLDIER'S MEDAL

PURPLE HEART

GOOD CONDUCT

AMERICAN DEFENSE

MEDAL OF HONOR

UNIT CITATION

ASIATIC-PACIFIC THEATER

AMERICAN THEATER

**EUROPEAN-AFRICAN-
MIDDLE EASTERN THEATER**

DISTINGUISHED SERVICE CROSS

DISTINGUISHED SERVICE MEDAL

LEGION OF MERIT

SILVER STAR

DISTINGUISHED FLYING CROSS

AIR MEDAL

HISTORICAL HIGHLIGHTS

On Aug. 1, 1907, an Aeronautical Division "to study the flying machine and the possibility of adapting it to military purposes" was established in the Office of the Chief Signal Officer, U. S. Army. One officer and 2 enlisted men were assigned to the division. There were no airplanes.

Late in 1907 the Army asked for bids for an airplane capable of flying for 60 minutes and of attaining a speed of 40 miles per hour while carrying 2 men whose combined weight did not exceed 350 pounds. It was further specified that the airplane be so constructed that "it permit an intelligent man to become proficient in its use within a reasonable length of time." On Feb. 10, 1908, the contract was signed for the Wright brothers' plane.

First Airplane—The first airplane delivered by the Wrights crashed during trial flights at Fort Myer, Va., in Sept. 1908, injuring Orville Wright and killing Lt. Thomas E. Selfridge, his passenger. Until the accident, however, the plane had performed well, and the Wrights were given a second chance. In June 1909, they returned to Fort Myer with a new biplane. It had approximately a 40-foot wing spread and a wing area of 500 square feet. It weighed 800 pounds empty. Two propellers, mounted in the rear, were chain-driven by a small gasoline engine. The landing gear consisted of a pair of runners. There was no armament of any kind. Orville Wright piloted the plane with Lt. (later Brig. Gen.) Frank P. Lahm riding as passenger. Wright kept the plane aloft for one hour, 20 minutes and 40 seconds. In another test flight he achieved an average speed of 42.583 miles per hour for a 5-mile flight from Alexandria to Fort Myer, Va. The Army accepted it—the world's first military airplane.

Under the terms of the contract the Wright brothers had to teach 2 Army officers to pilot the airplane. Lts. Lahm and F. E. Humphreys were the first students. Lt. (later Maj. Gen.) Benjamin Foulois was the next pilot trained. When Lts. Lahm and Humphreys were called back to their respective posts in the Cavalry and Engineers, Lt. Foulois (who had instruction flights) became the only officer available for flying duty. In the months that followed a few more pilots were trained—among them Lt. Henry H. Arnold, now Commanding General of the AAF.

World War—When we went to war on April 6, 1917, the Aviation Section had 65 officers (35 of them fliers) and 1087 enlisted men. The total of our airplanes was 55, all of which were obsolete compared to the planes being used over the Western Front. However, $640,000,000—largest sum ever appropriated for a single purpose to that date—was voted by Congress on July 24, 1917, for the development of military aviation.

In the closing months of the war our air squadrons chalked up an impressive record in aerial combat (see summary page 345). Observation, the original concept of an airplane's military usefulness, became a secondary function. The airplane was recognized as a weapon in itself. Army aeronautics was separated from the Signal Corps in May 1918. In August a Director of Air Service was appointed with control over both the Bureau of Military Aeronautics and the Bureau of Aircraft Production. In June 1920, the Army Air Service was created.

Peacetime Accomplishments—The 23 years between wars, in spite of the small number of personnel and limited appropriations, was a period of progress for the Army's air arm. New techniques, tactics and equipment were tested. Strides forward were made in such technical developments as instrument flying, aerial photography and communications. From peacetime research came almost all of our present-day combat planes. High level precision bombing was developed. Aerial formations and tactics were evolved. Perhaps most important was the formation of a small body of devoted and highly skilled men who knew aviation from top to bottom. They were the men who organized the program for training the hundreds of thousands recruited for air duty when war came again.

Reorganizations—In 1926 the Air Service was renamed the Air Corps and an expansion program was authorized. This was followed by several reorganizations until on March 9, 1942, the present AAF was established as one of the 3 main branches of the Army.

Following is a chronological record tracing the development of land-based military aviation in the United States up to the attack on Pearl Harbor. (For an AAF war calendar, see page 329.)

1861: APRIL 19. Inaugurating air service with the Army, civilian aeronaut James Allen, 1st Rhode Island State Militia, makes balloon ascent in Washington, D. C.

JUNE 22-24. Civilian aeronaut T. C. Lowe and Army officers make first military reconnaissance ascents at Arlington and Falls Church, Va.; telegraph used from balloon.

SEPT. 24. Lowe directs Union Army artillery fire by telegraph from a balloon at Ft. Corcoran, Washington, D. C., against Confederate targets in Virginia.

1862–63: Continuous tactical observations made from Union Army balloons until discontinuance of service in June, 1863; similar observations also made by Confederates.

1892: First military aeronautic organization in this country is established by U. S. Army with attachment of balloon section to Signal Corps telegraph units.

1893–97: Aerial photography and air-to-ground telephony practiced. A balloon park established at Ft. Logan, Colo.

1898: $50,000 allotted for Army aviation for 1899 (to S. P. Langley for experiments in aerodynamics).

JUNE 30. Army balloon observations reveal Spanish fleet in Santiago Harbor.

NOV. 9. Construction of man-carrying power airplane authorized with allotment of $25,000 by U. S. Army to S. P. Langley.

1902: MAY 6. Army balloon unit organized at Fort Myer, Va.

1903: DEC. 17. First controlled power airplane flights made by Orville and Wilbur Wright at Kitty Hawk, N. C.

1906: SEPT. 30. First Gordon Bennett balloon race, Paris, won by Lt. F. P. Lahm, U. S. Army.

1907: AUG. 1. Aeronautical Division established in Office of Chief Signal Officer to have charge of all matters pertaining to military ballooning, air machines and all kindred subjects.

DEC. 16. Chief Signal Officer calls for bids on lighter-than-air "airship."

DEC. 23. Bids on heavier-than-air "flying machine" called for by Chief Signal Officer.

1908: $30,000 appropriated for Army aviation for 1909.

FEB. 10. Formal contract for Army's first flying machine signed by Signal Corps and the Wright brothers.

MAY 19. Lt. T. E. Selfridge, U. S. Army, first military man to fly a heavier-than-air machine, pilots the aircraft "White Wing" of Dr. Alexander Graham Bell's Aerial Experiment Association.

JUNE 30. Air strength, U. S. Army (Signal Corps): 3 officers, 10 men, all in balloon troops.

SEPT. 3. First test flight of flying machine made at Ft. Myer, Va., by Orville Wright.

SEPT. 9. First Army passenger carried in "Wright Flyer" is Lt. F. P. Lahm, during trials at Ft. Myer, Va.

SEPT. 17. Lt. T. E. Selfridge killed and Orville Wright injured during trial flights of flying machine at Ft. Myer, Va. Delivery of machine postponed.

1909: AUG. 2. Wright airplane accepted by Army after new tests at Ft. Myer, Va.

OCT. 26. First Army man to solo the Army's first airplane is Lt. F. E. Humphreys; second, Lt. F. P. Lahm, both after about 3 hours' pilot instruction by Wilbur Wright at College Park, Md.

1910: JAN. 10-20. Weight dropping experiments from an airplane conducted by Lt. P. W. Beck at Los Angeles.

JUNE 30. Air strength, U. S. Army: 1 officer, 9 enlisted men; 1 Wright airplane, 1 Baldwin airship, 3 captive balloons.

AUG. 10. Tricycle landing gear fitted to Army airplane by Lt. B. D. Foulois and civilian mechanic O. G. Simmons.

AUG. 20. Firing of rifle from airplane demonstrated at Sheepshead Bay, N. Y., by Lt. J. E. Fickel.

1911: JAN. 7-25. Live bombing (use of real bombs) demonstrated at San Francisco, Calif. by Lt. M. S. Crissy. Radio messages transmitted from airplane by Lt. P. W. Beck.

MAR. 3. Appropriation for air operations, $125,000, authorized for Army for fiscal year 1912.

MAR. 3. 106-mile non-stop flight from Laredo to Eagle Pass, Tex., made by Lt. B. D. Foulois and civilian pilot P. W. Parmalee in Wright airplane.

MAY 20. Army's first pilot training school opens at College Park, Md.; bids opened for airplane hangars.

SEPT. 26. Official 3-man world flight endurance record set by Lt. T. DeW. Milling in Wright airplane at Nassau Boulevard, L. I., N. Y. Time: 1:54:42.

OCT. 10. Riley E. Scott bombsight and dropping device tested at College Park, Md. from Wright airplane flown by Lt. Milling.

OCT. 14. Air strength, U. S. Army (Signal Corps): 6 officers with civil FAI (Federation Aeronautique Internationale) airplane certificates; 5 airplanes; 3 captive balloons.

DEC. 31. 15 airplanes purchased by the Army in 1911.

1912: MAR. 11. Army air school opens in the Philippines.

JUNE 1. 6540 ft. altitude record set by Lt. H. H. Arnold (Burgess-Wright airplane).

JUNE 7-8. Aerial firing with machine gun demonstrated by Capt. C. deF. Chandler at College Park, Md. from Wright airplane flown by Lt. Milling.

AUG. 24. $100,000 appropriated for Army air operations for fiscal year 1913.

OCT. 9. First competition for Mackay Trophy; won by Lt. H. H. Arnold.

1913: FEB. 28. Air-ground cooperation practiced at Texas City, Tex., in 2nd Division maneuvers.

MAR. 2. $125,000 appropriated for air for fiscal year 1914; flying pay authorized, 35% over base pay.

MAR. 28. Official American 2-man cross-country duration and distance records established by Lts. Milling and W. C. Sherman. Route: Texas City to San Antonio, Tex. Distance: 220 miles. Flying time: 4:22:00.

1914: FEB. 14. American non-stop duration and distance closed circuit records set at San Diego, Calif., by Lt. T. F. Dodd and Sgt. H. Marcus (Burgess-Renault 70). Distance: 244.18 miles. Flying time: 4:43:00.

FEB. 23. Automatic attached back-pack type parachute demonstrated by Charles Broadwick.

JULY 18. Aviation Section (Signal Corps) is created by Congress. Strength limited to 60 officers, 260 men. Ratings authorized: Military Aviator (MA), Junior Military Aviator (JMA), Aviation Mechanician (AM). Flight pay: 25%, 50% and 75% increase over base pay to students, JMAs and MAs respectively.

SEPT. 1. First Aero Squadron is organized at San Diego, Calif., with 16 officers, 77 enlisted men; 8 airplanes.

OCT. 8. 16,798 ft. official American one-man altitude record set by Capt. H. LeR. Muller (Curtiss 90).

DEC. 1-16. "First radio message ever received in an airplane," at Manila, P. I. from Corregidor station, credited to pilot Lt. H. A. Dargue and Lt. J. O. Mauborgne, designer of the set.

DEC. 23. Mackay Trophy for reconnaissance competition won by Capt. T. F. Dodd and Lt. S. W. Fitzgerald.

1915: JAN. 15. New official American one-man duration record is set at San Diego, Calif. by Lt. B. Q. Jones (Burgess-Renault 70). Flying time: 8:53:00.

MAR. 3. National Advisory Committee for Aeronautics created to supervise and direct the scientific study of flight problems, with a view to their practical solution.

MAR. 4. $200,000 appropriated for air for fiscal year 1915.

MAR. 12. Official world 3-man duration record set by Lt. B. Q. Jones, San Diego. Flying time: 7:05:00. Mackay Trophy awarded for record flights.

1916: JAN. 17. Strength, Aviation Section (Signal Corps): 23 MAs and JMAs, 25 aviation students, 1 non-flying officer; 25 airplanes.

MAR. 13-AUG. 15. Air operations conducted with General Pershing's punitive expedition by First Aero Squadron, Major Foulois commanding; 540 flights made in Mexico for carrying mail and messages; reconnaissance; photographic work covering over 19,-000 miles.

MAR. 21. Organization of Escadrille Americaine, or Nieuport 124, is authorized by French Air Department; popularly known as Lafayette Escadrille.

MAR. 31. $500,000 allocated to Aviation Section (Signal Corps), under 1916–17 Emergency Act.

AUG. 29. $18,681,666 appropriated for air for fiscal year 1917.

OCT. 27. For fiscal year 1918 the Chief Signal Officer asks for enlisted strength of 3320 for 10 aero squadrons, 6 observation balloon companies, a proving ground and necessary schools.

1917: MAR. 29. Air program calls for 1850 aviators and 300 balloonists for an Air Service of 16 aero squadrons, 16 balloons, 9 schools. Estimated cost: $54,250,000.

APR. 6. Declaration of war. Aviation Section (Signal Corps) comprises 35 pilots, 1087 enlisted men, 55 training airplanes, 7 tactical squadrons, organized or in process. Flying schools in operation at Mineola, N. Y., San Diego, Calif., Memphis, Tenn. (winter 1916–17), Essington, Pa., with a balloon school at Fort Omaha, Neb.

MAY 12. $8,300,000 appropriated for Army aeronautics.

MAY 16. Flying fields approved for San Antonio, Tex.; Fairfield, Ohio; Mt. Clemens, Mich.; Belleville, Ill.

MAY 29. Liberty engine project initiated to produce standard engine in 8 and 12 cylinder models (the 8 was discontinued early).

JUNE 15. $32,000,000 allocated to Signal Corps for air operations under Emergency Act.

JUNE 28. Langley Field, Va., authorized as experimental station.

JUNE 30. Lt. Col. Wm. Mitchell becomes Aviation Officer, AEF.

JULY 11. Gen. Pershing calls for 69 balloon companies in France by late summer, 1918.

JULY 24. $640,000,000 appropriated for air. Aviation Section is authorized to expand to 9989 officers, 87,083 enlisted men. Flying ratings and pay revised.

JULY 28. First American Aero Sq to reach AEF, the 29th Provisional (later 400th Construction) Sq, docks at Liverpool.

AUG. 22. Air-to-ground radiophone sets go into production stage.

AUG. 25. Liberty 12 engine ends 50 hr. test, delivering 320 hp.

SEPT. 1. First Aero Sq, commanded by Maj. R. Royce, arrives in France, and assigned to First Division.

SEPT. 2. First American detachment for flying training arrives in England.

SEPT. 20. Balloon Section, AEF, created under Maj. J. W. East.

· SEPT. 28. Initial flying training in AEF begins at Foggia, Italy.

OCT. 18. McCook Field, Dayton, Ohio, established as experimental laboratory pending preparation of Langley Field, Va.

1918: FEB. 18. 103rd Pursuit Sq, AEF, formed with members of Lafayette Escadrille, begins operations at front under tactical control of the French.

MAR. 19. First operations across the lines made by 94th Sq of First Pursuit Gp.

APR. 6. Night aerial photos by magnesium flares made by Lts. J. C. McKinney and Norbert Carolin.

APR. 14. 94th Sq of the First Pursuit

Gp brings down first 2 enemy airplanes by AEF.

MAY 9. Flight surgeons organized and assigned to U. S. flying fields.

MAY 11. First American-made airplane (DH4-Liberty) is received by AEF.

MAY 15-AUG. 12. Government's first permanent airmail route (Washington to New York) is flown by Army pilots until taken over by the Post Office Department.

MAY 20. Army aeronautics severed from the Signal Corps and 2 air departments created: Bureau of Military Aeronautics and Bureau of Aircraft Production.

MAY 29. Brig. Gen. M. M. Patrick appointed Chief of Air Service, AEF; Brig. Gen. B. D. Foulois, Chief of Air Service, 1st Army; Col. Wm. Mitchell, Chief of Air Service, 1st Corps.

JUNE 12. First AEF day bombing done by 96th Aero Sq on Dommary-Baroncourt yards.

JUNE 20. First detachment of bombing pilots arrives at Italian front, Capt. F. H. LaGuardia commanding.

JULY 8. $124,304,758 appropriated for Army aviation.

JULY 18-AUG. 7. In battle of Chateau-Thierry, AEF flies 3790 hours; 3 balloon companies participate.

AUG. 10. First U. S. Army AEF organized, including First Army Air Service to which are assigned 3 fighter groups; the 96th Bombing Sq; 2 Army and 9 corps observation squadrons; 15 balloon companies.

AUG. 28. A Director of Air Service appointed to administer the 2 new bureaus of Military Aeronautics and Aircraft Production.

SEPT. 12-15. Greatest air armada to date—1481 planes—participates in

St. Mihiel drive; AEF flies 3593 hours in artillery direction, observation, day and night bombing, ground strafing and air combat.

SEPT. 18. World altitude record (unofficial) of 28,899 ft. set by Maj. R. W. Schroeder (Bristol-300 Hispano) at Dayton, Ohio.

SEPT. 26-NOV. 11. Meuse-Argonne offensive. AEF operations include day and night observation and bombardment, strafing, day bombing in formation by groups and air combat. Americans fly 18,505 hrs.

OCT. 9. Meuse-Argonne offensive. 32 tons of bombs dropped on cantonment district between La Wavrille and Damvillers, in highest concentration of air forces to date, with more than 250 bombers and 100 pursuits.

OCT. 12. Oxygen tanks ordered carried on all American flights over lines. American Air Service engages in its first night fighting of the war.

NOV. 4. $60,000,000 appropriated for Air Service.

NOV. 11. Armistice.

SUMMARY—WORLD WAR I: Upon cessation of hostilities, assigned to armies were 45 American squadrons as follows: 20 fighter, 6 day bombardment, 1 night bombardment, 18 Army or corps observation; these comprised 767 pilots, 481 observers, 23 aerial gunners and 23 balloon companies. These squadrons were equipped with 740 airplanes; 12 squadrons were equipped with American-made airplanes powered with Liberty engines. In the Zone of Advance the American Army had received a total of 2698 airplanes, of which 668 were American-made. Air Service pilots shot down 755 officially confirmed enemy airplanes, 71 enemy balloons. Our losses were 357 airplanes and 43 balloons.

U. S. Aces credited with 10 enemy aircraft or over:

NAME	RANK	LAST ORG.	AIR-PLANES	BAL-LOONS	TO-TAL
Rickenbacker, Edward V., Columbus, Ohio	Capt.	94	21	4	25
*Luke, Frank, Phoenix, Ariz.	2nd Lt.	27	4	14	18
Vaughn, George A., Brooklyn, N. Y.	1st Lt.	17	12	1	13
Kindley, Field E., Gravette, Ark.	Capt.	148	12	..	12
Springs, Elliott W., Lancaster, S. C.	Capt.	148	12	..	12
Landis, Reed G., Chicago, Ill.	Capt.	25	9	1	10
*Putnam, David E., Brookline, Mass.	1st Lt.	139	10	..	10
Swaab, Jacques M., Philadelphia, Pa.	Capt.	22	10	..	10

* Killed in combat.

Army Air Service units, participating in 215 bombing raids, dropped over 255,000 lbs. of explosives; flew 35,000 hrs. over the lines; took nearly 18,000 photographs of enemy positions, from which 585,000 prints were made by photographic sections. They regulated artillery fire, supported ground attack, strafed and bombed enemy batteries, convoys and troops.

Of 35 balloon companies in France with 466 officers and 6365 men, 23 companies served with armies at the front, made 1642 ascensions with 3111 hrs. in the air. They made 316 artillery adjustments, reported 12,018 shell bursts, sighted 11,856 enemy airplanes, reported enemy balloon ascensions 2649 times, enemy batteries 400 times, enemy traffic on roads and railroads 1113 times, explosions and destructions 597 times.

Outstanding technical developments during the war period were: Liberty engine, oxygen mask equipped with telephone connections, cotton airplane and balloon fabric, electrically heated clothing, wireless telephone for air-ground communications, automatic camera, helium gas, armored pilot seat, 8-machine gun ground-strafing airplane, aero-medical research.

NOV. 14. Brig. Gen. Wm. Mitchell made Chief of Air Service, 3rd Army.

DEC. 23. Maj. Gen. C. T. Menoher appointed Director of Air Service.

1919: JAN. 18. Monoplane altitude record of 19,500 ft. established by Maj. R. W. Schroeder (Loening-Hispano 300).

MAR. 10. Brig. Gen. Wm. Mitchell succeeds Maj. Gen. W. L. Kenly as Director of Military Aeronautics under the Director of Air Service.

MAR. 15. Civil Operations Branch, Office of the Director of Military Aeronautics, created to supervise civil activities of the Air Service.

APR. 19. American distance cross-country record set in non-stop flight, Chicago-New York, by Capt. E. F. White and mechanic H. M. Schaefer (DH4-Liberty 400). Distance: 738.6 miles. Time: 6:50:00.

APR. 28. First jump from airplane with free type backpack parachute (later adopted as standard) made at Mc-Cook Field, Dayton, Ohio, by Leslie Irving from plane flown by Floyd Smith, designer of the parachute.

MAY 2-15. 5-plane formation directed by radiophone with interplane radiophone communication at Southeastern Air Congress, Macon, Ga.

JUNE 1. Aerial forest fire patrol initiated in California.

JULY 11. $25,000,000 appropriated for Air Service for fiscal year 1920.

JULY 24-NOV. 9. Coastal and border-circuit flight of U. S. accomplished by Lt. Col. R. S. Hartz and Lt. E. E. Harmon and crew. (Martin Bomber-2 Liberty 400.) Distance: 9823 miles. Flying time: 114:25:00.

SEPT. Dive bombing demonstrated by Lt. L. B. Sweeley (DH4B-Liberty) at Aberdeen Proving Grounds, Md.

SEPT. 6. New unofficial world altitude 2-man record of 28,250 ft. set by Maj. R. W. Schroeder and Lt. G. E. Elfrey (Lepere-Liberty 400) at Dayton, Ohio.

SEPT. 17. Provision made by Act of Congress for 1200 emergency officers for the Air Service, 85% of them to be fliers.

OCT. 4. Official world 2-man altitude record of 31,821 ft. set by Maj. R. W. Schroeder and Lt. G. E. Elfrey (Lepere-Liberty 400 supercharged) at Dayton, Ohio.

DEC. 31. Notable technical developments of the year as reviewed by McCook Field, Dayton, Ohio, are leakproof tanks; free parachute pack; development of the DH9A; the Martin bomber; 3 SS fighters and XB1A observation planes; reversible and variable pitch propeller; supercharger; siphon gasoline pump; fins and floats for emergency water landing; and a 37 mm cannon in Martin bomber, "the first cannon mounted and fired in an American-built airplane."

1920: JAN. 20. Record radio reception, 175 miles from airplane, achieved during 37th Infantry maneuvers, Ft. McIntosh, Tex.

FEB. 27. Official world altitude record of 33,113 ft. set by Maj. R. W. Schroeder (Lepere-Liberty 400) at McCook Field, Dayton, Ohio.

APR. 12. 8 machine guns fitted in tests to remodeled DH4s: 2 fixed synchronized, 2 fixed through pilot's floor, 2 flexible on upper mount, 2 mounted in rudimentary floor turret.

APR. Initial tests made of gyroscopic compass.

MAY 18. Antitank bombs (from DH4) and 37 mm cannon (from Martin) tested against tanks from 100 ft. altitude by Lts. H. R. Harris and O. G. Kelly.

MAY 21. $1,539,300 appropriated for the Air Service for seacoast defenses.

MAY 26. GAX (twin-Liberty engine armored triplane) armed with 8 machine guns and 37 mm cannon tested at McCook Field, Dayton, Ohio.

JUNE 4. Army Reorganization Bill creating an Air Service with 1514 officers and 16,000 enlisted men is approved. New rating of "Airplane Pilot" supersedes former ratings. Flying pay 50% above base pay authorized.

JUNE 5. $33,435,000 appropriated for Air Service; act limits Air Service to land bases.

JUNE 8. Parachute jump of about 19,800 ft. by Lt. J. H. Wilson initiates series of high altitude jumps.

JULY 1. "Cannon engine," shooting 37 mm shells through propeller shaft, produced by Wright Aeronautical Corp.

JULY 17-20. Flight of 9329 miles, with Capt. St. Clair Streett commanding (4 DH4B-Liberty 400), made from Mitchel Field, N. Y., to Nome, Alaska and return to gain knowledge in aerial navigation, air route organization and movement of aircraft over great distances.

SEPT. 3. New Martin light bomber MB-2 (2 supercharged Liberty 400 engines) tested with 1000-lb. torpedo and 4 aboard.

SEPT. 11. 3 airships fly formation under radio direction, Langley Field, Va.

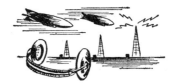

SEPT. 24. Air Service strength this date: 896 flying officers, 275 non-flying, 7846 enlisted men.

NOV. 25. Pulitzer race won by Lt. C. C. Moseley (Verville-Packard 600) at Mitchel Field, N. Y. Distance: 132 miles. Speed: 178 mph.

DEC. 31. Major accomplishments listed by Air Service engineering division are: the GAX armored attack plane; the Verville-Packard racer; Packard engines 160, 300 and 600; 700 hp "W" engine; the new Martin bomber; the miniature Messenger airplane; and aerial firing of 37 mm cannon.

1921: Studies of strategic employment of aviation reveal the need for 2 classifications of military airpower, "Air Service" and "Air Force"; Tables of Organization for the Air Service based on enlisted strength of 16,000 is approved by War Department.

FEB. 12. First section of American "model" Airways route from Washington, D. C., to Dayton, Ohio inaugurated.

FEB. 21-24. Eastbound transcontinental flight from Rockwell Field, Calif. to Pablo Beach, Jacksonville, Fla. made by Lt. W. D. Coney. Distance: 2180 miles. Flying time: 22:27:00.

MAR. 15. Indicated altitude flight to 30,000 ft. made by Lt. J. A. Macready and R. F. Langham (Lepere-Liberty 400 supercharged).

MAY 6. First Provisional Air Brigade organized at Langley Field, Va.

JUNE 10-17. Series of 14 flights in and about Grand Canyon, descending 4500 feet below the rim, leads to recommendations on aerial reconnaissance.

JUNE 30. $19,200,000 appropriated for Air Service for fiscal year 1922. Air strength: 975 officers; 2820 airplanes; 38 free balloons; 250 observation balloons; 12 non-rigid airships.

JULY 13-21. In a series of Army-Navy bombing tests, captured German destroyer G-102, light cruiser FRANKFURT, and battleship OSTFRIESLAND are sunk.

SEPT. 23-26. Day and night bombardment test flights result in sinking of the battleship ALABAMA by 2000-lb. bomb.

SEPT. 28. Official world altitude record of 34,508 ft. set by Lt. J. A. Macready (Lepere-Liberty 400 supercharged); Mackay Trophy awarded.

SEPT. 28. A 4300-lb. bomb dropped from 4000 ft. by Capt. N. Carolin and bombardier Sgt. S. Smink (Handley-Page O-400—2 Liberty 400s) in tests at Aberdeen Proving Grounds, Md.

NOV. 15. Initial flight of ROMA, largest American semi-rigid airship in existence, made at Langley Field, Va., with Capt. D. Mabry commanding.

DEC. 31. Notable technical developments reported by McCook Field, Dayton, Ohio: 50-hr. test of the 700 hp "W" engine of 1920; the 300 hp cannon Wright plane sand test; model test of 350 hp Wright-engined Loening fighter; the 700 hp "W" engined Gallaudet day bomber test; development of 4000-lb. bomb racks and electrical synchronizer.

1922: MAY 31. National Balloon Race won by Maj. O. Westover, Lt. C. F. Bond, aide. Distance: 866.5 miles from starting point at Milwaukee, Wis.

JUNE 12. 24,206 ft. parachute jump made by Capt. A. W. Stevens from a Martin bomber piloted by Lt. L. Wade, at Dayton, Ohio.

JUNE 16. Series of night cross-country flights, Bolling Field, D. C. to Langley Field, Va., and return, are initiated by Lt. C. L. Bissell.

JUNE 16. Berliner helicopter demonstrated at Washington, D. C.

JUNE 20. Border to border flight, Kelly Field, San Antonio, Tex., to Selfridge Field, Mich., accomplished by Lt. D. Dunton (DH4B-Liberty 400). Distance: 1350 miles. Elapsed time: 40:25:00. Flying time: 16:10:00. Average speed, 84.5 mph.

JUNE 30. $12,895,000 appropriated for Air Service for fiscal year 1923. Air strength: 958 officers; 1681 serviceable airplanes; 55 free balloons and 448 observation balloons; 13 non-rigid airships.

AUG. 1. The First Pursuit Gp removes complement of 21 airplanes from Ellington Field, Houston, Tex. to Selfridge Field, Mich. Flying time: 16:10:00.

AUG. 1. 87 airplanes engaged in fire patrol over national forests.

AUG. 2. Unofficial 3-man altitude record of 23,350 ft. set at McCook Field, Dayton, Ohio by Lt. L. Wade, Capt. A. W. Stevens and Sgt. Langham in supercharged bomber.

SEPT. 4. First transcontinental crossing within 24 hrs. made by Lt. J. H. Doolittle (rebuilt DH4B-Liberty 400), Pablo Beach, Fla. to Rockwell Field, San Diego, Calif. Distance: 2163 miles. Elapsed time: 22:35:00. Flying time: 21:20:00.

SEPT. 14. First trial of the LWF Owl, largest American bomber to date, made at Mitchel Field, N. Y.

SEPT. 14-23. First transcontinental airship flight is made by the non-rigid C2, Langley Field, Va. to Ross Field, Arcadia, Calif., with Capt. G. W. McEntire commanding.

OCT. 1. During a 2-month mapping project in Tennessee, Capt. A. W. Stevens and Lt. G. W. Polk photograph 5000 square miles.

OCT. 6. Unofficial world duration record set by Lts. J. A. Macready and O. G. Kelly (Fokker T2-Liberty 375) at

Rockwell Field, San Diego, Calif.
Time: 35:18:30.

OCT. 13. Liberty Engine Trophy Race won by Lt. T. J. Koenig (Lepere-Liberty 400). Speed: 128.8 mph over 257.7 mile course.

OCT. 14. Pulitzer Trophy Race won by Lt. R. L. Maughan (Army Curtiss racer-D 12 Curtiss 375). Speed: 205.8 mph over 250 km course.

OCT. 14. John L. Mitchell Trophy won by Lt. Donald F. Stace (Thomas-Morse MB-3Wright 300). Speed: 147.8 mph over 200 km course.

OCT. 18. World's speed record of 222.96 mph for 1 km set by Brig. Gen. Wm. Mitchell (Curtiss Racer used by Lt. Maughan in Pulitzer Race).

NOV. 14. Unofficial American distance record set by Lts. O. G. Kelly and J. A. Macready (Fokker T2-Liberty 375), in non-stop flight, San Diego, Calif. to Ft. Benjamin Harrison, Ind. Distance: 2060 miles.

DEC. 18. DeBothezat helicopter test-flown 1 min. 42 sec. by Maj. T. H. Bain, McCook Field, Dayton, Ohio.

1923: JAN. 31. Armored GAX triplane flown to 6000 ft. altitude at Kelly Field, San Antonio, Tex., by Lt. D. V. Gaffney.

FEB. 6. New 12-plane airship D2 (190,-000 cu. ft.—2 Wright 180s) test-flown at Scott Field, Ill., by Lts. H. H. Holland, A. Thomas and D. L. Hutchins. Time: 1:04:00.

MAR. 1. TC1, largest American non-rigid airship, delivered.

MAR. 2. $12,626,000 appropriated for Air Service for 1924.

MAR. 3-APR. Approximately 6000-mile San Antonio-Puerto Rico-Washington flight made by 6 DH4Bs, Capt. T. G. Lanphier commanding.

MAR. 5. Auxiliary jettisonable belly tank, fitted to bomb rack of MB3A at Selfridge Field, Mich., increases flying radius to about 400 miles.

MAR. 29. 167.769 mph speed record for 500 km set at McCook Field, Dayton, Ohio, by Lt. A. Pearson (Verville Sperry R3-Wright 350).

MAR. 29. 236.587 mph world maximum speed record set by Lt. R. L. Maughan (Curtiss 465) at McCook Field, Dayton, Ohio; 127.42 mph world speed record for 1000 km is set by Lts. H. R. Harris and R. Lockwood (DH4L-Liberty 400) at same time.

APR. 16-17. Non-refueled world duration and distance records set by Lts. J. A. Macready and O. G. Kelly (Fokker T2-Liberty 375) at Dayton, Ohio. Duration: 36:04:34. Distance: 2516.55 miles.

APR. 17. World's speed records of 114.35 mph for 1500 km and 114.22 mph for 2000 km set by Lt. H. R. Harris (DH4L-Liberty 375).

MAY 2-3. First non-stop transcontinental flight, New York to San Diego, Calif., accomplished by Lts. O. G. Kelly and J. A. Macready (Fokker T2-Liberty 375). Distance: 2520 miles. Flying time: 26:50:00. DFC and Mackay Trophy awarded.

MAY 26. Non-stop transcontinental south-north flight, Ellington Field, Houston, Tex. to Gordon, Ontario, made by Lt. H. G. Crocker (DH4B-Liberty 400). Flying time: 11:55:00.

JUNE 20. First flight of first all-metal plane (Gallaudet CO1-Liberty 400), designed by engineering division, made at McCook Field, Dayton, Ohio.

JUNE 28-29. New refueled world's speed records of 85.10 mph for 2500 km and 84.49 mph for 3000 km set by Lts. L. H. Smith and J. P. Richter (DH4B3-Liberty 400).

JUNE 30. Cited among engineering developments of the fiscal year 1923 are: Curtiss and Elias 2-engined night bombers; inverted, and air-cooled Liberty engines; Douglas world cruise planes; Curtiss PW8, Boeing PW9 planes, Curtiss D12 tandem, 375 hp engine.

JULY 1. Air Service strength: 867 officers, 9578 enlisted men; 1364 airplanes.

JULY 4-5. National Balloon Race at Indianapolis, Ind. won by Lts. R. S. Olmstead and J. W. Shoptaw. Distance: 449.5 miles.

JULY 10. Night motion pictures made from ground of searchlight-illuminated planes flying at 3000 ft. at Ft. Totten, N. Y.

AUG. 22. Initial flight of Barling bomber (6 Liberty 400 engines), largest airplane made in U. S., accomplished at Wright Field, Dayton, Ohio. Pilot, Lt. H. R. Harris.

AUG. 27-28. New world's refueled duration and distance record of 37:15:14.8 for 3293.26 miles set by Lts. L. H. Smith and J. P. Richter (DH4B-Liberty 400) at Rockwell Field, San Diego, Calif.

SEPT. 5. Destruction by bombing of condemned naval-vessels NEW JERSEY and VIRGINIA is accomplished during Army bombing tests, Cape Hatteras, Va.

SEPT. 13-DEC. 14. Double transcontinental tour, anticipating national airways, is made by Lts. J. F. Whiteley and H. D. Smith and crew (Martin-2 Liberty 400), Langley Field, Va. to San Diego, Calif., and return. Distance: 8000 miles.

OCT. 3-6. At National Air Races at St. Louis, Mo.: Liberty Engine Builders Trophy won by Lt. C. McMullen (CO4-Liberty 400); speed: 139.03 mph. General William Mitchell Trophy event won by Capt. B. E. Skeel (MB3-H3 Wright 300). Speed: 146.44 mph.

1924: MAR. 7-12. Flight navigated on instruments from McCook Field, Dayton, Ohio to Mitchel Field, N. Y. accomplished by Lt. E. H. Barksdale and navigator .B. Jones (DH4B-Liberty 400). Distance: 575 miles.

APR. 6-SEPT. 28. First round-the-world air tour, first trans-Pacific flight and first westbound Atlantic crossing are made by Air Service officers (Douglas-Liberty 400 bombers). Distance from start at Seattle: 26,345 route miles. Elapsed time: 175 days. Flying time: 363 hrs. For this flight the Collier

Trophy awarded to the Air Service; Mackay Trophy and DSM awards made to Capt. L. H. Smith and Lts. L. Wade, L. P. Arnold, E. H. Nelson, J. Harding and H. H. Ogden.

JUNE 7. $12,798,576 appropriated for the Air Service.

JUNE 23. Daylight transcontinental flight, New York to San Francisco, accomplished by Lt. R. L. Maughan (Curtiss PW8—D12 Curtiss 450). Distance: 2670 miles. Time: 21:48:-30.

JULY 6. New speed record set between Rockwell Field, San Diego, and San Francisco, Calif., by Maj. H. H. Arnold. Distance: 500 miles. Time: 4:25:00.

AUG. 6-14. 6765-mile cross-country circuit, Dayton—San Diego and return, made by Lt. J. H. Doolittle (DH4L-Liberty 400).

OCT. 2-4. Air race winners at Wright Field, Dayton, Ohio include: Liberty Engine Builders Trophy, Lt. D. G. Duke (DH4B-Liberty 400), speed 130.34 mph over 180-mile course; John L. Mitchell Trophy, Lt. C. Bettis (Curtiss PW8—D12HC Curtiss 460), speed 175.41 mph over 200 km course; Pulitzer Trophy Race, Lt. H. H. Mills (Verville Sperry—D12-AHC Curtiss 520), speed 216.55 mph over 200 km course.

1925: FEB. 8. Tests made of glider targets for aerial machine gun practice, Langley Field, Va.

JUNE 26. New Berliner helicopter flown at Washington, D. C. by Lt. H. R. Harris.

AUG. 1. First of new series, the Curtiss Condor night bomber, is flown at Mitchel Field, N. Y.

SEPT. 15. RS1, first great semi-rigid helium airship to be constructed in

America, completed at Scott Field, Ill.

OCT. 8-10. National Air Races, Mitchel Field, N. Y.: 200 km Pulitzer Race won by Lt. C. Bettis (Curtiss R3C1 —V1400 Curtiss 619); speed: 248.9 mph. New world speed records of 249.342 mph for 100 km, and 248.-975 mph for 200 km are set. Mackay Trophy awarded. John L. Mitchell Trophy Race won by Lt. T. K. Matthews (Curtiss PW8—D12 Curtiss 400); speed: 161.47 mph over 120 mile course.

OCT. 26. Schneider Seaplane Trophy Race, Baltimore, Md., won by Lt. J. H. Doolittle (Curtiss R3C2— V1400 Curtiss 619). Speed: 232.57 mph over 350 km course. Mackay Trophy awarded.

NOV. 20. Night photographs from Martin bomber taken by Lt. G. W. Goddard, Rochester, N. Y., using 50-lb. magnesium bombs.

DEC. 31. Developments of the year include: Curtiss PW1 and Boeing PW9 fighters to supersede the PW8; the Huff-Daland light bomber XLB1 with 5 machine guns; the Curtiss observation XO1; the Thomas-Morse all-metal observation plane; the Consolidated PT1 and Huff-Daland AT1 for training; and the Douglas C1 transport (Liberty 400). Engine developments in the 600 hp Curtiss, the 500 Packard, the geared Packard 800, the air-cooled Liberty, and the 1200 hp "X" engines. 6 to 10 machine guns mounted on ground-strafing planes, standardized airway light beacons, the radio beacon, the 5-lens camera, oleo-pneumatic shock absorbers and brakes are additional developments.

1926: JAN. 29. American altitude record of 38,704 ft. set by Lt. J. A. Macready (XCO5A-Liberty 400), Dayton, Ohio.

FEB. 11. Skip-bombing tests reported at Kelly Field, San Antonio, Tex., where Lt. R. G. Zettel has conducted practice at 20 to 25 ft. to determine rolling and bounding characteristics of bombs.

APR. 15. $15,256,964 appropriated for the Air Service for fiscal year 1927.

JUNE 30. Strength of Air Service: 919 officers, 8583 enlisted men, 142 flying cadets. 118 new planes delivered during fiscal year 1926.

JULY 2. Air Corps Act becomes law. The Air Service is redesignated Air Corps. A 5-year expansion program initiated for 1514 officers, 16,000 enlisted men; 1800 serviceable planes.

SEPT. 4-11. National Air Races, Philadelphia, Pa.: Liberty Engine Builders Trophy won by Lt. O. S. Stephens (O1-D12 Curtiss 400). Speed: 142.-26 mph.

DEC. 21-MAY 2, 1927: Pan-American Goodwill flight from San Antonio, Tex. around South America to Washington, D. C. with Maj. H. A. Dargue commanding 4 Loening amphibians (Liberty 400). Distance: 22,065 miles. Mackay Trophy and DFC awarded.

1927: FEB. 23. $20,602,594 appropriated for Air Corps for fiscal year 1928.

MAR. 9. 2 world altitude records and 3 American records broken in 28,510 ft. ascension by Capt. H. C. Gray at Scott Field, Ill.

MAY 4. 42,470 ft. unofficial altitude in free balloon reached by Capt. H. C. Gray.

MAY 25. Outside loop accomplished by Lt. J. H. Doolittle.

JUNE 28-29. First non-stop Hawaii flight, Oakland, Calif. to Wheeler Field, Honolulu, made by Lts. L. J. Maitland and A. F. Hegenberger (Fokker C2-3 Wright 220). Distance: 2407 miles. Flying time: 25:50:00. Navigation is accomplished by directional beacons at San Francisco and Maui. Mackay Trophy awarded in

1929. DFC also awarded for this flight.

JUNE 30. Strength of the Air Corps: 960 officers, 8857 enlisted men, 123 flying cadets.

JULY 5-8 Transcontinental flight from Bolling Field, D. C. to Rockwell Field, Calif., made by Majs. C. Spaatz, R. Royce and J. H. Jouett.

SEPT. 19-24. National Air Derby: Liberty Engine Builders Trophy won by Lt. H. A. Johnson (Curtiss XO13A). Speed: 170.156 mph.

OCT. 12. Wright Field, Dayton, Ohio, formally dedicated, and the Materiel Division moves from McCook Field to the new site. The John L. Mitchell Trophy Race won by Lt. I. A. Woodring, 1st Pursuit Group, during the ceremonies. Speed: 158.968 mph.

DEC. 14. Maj. Gen. J. E. Fechet succeeds Maj. Gen. M. M. Patrick as Chief of Air Corps; Brig. Gen. B. D. Foulois, Asst. Chief.

1928: FEB. 18. $3,882,975 authorized for new primary flying center at San Antonio, Tex., out of an authorized appropriation of nearly $7,000,000.

MAR. 1-9. Amphibian transcontinental flight, New York City to Rockwell Field, Calif., made by Lt. B. R. Dallas and Beckwith Havens (Loening amphibian inverted Liberty 400). Distance: about 3300 miles. Elapsed time: 32:45:00.

MAR. 10. $900,000 authorized for completion of Wright Field, Dayton, Ohio, experimental laboratory.

MAR. 23. $25,428,564 appropriated for Air Corps for 1929.

APR. 26. Receivers, radio beacon, 2-way telephone between air and ground, and other radio equipment tested in a radio laboratory airplane (C2 transport); Capt. O. P. Echols and Lt. L. M. Wolfe, pilots.

MAY 12-16. Record cross-country flight for single-seater planes from France Field, C. Z. to Bolling Field, D. C. made by Lts. R. W. Douglas and J. E. Parker (Boeing PW9-D12 Curtiss).

MAY 30-31. National Balloon Race from Pittsburgh, Pa. won by Capt. W. E. Kepner and Lt. W. O. Eareckson. Distance: 261.5 miles.

JUNE 16. Successful tests made at Wright Field, Dayton, Ohio, of superchargers designed to give sea level pressure at 30,000 ft., and of a new liquid oxygen system for high altitude flying.

JUNE 30-JULY 1. International Gordon Bennett Balloon Race, Detroit, Mich., won by U. S. for third successive time, insuring permanent possession of trophy; pilot, Capt. W. E. Kepner; aide, Lt. W. O. Eareckson. Distance: 460.9 miles.

SEPT. 12. National Air Races: John L. Mitchell Trophy won by Lt. B. H. Lawson. Distance: 120 miles. Speed: 154.74 mph.

OCT. 19. 6-man machine gun team parachutes from 6-airplane formation over Brooks Field, Tex.; sets up equipment in 3 minutes.

1929: JAN. 1-7. Unofficial record for refueled endurance airplane flight set by Maj. C. Spaatz and Capt. I. C. Eaker in QUESTION MARK (Fokker C2-3 Wright 220) over Los Angeles Airport. Flying time: 150:40:15.

JAN. 9-16. C-2 Army transport, first airplane ferried by Army Air Corps to foreign station, flies from Wright Field, Dayton, Ohio to France Field, C. Z., about 3130 miles; Maj. P. T. Beck commanding.

FEB. 23. Special goggles, electrically heated gloves and a device for warming oxygen before use announced by Materiel Division, Wright Field, Dayton, Ohio.

MAR. 3. Night photographs of White House and Capitol, developed in air, are taken to American Telegraph & Telephone Co., then wired to principal U. S. cities; airmen, Capt. A. W. Stevens and Lt. J. D. Corkille (O2-observation plane equipped with K-3 camera).

APR. 18-21. Flight from Bolling Field, D. C. to Havana, Cuba, and return made by Capt. W. F. Kraus and Lt. J. E. Upston. Flying time: southbound, 13:25:00; return, 11:00:00.

AUG. 2. Formation flight delivery made from factory to foreign service: 4 LB-6 bombers, Keystone factory, Bristol, Pa., to France Field, C. Z. Distance: about 4250 miles.

AUG. 12. Colored motion pictures from the air reported made by Capt. A. W. Stevens.

1930: JUNE 20-21. Randolph Field, San Antonio, Tex. dedicated.

NOV. 6. Medal of Honor presented Capt. Edward V. Rickenbacker in recognition of World War I service.

1931: AUG. 31. Air Corps Tactical School transferred from Langley Field, Va., to Maxwell Field, Montgomery, Ala.

NOV. 3. Cross-country flight at 20,000 ft., from Selfridge Field, Mich. to Washington, D. C., completed by 94th Pursuit Squadron, all pilots using liquid oxygen. Flying time: 2:05:00.

DEC. 18. Lt. W. A. Cocke, in Hawaii, makes world duration record for gliders. Time: 21:34:15.

DEC. 22. Maj. Gen. B. D. Foulois takes oath as Chief of Air Corps.

1932: MAY 9. First blind flight without a check pilot aboard and solely on instruments made by Lt. A. F. Hegenberger, Dayton, Ohio. Awarded Collier Trophy.

SEPT. 21. Intensity of cosmic rays at various altitudes tested by personnel of 11th Bombardment Squadron (Condor bomber) in flights from March Field, Calif.

DEC. 17. Frank Luke Trophy, presented by Arizona American Legion, accepted for War Dept. by Lt. Col. H. H. Arnold.

1933: Formal design proposals made for the Boeing B-17 heavy bomber.

FEB. 17. Mackay Trophy awarded Maj. Gen. B. D. Foulois for flight leadership during Air Corps exercises and maneuvers during 1931.

MAY 29. First class of "instrument landing" fliers demonstrate expertness at Wright Field, Dayton, Ohio.

1934: FEB. 19. Army Air Corps starts flying domestic airmail by Presidential Order.

MAY 22. Mackay Trophy for 1933 is awarded Capt. W. T. Larson for development of procedures of aerial frontier defense involving instrument takeoffs and landings on land and sea, and instrument flying over water.

JUNE 1. Army Air Corps terminates air mail operations.

JUNE 18. Contract made with Boeing Aircraft Co. for design data, mock-up and wind tunnel test of B-17.

JULY 19-AUG. 20. Flight from Bolling Field, D. C. to Fairbanks, Alaska and return accomplished by 10 Martin bombers (B-10), Lt. Col. H. H. Arnold commanding. Distance: 8290 miles. Flying time: northbound, 25:-30:00; southbound, 26:00:00. Mackay Trophy and DFC awarded to Lt. Col. H. H. Arnold.

JULY 28. 60,613 ft. altitude reached in Air Corps-National Geographic Society Stratosphere Balloon Flight by Maj. W. E. Kepner and Capts. A. W. Stevens and O. A. Anderson; all receive DFC.

1935: MAR. 1. General Headquarters Air Force is organized under command of Brig. Gen. Frank M. Andrews.

MAY 21. Hickam Field, near Fort Kamehameha, Hawaii, dedicated.

AUG. 24. 3 new world seaplane records are established in flights from Langley Field, Va. to Bennett Field, N. Y. and return, by Brig. Gen. F. M. Andrews (Martin B-12W bomber, with pontoon flotation gear replacing landing wheels).

AUG. 28. Automatic radio navigation equipment comprising Sperry automatic pilot mechanically linked to standard radio compass is tested by equipment branch, Wright Field, Dayton, Ohio.

NOV. 11. 72,394.795 ft. world record balloon ascent made by Capts. A. W. Stevens and O. A. Anderson, Rapid

City, S. D., in cooperation with National Geographic Society; Hubbard gold medal awarded.

DEC. 1-2. Mass flight of 29 bombardment planes of 7th Bombardment Group made from Hamilton Field, Calif. to Vero Beach, Fla. Elapsed time: 21:50:00.

DEC. 24. Brig. Gen. Oscar Westover appointed Chief of Air Corps with rank of major general.

DEC. 27. Aerial bombardment diverts Mauna Loa lava flow from waterworks at Hilo, Hawaii.

DEC. 28. Brig. Gen. H. H. Arnold becomes Asst. Chief of Air Corps.

DEC. 31. Device insuring automatic fuel transfer in airplanes with reserve fuel tanks developed by Air Corps Materiel Division.

1936: JUNE 24. Amendment to Air Corps Act of July 2, 1926 increases serviceable planes from 1800 to 2320.

JUNE 29. World's airline distance record for amphibians set by Maj. Gen. Frank M. Andrews and Maj. John Whiteley and crew (Douglas YOA 5-2 Wright 800) in flight from San Juan, Puerto Rico to Langley Field, Va. Distance: 1,429.685 miles.

DEC. 14-18. Goodwill flight made to Bogota, Colombia by 5 B-10Bs, 7th Observation Squadron, France Field, C. Z.

1937: FEB. 4-11. Longest overwater flight of land planes to date made by 96th Bombardment Squadron, 2nd Bombardment Group, during a trip from Langley Field, Va. to Albrook Field, C. Z.

MAR. 1. First Y1B-17A (Flying Fortress) delivered to 2nd Bombardment Group, Langley Field, Va.

JULY 1. Air Corps assumes responsibility for weather service activities of aerial arm and for providing weather forecasts required by divisions and higher headquarters; First, Second and Third Weather Squadrons established.

DEC. 2. XB-15, largest bombardment plane to date, leaves Boeing plant at Seattle, Wash. for Wright Field, Dayton, Ohio for test.

1938: FEB. 27. Goodwill flight, Langley Field, Va. to Buenos Aires, Argentina, completed by 6 B-17s. Flying time: southbound, 33:30:00; return, 33:45:00.

APR. 13. Expansion of Air Corps to 2092 commissioned officers authorized by Congress.

APR. 20. First class in Air Corps school for autogiro training and maintenance opens at Patterson Field, Ohio.

JUNE 11. Expansion of Air Corps to 21,500 enlisted men authorized.

JULY 28. 278 mph average speed in transcontinental flight achieved by Lt. H. L. Neely (Seversky P-35). Elapsed time: 11:29:00. Flying time: 9:54:00.

AUG. 3-12. Goodwill mission from Langley Field, Va. to Bogota, Colombia, made by 3 B-17s of 2nd Bombardment Group.

AUG. 6. Delivery made of B-15 bombardment airplane (wing spread 150 ft.; four 1000 hp engines) to 2nd Bombardment Gp.

AUG. 19. First transcontinental non-stop flight by B-18 bomber made from Hamilton Field, Calif. to Mitchel Field, N. Y. Fying time: 15:38:00.

SEPT. 15. Announcement made of Collier Trophy award to Army Air Corps for development of pressurized cabin substratosphere plane.

SEPT. 21. Daedalian and Colombian Trophies awarded 19th Bombardment Gp, March Field, Calif. for record of 10,942 flying hrs. with only one accident.

SEPT. 22. Maj. Gen. H. H. Arnold appointed Chief of the Air Corps.

OCT. 14. Mackay Trophy for 1937 awarded Capts. G. J. Crane and G. V. Holloman for development of airplane automatic landing system.

OCT. 26. 350 mph average speed achieved by new Army pursuit plane during flight from Dayton, Ohio to Buffalo, N. Y.; pilot, Lt. B. S. Kelsey.

1939: JAN. 12. President Roosevelt asks

Congress for revision of authorization for Army airplanes, an appropriation of $300,000,000 for plane purchases and for authorization to train 20,000 civilian pilots a year.

MAR. 1. To insure coordination of expansion activities and immediate availability of an operating staff in the event of war, the GHQ Air Force placed under the Chief of the Air Corps; command duties of the Commanding General, GHQ Air Force, are not affected.

APR. 3. Expansion bill signed by President. Authorizes 6000 airplanes for Air Corps and appropriation of $300,-000,000. Bill provides for calling Air Corps Reserve officers to active duty. Peacetime strength of Air Corps, Regular Army, increased to 3203 officers and 45,000 enlisted men.

MAY. First 4-blade controllable pitch propeller known to be built in U. S. is installed on a P-36A at Wright Field, Ohio.

JUNE 1. 72 civilian instructors from 9 civilian elementary flying schools report for 2-weeks' course at Randolph Field, Texas, preparatory to the inauguration on July 1, 1939 of the plan to utilize civilian flying schools for the primary training of Air Corps flying cadets.

JUNE 27. Civilian Pilot Training Act authorizes Civil Aeronautics Authority to train civilian pilots.

JUNE 30. War Department announces Air Corps enlisted strength to be increased by 25,794 during fiscal year 1940; about 19,000 to be trained as technical specialists.

JULY 1. Air Corps Primary Pilot Training in Civil Contract Schools begins.

JULY 30. U. S. regains world record for payload-carrying when Maj. C. V. Haynes and Capt. W. D. Old fly Army Boeing B-15 to 8200 ft. with payload of 15½ tons at Wright Field, Ohio.

AUG. 1. The Y1B-17A, flown by Capts. C. S. Irvine and Pearl Robey over a closed course of 1000 km (621 miles) and carrying a payload of 5000 kilograms (5½ tons), averages 259 mph, new international record.

AUG. 7. War Department announces award of contracts totaling $366,-386.80 to 7 civilian schools; program calls for training of 1000 airplane and engine mechanics.

NOV. 7. Mackay Trophy for 1938 is awarded 2nd Bombardment Group for 10,000 mile flight from Langley Field, Va. to Buenos Aires, Argentina.

NOV. 20-21. Total of 71,133 miles of night flying reported by the Air Corps Advanced Flying School, Kelly Field, Tex.

1940: JAN. 23. In the first American test of the practicability of moving a complete troop unit by air, a battalion of 65th Coast Artillery is transported 500 miles by the 7th Bombardment Group, Hamilton Field, Calif.

FEB. 2. Initial tests announced for XB-24, 4-engined bomber, at Lindbergh Field, San Diego, Calif.

FEB. 12. Plans announced for Air Corps stations at Fairbanks and Anchorage, Alaska.

MAR. 25. Sales of modern types of Army combat airplanes to anti-Axis governments by Air Corps contractors authorized under a "liberalized release policy," as a means for expanding future Air Corps production facilities.

APR. 14. First Air Corps detachment assigned to Alaskan station arrives at Fairbanks.

MAY 23-25. First demonstration of complete military maneuvers simulating European combat operations are held at Barksdale Field, La., by 320 Army aircraft during Third Army maneuvers.

JUNE. War Department announces plans

for training 7000 pilots and 3600 bombardiers and navigators annually.

JUNE 21. Kelly Field, Tex. graduates class of 236, largest in its history.

JUNE 29. Program of 12,835 airplanes (54 combat groups) by April 1, 1942 approved as the "Army's first aviation objective for training, organization and procurement."

JULY. $7,500,000 building program nears completion at Scott Field, Ill.; $9,364,000 is allotted Moffet Field, Calif., for conversion to West Coast Air Corps Training Center.

JULY 2. All existing limitations suspended during fiscal year 1941 on the number of flying cadets in the Air Corps, the number and rank of Reserve Air Corps officers who may be ordered to extended active duty, and on the number of serviceable airplanes, airships, and free and captive balloons that may be equipped and maintained.

JULY 8. 3 Air Corps Training Centers established; Air Corps Training Center at Randolph Field, Tex. redesignated Gulf Coast Training Center, and Southeast and West Coast Training Centers established with headquarters at Maxwell Field, Ala. and Moffet Field, Calif. respectively.

JULY 16. First bombardier training in Air Corps Schools begins at Lowry Field, Colo., with the entrance of the first class of bombardier instructors.

AUG. 10. War Department announces opening of navigator's course conducted by Pan-American Airways at Miami, Fla. with initial enrollment of 50.

AUG. 21. Contracts announced amounting to $10,893,248.94 awarded to civilian schools, putting into effect the program for the training of 7000 pilots and 3448 mechanics annually.

SEPT. 7. First awarding of Getulio Vargas Cup for outstanding contribution to goodwill among the Americas upon the 118th anniversary of Brazilian Independence, to 2nd Bombardment Group for the flight to Brazil in November 1939. Awarded at New York Worlds Fair.

OCT. 23. Announcement made that several Boeing B-17Cs are delivered to Wright Field, Ohio for flight tests.

OCT. 24. Northeast, Southeast, Northwest and Southwest Air Districts constituted for the purposes of decentralizing training and tactical control.

OCT. 25. Maj. Gen. H. H. Arnold designated Acting Deputy Chief of Staff for Air.

NOV. First navigator training in Air Corps schools begins at Barksdale Field, La.

NOV. 1. Hq and Hq Sq, Hawaiian Air Force, activated.

NOV. 19. GHQ Air Force removed from jurisdiction of the Chief of the Air Corps and as an element of the field forces, is placed under the command of the general commanding the field forces.

NOV. 20. Hq and Hq Sq, Panama Canal Air Force, activated.

NOV. 21-23. Announcement of flight tests of B-25 and B-26 made.

1941: JAN. 16. Hq and Hq Squadrons Northeast, Northwest, Southeast and Southwest Air Districts activated.

MAR. 26. Air Districts redesignated as Air Forces: Northeast as 1st, Northwest as 2nd, Southeast as 3rd and Southwest as 4th; Air Corps Technical Training Command established.

MAY 6. Philippine Department Air Force activated and placed under Brig. Gen. Henry B. Claggett.

MAY 15. Air Corps Specialized Flying School at Eglin Field redesignated Air Corps Proving Ground.

MAY 29. Air Corps Ferrying Command established.

JUNE 3. Grade of aviation cadet created.

JUNE 4. Grade of aviation student created.

JUNE 20. The Army Air Forces is created to coordinate the activities of the Air Force Combat Command (formerly GHQ Air Force) and the office of the Chief of the Air Corps; Maj. Gen. H. H. Arnold is named Chief, Army

Air Forces; Maj. Gen. G. H. Brett, Chief of the Air Corps; and Lt. Gen. D. C. Emmons, Commanding General, Air Force Combat Command.

JUNE 27. The B-19, "flying laboratory" of the AAF, makes first test flight.

JULY 1. North Atlantic Transport Service, for aerial transport of passengers and freight, inaugurated in a B-24 piloted by Col. C. V. Haynes, in flight from Bolling Field, D. C.

AUG. 12. AAF submits Air War Plan No. 1 to War Department in answer to request from the President.

SEPT. In the first movement of heavy bombers by air across western Pacific, 9 B-17s fly from Hawaii to the Philippines.

SEPT. 2. Hq and Hq Sq, 5th Air Support Command, activated.

SEPT. 11. First use of paratroopers in large-scale maneuvers is announced.

SEPT. 29. First class begins training in heavy bombardment crew school.

OCT. 17. Air Corps Maintenance Command becomes Air Service Command.

OCT. 23. Increase in AAF expansion program from 54 to 84 combat groups announced by War Department.

OCT. 30. Record-making world-circling flight in a B-24 carrying members of Harriman Mission is completed at Bolling Field, D. C. Pilot: Maj. A. V. Harvey. Elapsed time: 17 days. Distance: 24,700 miles.

NOV. 21. First of 16 B-24s, the first tactical planes piloted to overseas destination by Army Air Forces personnel, leaves Bolling Field, D. C. for the British at Cairo.

NOV. 22. 35 heavy bombers, all B-17s, now in the Philippines.

DEC. 7. Japanese attack Pearl Harbor. (For a chronological report of events from Dec. 7, 1941, to March 15, 1944, see War Calendar, page 329.)

Note: Where original records were not available for verification, the information in Historical Highlights is subject to revision based on research.

APPENDIX **

A SELECTED BIBLIOGRAPHY OF AVIATION

Any attempt to compile a complete bibliography of aviation would involve several shelves of volumes the size of this book. The following list is quite deliberately a selection focusing attention on only one small part of the publications in the field: new American publications which present in readable fashion important information on the various aspects of the Army Air Forces and the aviation scene today. Current official publications have been of necessity omitted because of their restricted nature. Specific references to important magazine articles have not been included due to space limitations. Even with these omissions, the following bibliography can serve as a guide to important recent literature of aviation and the Army Air Forces. Most of the books are currently available either through bookstores or libraries. Those no longer available for purchase are marked with the * symbol. In sections 8 and 9 the † symbol indicates books written for the non-technical reader.

1. STANDARD BIBLIOGRAPHIES IN THE FIELD OF AERONAUTICS

Dennis, Willard K. AN AERONAUTICAL REFERENCE LIBRARY. N. Y., Special Libraries Association, 1943. $1.00

U. S. Smithsonian Institution. BIBLIOGRAPHY OF AERONAUTICS, compiled by Paul Brockett. Washington, Smithsonian Institution, 1910. (Published as Vol. 55 of the Institution's Miscellaneous Collections. Records the literature to 1909)

U. S. National Advisory Committee for Aeronautics. BIBLIOGRAPHY OF AERONAUTICS. Washington, Government Printing Office, 1921-1936.

(13 volumes to date. Records the literature from 1909 through 1932)

U. S. Works Progress Administration. BIBLIOGRAPHY OF AERONAUTICS. N. Y., W. P. A., 1936-1941. 51 vols. (Continued by the following item)

U. S. Library of Congress, Division of Aeronautics. AERONAUTICAL INDEX. N. Y., Institute of the Aeronautical Sciences, 1939, 1943. (Records the literature for the years 1938 and 1939)

**Please note that the publications and prices listed herein were current in 1944, and as such, may no longer be available for purchase.

2. HISTORY

Arnold, Henry H., and Eaker, I. C. THIS FLYING GAME, N. Y., Funk & Wagnalls, 1944. $3.00

Bruno, Harry. WINGS OVER AMERICA. N. Y., McBride, 1942. $3.00

Chandler, Charles de F., and Lahm, F. P. HOW OUR ARMY GREW WINGS. N. Y., Ronald, 1943. $3.75

Cleveland, Reginald M. AMERICA FLEDGES WINGS, THE HISTORY OF THE DANIEL GUGGENHEIM FUND FOR THE PROMOTION OF AERONAUTICS. N. Y., Pitman, 1942. $2.50

* Goldstrom, John. NARRATIVE HISTORY OF AVIATION. N. Y., Macmillan, 1930. $4.00

Grey, Charles G. HISTORY OF COMBAT AIRPLANES. Northfield, Vt., Norwich University, 1941. $1.00

Herzberg, Max J., and others. HAPPY LANDINGS. Boston, Houghton, 1942. $2.50

Johnston, S. Paul. FLYING SQUADRONS, A GRAPHIC HISTORY OF THE U. S. ARMY AIR FORCES. N. Y., Duell, Sloan & Pearce, 1942. $3.50

Johnston, S. Paul. HORIZONS UNLIMITED. N. Y., Duell, Sloan &

Pearce, 1941. $3.75

Leyson, Burr W. AMERICAN WINGS. N. Y., Dutton, 1943. $2.00

McCoy, John T. PICTORIAL HISTORY OF THE ARMY AIR FORCES. N. Y., Duell, Sloan & Pearce, 1944. $3.00

Milbank, Jeremiah. FIRST CENTURY OF FLIGHT IN AMERICA; AN INTRODUCTORY SURVEY. Princeton, N. J., Princeton University, 1943. $2.75

Miller, Francis T. WORLD IN THE AIR, THE STORY OF FLYING IN PICTURES. N. Y., Putman, 1930. 2 vols. $10.00

Puffer, Claude E. AIR TRANSPORTATION. Philadelphia, Blakiston, 1941. $3.75

Rickenbacker, Edward V. FIGHTING THE FLYING CIRCUS. N. Y., Stokes, 1919. $2.00

Smith, Henry L. AIRWAYS; THE HISTORY OF COMMERCIAL AVIATION IN THE UNITED STATES. N. Y., Knopf, 1942. $3.50

Wood, John W. AIRPORTS, SOME ELEMENTS OF DESIGN AND FUTURE DEVELOPMENT. N. Y., Coward-McCann, 1940. $12.50

3. BIOGRAPHY

Driggs, Laurence L. HEROES OF AVIATION. Boston, Little, Brown, 1928. $2.50

* Fraser, Chelsea C. FAMOUS AMERICAN FLYERS. N. Y., Crowell, 1942. $2.00

Fraser, Chelsea C. HEROES OF THE AIR. N. Y., Crowell, 1942. $2.50

* Gardner, Lester D., ed. WHO'S WHO IN AMERICAN AERONAUTICS, THE BLUE BOOK OF AMERICAN AIRMEN. N. Y., Gardner, 1922–1928. 3 editions. $2.00

Gauvreau, Emile, and Cohen, Lester. BILLY MITCHELL, FOUNDER OF OUR AIR FORCE AND PROPHET WITHOUT HONOR. N. Y., Dutton, 1942. $2.50

* Hall, James N., and Nordhoff, C. B.

LAFAYETTE FLYING CORPS. Boston, Houghton, 1920. 2 vols. $15.00. Vol. 1 Biographies of Personnel, Vol. 2 Narrative History.

* Hoagland, Roland W., ed. BLUE BOOK OF AVIATION, A BIOGRAPHICAL HISTORY OF AMERICAN AVIATION. Los Angeles, Hoagland, 1932. $15.00

Kelly, Fred C. WRIGHT BROTHERS. N. Y., Harcourt, 1943. $3.50

Levine, Isaac D. MITCHELL, PIONEER OF AIR POWER. N. Y., Duell, Sloan & Pearce, 1943. $3.50

* Maitland, Lester J. KNIGHTS OF THE AIR. N. Y., Doubleday, 1929. $3.50

Mann, Carl. LIGHTNING IN THE SKY, THE STORY OF JIMMY DOOLITTLE. N. Y., McBride, 1943. $2.75

Mingos, Howard. AMERICAN HEROES OF THE WAR IN THE AIR. N. Y., Lanciar, 1943. Vol. 1. $10.00

Shenton, Edward. ON WINGS FOR FREEDOM. Philadelphia, Macrae-Smith, 1942. $2.00

Writers' Program. WHO'S WHO IN AVIATION, A DIRECTORY OF LIVING MEN AND WOMEN WHO HAVE CONTRIBUTED TO THE GROWTH OF AVIATION IN THE UNITED STATES, 1942–1943. Chicago, Ziff-Davis, 1942. $5.00

4. THE ARMY AIR FORCES TODAY

Army Air Forces. OFFICIAL GUIDE TO THE AAF. N. Y., Pocket Books; 1944. $.25. Simon and Schuster, 1944. $2.50

Army Air Forces Training Command. WINGS FOR COMBAT, THE STORY OF THE TRAINING OF AN AIR FORCE. Brooklyn, Ullman Co., 1943. $.90

Arnold, Henry H., and Eaker, I. C. ARMY FLYER, N. Y., Harper, 1942. $2.50

Arnold, Henry H., and Eaker, I. C. WINGED WARFARE, N. Y., Harper, 1941. $3.00

Collison, Thomas. FLYING FORTRESS, THE STORY OF THE BOEING BOMBER. N. Y., Scribner's, 1943. $2.50

DeLonge, Merrill E. MODERN AIRFIELD, PLANNING AND CONCEALMENT. N. Y., Pitman, 1943. $4.00

Ford, Corey, and MacBain, Alastair. FROM THE GROUND UP. N. Y., Scribner's, 1943. $2.50

* Graham, Frederick P., and Kulick, H. W. HE'S IN THE AIR CORPS NOW. N. Y., McBride, 1942. $2.50

Hartney, Harold E. WHAT YOU SHOULD KNOW ABOUT OUR AIR FORCES. N. Y., Norton, 1942. $2.50

Hibbits, John J. TAKE 'ER UP ALONE, MISTER! as told to F. C. Rechnitzer. N. Y., McGraw-Hill, 1943. $2.50

Ind, Allison. BATAAN, THE JUDGMENT SEAT, THE SAGA OF THE PHILIPPINE COMMAND OF THE UNITED STATES ARMY AIR FORCE. MAY 1941 TO MAY 1942. N. Y. Macmillan, 1944. $3.50

Knox, John. WINGS OF WAR, THE STORY OF AIR TRANSPORT. N. Y., Macmillan, 1944. $3.00

Lent, Henry B. BOMBARDIER, TOM DIXON WINS HIS WINGS WITH THE BOMBER COMMAND. N. Y., Macmillan, 1943. $2.00

Leyson, Burr W. WINGS FOR OFFENSE. N. Y., Dutton, 1942. $2.50

LOOK (magazine). AIRPOWER. N. Y., Duell, Sloan & Pearce, 1943. $2.75

Miksche, Ferdinand O. PARATROOPS. N. Y., Random House, 1943. $2.50

Rathbone, Alfred D. HE'S IN THE PARATROOPS Now. N. Y., McBride, 1943. $2.50

Ryan, Richard N. SPIN IN, DUMBWHACKS. Philadelphia, Lippincott, 1943, $1.75

Sagendorph, Kent. THUNDER ALOFT, U. S. AIR POWER TODAY—TOMORROW. Chicago, Reilly & Lee, 1942. $2.50

Sears, Hugh. WHAT'S NEW IN THE AIR CORPS? N. Y., Grosset & Dunlap, 1941. $.50

Steinbeck, John. BOMBS AWAY, THE STORY OF A BOMBER TEAM. N. Y., Viking, 1942. $2.50

Winter, William. ARMY AIR COMMANDS. N. Y., Crowell, 1944. $2.00

Writers' Program, Texas. RANDOLPH FIELD, A HISTORY AND GUIDE. N. Y., Devin-Adair, 1942. $2.00

5. THEORY OF AIR WARFARE

Ayling, Keith. COMBAT AVIATION. Harrisburg, Pa., Military Service, 1943. $2.00

Blunt, Vernon E. R. USE OF AIR POWER. Harrisburg, Pa., Military Service, 1943. $1.00

Caldwell, Cyril C. Air Power and Total War. N. Y., Coward-Mc-Cann, 1943. $2.50

De Seversky, Alexander P. Victory through Air Power. N. Y., Simon & Schuster, 1942. $2.50

Douhet, Giulio. Command of the Air. N. Y., Coward-McCann, 1942. $4.00

Drake, Francis V. Vertical Warfare. N. Y., Doubleday, 1943. $3.00

Hershey, Burnet. Air Future, a Primer of Aeropolitics. N. Y., Duell, Sloan & Pearce, 1943. $2.75

Huie, William B. Fight for Air Power. N. Y., L. B. Fischer, 1942. $2.50

Lee, John G. Fighter Facts and Fallacies. N. Y., Morrow, 1942. $1.25

Michie, Allan A. Air Offensive against Germany. N. Y., Holt, 1943. $2.00

Miksche, Ferdinand O. Attack, a Study of Blitzkreig Tactics. N. Y., Random House, 1942. $2.50

* Mitchell, William. Winged Defense, the Development and Possibilities of Modern Air Power —Economic and Military. N. Y., Putnam, 1925. $2.50

Williams, Alford J. Airpower. N. Y., Coward-McCann, 1940. $3.50

Ziff, William B. Coming Battle of Germany. N. Y., Duell, Sloan & Pearce. 1942. $2.50

6. MILITARY AIRPLANES

Booth, Harold H. Book of Modern Warplanes, a Collection of Paintings of the World's Latest Fighting Planes. N. Y., Garden City, 1942. $1.00

Guthman, L. C. Aeronautics Aircraft Spotters' Handbook. N. Y., National Aeronautics Council, 1943. $1.00

Kinert, Reed C. America's Fighting Planes in Action. N. Y., Macmillan, 1943. $2.50

Law, Bernard A. Fighting Planes of the World. N. Y., Random House, 1942. $1.00

Leyson, Burr W. Warplane and How it Works. N. Y., Dutton, 1943. $2.50

Ott, Lester. Aircraft Spotter. N. Y., Dodd, Mead, 1943. $1.00

Pitkin, Walter B. What's That Plane? Washington, Infantry Journal, 1942. $.25

Saville-Sneath, R. A. Aircraft Recognition. Washington, Infantry Journal, 1943. $.25

Winter, William J. War Planes of All Nations. N. Y., Crowell, 1943. $2.50

7. AIR NARRATIVES OF WORLD WAR II

Balchen, Bernt, and others. War Below Zero. Boston, Houghton, 1944. $2.50

Childers, James S. War Eagles, the Story of the Eagle Squadron. N. Y., Appleton, 1943. $3.75

Donahue, Arthur G. Tally-Ho! Yankee in a Spitfire. N. Y., Macmillan, 1941. $2.50

Ford, Corey. Short Cut to Tokyo, the Battle for the Aleutians. N. Y., Scribner's, 1943. $1.75

Greenlaw, Olga S. Lady and the Tigers. N. Y., Dutton, 1943. $3.00

Hardison, Priscilla, and Wormser, Anne. Suzy-Q. Boston, Houghton, 1943. $2.00

Hotz, Robert B., and others. With General Chennault, the Story of the Flying Tigers. N. Y., Coward-McCann, 1943. $3.00

Kennerly, Byron. The Eagles Roar! N. Y., Harper, 1942. $3.00

Lawson, Ted W. Thirty Seconds over Tokyo. N. Y., Random House, 1943. $2.00

Mims, Sam. CHENNAULT OF THE FLYING TIGERS. Philadelphia, Macrae-Smith, 1943. $2.00

Redding, John M., and Leyshon, Harold I. SKYWAYS TO BERLIN, WITH THE AMERICAN FLYERS IN ENGLAND. Indianapolis, Bobbs-Merrill, 1943. $2.75

Rickenbacker, Edward V. SEVEN CAME THROUGH. N. Y., Doubleday, 1943. $1.50

River, Walter L. MALTA STORY, BASED ON THE DIARY AND EXPERIENCES OF LIEUTENANT HOWARD M. COFFIN. N. Y., Dutton, 1943. $2.50

Scott, Robert L., Jr. GOD IS MY CO-PILOT. N. Y., Scribner's, 1943. $2.50

Taggart, William C., and Cross, Christopher. MY FIGHTING CONGREGATION. N. Y., Doubleday, 1943. $2.75

TARGET: GERMANY, THE ARMY AIR FORCES' OFFICIAL STORY OF THE VIII BOMBER COMMAND'S FIRST YEAR OVER EUROPE. N. Y., Simon & Schuster, 1943. $1.00 and $2.00

Whelan, Russell. FLYING TIGERS. N. Y., Viking, 1943. $2.50

White, William L. QUEENS DIE PROUDLY. N. Y., Harcourt, 1943. $2.50

Whittaker, James C. WE THOUGHT WE HEARD THE ANGELS SING. N. Y., Dutton, 1943. $1.50

8. THEORY OF FLIGHT AND PILOT TRAINING

Barringer, Lewin B. FLIGHT WITHOUT POWER, THE ART OF GLIDING AND SOARING. N. Y., Pitman, 1942. $3.00

† Black, Archibald. STORY OF FLYING. N. Y., Whittlesey, 1943. $2.50

Chapin, Mary K. WHY MEN CAN FLY. N. Y., Reynal & Hitchcock, 1943. $2.50

† Clevenger, Cloyd P. MODERN FLIGHT. N. Y., Noble, 1941. $2.95

Columbia University. Teachers College. Aviation Education Research Group. SCIENCE OF PRE-FLIGHT AERONAUTICS. N. Y., Macmillan, 1942. $1.32. (Air-Age Education Series, includes a bibliography of this series)

† * Floherty, John J. AVIATION FROM SHOP TO SKY. Philadelphia, Lippincott, 1941. $2.00

† Gann, Ernest K. GETTING THEM INTO THE BLUE. N. Y., Crowell, 1942. $2.00

† Hall, Charles G. HOW A PLANE FLIES. ARE YOU SURE YOU KNOW? N. Y., Funk & Wagnalls, 1942. $2.00

Hartney, Harold E. COMPLETE FLYING MANUAL. N. Y., National Aeronautics Council, 1940. $1.25

† Hunt, Jack, and Fahringer, Ray. STUDENT PILOT HANDBOOK. N. Y., Books, 1943. $2.50

† Jordanoff, Assen. YOUR WINGS. N. Y., Funk & Wagnalls, 1942. $3.00

† Knerr, Hugh J. STUDENT PILOT'S TRAINING PRIMER. N. Y., Van Nostrand, 1941. $1.75

Manley, Gardner B. AVIATION FROM THE GROUND UP. Chicago, Drake, 1940. $3.00

Niles, Alfred S., and Newell, J. S. AIRPLANE STRUCTURES. N. Y., Wiley, 1943. 2 vols. $9.00

Page, Victor W. A. B. C. OF AVIATION. N. Y., Henley, 1942. $2.50

Peck, James L. H. SO YOU'RE GOING TO FLY. N. Y., Dodd, Mead, 1941. $2.50

Robinson, Pearle T., and others. BEFORE YOU FLY, ESSENTIALS OF AERONAUTICS. N. Y., Holt, 1943. $2.00

Shields, Bert. AIR PILOT TRAINING. N. Y., McGraw-Hill, 1943. $3.50

† Stieri, Emanuele. GLIDERS AND GLIDER TRAINING. N. Y., Duell, Sloan & Pearce, 1943. $3.00

Stout, William B., and Reck, F. M. TOMORROW WE FLY. N. Y., Crowell, 1943. $2.00

Turner, Roscoe, and Dubuque, J. H. WIN YOUR WINGS. Chicago, Drake, 1943. 2 vols. $6.00

9. TECHNICAL HANDBOOKS

AVIATION TRAINING SERIES

Flight Preparation Training Series. N. Y., McGraw-Hill, 1943. AEROLOGY FOR PILOTS. $1.25. AIR NAVIGATION. Parts 1-3, 5. $4.25. EFFECTS OF FLIGHT, PHYSICAL AND MENTAL ASPECTS. $.60. MATHEMATICS FOR PILOTS. $.75. OPERATION OF AIRCRAFT ENGINES. $.90. PHYSICS MANUAL FOR PILOTS. $.90. PRINCIPLES OF FLYING. $1.50

Wright, Bailey A., and others. FLIGHT, GENERAL SURVEY OF FUNDAMENTALS OF AVIATION. Chicago, American Technical Society, 1941–1942. AIRCRAFT ENGINES. $3.25. CONSTRUCTION AND .MAINTENANCE. $2.50. FIRST PRINCIPLES. $2.50. METEOROLOGY, AIRCRAFT INSTRUMENTS, AND NAVIGATION. $3.25

AERIAL PHOTOGRAPHY AND MAP READING

Eardley, Armand J. AERIAL PHOTOGRAPHS, THEIR USE AND INTERPRETATION. N. Y., Harper, 1942, $2.75

Field, Richard M., and Stetson, H. T. MAP READING AND AVIGATION; AN INTRODUCTION. N. Y., Van Nostrand, 1942. $2.50

† Heavy, William F. MAP AND AERIAL PHOTO READING SIMPLIFIED. Harrisburg, Pa., Military Service, 1943. $1.00

Sharp, Howard O. PHOTOGRAMMETRY. N. Y., Wiley, 1943. $3.50

AVIATION ENGINES AND MECHANICS

Colvin, Fred H. AIRCRAFT HANDBOOK. N. Y., McGraw-Hill, 1942. $5.00

† Hylander, Clarence J. FLYING POWER. N. Y., Macmillan, 1943. $2.00

† Jordanoff, Assen. MAN BEHIND THE FLIGHT, A GROUND COURSE FOR AVIATION MECHANICS AND AIRMEN. N. Y., Harper, 1942. $3.50

Manley, Gardner B. AIRCRAFT POWERPLANT MANUAL. Chicago, Drake, 1942. $4.00

Norcross, Carl, and Quinn, J. D. AVIATION MECHANIC. N. Y., McGraw-Hill, 1941. $3.50

AVIATION MATHEMATICS

Ayres, Frank, BASIC MATHEMATICS FOR AVIATION. Boston, Houghton, 1943. $3.00

MEDICAL ASPECTS OF AVIATION

Barr, Eugene O. FLYING MEN AND MEDICINE: THE EFFECTS OF FLYING UPON THE HUMAN BODY. N. Y., Funk & Wagnalls, 1943. $2.50

Grow, Malcolm C. FIT TO FLY, A MEDICAL HANDBOOK. N. Y., Appleton, 1941. $2.50

Kafka, M. Martyn. FLYING HEALTH. Harrisburg, Pa., Military Service, 1942. $2.00

† Zim, Herbert S. MAN IN THE AIR, THE EFFECTS OF FLYING ON THE HUMAN BODY. N. Y., Harcourt, 1943. $3.00

METEOROLOGY

Eaton, Elbert L. WEATHER GUIDE FOR AIR PILOTS. N. Y., Ronald, 1943. $2.00

Harrison, Louis P. METEOROLOGY. N. Y., National Aeronautics Council, 1942. $2.00

† Jordanoff, Assen. THROUGH THE OVERCAST. N. Y., Funk & Wagnalls, 1943. $3.00

† Sloane, Eric. CLOUDS, AIR AND WIND. N. Y., Devin-Adair, 1941. $3.00

Wenstrom, William H. WEATHER AND THE OCEAN OF AIR. Boston, Houghton, 1942. $4.50

MODEL AIRPLANES

Stieri, Emanuele. BUILDING MODEL WAR PLANES FOR THE ARMY AND NAVY. N. Y., Duell, Sloan & Pearce, 1943. $2.50

Stieri, Emanuele. SUPPLEMENT TO BUILDING MODEL WAR PLANES FOR THE ARMY AND NAVY. (60 full-size construction patterns.) N. Y., Duell, Sloan & Pearce, 1943. $1.25

NAVIGATION AND INSTRUMENT FLYING

Hurt, Haworth W., and Wolf, C. A. FLIGHT INSTRUMENTS. N. Y., National Aeronautics Council, 1942. $1.00

Lyon, Thoburn C. AERIAL NAVIGATION. N. Y., National Aeronautics Council, 1942. $1.50

Smith, Frederick H. FLYING BY INSTRUMENTS. N. Y., National Aeronautics Council, 1942. $1.50

Weems, Philip V. H. AIR NAVIGATION. N. Y., McGraw-Hill, 1943. $4.50

† Zim, Herbert S. AIR NAVIGATION. N. Y., Harcourt, 1943. $3.00

PARACHUTES

Fechet, James E., and others. PARACHUTES. N. Y., National Aeronautics Council, 1942. $1.00

† Zim, Herbert S. PARACHUTES. N. Y., Harcourt, 1942. $2.50

RADIO AND AVIATION

Fechet, James E., and others. RADIO IN AIRMANSHIP, N. Y., National Aeronautics Council, 1943. $1.00

Morgan, Howard K. AIRCRAFT RADIO AND ELECTRICAL EQUIPMENT. N. Y., Pitman, 1941. $4.50

10. LITERATURE OF FLIGHT

Benet, William R. WITH WINGS AS EAGLES, POEMS AND BALLADS OF THE AIR. N. Y., Dodd, Mead, 1940. $2.00

Collison, Thomas. THIS WINGED WORLD; AN ANTHOLOGY OF AVIATION FICTION. N. Y., Coward-McCann, 1943. $3.50

Hart, Moss. WINGED VICTORY, THE AIR FORCE PLAY. N. Y., Random House, 1943. $2.00

Lindbergh, Anne M. LISTEN! THE WIND. N. Y., Harcourt, 1938. $2.50

Lindbergh, Anne M. NORTH TO THE ORIENT. N. Y., Harcourt, 1935. $2.50

Rodman, Selden. POETRY OF FLIGHT, AN ANTHOLOGY. N. Y., Duell, Sloan & Pearce, 1941. $2.50

Saint Exupery, Antoine de. AIRMAN'S ODYSSEY. N. Y., Reynal & Hitchcock, 1943. $3.00. (Includes WIND, SAND AND STARS, NIGHT FLIGHT, and FLIGHT TO ARRAS)

11. YEARBOOKS AND DICTIONARIES

YEARBOOKS

AEROSPHERE. N. Y., Aircraft Publications, 1939–1944. Vol. 4, 1944. $15.00

AIRCRAFT YEARBOOK. N. Y., Aeronautical Chamber of Commerce of America 1919–1943. Vol. 25, 1943. $5.00 (Vol. 26 to be published June 1944.)

AMERICAN AVIATION DIRECTORY. Washington, American Aviation Associates, 1940–1943. Vol. 7, 1943. $5.00

Andrews, Phillip. AIR NEWS YEARBOOK. N. Y., Duell, Sloan & Pearce, 1942. $3.75 (Vol. 2 to be published June 1944.)

Cleveland, Reginald M., and Graham, Frederick P. AVIATION ANNUAL OF 1944. N. Y., Doubleday, 1943. $3.50

Cooke, David C. AIRCRAFT ANNUAL: 1944. N. Y., McBride, 1943. $3.00

Cooke, David C., and Davidson, Jesse. MODEL PLANE ANNUAL. N. Y., McBride, 1941–1943. Vol. 2, 1943. $2.50

Cooke, David C. (formerly edited by Frederick P. Graham and Reginald M. Cleveland.) YOUNG AMERICA'S AVIATION ANNUAL. N. Y., McBride, 1940–1943. Vol. 4, 1943. $2.50

JANE'S ALL THE WORLD'S AIRCRAFT. N. Y., Macmillan, 1909–1943. Vol. 32, 1943. $19.00

DICTIONARIES

Ahrens, Lothar. DICTIONARY OF AERONAUTICS; English, French, German, Italian, Spanish. N. Y., Frederick Ungar, 1943. $5.00

Baughman, Harold E. AVIATION DICTIONARY AND REFERENCE GUIDE. Glendale, California, Aero Publishers, 1942. $6.50

Jordanoff, Assen. JORDANOFF'S ILLUSTRATED AVIATION DICTIONARY. N.Y., Harper, 1942. $3.50

Thorpe, Leslie A. SIMPLIFIED DEFINITIONS AND NOMENCLATURE FOR

AERONAUTICS, A MODERN AERONAUTICAL DICTIONARY. San Francisco, Aviation Press, 1942. $2.00

U. S. Army Air Forces, Director of Intelligence Service. DICTIONARY OF AERONAUTICAL TERMS; ENGLISH, JAPANESE, FRENCH, GERMAN. Washington, Government Printing Office, 1942. $.35

12. MAGAZINES

AERO DIGEST. N. Y., Aeronautical Digest Publishing Corporation. Semimonthly, 1921–date.

AERONAUTICAL ENGINEERING REVIEW. N. Y., Institute of the Aeronautical Sciences. Monthly, 1942–date.

AIR FACTS. N. Y., Air Facts Inc. Monthly, 1938–date.

AIR NEWS. N. Y., Phillip Andrews. Monthly, 1941–date.

AIR PILOT AND TECHNICIAN (formerly Sportsman Pilot). N. Y., F. A. Tichenor. Monthly, 1929–date.

AIR TECH. N. Y., Phillip Andrews. Monthly, 1942–date.

AIR TRAILS. N. Y., Street & Smith. Monthly, 1915–date.

AIR TRANSPORT. N. Y., McGraw-Hill. Monthly, 1943–date.

AMERICAN AVIATION. Washington, American Aviation Associates. Semimonthly, 1937–date.

AUTOMOTIVE AND AVIATION INDUSTRIES. Philadelphia, Chilton Co. Semi-monthly, 1899–date.

AVIATION. N. Y., McGraw-Hill. Monthly, 1916–date.

AVIATION NEWS. N. Y., McGraw-Hill.

Weekly, 1943–date.

FLYING. Chicago, Ziff-Davis. Monthly, 1927–date.

JOURNAL OF THE AERONAUTICAL SCIENCES. N. Y., Institute of the Aeronautical Sciences. Quarterly, 1934–date.

JOURNAL OF AVIATION MEDICINE. St. Paul, Minn., Bruce Publishing Co., Bi-monthly, 1930–date.

MODEL AIRPLANE NEWS. Mount Morris, Ill., Air Age Inc. Monthly, 1929–date.

NATIONAL AERONAUTICS. Washington, National Aeronautic Association. Monthly, 1923–date.

SKYWAYS. N. Y., Henry Publishing Co. Monthly, 1942–date.

SOUTHERN FLIGHT. Dallas, Texas, Air Review Publishing Corp. Monthly, 1934–date.

U. S. AIR SERVICES. Washington, Air Service Publishing Co. Monthly, 1919–date.

WESTERN FLYING. Los Angeles, Occidental Publishing Co. Monthly, 1926–date.

AAF personnel, both commissioned and enlisted, each month are furnished copies of Air Force, the Official Service Journal of the U. S. Army Air Forces. Popularly styled for general interest, Air Force keeps personnel informed on tactical, technical and organizational developments within the AAF and on other pertinent information regarding the air war. Its articles are contributed by AAF officers and men, and it serves as a medium for the exchange of ideas and information among both flying and ground personnel. Air Force is distributed without charge on a pro-rated basis through station and field channels.

ABBREVIATIONS

Below are listed abbreviations found in this book and a few others commonly used in the AAF:

AA—antiaircraft
AACS—Army Airways Communications System
AAF—Army Air Forces
AAFAS—Army Air Forces Aid Society
AAFSAT—Army Air Forces School of Applied Tactics
AAFTAC—Army Air Forces Tactical Center
AAFTAD—Army Air Forces Training Aids Division
AAFTC—Army Air Forces Training Command
AC—Air Corps
A/C—aviation cadet
ACER—Air Corps Enlisted Reserve
AEAF—Allied Expeditionary Air Forces (Europe)
AFCE—Automatic Flight Control Equipment
AFSWA—Assistant Secretary of War for Air
AGF—Army Ground Forces
AGO—Adjutant General's Office
AJA—Air Judge Advocate
AM—Air Medal, Airplane Mechanic
ANC—Army Nurse Corps
ANSCOL—Army-Navy Staff College
APO—Army Post Office
AR—Army Regulation
ASC—Air Service Command
ASF—Army Service Forces
ASN—Army serial number
ATC—Air Transport Command
ATS—Army Transport Service
AUS—Army of the United States
AVG—American Volunteer Group (Flying Tigers)
AWC—Army War College

AWC—Aircraft Warning Corps
AWOL—absent without official leave
AWS—Aircraft Warning Service
AWVS—American Women's Voluntary Services

BOQ—bachelor officers' quarters
BPR—Bureau of Public Relations
BTC—Basic Training Center

CAA—Civil Aeronautics Administration
CAP—Civil Air Patrol
CAVU—ceiling and visibility unlimited
CBI—China-Burma-India Theater of Operations
CCRC—Combat Crew Replacement Center
CFE—contractor furnished equipment
CG—Commanding General
CO—Commanding Officer
CWS—Chemical Warfare Service

DFC—Distinguished Flying Cross
D/R—dead reckoning
DSC—Distinguished Service Cross
DSM—Distinguished Service Medal

EM—enlisted man
ETA—estimated time of arrival
ETO—European Theater of Operations

F/O—flight officer
FM—field manual
FTC—Flying Training Command

GCI—ground controlled interception
GCT—general classification test; Greenwich Civil Time

APPENDIX

GFE—government furnished equipment
GHQ—General Headquarters
G.I.—Government issue
GOC—Ground Observer Corps
Gp—Group
GSC—General Staff Corps

HE—high explosive
hp—horsepower
Hq—headquarters

IAS—indicated airspeed

JAC—Joint Aircraft Committee

LM—Legion of Merit

MH—Medal of Honor
MOS—military occupational specialty
MP—Military Police
mph—miles per hour
MTU—mobile training unit

NAAF—Northwest African Air Forces
NAAFW—National Association of Air Forces Women
NACA—National Advisory Committee for Aeronautics
NCO—noncommissioned officer
NSLI—National Service Life Insurance

OC(S)—Officer Candidate (School)
OD—officer of the day; olive drab
ORC—Officers' Reserve Corps
OSW—Office Secretary of War
OTS—Officer Training School
OTU—Operational Training Unit

PD—Port of Debarkation
PDI—pilot direction indicator
PGC—Proving Ground Command
PH—Purple Heart
POE—Port of Embarkation
POM—Preparation for Overseas Movement
POW—prisoner of war
PRO—Public Relations Officer

QM(C)—Quartermaster (Corps)

RA—Regular Army
RAAF—Royal Australian Air Force
RAF—Royal Air Force (Great Britain)
RCAF—Royal Canadian Air Force
RNZAF—Royal New Zealand Air Force
rpm—revolutions per minute
RTC—Replacement Training Center
RTU—Replacement Training Unit

SAAF—South African Air Force
SHAEF—Supreme Headquarters of the Allied Expeditionary Forces (Europe)
SM—Soldier's Medal
SOP—standard operating procedure
Sq—Squadron

TCC—Troop Carrier Command
T/E—table of equipment
TM—technical manual
TO—technical order
T/O—table of organization
TTC—Technical Training Command
TV—terminal velocity

UR—unsatisfactory report
USAAF—U. S. Army Air Forces
USMA—U. S. Military Academy
USSTAF—U. S. Strategic Air Forces (Europe)

VHF—very high frequency
VOCO—verbal orders commanding officer
VOQ—visiting officers' quarters
VP—variable pitch

WAC—Women's Army Corps
Wac—a member of the WAC
WASP—Women's Airforce Service Pilots
Wasp—a member of the WASP
WD—War Department
WO—warrant officer

ZI—zone of interior

AAF VERNACULAR

The language of the AAF has been expanded by the addition of words and phrases peculiar to aircraft and aerial combat. The expressions given below are only a few examples chosen from those most common and most widely used. Some of them will undoubtedly serve only for the duration; others may find a permanent place in our language. Many of them have other meanings.

baksheesh—*easy mission; no enemy encountered.*
bandits—*enemy planes.*
bathtub—*ball turret.*
belly landing—*landing without wheels.*
big friends—*bombers.*
big jeep—*large bomber.*
biscuit gun—*imaginary appliance for shooting food to pilots who are having difficulty in landing.*
bogie—*unidentified aircraft.*
bomb-up—*loading with bombs.*
buzz—*dive low over an area.*

cadet widows—*girls who date many cadets.*
chairborne troops—*non-flying AAF personnel.*
chauffeur—*pilot*
Chinese landing—*landing with one wing low.*
clocks—*instruments on panel in cockpit.*
coffee grinder—*aircraft engine.*
conk—*sudden stopping of engine during flight.*
crab—*apparent sidewise motion of an airplane with respect to ground when flying with a side wind.*

dodo—*aviation cadet who has not yet soloed.*
dry run—*practice, or dress rehearsal for operations.*

eggs—*bombs.*

fans—*propellers.*
flak happy — *condition resulting from combat fatigue.*
flying coffin—*dilapidated plane.*

gaggle—*group of aircraft in formation.*
geese—*bombers in formation.*
get cracking—*show action; hurry up.*
glory wagon—*Flying Fortress.*
greenhouse—*glass enclosure, usually bombardier compartment.*
ground-gripper—*non-flying personnel.*

hangar flying—*conversation about flying and kindred subjects.*
hangar pilot—*one who does his best "flying" in conversation.*
hanging on props—*near point of stall.*
hang out the laundry—*dropping paratroops.*
hedge-hop—*flying below level of obstacles and hopping over them.*
hemp stretcher—*member of balloon outfit.*
hit the silk—*bail out.*
hot pilot—*fighter pilot whose ability is recognized as superlative; fighter pilot show-off or braggart.*
hot-plane—*aircraft needing careful handling with high takeoff or landing speed.*

368

in the drink—*forced down at sea.*

junior birdman—*recipient of Air Medal.*
junior prom—*hot mission.*

kiwi—*a non-flying officer.*

madhouse—*control tower.*
Mae West—*inflatable life vest.*
Messerschmitt Maytag — *light, low horsepower liaison type aircraft; check ship in washout flight.*
milk-run—*routine mission flown repeatedly.*
mustard cluster—*mythical award for poor bombing.*

on the beam—*acting effectively or satisfactorily.*
on the deck—*minimum altitude; near the ground or water.*
overcoat—*parachute.*

PDI chaser—*pilot.*
peashooter—*fighter pilot or fighter plane.*
peel-off—*to turn a corner, or leave a group of friends.*
pencil pusher—*navigator.*
photo Joe—*pilot of single seat photographic aircraft.*
picklebarrel—*shack or target in bombardier training.*
prop wash—*gossip.*
Purple Heart corner—*outside-plane in lowest flying element of bomber formation.*

rainmaker—*meteorologist.*
raunchy—*sloppy flying technique.*
ribbon happy—*airman with extreme interest in his decorations or in collecting them.*

Roger—*all right (OK); "I understand"; "I have received all of your last (radio) transmissions."*

short-snorter—*member of unofficial fraternity relating to accomplishment of trans-oceanic flight. Many concepts of origin and eligibility to membership. Members exchange signatures on paper money attached together, usually from various countries in which they have served.*
socked in—*ceiling zero.*
solid bundle of blitz—*large formation of enemy aircraft.*
spinning your wheels—*wasting time or energy and accomplishing nothing.*
static-bender—*radio operator.*
stooge—*copilot.*
stratosphere Joe—*a tall man.*
stuff—*clouds or weather.*
sweat it out—*to wait expectantly.*

tail-end or (low-hole) Charlie—*wing man in formation.*
togglier—*bombardier.*
Tojo—*soldier who is reading technical orders (tech order Joe).*
Tokyo tanks—*auxiliary gas tanks.*
truck driver—*transport pilot.*

washing machine—*flight commander's airplane for aviation cadet qualification flights; a plane in which an unsuccessful cadet is "washed out."*
washout—*one who has been eliminated from flying training.*
wilco—*will comply; will do; "Your last message (or message indicated) has been received, understood and (where applicable) will be complied with."*

INDEX